A Reformed View of Freedom

A Reformed View of Freedom

The Compatibility of Guidance Control and Reformed Theology

Michael Patrick Preciado

FOREWORD BY
Paul Helm

☙PICKWICK *Publications* • Eugene, Oregon

A REFORMED VIEW OF FREEDOM
The Compatibility of Guidance Control and Reformed Theology

Copyright © 2019 Michael Patrick Preciado. All rights reserved. Except for brief quotations in critical publications or reviews, no part of this book may be reproduced in any manner without prior written permission from the publisher. Write: Permissions, Wipf and Stock Publishers, 199 W. 8th Ave., Suite 3, Eugene, OR 97401.

Pickwick Publications
An Imprint of Wipf and Stock Publishers
199 W. 8th Ave., Suite 3
Eugene, OR 97401

www.wipfandstock.com

PAPERBACK ISBN: 978-1-5326-5892-1
HARDCOVER ISBN: 978-1-5326-5893-8
EBOOK ISBN: 978-1-5326-5894-5

Cataloguing-in-Publication data:

Names: Preciado, Michael Patrick, author. | Helm, Paul, foreword.

Title: A reformed view of freedom : the compatibility of guidance control and reformed theology / by Michael Patrick Preciado ; foreword by Paul Helm.

Description: Eugene, OR: Pickwick Publications, 2019 | Includes bibliographical references.

Identifiers: ISBN 978-1-5326-5892-1 (paperback) | ISBN 978-1-5326-5893-8 (hardcover) | ISBN 978-1-5326-5894-5 (ebook)

Subjects: LCSH: Free will and determinism—Religious aspects—Christianity | Providence and government of God—Christianity | Responsibility | Calvinism | Philosophy and religion

Classification: BT135 P72 2019 (print) | BT135 (ebook)

Manufactured in the U.S.A. 06/07/19

To Alexandra, Michael Jr., and Kirsten

Contents

Foreword by Paul Helm | ix
Acknowledgements | xiii
Introduction | xv

CHAPTER ONE: Frankfurt Examples and Moderate Reasons-Responsiveness | 1
CHAPTER TWO: Mechanism Ownership | 38
CHAPTER THREE: Decree, Foreknowledge, and Providence | 61
CHAPTER FOUR: Rational Spontaneity and the Sensus Divinitatis | 140
CHAPTER FIVE: Jonathan Edwards and the Reformed Tradition | 183

Conclusion | 217
Appendix: Criticisms of Fischer and Ravizza | 219
Bibliography | 275

Foreword by Paul Helm

THE ROAD OF THE interaction of Christian theology with philosophy has been long and sometimes rocky. Maybe it began with Paul at Athens, with his assertion that Epimenides (c. 600 BC) wrote that God is the one in whom "we live and move and have our being" (Acts 17:28). Augustine leant on Plato, Calvin cited the Stoics, the Reformed Orthodox were indebted to the medieval scholastics who relied on Aquinas, and Aquinas on Aristotle, and so on.

Mike Preciado's splendid book continues this tradition. He uses contemporary work on determinism to elucidate the relationship of our wills with the decree of God, supporting the Reformed position. And particularly with the help of this work he offers elucidations of basic human moral responsibility in a deterministic world.

There is determinism, and there is compatibilism. The compatibilist is a determinist who argues that determined actions may be actions that the agent is responsible for, praised if good, blamed if bad. Mike argues that work done by two contemporary philosophers, John Martin Fischer and Mark Ravizza, SJ, as it happens supports the compatibilism of the Westminster Confession and of confessional Reformed Theology more generally in arguing that under certain conditions determinism is consistent with personal accountability, hence compatibilism. Fischer and Ravizza call their position "Guidance Control." The first aspect of guidance control is "reasons-responsiveness," the second is "mechanism ownership."

Each of these positions in a more rudimentary form will be found by the diligent student of confessional Reformed theology. The purpose of the first chapter of his book is to familiarize the reader with Fischer and Ravizza's unique brand of reasons-responsive theory. In chapter 2, the author presents their conception of mechanism ownership, the second aspect of guidance control. These correspond to our intuitions that responsibility has to do with the degree of our responsiveness to reasons (a responsiveness that babies lack) and that we have an awareness of our ownership of our "mechanism," our body and its connection to our mind. Though God may decree that we have lunch, it is not then God who has lunch for us, but we have it for ourselves. I cannot in raising my own arm raise your arm, and so on. These are features that ground our responsibility for our actions.

The author spends the first two chapters (and the Appendix) expounding this philosophical position, Guidance Control, in a purely philosophical way. These chapters are examples of contemporary analytic philosophy, neat and at full strength. They are executed clearly and with full knowledge of the discussion that has grown up around these proposals. Granted, this will not be every reader's cup of tea. However for such readers Mike has provided a useful précis of the conclusions at the beginning, in his Introduction. It must be said, however, that his full exposition and a clear, step by step account, will enlighten any non-philosopher who is prepared to take their time over the technicalities. Mike suggests that the non-philosopher first skip chapters 1 and 2, until they have read the other chapters, 3–5. and this is probably wise counsel. In philosophy, as in much else, practice makes perfect.

In these later, theological chapters, the author considers relevant parts of Reformed theology in the light of Guidance Control, showing his ability not only as a philosopher but a Reformed theologian. In these chapters he expertly shows how these contemporary developments of the philosophy of compatibilism can apply to Reformed theology, offering understanding of the Westminster Confession on the divine decree, divine foreknowledge, and providence, and the position of Jonathan Edwards in his book on the freedom of the will. He then applies this theology to illuminate a range of discussions on free will in Reformed theology by a critical consideration of Richard Muller's view that compatibilism represents a "parting of the ways" in the history of Reformed theology.

Philosophy is not divine revelation. For the Christian that revelation takes priority. Nevertheless philosophy can be an illuminating tool in understanding doctrines of the faith, and offering support for them. So long as it is not the master.

So the heart of the book centers on the claim that Reformed anthropology is deterministic, pivoting on the divine eternal decree. More exactly it is compatibilistic in that under certain conditions a deterministic action is praiseworthy or blameworthy, that is, a person has responsibility. In some sense the agent uniquely "owns" those actions for which he is responsible, and which are not the result of coercion or mere reflexes, for example. One way that this can be illustrated, is in the Confession's closing statement on God's eternal decree:

> Although, in relation to the foreknowledge and decree of God, the first cause, all things come to pass immutably and infallibly;

yet, by the same providence, he ordereth them to fall out *according to the nature of second causes, either necessarily, freely, or contingently.* (WCF 5:2)

The decree of God, the first cause, is nuanced; it takes into account the natures of what is caused, and in the laconic wording of the Confession, God the first cause "rendereth them to fall out" accordingly. It is the nature of human nature that we have responsive control. Of course not all the changes that we undergo are cases of responsive control. If I have lost a leg, I cannot respond to the command to run, but then I am not blamed when I stumble along. We can see here, incidentally, how the question of human responsibility connects with what both the Reformed Orthodox, and Jonathan Edwards as well, called cases of moral and natural ability and inability. These distinctions when they are worked out by them, can be thought of as their way of pointing to the kinds and limits of responsive control, and therefore of human responsibility.

Preciado examines the position of the WCF not only on the decree, divine foreknowledge, and predestination, but also on the creation of mankind with a *sensus divinitatis*, a topic that seems to be downplayed by Reformed theologians at the present. He commendably shows that the WCF and Jonathan Edwards both emphasize this as the locus of human responsibility, though I think this is frequently overlooked in Edwards's case.

The sensus divinitatis is the evidence that as creatures in God's image (though fallen) with particular ranges of responsiveness, the behavior of the conscience is part of our creaturely endowment. Mike notes that besides his commitment to compatibilism (for which he is best known), in *The Freedom of the Will*, Edwards has strong statements of the *sensus divinitatis*. His citation of Edwards's Miscellany 533 is peculiarly apt, with its stress on personal accountability to God based on his law implanted innately in the conscience.

The chapter on Edwards also takes issue with Richard Muller's view that Edwards's compatibilism distinguishes him from his theological antecedents. In brief, Mike argues that from a commitment to predestination and divine providence, human compatibilism follows, and that Muller's attempt to find a mid-way position between libertarianism and determinism in what he refers to as our possession of "multiple potencies" does not succeed in identifying a "third way."

Mike Preciado is to be congratulated on his new book. It is a model of Christian apologetics, of an intensive examination of one set of interrelated topics in Christian theology by a person who knows what he is doing, both in philosophy and theology.

Acknowledgements

I would like to thank Andrew McGowan and Innes Visagie for overseeing the dissertation which later became this book. I appreciated their helpful feedback. I would also like to thank John Martin Fischer for reviewing some of the chapters of this book when it was in dissertation form. He gave me very valuable feedback. In addition, I would also like to thank Paul Helm. He encouraged me to seek publication of this work and to add a chapter on Jonathan Edwards. His feedback was invaluable.

Most of all I would like to thank my beloved wife Alexandra for all her support, patience, and thoughtfulness during this project. I could not have done it without her.

Introduction

OVER THE COURSE OF the past fifty years or so, an explosion of literature in the study of free will and moral responsibility has appeared. Analytic philosophers have discussed these issues in detail and have provided much material that could be beneficial to reformed theologians and philosophers. Yet few, if any, reformed theologians and philosophers have mined these resources. Many are unaware of these resources or they think that they are not compatible with reformed theology. Therefore, there is a need for a study focused on asking whether reformed theology is compatible with these resources. More specifically, there is a need for a study focused on asking whether reformed theology is compatible with one of the most highly regarded theories of freedom and moral responsibility, that of John Martin Fischer and Mark Ravizza.

Fischer and Ravizza call their theory guidance control. It is the purpose of this book to ask the question, "Is guidance control compatible with reformed theology?" In this book, I will argue for an affirmative answer. I believe that an affirmative answer opens the door for reformed theologians and philosophers to make use of these resources. In the course of answering this question, a few other important issues will be illuminated. We will see that reformed theology is theological determinism. We will see that reformed theology is compatibilism or semi-compatibilism. We will see that there is no substantial departure between Jonathan Edwards and the reformed orthodox on the issue of free will and moral responsibility. These propositions have been recently denied by the Utrecht School and Richard Muller.

The purpose of this book is threefold. First and foremost, to establish compatibility between guidance control and reformed theology on the issues of freedom and moral responsibility. This will be done by establishing that reformed theology denies the sourcehood and alternative possibilities conditions, by establishing that rational spontaneity is a primitive form of reasons-responsive theory and by establishing that reformed theology and guidance control have a similar subjectivist condition. I will define these concepts shortly.

An important consequence follows, namely that reformed theology is broadly compatible with most, if not all, other compatibilist and semi-compatibilist theories. In addition, reformed theology is compatible with most, if not all, other reasons-responsive theories. This is important because it reveals that reformed philosophers and theologians have a wealth of material from which they can draw in contemporary analytic philosophy. This conclusion also rebuts the Utrecht School's and Richard Muller's denial that reformed theology is compatibilism.

The second purpose of this book is to elucidate the reformed orthodox view of freedom and moral responsibility. I will accomplish this by stating the reformed orthodox view in their own terms as well as in the terms of contemporary analytic philosophy. This will allow reformed theologians and philosophers to see what the reformed view amounts to in light of current debates in contemporary philosophy.

The third purpose of this book is to show that there is basic continuity between the reformed orthodox and Jonathan Edwards with regard to freedom and moral responsibility. It will be argued that there are some differences, however, they hold substantially the same position. This conclusion rebuts Richard Mullers's contention that there was a parting of ways between Edwards and the reformed orthodox.

This book began as my doctoral dissertation. In the process of preparing it for publication, I have made some changes to the original. First, I added a new chapter on Jonathan Edwards and the reformed tradition. Second, I moved chapter three of the dissertation to an appendix in this book. In this appendix, I explain how one could philosophically defend guidance control. This is not intended to be an exhaustive defense. It is intended merely to show the plausibility of guidance control. In the course of this defense, I suggest two areas of departure from Fischer. First, that we adopt an agent as opposed to a mechanism-based view of guidance control. Second, that we adopt a hard line as opposed to a soft line approach to manipulation cases. All this is explained in the appendix. Third, I have added a new introduction and conclusion. Finally, I have made minor modifications to the body of the book to make for an easier read.

The argument of this book will unfold in five chapters. In chapter one, I present Fischer and Ravizza's conception of moderate reasons-responsiveness. This is the first aspect of guidance control. The purpose of this chapter is to familiarize the reader with Fischer and Ravizza's unique brand of reasons-responsive theory. In chapter two, I present Fischer and Ravizza's conception of mechanism ownership. This is the second aspect of guidance control. In chapter three, I begin to argue for the compatibility of guidance control with reformed theology. I argue that the reformed doctrines of decree, foreknowledge, and providence deny the sourcehood and alternative possibilities conditions. The denial of these two conditions establishes a broad compatibility with all compatibilist and semi-compatibilist theories of freedom and moral responsibility. In particular, it establishes broad compatibility with guidance control. In chapter four, I argue for a more specific compatibility between guidance control and reformed theology. In particular, I argue that the reformed doctrine of rational spontaneity is a form of reasons-responsive theory. This establishes compatibility with moderate reasons-responsiveness. It also establishes that reformed theology is compatible with other reason-responsive theories in the literature. In addition, I argue that the reformed doctrine of the *sensus divinitatis* implies a similar subjectivist condition to that of mechanism ownership. In this way, reformed theology is compatible with mechanism ownership. Finally, in chapter five, I argue that the reformed orthodox view of freedom and moral responsibility is substantially the same as the view of Jonathan Edwards. This is accomplished by arguing that Edwards denies the sourcehood and alternative possibilities conditions, that he affirms a type of reasons-responsive theory and that he affirms a type of subjectivist condition. In addition, I survey the debate between Richard Muller and Paul Helm. I point out the continuity and discontinuity between Edwards and the reformed orthodox. I end by challenging Richard Muller on what Paul Helm calls the crux of the matter. I challenge the notion that Muller's multiple potencies marks a major teaching of the reformed orthodox from which Edwards parted ways.

At this point, I would like to offer the reader two different reading strategies. I offer these strategies to facilitate easier reading for those with different interests. The first reading strategy is just to plow through the book from the introduction through the appendix. This strategy is offered for those who are interested in a more detailed account of how Fischer and Ravizza arrive at their view and how it can be philosophically defended. The first two chapters are largely exegesis of guidance control. I felt the need to let Fischer and Ravizza speak in their own words as much as possible. I personally find an exegesis like this helpful because many important details can be lost in a basic summary.

The second strategy is to skip chapters one, two and the appendix. I will give a brief summary of guidance control at the end of this introduction. One could read that summary and then read chapters three, four and five. This strategy is offered for those that are not as interested in how Fischer and Ravizza arrive at guidance control and are not as interested in how it can be philosophically defended. Both reading strategies will enable the reader to profit from this book according to their own interests.

Before I move to a summary of guidance control, I feel the need to explain the title of this book. The title is intended to communicate that guidance control is one way in which a philosopher or theologian can extend and elaborate upon the reformed view of freedom and moral responsibility. However, it is not the only way. This is why I titled it *A Reformed View of Freedom* and not *The Reformed View of Freedom*. As I have mentioned, there are other compatibilist, semi-compatibilist and reason-responsive views out there that are compatible with reformed theology and may be better extensions and elaborations of reformed theology. The use of the indefinite article in the title is meant to communicate this fact. At the same time, I do believe that guidance control holds out the most promise. This is why I have chosen to examine it in relation to reformed theology.

I would like to begin my basic summary of guidance control by defining key concepts that will govern this book. These key concepts are more important for seeing the compatibility of guidance control and reformed theology than the specific details of guidance control. This is why I am choosing to summarize them up front. If one grasps guidance control along these lines, then one will be in a good position for seeing the compatibility of guidance control, reformed theology and Jonathan Edwards. At this point, I am not going to rigorously define these concepts. Rather, I am going to state them in a very basic manner. This will enable the reader to have a quick and basic grasp of what drives this book. Throughout the course of the following chapters, these concepts will be more rigorously defined.

The first is the sourcehood condition. This is the idea that an agent must be the ultimate source of his actions if he is to be properly regarded as free and morally responsible. The agent's actions must terminate in the agent and not in something outside of him such as God's decree or the laws of physics.

The second concept is the alternative possibilities condition. This is also known as the principle of alternative possibilities or PAP. It states that an agent must have the ability to do otherwise if he is to be genuinely regarded as free and morally responsible. We will see that there are numerous senses of "could have done other." Reformed theology denies that an agent could have done other than what God decreed, foreknew and controls by His providence. This will be made more precise throughout the book.

The third concept is reasons-responsiveness. This is the idea that an agent is free and morally responsible if he is able to respond to reasons in an appropriate manner. There are various views as to what constitutes responding to reasons in an appropriate manner. These details are not important at this point. One just needs to understand that reason-responsiveness means that freedom and moral responsibility are understood in terms of the ability to respond to reasons in a certain way.

The fourth concept is the subjectivist condition. This is the idea that a free and morally responsible agent must view himself in a certain way. Typically, he must view himself as an agent that can properly be blamed or praised. It is not only the case that the objective conditions for freedom and moral responsibility must be met, but it is also the case that the agent must have this subjective view of himself. If he lacks this subjective view of himself, then he is not free and morally responsible.

Having defined these basic concepts, we can now move to a summary of guidance control. As I mentioned, the specific details of guidance control need not be digested in order to see the compatibility of guidance control, reformed theology and Jonathan Edwards. This is why I am contenting myself to give a very basic overview of guidance control here. If one has chosen the second reading strategy, this will be sufficient to follow chapters three, four and five.

A very common approach to freedom and moral responsibility makes use of PAP. The basic idea is that for an agent to be free and thus morally responsible, the agent must have been able to do otherwise. Fischer and Ravizza reject this idea. They do so, in large part, on the basis of Frankfurt style counter examples (FSCs). FSCs are thought experiments that purport to give a logically possible example wherein an agent is free and morally responsible but did not have the ability to do otherwise. If these thought experiments work, then they show that PAP is not necessary for freedom and moral responsibility. Fischer and Ravizza maintain that FSCs do work.

It would be helpful to give a very basic FSC in order to see what motivates Fischer and Ravizza. Imagine a scenario where Black wants Jones to vote for Hillary Clinton. Black wants to ensure that Jones votes for Clinton, so he goes to great lengths to ensure that Jones does. Unbeknownst to Jones, Black has secretly installed a device in Jones brain where Black can monitor Jones thoughts and force Jones to vote for Clinton if necessary. Black can monitor Jones thoughts so that if Jones is about to vote for Trump, Black can flip a switch and force Jones to vote for Hillary. On election day, Jones walks into the voting booth and votes for Clinton on his own accord. Black never has to flip the switch forcing Jones to vote for Clinton. In light of this FSC, it appears that Jones freely and morally responsibly voted for Clinton even though he could not have done otherwise. He could not have done otherwise because Black was always lurking in the background ready to flip the switch that would ensure that Jones voted for Clinton, but he never had to flip it.

FSCs such as the one above come in varying degrees of complexity. Yet they all have a basic structure. They seek to present a logically possible scenario, where the agent cannot do otherwise and where we have the intuition that the agent acted freely and morally responsibly. The above example is logically possible and it does invoke the intuition, among many, that Jones acted freely and morally responsibly.

This leads Fischer and Ravizza to ask why we have the intuition that the agent is free and morally responsible in FSCs? They answer this question by examining FSCs more closely. They find that what makes the agent free and morally responsible is what actually happens in the example, not the ability to do otherwise. Thus, they find in the actual sequence, the conditions of freedom and moral responsibility. These conditions are the content of guidance control. Guidance control consists of two parts. The first part is moderate reasons-responsiveness. The second part is mechanism ownership. I will briefly explain these two parts below.

Fischer and Ravizza have a long discussion of what it means for an agent to be moderately reasons-responsive. Briefly put, to be moderately reasons-responsive is to be regularly receptive to reasons and weakly reactive to reasons. To be regularly receptive to reasons means that the agent has the ability to recognize an understandable pattern of moral reasons. To be weakly reactive to reasons requires that there be one possible world where the agent would do otherwise. This is the first part of guidance control.

The second part of guidance control is mechanism ownership. Fischer and Ravizza call their view of mechanism ownership a subjectivist view. This view consists of three parts. First, an agent must view himself as an agent. He must see himself as causing some of his actions. Second, the agent must view himself as the fair target of the reactive attitudes. That is, he must view himself as the proper target of praise and blame. Third, the agent must base the first two parts of mechanism ownership on evidence.

This basic summary of guidance control is admittedly abstract. The details of this account are found in chapters one and two. However, it is not necessary to read those chapters in order to have an adequate enough understanding of guidance control to proceed. It is sufficient to know the positions guidance control and reformed theology take on the sourcehood condition, the alternative possibilities condition, reasons-responsiveness and the subjectivist view.

Let us first look at guidance control along the lines of these four concepts. First, guidance control denies the sourcehood condition. It denies that an agent must be the ultimate source of his actions in order to be free and morally responsible. Second, guidance control denies the alternative possibilities condition. It is not necessary that an agent have access to alternative possibilities in the actual sequence for him to be free and morally responsible. Third, guidance control affirms a type of reasons-responsive theory. It affirms that moderate reasons-responsiveness is necessary for free and morally responsible action. Fourth, guidance control affirms mechanism ownership as a subjectivist condition. That is, it is a necessary part of guidance control that the agent view himself along the lines of mechanism ownership.

Now let us see reformed theology along the lines of these four concepts. First, reformed theology denies the sourcehood condition. Human beings are not the ultimate source of their actions. Rather, God's decree, providence and foreknowledge are the ultimate source. Second, reformed theology denies the alternative possibilities condition. It is not the case that an agent has the ability to do otherwise than what God has decreed, foreknew and controls by his providence. God's decree, foreknowledge and providence cannot be thwarted. Third, reformed theology affirms a type of reasons-responsive theory. Their view of rational spontaneity is a primitive type of reasons-responsive theory. Fourth, reformed theology affirms a type of subjectivist condition. The sensus divinitatis holds that mankind has a knowledge of God and his law implanted within. This implies that every human being views himself as an agent that is properly praiseworthy and blameworthy. In addition, I will argue that the position of Jonathan Edwards is identical with reformed theology on these four concepts.

CHAPTER ONE

Frankfurt Examples and Moderate Reasons-Responsiveness

Introduction

THIS CHAPTER WILL EXPLORE Fischer and Ravizza's account of moral responsibility. They believe that the essence of moral responsibility is guidance control. An agent is morally responsible for his actions if he possesses guidance control when he commits them. Guidance control consists of two main parts. The first part is moderate reasons-responsiveness. The second part is mechanism ownership. Both of these are necessary for guidance control. In this chapter, I will discuss moderate reasons-responsiveness. In this chapter we will see that Fischer and Ravizza deny the sourcehood condition, deny the alternative possibilities condition and affirm a type of reasons-responsive theory. In the next chapter, I will discuss mechanism ownership. There we will see that Fischer and Ravizza affirm a subjectivist condition.

This chapter has five main parts. The first part will discuss the concept of control. This is important because moral responsibility relates directly to whether or not an agent has appropriate control over his actions. The second part will discuss reasons-responsiveness in general. Here we will see two accounts of reasons-responsiveness that are ultimately rejected: strong reasons-responsiveness (SRR) and weak reasons-responsiveness (WRR). In this section, Fischer and Ravizza will make some important refinements to these theories in order to come up with a more adequate account of reasons-responsiveness. The two main refinements deal with the concepts of "mechanism" and "tracing." The third part of this chapter is Fischer and Ravizza's account of moderate reasons-responsiveness. This account will be applied to three areas of human life for which we hold people responsible: (1) actions, (2) consequences, and (3) omission. In the third section, I will deal only with actions. The fourth and fifth sections will apply moderate reasons-responsiveness to consequences and omissions, respectively.

The Concept of "Control"

> I could certainly imagine waking up some morning to the newspaper headline, "Causal Determinism Is True!" (Most likely this would not be in the *National Inquirer* or *People*—but perhaps the *New York Times*). . . . I could imagine reading the article and subsequently (presumably over some time) becoming convinced that causal determinism is true—that the generalizations that describe the relationships between complexes of past events and laws of nature, on the one hand, and subsequent events, on the other, are universal generalizations with 100 percent probabilities. And I feel confident that this would not, nor should it, change my view of myself and others as (sometimes) free and robustly morally responsible agents—deeply different from other animals.[1]

Some philosophers believe that the truth of causal determinism (or determinism of any sort) is incompatible with many of the common-sense beliefs we have about ourselves. For example, it is incompatible with our belief that we are persons, incompatible with the belief that we are free, or incompatible with the belief that we are morally responsible. They see determinism as a threat to very important and fundamental beliefs. These beliefs are central to our way of life and the societies we have built.

John Martin Fischer and Mark Ravizza do not believe that the truth of causal determinism ought to change these beliefs. Their account of moral responsibility is motivated by a desire to preserve these common-sense beliefs. On their account, causal determinism can be true and we can preserve these beliefs. More specifically, their account attempts to show how our belief that we are morally responsible agents is compatible with the truth of causal determinism. Affirming this compatibility is a denial of the sourcehood condition. Though we will not explore it in this book, Fischer and Ravizza believe that their account of moral responsibility is also compatible with the falsity of causal determinism.[2]

In order to explore Fischer and Ravizza's theory, we first need to have a definition of "causal determinism." Peter Van Inwagen gives a basic definition of determinism:

---

1. Fischer, "Compatibilism," 44.

2. "Further, we shall suggest that our account of moral responsibility is consistent not only with the truth of causal determinism, but with its falsity as well; this renders moral responsibility optimally insulated from scientific discoveries about the form and implications of the laws of nature" (Fischer, *Responsibility and Control*, 26).

> Determinism is, intuitively, the thesis that, given the past and the laws of nature, there is only one possible future.[3]

The basic idea is that the past entails only one future. This definition is broad enough to incorporate a number of different types of determinism. Robert Kane writes:

> Doctrines of determinism have taken many historical forms. But there is a core idea running through all historical doctrines of determinism that reveals why they are a threat to free will—whether the doctrines be fatalistic, theological, logical, physical, psychological or social. According to this core idea:
>
> An event (such as a choice or action) is *determined* when there are conditions obtaining earlier (such as the decrees of fate or the foreordaining acts of God or antecedent causes plus laws of nature) whose occurrence is a sufficient condition for the occurrence of the event. In other words, it *must* be the case that, *if* these earlier determining conditions obtain, then the determined event will occur.[4]

This definition is broad enough to cover various forms of determinism and gives us a good understanding of the concept of "determinism." We can see from this definition that any affirmation of any type of determinism denies the sourcehood condition. The agent cannot be the ultimate source of his actions given determinism. Instead, depending on the type of determinism, the laws of physics, the decrees of God, etc. are the ultimate source of the agent's actions. Fischer and Ravizza's understanding of determinism fall under Kane's definition, though they make it more specific. Fischer defines it as follows:

> The thesis that, for any given time, a complete statement of the facts about that time, together with a complete statement of the laws of nature, entails every truth as to what happens after that time.[5]

This definition excludes any appeal to fate or God's decree as the determining past. Instead, it appeals to facts and laws of nature. These facts and laws entail every truth that happens in the future.

As I mentioned, many believe that the truth of causal determinism threatens, if not eliminates, moral responsibility. Their concerns center on the concept of "control." If causal determinism is true, then, it is argued,

---

3. Van Inwagen, *Essay on Free Will*, 65.
4. Kane, *Contemporary Introduction to Free Will*, 5–6.
5. Fischer, *Metaphysics of Free Will*, 9.

humans do not possess the proper sort of control over their actions. Intuitively, we tend to tie control and moral responsibility together. Most people would not judge a person to be morally responsible for an action that was "out of their control." Our common-sense conception of "moral responsibility" centers on "control." Therefore, in order to make progress toward a theory of moral responsibility, we must analyze the concept of "control" more closely. Once we do so, it will become clear that control is not incompatible with causal determinism. Only certain conceptions of control are incompatible with causal determinism.

With this understanding of causal determinism, we can proceed to a basic analysis of the concept of control. Philosophers analyze the concept of control in two main ways: (1) control as access to alternative possibilities and (2) control as being the appropriate source of one's actions. The first analysis of the concept of control has been labeled the "Principle of Alternative Possibilities" (PAP). Harry Frankfurt's famous essay, "Alternative Possibilities and Moral Responsibility," defines PAP as follows:

> A dominant role in nearly all recent inquiries into the free-will problem has been played by a principle which I shall call "the principle of alternative possibilities." This principle states that a person is morally responsible for what he has done only if he could have done otherwise.[6]

Carl Ginet states it more precisely:

> It is natural to embrace the following general principle, to which I will give the name 'the principle of alternative possibilities' (PAP for short): PAP: An agent S is morally responsible for its being the case that p only if S could have made it not the case that p.[7]

The PAP analysis of control states that an agent has control if and only if the agent could have done something other than what he did. This specific type of control is communicated by the phrase "could have." If the agent is to be legitimately held as a morally responsible agent, then it must have been within his power to refrain from action p. The agent must have had access to an alternative possibility, such as not p. PAP is supposed to be incompatible with causal determinism because causal determinism denies access to alternative possibilities. This means that causal determinism is incompatible

---

6. Frankfurt, "Alternative Possibilities and Moral Responsibility," 167.
7. Ginet, "In Defense of the Principle," 75.

with moral responsibility.[8] Fischer and Ravizza call this analysis of control regulative control.

We can illustrate regulative control by comparing it with a garden of forking paths. Imagine yourself in a garden and you are walking down one path. You come to a fork at the end of that path which branches off into two different directions. Both paths are open for you to take, but you can only choose one. In this garden, there are a number of these forking path options. This means that there are a number of alternative possibilities that could be taken. In other words, there is access to alternative possibilities. Fischer writes:

> When we take one path rather than another in a situation in which the other path is genuinely available to us, we say that we have a certain kind of *control* over our behavior. In this kind of circumstance, a person has the sort of control which involves alternative possibilities: he follows one path, and yet he *can* ("is able to," "has it in his power to") follow another path.[9]

Causal determinism rejects this picture of a garden of forking paths. Instead, it conceives of the future as having only one path. In light of this, it is clear how causal determinism threatens control if it is analyzed according to PAP. An agent in a causally determined world does not have the ability to do something other than what he did. So, we see that determinism must deny PAP.

---

8. There are philosophers that affirm both PAP and causal determinism. They are sometimes known by the label "Classical Compatibilism." They believe that there is an analysis of PAP that is compatible with causal determinism. One example of this is G. E. Moore's *Ethics*. In this book, he gives what has come to be known as the hypothetical analysis. If we apply this to PAP, Moore would be saying that the phrase "could have" in PAP is equivocal. A causal determinist could give an analysis of 'could have' or equivalent terms such as 'able,' that is compatible with causal determinism. His hypothetical analysis of "could have" states: "S was able to do otherwise" means "if S had willed (or chosen, or wanted, etc.) to do otherwise, then S would have done otherwise." This type of analysis had precursors in Hume, *Enquiry Concerning Human Understanding*, 104.

Contemporary philosophers that defend the compatibility of PAP and causal determinism are Berofsky, "Classical Compatibilism"; "Ifs, Cans, and Free Will"; Vihvelin, *Causes, Laws, and Free Will*. Vihvelin is not labeled as a classical compatibilist. Instead she is often labeled a New Dispositionalist. This is because she gives a dispositional account of free will.

Fischer and Ravizza avoid the issues of the compatibility of causal determinism and PAP by advocating Frankfurt Style Counterexamples (FSCs). FSCs purportedly show that PAP is false. If this is the case, then it is unnecessary to give an account of the compatibility of free will or moral responsibility with PAP.

9. Fischer, *Metaphysics of Free Will*, 4.

The second analysis of control deals with being the appropriate source of one's own actions. Derk Pereboom describes it as follows:

> In metaphysical terms, the sort of free will required for moral responsibility does not consist most fundamentally in the availability of alternative possibilities, but rather in the agent's being the causal source of her action in a specific way.[10]

This requirement sounds intuitive. If a murder occurred at 2:00 AM and I am one hundred miles away from the murder at that time, then it seems unreasonable to hold me responsible for committing the murder. It is unreasonable because I could not have been the causal source of that murder in the right way. The idea of the sourcehood requirement is that we cannot be held responsible for actions for which we are not the appropriate source.[11] This concept of control is analyzed not in terms of alternative possibilities, but in terms of being the proper causal source of our actions.

Some argue that determinism threatens this sort of control because, given determinism, agents are not the proper causal source of their action. In order to see this, let us return to Fischer's definition of causal determinism:

> The thesis that, for any given time, a complete statement of the facts about that time, together with a complete statement of the laws of nature, entails every truth as to what happens after that time.[12]

There are three parts of this definition: (1) a given time (call this T), (2) a complete statement of the facts about a given time (call this F), and (3) a complete statement of the laws of nature (call this L). Any truth after T, F,

---

10. Pereboom quoted in Timpe, *Free Will*, 121.

11. For the incompatibilist, this sourcehood requirement is some type of ultimacy. Robert Kane provides a good understanding of this: "*Free Will*, in the traditional sense I want to retrieve . . . is *the power of agents to be the ultimate creators (or originators) and sustainers of their own ends or purposes.* . . . To act freely is to be unhindered in the pursuit of your purposes (which are usually expressed by intentions; to will freely, in this traditional sense, is to be the ultimate creator (prime mover, so to speak) of your own purposes. . . . Its meaning can be captured initially by an image: when we trace the causal or explanatory chains of action back to their sources in the purposes of free agents, these causal chains must come to an end or terminate in the willings (choices, decisions, or efforts) of the agents, which cause or bring about their purposes. If these willings were in turn caused by something else, so that the explanatory chains could be traced back further to heredity or environment, to God, or fate, then the ultimacy would not lie with the agents but with something else" (Kane, *Significance of Free Will*, 4). Fischer and Ravizza will argue that this conception of sourcehood is too strong. For an extended discussion of this type of sourcehood, see Fischer, "Sourcehood."

12. Fischer, *Metaphysics of Free Will*, 9.

and L is entailed by T, F, and L. This means that the murder of Jones by Smith is entailed by T, F, and L. But if the murder of Jones by Smith is entailed by something outside of Smith (T, F, and L), then how could Smith be the appropriate causal source of Jones's murder? It could be argued that the real causal source of the murder was all of the facts (F) at a given time (T) together with all the laws of nature (L). This caused Jones's murder, not Smith. In other words, Jones did not have the appropriate control over his actions to be morally responsible for the murder. He did not have appropriate control because he was not the ultimate causal source. Determinism must deny the sourcehood condition understood as ultimate sourcehood.

In light of this, it would appear that causal determinism excludes the agent from "being the causal source of her action in a specific way."[13] As we will see, the phrase "specific way" will be important. Fischer and Ravizza do not think their specific concept of control is incompatible with being the appropriate causal source of our actions. Their specific concept of control is compatible with causal determinism. Fischer and Ravizza deny the sourcehood condition understood as ultimate sourcehood. Yet, they will affirm that an agent is an appropriate causal source if he acts with guidance control. This is a more modest view than ultimate sourcehood.

We have seen that the concept of control is analyzed in two parts: (1) PAP and (2) sourcehood. We have also seen how these two concepts of control can provide a challenge to the compatibility of causal determinism and moral responsibility. We will now see how Fischer and Ravizza respond to these two concepts of control. They respond in two ways. First, they answer the PAP (or the regulative control) analysis of control by appealing to the Frankfurt Style Counterexamples (FSCs). FSCs are supposed to show that PAP is not necessary for moral responsibility. Second, they answer the sourcehood analysis of control with their conception of guidance control. If they succeed, then they would have shown that causal determinism is compatible with moral responsibility.[14]

The first concept of control utilizes PAP. Carl Ginet defines PAP,

---

13. Timpe, *Free Will*, 121.

14. There are other confusions about determinism that cause people to be threatened besides PAP and the sourcehood requirement. Robert Kane has a good discussion of them. I will briefly list what they are without going into Kane's discussion: "1. Don't confuse determinism with constraint, coercion or compulsion.... 2. Don't confuse causation with constraint.... 3. Don't confuse determinism with control by other agents. ... 4. Don't confuse determinism with fatalism.... 5. Don't confuse determinism with mechanism" (Kane, *Contemporary Introduction*, 18–21). By 'mechanism' he means that agents are not machines running mechanically nor robots nor computers.

> PAP: An agent S is morally responsible for its being the case that p only if S could have made it not the case that p.[15]

There have been a number of responses to this concept of control in the literature. Some argue that it is false because our ordinary practices of holding people responsible do not rely on alternative possibilities.[16] Others give different types of arguments to show that alternative possibilities are not necessary for moral responsibility.[17] Still others appeal to the Frankfurt Style Counterexamples.[18] Fischer and Ravizza attempt to respond to PAP by appealing to Frankfurt Style Counterexamples.

These counterexamples are named after the philosopher Harry G. Frankfurt. In 1969, he published a very important paper called "Alternative Possibilities and Moral Responsibility."[19] In it, Frankfurt challenged the idea that access to alternative possibilities is necessary for freedom and moral responsibility. Frankfurt provided counterexamples to PAP. In these counterexamples, the agent was intuitively morally responsible and it was supposed that the agent did not have access to an alternative possibility.[20] Let us look at an FSC by John Martin Fischer:

> Because he dares to hope that the Democrats finally have a good chance of winning the White House, the benevolent but elderly neurosurgeon, Black, has come out of retirement to participate in yet another philosophical example . . . he has secretly inserted a chip in Jones's brain that enables Black to monitor and control Jones's activities. Black can exercise this control through a sophisticated computer that he had programmed so that, among

---

15. Ginet, "In Defense of the Principle," 75.
16. Wallace, *Responsibility and the Moral Sentiments*.
17. Dennett, *Elbow Room*; *Freedom Evolves*.
18. Fischer, *Metaphysics of Free Will*.
19. Frankfurt, "Alternative Possibilities and Moral Responsibility."
20. The counterexample strategy is an important way to argue against a rule or principle. Meghan Griffith explains how this works: "A counter-example is a scenario (often fictional, sometimes quite fanciful) that disproves a rule. It illustrates a case in which the rule does not hold. The Principle of Alternative Possibilities says that a person is responsible/free *only* if she could have done otherwise. This means that to disprove the rule, someone can give an example in which a person is responsible but could not have done otherwise. Thus, it's not *only* if able to do otherwise that a person is responsible. There might be occasions on which a person is responsible anyway. Maybe these aren't the usual; cases, but even one counterexample is enough. The principle is supposed to hold in general. It is supposed to tell us what has to be true in order for someone to be responsible. It says that there had to have been an alternative. If there is a scenario in which our intuitions tell us that a person is responsible without having alternatives, then the principle does not generally hold" (Griffith, *Free Will*, 43).

other things, it monitors Jones's voting behavior. If Jones were to show any inclination to vote for McCain (or, let us say, anyone other than Obama), then the computer, through the chip in Jones's brain, would intervene to assure that he actually decides to vote for Obama (as Black, the old progressive, would prefer), the computer does nothing but continue to monitor—without affecting—the goings-on in Jones's head.

Now suppose that Jones decides to vote for Obama on his own, just as he would have if Black had not inserted the chip in his head. It seems, upon first thinking about this case, that Jones can be held morally responsible for his choice and act of voting for Obama, although he could not have chosen otherwise and he could not have done otherwise.[21]

Counterexamples like this pose a challenge to PAP. In order to see this challenge, we must observe three things. First, Jones has no alternative possibilities. This is the role that Black fulfills in the example. Black has inserted a chip in Jones's brain and this chip enables Black to monitor and control Jones's activities. If the chip detects that Jones will vote for McCain, then the computer, through the chip, will cause Jones to vote for Obama. Black, the computer, and the chip eliminate Jones's alternative possibilities.[22] Second, Jones acts on his own. Though Black has all his equipment to ensure that Jones votes for Obama, he never needs to intervene. Jones decides on his own to vote for Obama. This is an important aspect of the counterexample. The idea is that Jones's voting for Obama, with Black's equipment in place, is no different than his voting for Obama without Black or any of his equipment. Third, this counterexample evokes the intuition that Jones is morally responsible for voting for Obama. As Fischer puts it, "It seems, upon first thinking about this case, that Jones can be held morally responsible for his choice and act of voting for Obama, although he could not have chosen otherwise and he could not have done otherwise."[23]

---

21. Fischer, "Frankfurt Cases," 34. As a historical point, John Locke had a precursor to FSCs: "Suppose a man be carried, whilst fast asleep, into a room, where is a person he longs to see and speak with; and be there locked fast in, beyond his power to get out: he awakes, and is glad to find himself in so desirable company, which he stays willingly in, i.e., prefers his stay to going away. I ask, is not this stay voluntary? I think, nobody will doubt it: and yet being locked fast in, 'tis evident he is not at liberty not to stay, he has not freedom to be gone" (Locke, *Essay Concerning Human Understanding*, 96).

22. Fischer will later argue that FSCs do not eliminate all alternative possibilities. However, he does not view this as a problem because they do eliminate all robust alternative possibilities. I will discuss this in the appendix of this book.

23. Fischer, "Frankfurt Cases," 34.

There is a further distinction that needs to be made in order to analyze this counterexample. It is the distinction between the actual sequence of events and the alternative sequence of events. The actual sequence is what actually happened in the counterexample. The actual sequence consisted of Jones voting for Obama on his own. In the actual sequence, we have the intuition that Jones is morally responsible. The alternative sequence is the sequence of Black's intervention. This sequence consists of Black, via the computer and the chip, intervening to cause Jones to vote for Obama. In the alternative sequence, we have the intuition that Jones is not morally responsible. This is because Black forced him to vote for Obama.[24]

If FSCs are successful, then they teach us that PAP is false and regulative control is not the type of control necessary for moral responsibility. However, FSCs are controversial. Some philosophers defend them[25] and others are critical of them.[26] I believe that they are successful; however, that discussion will take place in the appendix.

The second analysis of the concept of control centers on the sourcehood requirement. It is argued that we must be the appropriate source of our actions if we are to be morally responsible agents. Generally speaking, it is not sufficient to be *a* source of our actions, but we must be *the ultimate* source of our actions. If something outside of the agent is the ultimate

---

24. It is important that we understand that FSCs are not supposed to be real life scenarios. They are counterexamples or thought experiments. Matthew Iredale writes: "You may still want to object to it and argue that under normal circumstances figures like Black do not arise, and so we ordinarily *can* decide otherwise. But such a response misses the point of the example. It does not just seek to show that if a figure like Black were around that we could not decide otherwise, but rather to show that it is *logically possible* that a person can be in a position in which they *cannot* decide otherwise, and yet in which we would still wish to regard them as morally responsible. It is logically possible that there are situations in which being able to do otherwise is not a necessary condition of moral responsibility; situations in which ascriptions of moral responsibility do not rest upon PAP but purely upon other conditions. But (and this is the point) if we can describe the conditions of moral responsibility adequately without reference to PAP in *this* example, then we can do it in all situations, including real-life situations. And so we can conclude that the ability to choose otherwise is of no relevance whatsoever to moral responsibility" (Iredale, *Problem of Free Will*, 63).

25. Fischer, "Responsibility and Control"; "Responsibility and Failure"; *Metaphysics of Free Will*; "Responsibility and Self-Expression"; "Recent Work on Moral Responsibility"; "Responsibility and Agent-Causation"; "Responsibility and Alternative Possibilities"; "Frankfurt Cases"; *My Way*; Fischer and Ravizza, *Responsibility and Control*.

26. Kane, *Free Will and Values*; *Significance of Free Will*; Widerker, "Libertarianism and Frankfurt's Attack"; "Responsibility and Frankfurt-Type Examples"; Ginet, "In Defense of the Principle"; Wyma, "Moral Responsibility"; Goetz, "Frankfurt-Style Counterexamples"; Van Inwagen, *Essay on Free Will*; "Fischer on Moral Responsibility"; "Moral Responsibility"; O'Connor, "Alternative Possibilities and Responsibility"; McKenna, "Alternative Possibilities"; Ekstrom, "Protecting Incompatibilist Freedom."

source of the agent's actions (i.e., the facts of the universe together with laws of nature or the decree of God), then the agent cannot be morally responsible for those actions. Fischer disputes that this is the case. He writes:

> It is uncontentious that we want to be the "initiators" or "ultimate sources" of our behavior, in some suitable sense, and that a morally responsible agent must meet some conditions that capture these ideas appropriately. It is, however, controversial whether the relevant idea of sourcehood entails the strong sort of "self-creation" that seems to be envisaged by Strawson, Smilansky and even Kane. . . . I shall suggest that their views may depend on an inappropriate and unduly demanding picture, according to which the locus of control must be entirely "internal" to the agent, in order for there to be robust, genuine moral responsibility.[27]

Fischer and Ravizza believe that the idea of "ultimate sourcehood" as understood by Strawson, Smilansky, and Kane is too strong. Therefore, they adopt another notion of sourcehood that is appropriate for moral responsibility but not as strong as "ultimate sourcehood." Fischer and Ravizza's concept of "guidance control" is such a notion. In the remainder of this chapter and the next, I will describe Fischer and Ravizza's concept of guidance control as an answer to the sourcehood requirement for moral responsibility. They argue that guidance control is the kind of control necessary for moral responsibility and that it is compatible with causal determinism.

In giving their description of guidance control, FSCs motivate Fischer and Ravizza. Why do we have the intuition that Jones is morally responsible in this case? In the example, Black wants Jones to vote for Obama. He has taken all the precautions necessary to ensure that Jones will vote for Obama. Black, the chip, and the computer, will all ensure that Jones votes for Obama if necessary. Yet, we see that Jones votes for Obama on his own, without any intervention. A distinction was made between the actual sequence and the alternative sequence. In order to see why Jones is morally responsible, Fischer and Ravizza argue that we need to analyze the actual sequence. In other words, they are interested in analyzing the details of what actually happened in the Frankfurt example. The reason for this is that we intuitively hold the agent responsible when the actual sequence is actualized. What is it about the actual sequence that makes us think the agent is responsible? Clearly it is not access to alternative possibilities. The analysis of the actual sequence points Fischer and Ravizza to their concept of guidance control. In short, the agent in the actual sequence is responsible because he has guidance control and

---

27. Fischer, "Sourcehood," 163.

guidance control is all that is necessary for moral responsibility. Fischer and Ravizza briefly define guidance control as follows:

> One might then employ the following condition as part of a theory that distinguishes the relatively clear cases of moral responsibility from the cases of a lack of it: an agent exhibits guidance control of an action insofar as the mechanism that actually issues the action is his own, reasons-responsive mechanism.[28]

There are two main components of guidance control: (1) moderate reasons-responsiveness and (2) mechanism ownership.[29] In the remainder of this chapter, I will discuss moderate reasons-responsiveness. In the next chapter I will discuss mechanism ownership.[30]

---

28. Fischer and Ravizza, *Responsibility and Control*, 39.

29. Fischer and Ravizza refine the notion of reasons-responsiveness to ultimately be moderate reasons-responsiveness.

30. *Responsibility and Control: A Theory of Moral Responsibility* is the main work in which Fischer and Ravizza elaborate their theory of guidance control. This book does not have a defense of FSCs. Fischer and Ravizza operate on the presumption that FSCs confirm that PAP is false. It is important to note that the success of guidance control does not depend on the success of FSCs. FSCs point us in the direction of an analysis of the actual sequence and this points us to the theory of guidance control, but if FSCs do not show that PAP is false, this does not mean that guidance control fails. There are other ways to argue against PAP. Also, if regulative control is not shown to be false, there are other ways to defend guidance control. Michael McKenna provides us with an idea of how this might be done. He writes: "Still, this incompatibilist success would not itself *rule out* Fischer and Ravizza's compatibilist claim that it is *guidance* control and *not* regulative control which explains our judgment that the agent is morally responsible in a Frankfurt example. It is open to Fischer and Ravizza to provide a *positive* account of the freedom-relevant condition as the basis for why . . . Sam is morally responsible for killing the mayor. *Assuming* that Fisher and Ravizza are operating from this dialectical space, what they must do is advance their own account of control, despite the fact that their opponents have a more intuitive 'spin' on the disputed examples.

The defender of guidance control, however, might argue that guidance control is (minimally) on equal footing with regulative control in terms of which conception is more natural or intuitive. Suppose that, contrary to the incompatibilist advocate of regulative control, the defender of guidance control is right about this. Since, in the Frankfurt cases, an agent exhibits both regulative *and* guidance control, it is then a matter of dispute which conception of freedom better explains the agent's responsibility. Given *this* compatibilist line of defence, the proponent of guidance control might argue that Frankfurt examples still invite us to consider what kind of freedom an agent would retain *if it were true* that she had no alternatives open to her at the time of action. Although, she might concede, the examples do not offer clear cases in which an agent is morally responsible but cannot do otherwise, they draw out the fact that there are indeed two different kinds of control worthy of attention. In light of this, she can argue that there are powerful theoretical advantages to advancing the variety which is less metaphysically taxing, i.e., the variety which does not require alternative possibilities.

Even if Frankfurt's strategy ultimately fails under . . . scrutiny . . . the most that the

Reasons-Responsiveness

Before moving to an exposition of Fischer and Ravizza's theory, it would be helpful to better situate it. Fischer and Ravizza are semi-compatibilists. This means that they believe causal determinism is not compatible with free will, but it is with moral responsibility.[31] It is important to understand that what they mean by free will is regulative control. Causal determinism is incompatible with free will as understood as the agent's metaphysical accessibility to alternative possibilities. However, one could believe that causal determinism is incompatible with PAP and yet believe that it is compatible with other definitions of free will. For example, the classical compatibilists defined free will as,

> (1) to have the *power* or *ability* to do what we want or desire to do, which in turn entails (2) an *absence of constraints* or impediments (such as physical restraints, coercion, and compulsion) preventing us from doing what we want.[32]

This definition of free will is compatible with causal determinism. We could also define free will simply as "the ability to respond to reasons." In this case, Fischer and Ravizza would believe free will is compatible with causal

---

incompatibilist can claim is that there are no clear defeaters to their incompatibilist conception of control. She cannot claim that guidance control has been proven inadequate for moral responsibility. She might claim that regulative control is intuitively the more compelling kind of control. But at best, this would shift the burden of proof to Fischer and Ravizza to show what advantages could be gained by opting for the less natural variety. On the other hand, even if Fischer and Ravizza were to grant that the Frankfurt strategy was unsuccessful, they might argue that, intuitively, guidance control is just as appealing as regulative control. In either the case in which guidance control is taken to be at an intuitive disadvantage with regard to regulative control, or in the case in which guidance control is taken to remain on an intuitive par with regulative control, what Fischer and Ravizza must do, and what they in fact do, is defend a full account of guidance control. Theirs is a book that overlooks the finer points of the debate over the Frankfurt examples. However the chips fall for the semi-compatibilist as regards this debate, Fischer and Ravizza advance a positive expression of guidance control as the freedom-relevant condition for moral responsibility" (McKenna, "Assessing Reasons-Responsive Compatibilism" 89–114).

31. Traditionally, free will and moral responsibility were connected. Harry Frankfurt's counter examples changed this situation. After Frankfurt, philosophers separated free will and moral responsibility. This made it possible for positions like Fischer and Ravizza's semi-compatibilism. Michael McKenna defines semi-compatibilism this way, "Semi-compatibilism holds that determinism is incompatible with the freedom to do otherwise but compatible with moral responsibility" (McKenna, "Assessing Reasons-Responsive Compatibilism," 91).

32. Kane, *Free Will*, 13. Kane calls this "classical compatibilism" and identifies adherents such as Hobbes, Hume, and Mill.

determinism.³³ Nonetheless, semi-compatibilism is the label given to Fischer and Ravizza and thus the category in which they are placed.

Within the compatibilist and semi-compatibilist categories there are reasons-responsive theories of moral responsibility. According to these views, an agent is morally responsible if the agent is appropriately responsive to reasons.³⁴ Michael McKenna puts it more precisely:

> Reasons-responsive theories account for free will in terms of the relation between an agent and her reasons for action; free agents are those who, when acting intentionally, are in some manner sensitive to a suitable range of reasons for action.³⁵

Exactly what it means to be "appropriately responsive to reasons" differs among philosophers. Fischer and Ravizza will describe that this means being moderately reasons-responsive. Their view is regarded as the gold standard of reasons-responsive theories.³⁶

As we have seen, Fischer and Ravizza's account of moral responsibility centers on the concept of control. Their guidance control view consists of two parts: moderate reasons-responsiveness and mechanism ownership. We now turn to a discussion of moderate reasons-responsiveness. Fischer and Ravizza believe that their view of control is an articulation of our pre-reflective notions. This means that both elements of guidance control are what human beings already take to be the type of control necessary for moral responsibility. However, most humans do not have these pre-reflective notions clearly articulated. Therefore, Fischer and Ravizza set out various examples in order to bring to consciousness these pre-reflective notions. Their method will be to set out two notions of reasons-responsiveness—strong reasons-responsiveness (SRR) and weak

---

33. Michael McKenna both shows the various conceptions of free will and that the ability to respond to reasons is a legitimate sense. "What I mean by a free act is similar to what Frankfurt means by *acting of one's own free will* . . . or what Fischer and Ravizza mean by acting with *guidance control* " (McKenna, "Contemporary Compatibilism," 176.

34. For iterations of this view, see Dennet, *Elbow Room*; Fischer, *Metaphysics of Free Will*; Fischer and Ravizza, *Responsibility and Control*; Haji, *Moral Appraisability*; Wolf, *Freedom Within Reason*.

35. McKenna, "Contemporary Compatibilism,"175.

36. The Stanford Encyclopedia of Philosophy says: "Many working on the topics of free will and moral responsibility now regard Fischer's developed account to be the gold standard for cutting edge defenses of compatibilism" (McKenna and Coates, "Compatibilism"). Derk Pereboom also writes, "John Martin Fischer's theory of moral responsibility is one of the great compatibilisms in the history of philosophy, standing alongside of Aristotle, David Hume and Harry Frankfurt, for example, and of these it is arguably the most thoroughly developed" (Pereboom, "Reasons-Responsiveness," 198).

reasons-responsiveness (WRR)—which are at opposite ends of a spectrum. Then they will give examples that show that there is something right and something wrong with these notions. After this they will articulate their notion of moderate reasons-responsiveness as a refinement of the strengths and weaknesses of SRR and WRR.

The first end of the spectrum is SRR. Fischer and Ravizza define it as follows:

> If K were to operate and there were sufficient reason to do otherwise, the agent would *recognize* the sufficient reason to do otherwise and thus *choose* to do otherwise and *do* otherwise.[37]

In this quotation, K refers to the mechanism that issues in the action. Fischer defines 'mechanism' as follows: "By 'mechanism' I simply mean, roughly speaking, 'way'—I do not mean to reify anything."[38] Thus, K refers to the way in which the action came about. Seth Shabo defines it more precisely as, "a process that issues in action, such as practical reason or non-reflective habit."[39]

According to Fischer and Ravizza, an agent is SRR if three things occur. First, the agent must recognize that there is a sufficient reason to do otherwise. Second, the agent must choose to do otherwise. Finally, the agent must do otherwise. I have placed the word "must" here to highlight that SRR requires a tight fit between these three elements. If SRR obtains, then whenever there is a sufficient reason to do otherwise, the agent will recognize it, choose to act otherwise, and actually act otherwise. According to the SRR account, this is what it means to be reasons-responsive.

In order to make this relationship between reasons and actions clearer, Fischer and Ravizza identify three possible kinds of failure in SRR:

> The first kind of failure is a failure to be receptive to reasons. Here there are sufficient reasons (say) to perform some action, but the agent does not recognize these reasons. . . . The second kind of failure is a failure of reactivity—a failure to be appropriately affected by beliefs. . . . Finally, there is the failure successfully to translate one's choice into action; this sort of failure may reflect various kinds of physical incapacities or even (again) weakness of will.[40]

---

37. Fischer and Ravizza, *Responsibility and Control*, 41.
38. Fischer, "Frankfurt Cases," 30.
39. Shabo, "Fischer and Ravizza," 104.
40. Fischer and Ravizza, *Responsibility and Control*, 41–42.

Fischer and Ravizza believe that this concept of reasons-responsiveness is too strong because it does not account for weakness of the will. SRR has an overly tight fit between these three elements. We can see this clearly from a more precise definition of SRR. Shabo writes that an agent is SRR:

> If and only if the agent recognizes and reacts to such a reason at *every* world at which one is present.[41]

In this definition, an agent is SRR if and only if the agent does otherwise whenever there is a sufficient reason to do otherwise. This concept does not allow for weakness of will and yet our intuitions tell us that those guilty of weakness of will are morally responsible. Weakness of will occurs when an agent judges that he has a sufficient reason to do otherwise, yet he acts against this judgment. In order to illustrate this, Fischer and Ravizza give three examples of weakness of the will that cannot be accounted for by SRR. I will quote these examples more completely here because Fischer and Ravizza will return to them later.

The first example concerns a woman named Jennifer. She goes to a basketball game even though she has a sufficient reason not to go:

> To see this, imagine that as a result of the unimpaired operation of the normal human faculty of practical reasoning Jennifer decides to go (and goes) to the basketball game tonight, and that she has sufficient reason to do so. But suppose that she would have been "weak-willed" had there been sufficient reason not to go. That is, imagine that had there been a sufficient reason not to go, it would have been that she had a strict deadline for an important manuscript (which she couldn't meet, if she were to go to the game). She nevertheless would have chosen to go to the game, even though she would have recognized that she had sufficient reason to stay home and work. It seems that Jennifer actually goes to the basketball game freely and can reasonably be held morally responsible for going; and yet the actual-sequence mechanism which results in her action is not reasons-responsive in the strong sense. The failure of strong reasons-responsiveness here stems from Jennifer's disposition toward weakness of the will.[42]

This example is designed elicit the intuition that Jenifer is morally responsible for going to the basketball game even though she had a sufficient reason to refrain. If this is the intuition that is elicited, then this example shows that SRR is incorrect. The reason is because SRR tells us that Jennifer

---

41. Shabo, "Fischer and Ravizza," 104.
42. Fischer and Ravizza, *Responsibility and Control*, 42.

would be morally responsible if and only if she recognized the reason to not go to the game, chose to not go to the game, and did not go to the game. In this example, Jennifer did at least recognize the reason to not go to the game. However, she did not choose to not go to the game and actually refrained from going to the game. Yet we intuitively hold her morally responsible. Fischer and Ravizza identify this as an instance of weakness of the will and argue that this is incompatible with SRR.

The second example involves Jennifer devoting time in the afternoon to work for the United Way:

> And imagine that, if she had a sufficient reason to refrain, it would (again) have been her publication deadline. But imagine that she would have devoted her time to charity, even if she had had such a reason not to. Here it seems that Jennifer is both morally responsible and praiseworthy for doing what she does, and yet the actual mechanism is not strongly reasons-responsive.[43]

This example is designed to again elicit an intuition of moral responsibility and praiseworthiness. If this intuition is elicited, then it shows that SRR is incorrect. Jennifer's mechanism is not SRR, yet we hold her morally responsible and praiseworthy for donating time to the United Way in spite of a good reason not to devote her time.

The third example concerns Leonard stealing a book despite prudentially and morally sufficient reasons to do otherwise:

> Suppose Leonard steals a book from a store, knowing full well that it is morally wrong for him to do so and that he will be apprehended and thus that it is not prudent of him to do so. Nevertheless, the actual sequence may be responsibility-conferring; no factors that intuitively undermine moral responsibility may actually operate. (Of course, we assume here that there can be genuine cases of weak-willed actions that are free actions for which the agent can be held morally responsible). Here, then, is a case in which Leonard is morally responsible for stealing the book, but his actual-sequence mechanism is not strongly reasons-responsive: there actually is sufficient reason (both moral and prudential) to do otherwise, and yet he steals the book.[44]

Again, this example is designed to elicit the intuition of moral responsibility. Leonard has sufficient moral and prudential reasons not to

---

43. Fischer and Ravizza, *Responsibility and Control*, 43.
44. Fischer and Ravizza, *Responsibility and Control*, 43.

steal the book. However, he is not SRR and we intuitively hold him responsible for stealing the book.

The lesson to learn from these examples is that we have strong intuitions regarding moral responsibility, which are in conflict with SRR. The phenomenon of "weakness of the will" is common to human experience and we wish to hold people responsible for this. However, according to SRR, we could not hold people responsible for being weak willed. The reason for this is because even though they had sufficient reason to do otherwise and even though they recognized the sufficient reason to do otherwise, they did not choose to do otherwise and do otherwise. The tight fit between reasons and actions required by SRR excludes holding people responsible for weakness of the will. Fischer and Ravizza believe that such a tight fit is too strong to be necessary for moral responsibility. They believe that a looser fit would allow for things like weakness of the will.

In light of this, Fischer and Ravizza introduce the concept of WRR, which is motivated by the desire to have a looser fit between reasons and actions. Fischer and Ravizza define it as follows:

> In contrast, under weak reasons-responsiveness, we (again) hold fixed the actual kind of mechanism, and we simply require that there exist *some* possible scenario (or possible world) in which there is a sufficient reason to do otherwise, the agent recognizes this reason, and the agent does otherwise.[45]

According to Seth Shabo an agent is WRR:

> If and only if there is *some* possible world at which the agent recognizes and reacts appropriately to a sufficient countervailing reason.[46]

WRR requires a looser fit between reasons and actions. On this account of reasons-responsiveness, there only need be one possible world in which the agent recognizes and reacts to a sufficient reason to do otherwise. This differs from SRR because according to SRR, an agent must do otherwise in *every* world in which he recognizes a sufficient reason to do otherwise.

In order to illustrate the superiority of WRR, Fischer and Ravizza return to our previous three examples of weakness of will. Now they will illustrate a looser fit between reasons and actions. The first example was of Jennifer going to the basketball game:

---

45. Fischer and Ravizza, *Responsibility and Control*, 44.
46. Shabo, "Fischer and Ravizza," 104.

> Suppose, for instance, that Jennifer is told that she will have to pay one thousand dollars for a ticket to the game. In this situation, she presumably would not go to the game. Even though Jennifer is disposed to be weak-willed under some circumstances, there are other circumstances in which she would respond appropriately to sufficient reasons.[47]

WRR seems to account for this instance of weakness of the will. Even though Jennifer went to the game in spite of her recognition of a sufficient reason not to, there is at least one possible world where she would not go to the game. In this possible world, there is a sufficient reason to do otherwise (a one-thousand-dollar ticket price); Jennifer recognizes this reason and she does otherwise. WRR allows for Jennifer's mechanism to fail to act when it recognizes a sufficient reason to do otherwise, provided that her mechanism would act if it recognized a sufficient reason in at least one possible world. This allows for weakness of the will.

Fischer and Ravizza continue to illustrate the superiority of WRR by returning to the second example of Jennifer working for the United Way despite her publication deadline:

> Even though she would do so anyway if she had a publication deadline, she certainly would not work for the United Way if to do so she would have to sacrifice her job.[48]

Again, this fits in with WRR. There is a possible world where a sufficient reason to do otherwise exists (losing her job); Jennifer recognizes this reason to do otherwise and does otherwise.

The third example was of Leonard stealing a book. In this example, Fischer and Ravizza stress that there are moral and prudential reasons for Leonard not to steal the book. Even though Leonard actually does steal the book, "His actual mechanism might be responsive to at least *some* possible incentive not to steal."[49] If this were not the case, then we would not feel inclined to hold Leonard morally responsible. If there were no reason that would dissuade Leonard from stealing the book (perhaps his entire family dying as a result of his actions), then "the actual mechanism would seem to be inconsistent with holding him morally responsible for his actions. Arguably, this is because the agent here would not be exhibiting genuine control of his action."[50]

---

47. Fischer and Ravizza, *Responsibility and Control*, 45.
48. Fischer and Ravizza, *Responsibility and Control*, 45.
49. Fischer and Ravizza, *Responsibility and Control*, 45.
50. Fischer and Ravizza, *Responsibility and Control*, 45.

The lesson to learn from these three revised examples is that our intuitions about moral responsibility drive us in the direction of affirming that an agent's mechanism ought to be responsive to a sufficient reason to do otherwise in at least *one* possible world. Our intuitions drive us away from affirming that an agent's mechanism must respond to a sufficient reason to do otherwise in *every* possible world where the agent recognizes the reason (this is SRR). But they also drive us away from affirming that we can hold an agent responsible if his mechanism does not respond to a recognized sufficient reason to do otherwise in *any* possible world. In the former, control is too strong. In the latter, control does not exist. In WRR, control seems to be about right (though we will see that Fischer and Ravizza ultimately reject WRR).

In light of this, Fischer and Ravizza will provisionally adopt WRR to further the conversation. As this discussion progresses, they will add two refinements to the account. These refinements deal with the concepts of 'mechanism' and 'tracing.' I will first explain the concept of mechanism and then move on to the concept of tracing.

Fischer and Ravizza's account have made use of the term 'mechanism.' I noted earlier that a rough definition of mechanism is 'the way in which an action is brought about.' We can better understand the concept of mechanism by returning to FSCs, especially the distinction between the actual sequence and the alternative sequence. In these examples, the actual sequence proceeds "in the normal way or via the 'normal' process of practical reasoning."[51]

> In contrast, in the alternative scenario (which never actually gets triggered and thus never becomes part of the actual sequence of events in our world), there is (say) direct electronic stimulation of the brain—intuitively, a different way or different kind of mechanism. . . . The actually operating mechanism (in a Frankfurt-type case)—ordinary human practical reasoning, unimpaired by direct stimulation by neurosurgeons, and so forth.[52]

Thus, a mechanism is just the way an action came about. We can intuitively distinguish between the actual mechanism and the alternative

---

51. Fischer, "Guidance Control," 186. Michael Bratman elaborates on Fischer and Ravizza's understanding of 'mechanism': "The idea of a mechanism from which an action 'flows' is left fairly undeveloped. It is intended to include both a mechanism of practical reasoning, and 'nonreflective mechanisms of various kinds.' . . . Examples of such nonreflective mechanisms include irresistible urges . . . 'direct manipulation of the brain' by someone else . . . and habits that unreflectively issue in action" (Bratman, "Fischer and Ravizza," 453).

52. Fischer, "Guidance Control," 186–87.

mechanism in Frankfurt cases. According to Fischer and Ravizza, we can do this for each action, but there is no general way to do this before analyzing a specific action. They write,

> We cannot specify in a general way how to determine which mechanism is "the" mechanism that is relevant to assessment of responsibility. It is simply a presupposition of this theory as presented here that for each act, there is an intuitively natural mechanism that is appropriately selected as the mechanism that issues in action, for the purposes of assessing guidance control and moral responsibility.[53]

We have a rough and intuitive idea of what they mean by mechanism. In order for this description of mechanism to be complete, we need to add three refinements to it. The first one has to do with "sameness of mechanism." Fischer and Ravizza write:

> For a mechanism to be weakly reasons-responsive, there must be a possible scenario in which the same kind of mechanism operates and the agent does otherwise. But, of course, sameness of kind of mechanism need not require sameness of all details, even down to the "microlevel," just as nothing in "same kind of house" or "same kind of smile" requires sameness of all details. . . . Thus, the scenarios pertinent to reasons-responsiveness of an actual sequence mechanism may differ with respect both to the sort of incentives the agent has to do otherwise and the particular details of the mechanism issuing in action . . . Further, there is no plausibility to the suggestion that *all conditions in the past*—no matter how remote or irrelevant—must be included as part of the "mechanism that issues in action."[54]

This is a helpful clarification that appeals to our common sense. When we use phrases such as "same kind of house" or "same kind of smile," we do not mean "exactly the same in all details down to the sub-atomic level." Instead, there is a common sense understanding that "same kind of smile" contains some differences. This is important because "same kind of mechanism" will have different details imbedded in the context or possible world in which it issues in action.

The second refinement is that mechanism ought not to be construed as including "all conditions in the past." In other words, the entire history of the universe from the Big Bang up until the action performed does not

---

53. Fischer and Ravizza, *Responsibility and Control*, 47.
54. Fischer and Ravizza, *Responsibility and Control*, 52.

count as "the mechanism." At some point, we intuitively "cut off" past events in order to distinguish "the way" an action came about from "the entire history of the universe."

A third refinement is that WRR does not require that the possible worlds used to analyze mechanisms be accessible to the agent. Possible worlds or possible scenarios are used as a tool to clarify things; they are not actual metaphysical possibilities. Fischer and Ravizza write:

> Thus, we have associated moral responsibility with a dispositional or modal property. It is important to see that, whereas other possible worlds are relevant to ascertaining whether there is some actually operative dispositional feature (such as weak reasons-responsiveness), such worlds are *not* relevant in virtue of bearing on the question of whether some alternative sequence is *genuinely accessible* to the agent.
>
> On our approach to moral responsibility, then, other possible scenarios are relevant to the issue of whether the *actual sequence* has certain features (such as weak reasons-responsiveness). But it does *not* follow that our approach is committed to the claim that agents can have it in their power to *actualize* such scenarios—that is a quite different matter.[55]

This is important because Frankfurt's examples teach us that PAP is not necessary for moral responsibility. Thus, it could appear that making use of possible worlds contradicts this. However, possible worlds are a mere tool for analysis and not accessible alternatives.

There are five things to keep in mind when Fischer and Ravizza use the term mechanism. First, a mechanism is just the way in which an action came about. Second, mechanisms can be distinguished intuitively. Third, "sameness of mechanism" does not require all the exact details to be the same. Fourth, mechanisms do not require the inclusion of the entire past history of the universe. Fifth, mechanisms are analyzed by the tool of possible worlds. However, this does not mean the agent has access to these possible worlds.

Fischer and Ravizza now wish to give some application of their account with the example of an irresistible urge from a drug addict. This will enable us to see how WRR makes sense and it will allow them to add one more clarification: that of tracing. They write:

---

55. Fischer and Ravizza, *Responsibility and Control*, 53.

> We think intuitively that irresistible urges can be "psychologically compulsive" and can rule out guidance control and thus moral responsibility.[56]

If someone has a literally "irresistible urge," then they are not morally responsible. For example:

> When Jim acts on an irresistible urge to take the drug, there is some physical process of kind P taking place in his central nervous system. When a person undergoes this kind of physical process, we say that his urge is literally irresistible. And we believe that what underlies our intuitive claim that Jim is not morally responsible for taking the drug is that the relevant kind of mechanism issuing in Jim's taking the drug is of a physical kind P, and that a mechanism of kind P is not reasons-responsive.[57]

This example further supports the idea that we consider reasons-responsiveness to be essential to control and moral responsibility. An agent with a mechanism that is not reasons-responsive is an agent that we consider to be defective, even to the point of denying them responsibility. This intuition fits with what has already been seen concerning the alternative sequence in Frankfurt cases.

> Consider again, our claim that certain sorts of "direct manipulation of the brain" rule out moral responsibility. When scientists intervene and manipulate the brain in a way which is not reasons-responsive, this is sufficient to undermine an agent's moral responsibility for action.[58]
>
> Thus, the theory that associates moral responsibility with actual sequence reasons-responsiveness can help to explain our intuitive view that certain sorts of direct interventions in the brain are inconsistent with moral responsibility.[59]

---

56. Fischer and Ravizza, *Responsibility and Control*, 48.

57. Fischer and Ravizza, *Responsibility and Control*, 48. The point of this example is not to argue that all drug addicts act from irresistible urges when they take drugs and therefore are not morally responsible. It could be the case that drug addicts never experience a truly irresistible urge and thus are morally responsible. Fischer and Ravizza's point is that actions done from genuinely irresistible urges are not reasons responsive and this is why we have the intuition that an agent that acts from a genuinely irresistible urge is not morally responsible. This point stands regardless of whether or not drug addicts actually act from genuinely irresistible urges.

58. Fischer and Ravizza, *Responsibility and Control*, 48–49

59. Fischer and Ravizza, *Responsibility and Control*, 49.

An irresistible urge that arises from brain manipulation renders the agent's mechanism not reasons-responsive. Also, an irresistible urge arising from psychological compulsion renders an agent's mechanism not reasons-responsive. This fact enables us to account for why we think that some behaviors, such as an addict's drug use or actions from direct brain manipulation, are not responsible actions. However, this does present a challenge to Fischer and Ravizza's account. They solve this challenge by adding the refinement of tracing.

There is an obvious objection that can be raised. Think about the case where Max gets drunk and he gets behind the wheel of his car. He proceeds to drive and, in the process, kills a child with his car. The fact that Max was drunk means that he was not reasons-responsive. The drunken state rendered him unable to appropriately respond to reasons. Is this not an obvious problem? We intuit that Max is responsible in this case, but it seems like Fischer and Ravizza's theory requires that he is not. They respond:

> This is one case in a class of cases in which an agent's act at time T_1 issues from a reasons-responsive sequence, and this act causes his act at T_2 to issue from a mechanism that is not reasons-responsive. Further, Max can reasonably be expected to have known that his getting drunk at the party would lead to his driving in a condition in which he would be unresponsive. Thus, Max can be held morally responsible for his action at T_2 in virtue of the operation of a suitable sort of reasons-responsive mechanism at a prior time T_1.[60]

Fischer and Ravizza deal with this objection by arguing that we must trace a person's action backwards to see if it was produced at some point by a reasons-responsive mechanism:

> It is only when it is true that at no suitable point along the path to action did a reasons-responsive sequence occur that an agent will not properly be held responsible for his action.[61]

The tracing refinement to Fischer and Ravizza's account appeals to our common sense and gives their account greater explanatory power. In their final account, they will keep the refinements of tracing and the clarifications to the concept of mechanism. However, they will reject WRR in favor of moderate reasons-responsiveness (MRR). I will now discuss Fischer and Ravizza's concept of MRR.

---

60. Fischer and Ravizza, *Responsibility and Control*, 49–50.
61. Fischer and Ravizza, *Responsibility and Control*, 50.

Moderate Reasons-Responsiveness

Fischer and Ravizza have examined two types of reasons-responsiveness: SRR and WRR. They have found SRR to be too strong and they will find WRR to be too weak. In light of this, they further analyze the concept of moral responsibility in order to have a more adequate view. They write:

> In developing the richer notion, we shall emphasize the distinction between *recognition* of reasons and *reaction* to reasons (i.e., choosing in accordance with the reasons recognized). We shall argue that the requirements on reasons-recognition are more stringent than those on reasons-reactivity (for moral responsibility).[62]

Fischer and Ravizza will show the need for this distinction by examining the flaws of WRR. They begin by stating SRR and WRR more clearly:

> (SRR): Suppose that a certain kind K of mechanism actually issues in an action. Strong reasons-responsiveness obtains under the following conditions: if K were to operate and there were sufficient reason to do otherwise, the agent would *recognize* the sufficient reason to do otherwise and thus *choose* to do otherwise and *do* otherwise.
>
> (WRR): As with strong reasons-responsiveness, we hold fixed the operation of the actual kind of mechanism, and we then simply require that there exist *some* possible scenario (or possible world)—in which there is sufficient reason to do otherwise, the agent *recognizes* this reason, and the agent does otherwise.[63]

One of the difficulties with both of these formulations is that they do not require that the agent do otherwise *because* of the sufficient reason. It is one thing to say that there is a sufficient reason to do otherwise, but it is more important that the agent do otherwise *because* of that reason. SRR and WRR do not require this.

Fischer and Ravizza illustrate the necessity of this requirement. They ask us to consider a woman with a nervous tic that causes her to break her host's priceless Steuben egg.

> Imagine, for instance, a possible world in which instead of bringing about a broken glass egg, the nervous tic causes the woman to spill a tall pitcher of lemonade on her hosts lap—an

---

62. Fischer and Ravizza, *Responsibility and Control*, 63.
63. Fischer and Ravizza, *Responsibility and Control*, 63.

act that, coincidentally, there is good reason to perform, since the host's trousers have just been set ablaze by his cigarette ash.[64]

The problem with this illustration is that the requirements for WRR are satisfied, yet it does not seem that the woman is responsible for breaking the egg. The reason is that the agent doing otherwise must be appropriately connected to the reason to do otherwise.

> When we consider possible scenarios in which the actual mechanism operates, there is sufficient reason to do otherwise, and the agent does otherwise, we expect that the agent does otherwise *for that reason*.[65]

This is an important refinement to the account of reasons-responsiveness. It shows us that WRR is inadequate.

A second problem with WRR is that there is too loose a fit between reasons and actions. This is illustrated with another example that Fischer and Ravizza give. In this example, a person goes on a ferry and proceeds to kill everyone on the ferry with a saber. There is only one reason strong enough to keep him from doing this; that reason is if he sees someone on the ferry smoking a Gambier pipe. This example illustrates the satisfaction of WRR, but we have a tendency to think that this person is crazy and thus not morally responsible:

> The above example of the saber killer is puzzling largely because we cannot understand the saber killer's motivation and, in particular, why the presence of someone smoking a certain kind of pipe should count as the only reason strong enough to prevent the impending change.[66]

This illustrates a problem with WRR. The problem is that the particular reason to which the agent responds is not easily understandable.

Fischer and Ravizza give another example that illustrates a third problem with WRR. In this example, they return to the illustration of Jennifer going to the basketball game:

> But what if it were discovered that, although Jennifer would not attend the basketball game if the tickets cost one thousand dollars, she would go if the tickets cost two thousand dollars? To make the case more extreme, simply imagine that Jennifer would attend the game in every scenario except the one in which

---

64. Fischer and Ravizza, *Responsibility and Control*, 63.
65. Fischer and Ravizza, *Responsibility and Control*, 64.
66. Fischer and Ravizza, *Responsibility and Control*, 65.

the tickets cost one thousand dollars. At this point, Jennifer's behavior becomes nearly as puzzling as that of the saber killer. Although both of their mechanisms are weakly reasons-responsive, it is not intuitively clear that either is responsible for his or her action. Thus, it appears that weakly reasons-responsive behavior become problematic not only when the particular reason to which an agent responds is not easily understood, but also when the general *pattern* of an agent's responses is puzzling.[67]

These two examples demonstrate that WRR is not correct. It is not correct for three reasons. First, it does not require that the agent does otherwise for the sufficient reason to do otherwise. Second, it does not require that the reason for the agent to do otherwise be easily understandable. Third, it does not have a requirement that the agent's general pattern of response be understandable or not weird. Though WRR fails to be necessary for guidance control, it has enabled us to make progress towards an adequate account. The challenge, as Fischer and Ravizza put it, is as follows:

> The challenge apparently facing a responsiveness theorist, then, is to find something of a middle ground between SRR and WRR, in which there is sufficient structure in the profiles of responsiveness to reasons relevant to moral responsibility.[68]

The above discussion leads us to what Fischer and Ravizza regard as an adequate account of reasons-responsiveness. As we have seen, Fischer and Ravizza make a distinction between reasons-receptivity and reasons-reactivity. They will now explain this distinction and illustrate it with examples. The purpose of this is to develop a refined account of reasons-responsiveness that avoids the problems with SRR and WRR. They will call this moderate reasons-responsiveness (MRR). They define "reactivity to reasons" as "the capacity to *translate* reasons into choices (and then subsequent behavior)."[69] They define "receptivity to reasons" as "the capacity to recognize the reasons that exist."[70] The relationship between these two concepts is asymmetrical:

> We contend that the reactivity to reasons and receptivity to reasons that constitute the responsiveness relevant to moral responsibility are crucially *asymmetric*. Whereas a very weak sort

---

67. Fischer and Ravizza, *Responsibility and Control*, 66.
68. Fischer and Ravizza, *Responsibility and Control*, 68.
69. Fischer and Ravizza, *Responsibility and Control*, 69.
70. Fischer and Ravizza, *Responsibility and Control*, 69.

of reactivity is all that is required, a *stronger* sort of receptivity to reasons is necessary for this kind of responsiveness.[71]

Fischer and Ravizza illustrate this asymmetry with the example[72] of Brown and the non-addictive drug Plezu:

> Brown, unfortunately, is so fond of Plezu and so lacking in self-discipline that, although he recognizes that there are strong reasons *not* to take the drug every morning, he typically ends up passing his day on the couch. In fact, let us say that the only scenario in which Brown would not take Plezu is one in which he is told that injecting the drug once more would have an extremely grave consequence—death (a side effect of Plezu that threatens only longtime users).[73]

---

71. Fischer and Ravizza, *Responsibility and Control*, 69.

72. Patrick Todd and Neal Tognazzini clarify the receptivity/reactivity distinction. They begin with receptivity: "Receptivity is a modal property of mechanisms. To find out whether a particular kind of mechanism has this property... there must be counterfactual circumstances in which, holding fixed the kind of mechanism, the agent in question manages to recognize the sufficient reasons to do otherwise in that circumstance. So, to take a concrete example, suppose your actually operative mechanism issues in your purchasing a ticket to a Los Angeles Philharmonic concert for $50. In order for us to conclude that your actually operative kind of mechanism satisfies (RRcc), one thing we need to know is whether something like the following counterfactual is true: if the ticket were to have cost $5 million (and the same kind of mechanism were to have operated), you would have recognized that this fact is a sufficient reason not to buy the ticket. The truth of this counterfactual will give us a world (or sphere of worlds) at which you are preserved with sufficient reason to do otherwise, and you succeed in recognizing it. Thus your actually operative kind of mechanism is, in a weak sense, at least, receptive to reasons" (Todd and Tognazzini, "Problem for Guidance Control" 686).

Todd and Tognazzini next elaborate on reactivity: "If I cannot translate reasons into action, then no matter how reasons-responsive my mechanism is, I cannot properly be held morally responsible for what I do. F&R's account... of reasons-reactivity can be spelt out as follows:

WRca. An actually operative kind of mechanism is *weakly reactive to reasons* if and only if there is some possible scenario in which (1) there is a sufficient reasons to do otherwise; (2) the same kind of mechanism operates; (3) the agent recognizes the sufficient reason to do otherwise; (4) the agent thus chooses and does otherwise for that reason.

Clause (4) is crucial here. The first three clauses pick out one of the worlds that establish the mechanism's *receptivity;* if clause (4) is also satisfied at that world, then the mechanism is appropriately *reactive* as well. What makes this an account of *weak* reactivity to reasons is the fact that only *one* possible scenario is needed in which clauses (1)–(4) are satisfied. (Contrast this with (RRcc), according to which there must be a suitable *range* of worlds in which the agent recognizes sufficient reason to do otherwise). The reason for this is that reactivity is 'all of one piece'" (Todd and Tognazzini, "Problem for Guidance Control" 687).

73. Fischer and Ravizza, *Responsibility and Control*, 69–70.

We see in this example that Brown does recognize that there are strong reasons not to take the drug; this is the receptivity to reasons clause in Fischer and Ravizza's account. However, Brown often takes the drug; that is, he frequently gives in to weakness of the will. Yet he is not so weak willed that he would take the drug in every possible scenario. That is, his urge is not literally irresistible. The one possible scenario where he would not take the drug is if he knew that he would die. This is the reactivity to reasons clause in Fischer and Ravizza's account.

In light of this example, we see the asymmetry between receptivity to reasons and reactivity to reasons. In this case, we have strong intuitions to hold Brown responsible for taking the drug. Fischer and Ravizza say that is because Brown is strongly receptive to reasons, but weakly reactive to reasons. This illustrates the asymmetry they think is characteristic of guidance control. It is obvious to Brown that taking Plezu is bad, yet he is weak and frequently gives in to his weakness. However, he is not so weak that he would take the drug if he knew that it would kill him during the next use. Weak reasons reactivity just requires that there be one possible world or scenario where Brown would not take the drug. Fischer and Ravizza further clarify weak reasons reactivity:

> "Reactivity is all of one piece." That is, we believe that if an agent's mechanism reacts to *some* incentive to (say) do other than he actually does, this shows that the mechanism *can* react to *any* incentive to do otherwise. . . . This general capacity of the agent's actual-sequence mechanism—and *not* the agent's power to do otherwise—is what helps to ground moral responsibility. . . . The picture here is of one kind of mechanism with different "inputs." Further, the idea is that reactivity is all of one piece in the sense that the mechanism can react to all incentives, if it can react to one. . . . Our point is that, *holding fixed the actual kind of mechanism,* reactivity is all of one piece: if the mechanism can react to any reason to do otherwise, it can react to all such reasons.[74]

For Brown's mechanism to be weakly reactive to reasons, it must have at least one possible world where it chooses otherwise. In addition, since reactivity is "all of one piece," it follows that the mechanism has the capacity to respond to any reason to do otherwise.

With regard to reactivity, it must be only weakly responsive. However, with regard to receptivity, it must be regularly receptive to reasons. Fischer and Ravizza write:

---

74. Fischer and Ravizza, *Responsibility and Control*, 73–74.

> Regular-receptivity, then, is reasons-receptivity that gives rise to a minimally comprehensible pattern, judged from some perspective that takes into account subjective features of the agent (i.e., the agent's preferences, values, and beliefs) but is also *not simply* the agent's point of view. A comprehensible pattern of reasons-recognitions may, however, be utterly divorced from reality. Thus, we claim that the agent's answers in the imaginary interview must *also* be at least minimally "grounded in reality." . . . Regular receptivity to reasons, then, requires an understandable pattern of reasons-recognition, minimally grounded in reality.[75]

Fischer and Ravizza are now prepared to state the asymmetry more clearly:

> The asymmetry between reactivity and receptivity can now be stated crisply. In the case of receptivity to reasons, the agent (holding fixed the relevant mechanism) must exhibit an understandable pattern of reasons-recognition, in order to render it plausible that his mechanism has the "cognitive power" to recognize the actual incentive to do otherwise. In the case of reactivity to reasons, the agent (when acting from the relevant mechanism) must simply display *some* reactivity, in order to render it plausible that his mechanism has the "executive power" to react to the actual incentive to do otherwise. In both cases the pertinent power is a general capacity of the agent's mechanism, rather than a particular ability of the agent (i.e., the agent's possession of alternative possibilities—the freedom to choose and do otherwise).[76]

The account is not yet finished being refined. Fischer and Ravizza next consider borderline cases of moral responsibility. They argue that although intelligent animals, very young children, and psychopaths exhibit a certain pattern of reasons-responsiveness, they are not judged to be morally responsible. The reason for this is that they are not responsive to *moral reasons*:

> Although they may act on mechanisms that respond to instrumental or prudential reasons, they are not appropriately responsive to moral demands. We suggest that these individuals are not moral agents (not properly held morally responsible for their behavior) because they are without any understanding and appreciation of moral reasons.[77]

---

75. Fischer and Ravizza, *Responsibility and Control*, 73.
76. Fischer and Ravizza, *Responsibility and Control*, 75.
77. Fischer and Ravizza, *Responsibility and Control*, 76.

In light of this, they refine the account to include moral reasons:

> On this view, responsibility requires that (given the actual sequence mechanism) the agent recognize an understandable pattern of moral reasons; that is, just as the recognition of non-moral reasons must have a suitable *structure*, so must the recognition of moral reasons.... That is, the pattern in question must show that the agent (when acting on the actual mechanism) recognizes that other persons' claims give rise to moral reasons *that apply to him*. Without such a minimal receptiveness to moral reasons, agents would fail to be moral agents at all, and consequently would not be appropriate candidates for the reactive attitudes.[78]

Summary of Moderate Reasons-Responsiveness

The WRR account needed to be revised in order to make an explicit connection between reasons and actions. To this a clause was added to the account that read, "the agent does otherwise for that reason." The account also was refined in order to point out the asymmetry between receptivity to reasons and reactivity to reasons. The asymmetry tells us that receptivity to reasons is stronger than reactivity to reasons. A responsible agent must have a mechanism that is regularly receptive to reasons but only weakly reactive to reasons. There was also added to the account that mere reasons-responsiveness is not enough. The idea that a mechanism must be responsive to a range of reasons including moral reasons needed to be added. These refinements bring us to Fischer and Ravizza's summary of their account:

> This kind of responsiveness, then, requires that an agent act on a mechanism that is regularly receptive to reasons, some of which are moral reasons, and at least weakly reactive to reason.[79]

In order to make their account clearer, Fischer and Ravizza give a helpful taxonomy of the kinds of responsiveness that are relevant to responsibility. I will quote them at length:

> The first class of bodily movements ... is exemplified by tics, seizures, muscle spasms, and so forth. Such actions are not caused (in an appropriate way) by beliefs and desires, and thus they are not brought about via reasons-responsive mechanism. Clearly,

---

78. Fischer and Ravizza, *Responsibility and Control*, 77.
79. Fischer and Ravizza, *Responsibility and Control*, 82.

this kind of bodily movement is not one for which an agent is properly held responsible.

The second class of actions . . . is exemplified by the case of the sea captain who panics in a storm and is impelled to jettison his cargo by an irresistible fear. Such an action is intentional in the sense that it is produced (in an appropriate way) by the skipper's beliefs and desires; however, it is a forced action because the mechanism that produces it is not responsive to reasons. As a result, the captain is not morally responsible.

The next kind class of actions is illustrated by certain psychopaths, intelligent animals, and young children. Such agents act intentionally, and they may even act on mechanisms that respond to a range of nonmoral reasons. Nevertheless, they are still not responsible because they are not *moral* agents—they do not act on mechanisms that are receptive to moral demands.[80]

Next, there is a class of actions for which agents are appropriately held responsible. This class may be divided into at least two kinds of actions. The first kind—action under duress—is exemplified by the sea captain who deliberates and jettisons his cargo in order to save his vessel, and his decision does not stem from an irresistible urge. In this case, the skipper acts on a mechanism (normal practical reasoning) that is responsive to both moral and nonmoral reasons. Although the captain is responsible, he is not necessarily blameworthy,[81] since he acted under duress.

Finally, there are those actions for which agents are most clearly accessible to the reactive attitudes: "paradigmatic" cases of moral responsibility, on any account. These are intentional acts that are not done under duress

---

80. It is important to not be distracted by a particular example such as the psychopath. It may well be disputable that psychopaths are not morally responsible, yet that is beside the point. The issue is the agent not being able to respond to moral reasons. It could be the case that psychopaths are in fact able to respond to moral reasons. If this is the case, then they would be removed from this list. The point is that we do not regard people who are genuinely unable to respond to moral reasons as being morally responsible.

81. Fischer and Ravizza draw a distinction between moral responsibility and blameworthiness/praiseworthiness. The distinction basically comes to this: a person is morally responsible if he is an apt target for the reactive attitudes. A person is blameworthy/praiseworthy if the reactive attitudes can be justifiably applied to the person. For example, a person can be morally responsible in that he is an apt target for reactive attitude, yet he is not blameworthy or praiseworthy because he has done a morally neutral act or did not act at all. In this case, the captain acted from a mechanism that was responsive to moral and non-moral reasons. Thus, he was an apt target of the reactive attitude. However, his acting under duress rendered him not blameworthy. I take this to mean that we would not justifiably apply a negative reactive attitude towards him because intuitively we would not think it appropriate to do so given the circumstances.

and are produced via mechanisms that are responsive to a range of moral and nonmoral reasons.[82]

Responsibility for Consequences

Thus far, Fischer and Ravizza have given us their account of moral responsibility for actions. I have felt the need to be more thorough in describing this segment of their theory than the following two for consequences and omissions. The reason is that their account of responsibility for consequences and omissions largely builds upon their account of responsibility for actions. This is what we would expect for a unified theory of moral responsibility. Due to this, I can be briefer in describing the last two parts of their account.

People are held responsible for more than just their actions. They are also held responsible for the consequences of their actions. Fischer and Ravizza illustrate this with the example of the Exon Valdez disaster. In this example, the captain of the Exon Valdez was responsible for his actions of steering the ship, but he is also responsible for the consequences of what happened as a result of the way he steered it. The consequence of his actions was that massive amounts of oil spilled into the ocean and seriously damaged the wildlife and coastline.

Fischer and Ravizza want to be able to provide an account of holding people responsible for the consequences of their actions. This account must also be compatible with determinism. In order to do this, they build upon their account of moderate-reasons responsiveness. As we have seen, this account is compatible with determinism. Since this is the case, building upon this account will render responsibility for consequences that are also compatible with determinism. They begin their account by making an important distinction between consequence particulars and consequence universals:

> For example, in "Assassin" one can distinguish between the consequence-particular, the mayor's being shot, and the consequence-universal, *that the mayor is shot (in some way or another)*.[83]

The way in which these two are distinguished is via the actual causal path that occurs. In the case of consequence-particulars, a different causal path will yield a different causal-particular. However, in the case of consequence-universals, the same consequence-universal could be brought about through different causal paths.

82. Fischer and Ravizza, *Responsibility and Control*, 82–84.
83. Fischer and Ravizza, *Responsibility and Control*, 96.

As I mentioned, responsibility for consequences builds upon the account for responsibility for actions. Thus, Fischer and Ravizza state the following:

> An agent S has guidance control of a consequence-particular C just in case S has guidance control of some act A (i.e., A results from the agent's own, moderately reasons-responsive mechanism), and it is reasonable to expect S to believe that C will (or may) result from A.[84]

There are two parts of this account. The first part has to do with S's action. In order to be responsible for consequence-particulars, agent S must have acted in a responsible manner. Here we define "responsible manner" as "acting from the agent's own moderately reasons-responsive mechanism." This is the account that was previously made in responsibility for action. The second part has to do with the belief of the agent. The agent must believe that the consequence-particular C will or may result from A. This is also compatible with determinism because determinism does not rule out agents having beliefs.

Their account of consequence-universals also builds on their account of responsibility for actions. They write:

> Our approach to guidance control of consequence-universals builds on the account of guidance control of actions: but it does so in a different way than the account of guidance control of consequence-particulars. More specifically, it posits two interlocked and linked sensitivities: in order for an agent to have guidance control of a consequence-universal, its obtaining must result from a two-stage sequence that exhibits responsiveness. That is, the agent's bodily movement must issue from his own, moderately reasons-responsive mechanism, and the event in the external world must be suitably sensitive to the agent's bodily movement.[85]

Like the account of consequence-particulars, the account of consequence-universals has two parts. First, the agent's action or bodily movement must issue from his own, moderately reasons-responsive mechanism. As we have seen, this is compatible with determinism. The second part is that the event must be suitably sensitive to the agent's bodily movement. This second part requires some illustration to understand.

---

84. Fischer and Ravizza, *Responsibility and Control*, 121.
85. Fischer and Ravizza, *Responsibility and Control*, 121–22.

Fischer and Ravizza appeal to an illustration they call "Joint Assassins." In this example, Jack and Sam independently and at the same time shoot the mayor. Their bullets strike the mayor at the same time and each bullet is sufficient to kill the mayor. Sam is responsible for two consequence universals: (1) that the mayor is shot and (2) that the mayor is killed. But Fischer and Ravizza say that the event is not suitably sensitive to Sam's bodily movement. They write:

> But although Sam appears to be morally responsible for the state of affairs that the mayor is killed, the outer path from Sam's bodily movement to the event of the mayor's dying is *not* sensitive if Sam had not shot his gun, Jack would have anyway, and the mayor would have died anyway. (We assume that neither Sam nor Jack could prevent the other from shooting.) In "Joint Assassins" there are *two actually unfolding paths* that lead to the mayor's being killed. This explains why the mayor's being killed is not sensitive to Sam's bodily movement.[86]

Thus, by "the event in the external world must be suitable sensitive to the agent's bodily movement," Fischer and Ravizza basically mean that there must be only one unfolding path from the action to the event.

Responsibility for Omissions

Fischer and Ravizza further build their account of moral responsibility by extending it to omissions. They call their previous account of actions and consequences "positive agency." Omissions are different in that they are "negative agency." In positive agency, the agent does something. In negative agency, the agent fails to do something. There are two types of omissions: simple and complex. A simple omission is "the failure to move one's body in a certain way (where this can include failure to keep the body still)."[87] A complex omission:

> is not fully constituted by a bodily movement. For example, an individual's failure to cause an alarm to go off is a complex omission; intuitively, it involves not just a bodily movement, but also a relationship between the bodily movement and the alarm's not going off.[88]

---

86. Fischer and Ravizza, *Responsibility and Control*, 117–18.
87. Fischer and Ravizza, *Responsibility and Control*, 132.
88. Fischer and Ravizza, *Responsibility and Control*, 133.

Both simple and complex omissions can be related to the account of guidance control that Fischer and Ravizza have already laid out. As with consequences, the relation of omissions to guidance control shows that an agent can be responsible for omissions even if determinism is true. Fischer and Ravizza give the guidance control account for simple omissions first, then they give it for complex omissions:

> It is natural to say that one has guidance control of one's failure to do A (in case of a bodily omission) just in case one's actual bodily movement B (which fully constitutes the omission) issues from one's own, moderately reasons-responsive mechanism.[89]

This should sound familiar because it parallels their account of guidance control for actions. In other words, the only difference between actions and simple omissions is that one is positive agency and the other negative agency. This means that responsibility for simple omissions is basically the same as responsibility for actions.

In the case of complex omissions, things are a bit more complex. Fischer and Ravizza give their account:

> It is natural to say that an agent had guidance control of his failure to do A (where this is a complex omission) just in case: (1) his movement of his body in a certain way is moderately responsive to reason, and (2) the relevant event in the external world is suitably sensitive to his failure to move his body in a different way.[90]

This also should sound familiar in that this was basically the account given for responsibility for consequence-universals. Thus, since their account of consequence universals was consistent with determinism, it follows that so also is their account of responsibility for complex omissions.

Summary

Fischer and Ravizza have given us an account of moderate reasons-responsiveness for actions, consequences, and omissions that is compatible with determinism. It is compatible with determinism because it utilizes a concept of control that avoids the threats from alternative possibilities and from the sourcehood requirement. In the philosophical literature, it has been argued that determinism (of any kind) is not compatible with moral responsibility

---

89. Fischer and Ravizza, *Responsibility and Control*, 132.
90. Fischer and Ravizza, *Responsibility and Control*, 133.

because it denies that agents have the power to do other than what they have done. In other words, it denies PAP. Fischer and Ravizza respond to this by giving FSCs. In these examples, the agent could not do otherwise, yet we intuitively hold him responsible. This is evidence that our concept of moral responsibility does not require PAP.

The second threat that determinism supposedly brings is over sourcehood. Many philosophers have argued that if determinism is true, then we are not the appropriate source of our own actions. Since we are not the appropriate source of our own actions, we cannot be held responsible for them. Fischer and Ravizza respond to this by giving an account of sourcehood that is compatible with determinism and that accounts for all our intuitions for holding people responsible. This account centers on their concept of guidance control. A major element of guidance control is moderate reasons-responsiveness. The sourcehood objection is answered by denying ultimate sourcehood and affirming guidance control. An agent is an appropriate source of his actions, consequences, and omissions if they arise from the agent's own moderately reasons-responsive mechanism.

In light of this, Fischer and Ravizza have provided the first part of their account of guidance control. The second part is mechanism ownership. We now turn to this in the next chapter.

CHAPTER TWO

Mechanism Ownership

Introduction

FISCHER AND RAVIZZA'S ACCOUNT of guidance control has two main parts. Chapter one explained moderate reasons-responsiveness. There we saw that guidance control denies the sourcehood and alternative possibilities conditions and affirms a type of reasons-responsiveness. In this chapter, we will look at the second part of guidance control, mechanism ownership. Here we will see Fischer and Ravizza affirm and articulate a type of subjectivist condition. Fischer and Ravizza believe that these two parts form the necessary and sufficient conditions for moral responsibility. I will discuss mechanism ownership in six parts.

The first part is preliminary. In this section, I discuss the fact that Fischer and Ravizza present a notion of moral responsibility that is essentially historical. This distinguishes their view from other compatibilist views that are not historical. In the second part, I elaborate on a child's moral education according to Fischer and Ravizza. The purpose is to illuminate what it means for moral responsibility to be historical as well as what it means for an agent to take responsibility. In the third section, I will elaborate on the notion of taking responsibility. This notion is essential for Fischer and Ravizza's view of mechanism ownership. After these three sections, I turn to two objections Fischer and Ravizza raise against their view. These objections and the answers to them are intended to further illumine their account of mechanism ownership. In section four, I deal with the objection regarding people that fail to take responsibility. In section five, I deal with the objection that comes from manipulation cases. Section six discusses Fischer and Ravizza's subjectivist view as well as their view's relationship to causal determinism. This section ends with a brief summary of the three conditions for taking responsibility.

Moral Responsibility as a Historical Notion

Fischer and Ravizza want to distinguish their account of moral responsibility from other influential compatibilist accounts. They do this by arguing that their account is essentially historical. By this they mean that coming to take responsibility is not a matter of a current time slice notion, but rather a process:

> Someone's being morally responsible requires that the past be a certain way. . . . Thus, in order to establish whether the mechanism from which an agent acts is his own, we must attend to aspects of the history of the action. More specifically we have suggested that the past must contain a process of "taking responsibility." . . . It is part of the process by which a mechanism leading (say) to an action, becomes *one's own*.[1]

In order to better understand this, we need to briefly discuss a current time slice theory. No better one could be discussed than that of Harry Frankfurt's. In his essay, "Freedom of the Will and the Concept of a Person,"[2] Frankfurt outlines what has come to be known as a hierarchical model of freedom.

For Frankfurt, a person is free and responsible when his second order desires mesh with his first order desires. There are two levels of desires in the human psyche. A first order desire is a desire for action. For example, I could have a desire to run one mile to keep in shape. This first order desire does not need to lead to the action of running one mile, it just needs to be there in order to qualify as a first order desire. When I put this desire into action, then I am willing. In other words, when my desire to run one mile to keep in shape becomes actualized, then Frankfurt calls this "willing." Both the presence of the first order desire and the willing are different from a second order desire. The second order desire is a desire not for an action, but for the first order desire. I may have a first order desire to run one mile and even put this desire into action, but a second order desire is a desire to want that first order desire and the action that comes from it. When this mesh between second order desires and first order desires occurs, then I have free will and moral responsibility. Frankfurt writes:

> It is in securing the conformity of his will to his second-order volitions, then, that a person exercises freedom of the will. And it is in the discrepancy between his will and his second-order volitions, or his awareness that their coincidence is not his own

---

1. Fischer and Ravizza, *Responsibility and Control*, 207.
2. Frankfurt, "Freedom of the Will," 322.

doing but only a happy chance, that a person does not have this freedom feels its lack.[3]

What we see in Frankfurt is that freedom and responsibility depend upon a relationship or mesh between second order desires and first order desires. Fischer and Ravizza call this a current time slice theory because the history concerning how this relationship came about is not important for determining freedom and responsibility. All that matters for freedom and responsibility is that there is this mesh at a current time slice. If this mesh is there, then the person is free and responsible regardless of how these desires came about.

Fischer and Ravizza see a problem with this because it does not seem to be able to handle manipulation cases. Neal Judisch helpfully puts it this way:

> The concern is that an agent may have the right kind of internal psychical structure at a particular time even though the desires, values and preferences constituting that structure was instilled in her in a manner that seemingly *undercuts* her responsibility for acting as she does.[4]

For example, suppose that a clever scientist was able to electronically stimulate certain desires in the brain of a person. This scientist could stimulate both a first order and second order desire to want the first order desire. In this case, there is a mesh between the second order desire and the first order desire. According to Frankfurt's view, this person is free and responsible yet intuitively we think he is not. The mesh at a current time slice alone is not sufficient. Much more could be said about this, but Fischer and Ravizza's point is that we need a concept of moral responsibility that is historical in order to avoid manipulation problems such as this one. They begin their historical account by describing the moral education of a child.

The Moral Education of a Child

We have seen the importance of not appealing to the structure of one's psyche alone in order to determine responsibility. In place of a current time slice theory, Fischer and Ravizza appeal to the historical process of taking responsibility. Exactly what this is can be illumined by describing the general process of a child's moral education. This process is historical in that

---

3. Frankfurt, "Freedom of the Will," 332.
4. Judisch, "Responsibility, Manipulation, and Ownership," 116.

a child is not seen to be a morally responsible agent at birth or for years after birth. Instead, there is a process whereby a child becomes a responsible agent. The key factor is that the child comes to take responsibility by making the mechanism that issues in action his own. Once this is accomplished, the child sees himself as the source of his actions:

> The sense in which the child sees himself as the "source" of these upshots is that he sees that their occurrence is caused—in a certain characteristic way—by *him*. The child is brought to see that his desires, beliefs, and intentions result in actions and upshots in the world; these upshots are not the results of freakish accidents or other agents.[5]

Part of being a responsible agent is that we see or have a view of ourselves as the source of our actions. We tend to take this for granted until we encounter someone who does not see himself as the source of his actions. For example, suppose Frank committed the crime of murder. As he was interviewed, it was discovered that he did not see himself as the source of this crime. Though there were seven eyewitnesses that saw him do it and though there is a film that shows him stabbing the victim, he still does not see himself as the source of this crime. Instead, he may appeal to demon possession, alien manipulation, or something else as the source. Upon hearing this, we may diminish his responsibility, taking him to be a crazy person. We think this way because he does not see himself as the source of his action.

Part of the moral development of a child is that at some point, he comes to see himself as the source of his actions. In addition to this, the child must also see himself as the proper target of other people's praise or blame. This praise and blame from others are called reactive attitudes:

> If the young boy sees that he was not forced or tricked into opening the birthday presents, then he is encouraged to see that it is fair for his parents to blame him for doing so. Once a child has acquired this sort of view of himself, he can at least provisionally be *held* responsible for his behavior (which meets the other conditions for guidance control).[6]

It is not enough for the child to see himself as the source of his actions, but he must also see himself as both praiseworthy and blameworthy by others. To not see himself this way is a serious lack. For example, suppose that Frank does see himself as the source of the murder. However, he does not see himself as blamable for the murder. In fact, he finds it strange that

---

5. Fischer and Ravizza, *Responsibility and Control*, 208.
6. Fischer and Ravizza, *Responsibility and Control*, 209.

people would be angry, afraid, or repulsed by him. Though he sees himself as the source of the crime, he does not see himself as an apt target for the reactive attitudes. We tend to diminish Frank's responsibility because we think something is seriously wrong with him.

In the moral development of a child, once he sees himself as the source of his actions and sees himself as the apt target for reactive attitudes, then the parents expect the child to respond to their praise or blame in the appropriate manner. The idea is to instill within the child "an internal attitude towards himself that corresponds to the external attitude we adopt towards him."[7] If the child does not respond at all or in an inappropriate manner to praise or blame, we suspect that the child has not properly seen himself as the source of his actions in the right way.

We have seen that the moral education of a child consists of two things: First, viewing himself as the source of his actions and second, viewing himself as the apt target of the reactive attitudes. Fischer and Ravizza are appealing to a subjective experience in the child. We may think that the child is objectively responsible, but it is important that the child also view himself as responsible. This is a subjective experience that every responsible agent must have to be held morally responsible. Without viewing oneself both as the source and as an apt target of the reactive attitudes, the person diminishes in responsibility or is not responsible.

In light of the above discussion on a child's moral education, Fischer and Ravizza say that we can helpfully divide this into three stages "training, taking responsibility, and being held responsible:"[8]

> When parents treat their child as if he is responsible—taking certain attitudes toward him—they are engaging in moral *training*. This sort of training aims to induce a certain sort of view in the child, a view of himself as an agent and, in some situations, a fair target for praise or blame. Adopting this view is an important part of *taking responsibility*. Having adopted this sort of view, the child is ready to be *held responsible* (by others as well as himself). In practice, these stages are not neatly individuated; nor is the process a clearly defined, one-time operation. Rather, the different stages overlap with one another and compose a cycle that must be continually repeated in the process of becoming a fully morally responsible agent.[9]

---

7. Fischer and Ravizza, *Responsibility and Control*, 209.
8. Fischer and Ravizza, *Responsibility and Control*, 210.
9. Fischer and Ravizza, *Responsibility and Control*, 210.

At this stage in Fischer and Ravizza's theory, they want to focus on what it means for a child to "take responsibility."

Taking Responsibility

There are two things Fischer and Ravizza want to say about taking responsibility: First, what it means to take responsibility and second, the things for which we take responsibility. In the first, Fischer and Ravizza focus on the second stage of moral education, taking responsibility. The process of an agent taking responsibility is what makes the agent's actions his own. Carl Ginet helpfully summarizes what it means to take responsibility:

> They explain (section III) that taking responsibility has three ingredients: (1) the agent must see himself (a mechanism in him) as the source of his behavior, (2) he must accept that he is a fair target of the reactive attitudes as a result of how he exercises his agency (which presumably requires his believing that he is at least moderately reasons-responsive), and (3) this view of himself must be based in an appropriate way on the evidence. (1) and (2) seem to be snapshot properties; (3) the historically entailing ingredient.[10]

Fischer and Ravizza work through these points in more detail. It would be helpful to elaborate on them in order to better understand them. The first is that an agent must see himself as the source of his behavior:

> First, an individual must see himself as the source of his behavior in the sense we have specified. That is, the individual must see himself as an agent; he must see that his choices and actions are efficacious in the world. The agent thus sees that his motivational states are the causal source—in certain characteristic ways—of upshots in the world.[11]

It is important to understand that when Fischer and Ravizza appeal to the agent as the source of his behavior, they do not mean that he is the ultimate source, nor do they mean that nothing has caused or determined his actions. Instead, they mean that his actions spring from a mechanism that is moderately reasons-responsive and that the agent has taken ownership of this mechanism. Part of taking ownership is subjectively seeing or accepting that he caused the action that affects the world in certain ways. He truly believes that he is the causal source. As we will see later, this requires more

---

10. Ginet, "Working with Fischer and Ravizza," 238.
11. Fischer and Ravizza, *Responsibility and Control*, 210–11.

than simply uttering the words, "I am the causal source." Instead, it requires the belief that "I am the causal source."

The second condition consists of accepting that as an agent I am the apt subject of reactive attitudes:

> Second, the individual must accept that he is a fair target of the reactive attitudes as a result of how he exercises this agency in certain contexts.[12]

This condition requires a distinction because not everyone is prone to deep reflection on this. This means that there are two parts to this second condition:

> The first version deals with individuals who do not engage in significant metaphysical reflection about the relationship between causal determinism and the fairness of our social practices of applying the reactive attitudes.[13]

This is clearly the vast majority of people in the world. Most people take it for granted that they are morally responsible and the thought does not cross their minds that if causal determinism is true, then they may not be morally responsible. Even if they do reflect upon this issue, that reflection is not too deep and thus they do not really worry about not being morally responsible. Instead, they just go along with society and generally agree that there are certain situations where they are praiseworthy or blameworthy.

The second part of the second condition is significantly different. There are some people that engage in significant reflection on the issue of moral responsibility and causal determinism:

> And the second version pertains to those individuals who do in fact engage in such reflection.[14]

An example of this would be someone that holds to the position of hard determinism. After reflecting upon the issues, these people have concluded that causal determinism is true and that causal determinism is incompatible with free will and moral responsibility. In such cases, the person that holds this view does not see himself as a morally responsible person. Thus, they do not subjectively view themselves as apt targets for the reactive attitudes. These kinds of people are problematic according to Fischer and Ravizza's theory. They will return to this problem after further clarifying the rest of their theory.

---

12. Fischer and Ravizza, *Responsibility and Control*, 211.
13. Fischer and Ravizza, *Responsibility and Control*, 211.
14. Fischer and Ravizza, *Responsibility and Control*, 211.

Before we continue, it is important to understand that Fischer and Ravizza are not saying that an agent must always agree with the social attitude towards his behavior. This is not what they mean when they say that an agent must view himself as an apt candidate for the reactive attitudes. There can be and are cases where the reactive attitudes applied to one from the outside may not agree with the attitudes of the agent internally. That disconnect is allowable in Fischer and Ravizza's theory. It does not follow that every time someone or some group disapproves of an agent's behavior, the agent ought to feel or think that he did something wrong. Instead, Fischer and Ravizza are saying that there must be some sense on the part of the agent that he is part of the social game and it is fair for him to be praised or blamed for his behavior:

> At minimum, we expect our attitudes towards others to have some purchase. The fact that we might further blame someone who fails to react appropriately toward himself indicates that *we* believe the person is an appropriate candidate for the reactive attitudes. If, however, a person resolutely shows no moral response or *appreciation* of the moral force of the attitudes we take towards him, then eventually we must concede that he is not an appropriate partner in the conversation: he has not taken responsibility for himself. In this we can stop resenting him as a person, and begin treating him as we would a distasteful object or a dangerous (or annoying) animal.[15]

In other words, a responsible agent is one that views himself as subject to the reactive attitudes in general, even if he disagrees with the application of the reactive attitudes in a particular situation. What Fischer and Ravizza are guarding against is someone that "resolutely shows no moral response or appreciation of the moral force of the attitudes we take towards him."[16] This is someone that refuses to see himself as subject to the reactive attitudes. In this situation, something is clearly wrong with the person. They have not taken responsibility in the required sense and are acting like an animal, which we do not regard as morally responsible.

There is one last condition to Fischer and Ravizza's account of taking responsibility. It has to do with basing the first two conditions on the evidence:

---

15. Fischer and Ravizza, *Responsibility and Control*, 213.
16. Fischer and Ravizza, *Responsibility and Control*, 213.

> The third condition on taking responsibility requires that the individual's view of himself specified in the first two conditions be based, in an appropriate way, on the evidence.[17]

This means that the agent's view of himself should be based on the evidence of (1) "his experience with the effects of his choices and actions on the world"[18] and (2) "his view of himself as an apt target for reactive attitudes in certain contexts,"[19] which are based on what his parents and society have taught him.

This is what Fischer and Ravizza mean by "taking responsibility." There is one more feature of this that is important. It is that taking responsibility need not be a conscious or deliberative process:

> This process may involve conscious and deliberative reflection, but it need *not*. Just as a person who acts for a reason need not explicitly formulate the reason or consciously invoke it as an action guide, so a person can take responsibility in an implicit, nondeliberative way.[20]

This is important to understand. The process of taking responsibility is not necessarily conscious. As people grow up and become responsible agents, they are not always aware of these steps and they are not always aware of viewing themselves according to these three conditions. They function more like subconscious presuppositions. As we analyze situations of morally responsible actions, we see that they presuppose that an agent (1) views himself as the source, (2) views himself as an apt candidate for the reactive attitudes, and (3) bases (1) and (2) on the evidence.

We have seen how Fischer and Ravizza's account differs from a current time slice account like Frankfurt's. In Frankfurt's account, what mattered was the mesh between second order desires and first order desires. The history of how the agent got those desires is irrelevant. What matters is that the agent's second order desires "wanted" or "owned" the first order desires. This mesh happens in a current time slice. This is not the case with Fischer and Ravizza. As we have seen, the history of taking responsibility is important. At some point in history, the agent must meet the previously articulated three conditions on taking responsibility. This is a historical process and not a current time slice moment. The next question to ask is for what the agent takes responsibility.

---

17. Fischer and Ravizza, *Responsibility and Control*, 213.
18. Fischer and Ravizza, *Responsibility and Control*, 213.
19. Fischer and Ravizza, *Responsibility and Control*, 213.
20. Fischer and Ravizza, *Responsibility and Control*, 214.

The first thing to see is that an agent does not take responsibility for all of his actions regardless of the mechanism. Recall that a mechanism is just the way in which the action came about. There are a number of mechanisms that issue in actions. Fischer and Ravizza write:

> An agent's actions may be produced by a variety of different mechanisms; including the normal exercise of practical reason, nonreflective habit, and (for example) direct stimulation of the brain. When an agent takes responsibility, then, he obviously is *not* accepting responsibility for all his actions *whatever their source*; rather, he is accepting responsibility for only those actions which flow from a certain source. This idea can be framed more precisely by saying that *an agent takes responsibility for acting from a particular kind of mechanism.*[21]

An agent does not take responsibility for just any mechanism. The electronic stimulation of the brain is a mechanism that causes an action. However, a morally responsible agent does not take responsibility for this mechanism. Given our previous account of moderate reasons-responsiveness, we would say that the action springing forth from the electronic stimulation of the brain is not moderately reasons-responsive. That action would have occurred no matter what the reasons for doing otherwise. In addition to this, the agent does not take ownership of the electronic stimulation of the brain. It is not "his own" in the sense that he is not and does not view himself as the source of the action that springs from this mechanism.

However, a responsible agent would take responsibility for the mechanism and the actions that spring forth from the normal exercise of practical reason and non-reflective habit. In the moral education of a child, the parents praise or blame the child for actions that come from certain mechanisms; for example, practical reason and non-reflective mechanisms. If a child acts wrongly out of either of these mechanisms, the parents blame him. If he acts correctly, the parents praise him. The goal is to get the child to realize that acting from these mechanisms justly deserve praise or blame. At some point the child takes responsibility in the sense of taking ownership of the fact that behavior from these mechanisms can be praised or blamed:

> Having taken responsibility for behavior that issues from a kind of mechanism, it is almost as if the agent has some sort of "standing policy" with respect to that kind of mechanism. Thus, when the agent subsequently acts from a mechanism of that

---

21. Fischer and Ravizza, *Responsibility and Control*, 215.

kind, that mechanism is *his own* insofar as he has already taken responsibility for acting from that kind of mechanism.[22]

It is not the case that the agent must "take responsibility" every time he acts from these mechanisms. As we have seen, taking responsibility is not even necessarily a conscious thing, nor is it something that must be repeated. Instead, once the agent "takes responsibility" for a mechanism, then he always does.

Another important feature is that the agent need not know or understand all the details of the mechanism. As Fischer and Ravizza put it:

> To employ a metaphor, when one takes responsibility for acting from a kind of mechanism, it is as if one takes responsibility for the entire iceberg in virtue of seeing the tip of the iceberg.[23]

We all have these mechanisms from which our actions spring. However, we do not know the details regarding how these mechanisms work in their entirety. Fischer and Ravizza do not require that one know all this.

Failure to Take Responsibility

This account of taking responsibility opens Fischer and Ravizza to two criticisms. In exploring these criticisms, we will further illumine their account of mechanism ownership. The first criticism is that their account appears to give incentives not to take responsibility. The second criticism is that there may be cases of apparent responsibility in which the agent failed to take responsibility.

Regarding the first criticism, the question arises as to whether an agent could avoid responsibility by simply refusing to take responsibility. In other words, agents can easily refute the account by simply not taking responsibility. Fischer and Ravizza believe that this criticism can be resolved by understanding more clearly what they mean by taking responsibility:

> First, note that, on our view, taking responsibility is *not* just a matter of saying something, such as "I take responsibility." That is, taking responsibility—and not taking responsibility—need not line up with any kind of *verbal behavior* (or lack of verbal behavior). Indeed, on our view, taking responsibility is not even

---

22. Fischer and Ravizza, *Responsibility and Control*, 216.
23. Fischer and Ravizza, *Responsibility and Control*, 216–17.

an a*ction*; rather, it is (roughly) *coming to have a certain cluster of beliefs (in a certain way)*.[24]

In light of this, an agent cannot avoid taking responsibility by refusing to utter the words, "I take responsibility." Their account requires the negation of something deeper. It requires a failure to have "a certain cluster of beliefs."[25] This would not be an easy thing to do. We do not have the kind of control over our beliefs necessary to choose to avoid taking responsibility. In order to show this, Fischer and Ravizza distinguish between voluntary and non-voluntary beliefs as well as occurrent and dispositional beliefs. They write:

> Having a belief (or set of beliefs)—or not having a belief (or set of beliefs)—is typically *not* thought to be "voluntary" or up to an agent. Perhaps it is up to an individual whether he "entertains" or focuses on a particular belief, but it is not so clear that it is a voluntary matter whether one *has* a belief or set of beliefs. (Alternatively, one might say that whereas it may be in one's control which "occurrent beliefs" one has, it is not similarly in one's control which "dispositional beliefs" one has. And of course our account of taking responsibility specifies a set of *dispositional* beliefs). Thus, insofar as having the beliefs in question is not a voluntary matter; it is not evident that our account can be said to provide incentives for an agent to fail to take responsibility.[26]

It may not be the case that all of our beliefs are involuntary. That would depend on what we mean by voluntary. Certainly, we can acquire beliefs by making choices and ingraining those beliefs through developing habits. However, that is not relevant to Fischer and Ravizza's analysis. What is relevant is that they consider the cluster of beliefs surrounding taking responsibility to be dispositional beliefs. These would be more fundamental, subconscious beliefs that are ingrained in us. They could be ingrained in numerous ways: God could have put them there, society could have ingrained them there, our upbringing could have instilled them, etc. The point is that these beliefs cannot be simply turned off with the ease of a light switch, if at all. We may be able to consider these beliefs, but we may not be able to shed them. One thinks of the belief in the external world. No matter what our metaphysics, we cannot seem to help believing in the external world, nor can we seem to shed this belief. So also, conditions 1–3 of their account

---

24. Fischer and Ravizza, *Responsibility and Control*, 217.
25. Fischer and Ravizza, *Responsibility and Control*, 217.
26. Fischer and Ravizza, *Responsibility and Control*, 217–18.

of taking responsibility cannot be shed as easily, if at all. Since this is the case and since taking responsibility is dealing with dispositional beliefs, it follows that no one can fail to take responsibility by choosing to not have these dispositional beliefs.

However, even if these beliefs were of the sort that could be voluntarily (in some sense) avoided, Fischer and Ravizza do not think that their theory encourages people to do this. They write:

> We contend that our account of responsibility does *not* encourage agents to embark on programs designed to issue in the lack of the beliefs involved in taking responsibility. This is because the price of refusing to take responsibility may be as high as that of accepting responsibility.[27]

For example, if an agent does not believe that he is an agent (Fischer and Ravizza's first condition of taking responsibility), then he would not see himself as affecting the world. He would not view his actions as his. Instead, they would be viewed more as accidents. What would society think of a person like this? They would most likely view him as a danger and would seek to incarcerate him in order to protect the rest of society and himself. As Fischer and Ravizza put it:

> This forced sequestration surely is not something to be sought. Of course, to be treated as a dangerous animal, or an insane individual, is not something highly prized.[28]

If someone were incentivized to shed these dispositional beliefs, paying attention to the consequences would surely deter him. He would be treated as an insane person that would require confinement. Fischer and Ravizza conclude:

> An individual who genuinely does not see himself as an appropriate participant in the family of reactive attitudes will not be able to be a robust participant in important human relationships. Thus, to be cut off from meaningful human relationships, including any kind of true friendship, would also be a consequence of a failure to satisfy the second condition on taking responsibility; even a convicted felon has the possibility of friendship and meaningful connection with other persons—something that would be denied the individual who fails to take responsibility (in virtue of failing to satisfy the second condition).[29]

27. Fischer and Ravizza, *Responsibility and Control*, 218.
28. Fischer and Ravizza, *Responsibility and Control*, 219.
29. Fischer and Ravizza, *Responsibility and Control*, 219.

The objection that their account incentivizes people not to take responsibility is not likely.

Manipulation Cases

The second criticism Fischer and Ravizza face is that there are apparent cases where an agent seems responsible but upon further reflection, he is not. These are commonly called "manipulation cases." As we have seen, for Fischer and Ravizza, an agent must have taken responsibility in order for the agent to be morally responsible for his behavior. In taking responsibility, the agent makes the mechanism from which that behavior became one's own. In light of this, they raise a potential problem:

> In certain cases involving direct manipulation of the brain (and similar influences), it is natural to say that the mechanism leading to the action is not, in an important sense, the agent's own.[30]

If an agent were to have his brain electronically stimulated to perform a certain act, we would intuitively think that the person is not responsible for that act. This would be a case of manipulation that renders the agent not responsible for the action. In Fischer and Ravizza's account, they would say that the agent's action did not spring from a moderately reasons-responsive mechanism. That is, no matter what reasons were presented, the agent would do the same action because the electronic stimulation guarantees that action.

But what would they say if an agent did act from a moderately reasons-responsive mechanism, but that mechanism was implanted in a manipulative manner? Here is the problem:

> But it seems that the operation of a moderately reasons-responsive mechanism just prior to the action can *itself* be the product of a process that intuitively rules out moral responsibility. That is, it appears that a moderately reasons-responsive mechanism could be "implanted" by a scientist, or produced via direct electronic stimulation of the brain. What seems relevant is not only the fact that the mechanism issuing in the action is suitably reasons-responsive; what also matters is *how* that mechanism has been put in place. So, whereas responsiveness points us to the past, rather than solely to the current time slice, it does not make us look sufficiently *far* into the past. Responsiveness is

---

30. Fischer and Ravizza, *Responsibility and Control*, 230.

only *locally historical*; but various cases show that a more *globally historical* approach is needed.[31]

The reasons-responsiveness aspect of the theory alone is insufficient to handle this case because it is only locally historical and not globally historical. This means that we must look to another criterion—taking responsibility—in order to deal with cases like this. In order to illustrate this, Fischer and Ravizza propose a set of further manipulation cases.

In order to illustrate the benefits of their globally historical account of ownership, Fischer and Ravizza give us the example of Judith. Judith has secretly had a mechanism implanted in her brain a few days ago which causes her to have an irresistible desire. By using this mechanism, the scientist can stimulate Judith's brain in order to get her to have an irresistible desire to punch her best friend Jane the next time she sees her. Judith happens to run into Jane at the coffee shop not too long afterward. She experiences an irresistible urge to punch Jane and punches her. In this case, we would intuitively hold that Judith is not responsible. In Fischer and Ravizza's account, this is for two reasons:

> First, the mechanism leading to the action is not moderately reasons-responsive; by hypothesis, given the kind of stimulation of the brain that actually takes place, Judith has an irresistible urge to strike Jane. Thus, Judith would strike Jane, no matter what kinds of reasons to refrain were present.

The second reason is that she has not taken responsibility for the mechanism:

> And, whereas Judith can plausibly be thought to have taken responsibility for the mechanism of practical reason (uninfluenced by clandestine operations of scientists), it is *not* plausible to say that Judith has taken responsibility for the sort of mechanism that actually issues in her action; *this* sort of mechanism includes the manipulation of the scientist. Hence Judith *has* not (on our view) taken responsibility for the kind of mechanism that actually issues in the action, and thus cannot be deemed morally responsible for her action. In this case, *neither* component of the account of guidance control is satisfied, and since both components express necessary conditions on guidance control, there are *two reasons* (from our point of view) why she is not responsible for her action.[32]

---

31. Fischer and Ravizza, *Responsibility and Control*, 230–31.
32. Fischer and Ravizza, *Responsibility and Control*, 232.

The second illustration does not deal with irresistible desires, but extremely strong desires. Fischer and Ravizza refer to the Judith example once more. In this case, everything is the same as in the previous example. The only difference is that the scientist has not implanted a mechanism in her brain that gives her an irresistible desire to punch Jane. Instead, he has implanted a mechanism that gives Judith an extremely strong desire to punch Jane. The difference with the last case is obviously the intensity of the desire to punch Jane:

> The desire is so strong that Judith would punch Jane under every possible circumstance except ones in which Judith knows that if she were to punch Jane, she would thereby cause the deaths of large numbers of innocent people.[33]

The kind of manipulation is the same in the first and the second case with Judith; that is, a scientist has implanted a mechanism. The difference is that in the first case, the desire is irresistible and in the second case, the desire is extremely strong:

> Here the mechanism leading to Judith's action is indeed moderately reasons-responsive. What is crucial however is that (as in the first case) Judith has *not* taken responsibility for the kind of mechanism that actually issues in her action. Failing to meet the ownership condition on guidance control, Judith is not deemed morally responsible for her action, on our account.
>
> Our account of taking responsibility holds that agents typically have taken responsibility, in the past, for certain salient kinds of mechanisms; for example, agents have typically taken responsibility for the mechanism of practical reasoning (uninfluenced by subliminal advertising, direct electronic stimulation of the brain, and so forth), and unreflective habit (again, uninfluenced by such factors as subliminal advertising, direct electronic stimulation of the brain, and so forth). Given that Judith does not know about the manipulation of the scientist, and has not explicitly considered such manipulation, it is plausible to say that Judith has *not* taken responsibility for the kind of mechanism that actually issues in the action (the manipulation mechanism).[34]

At some point in the past, Judith took responsibility for her ordinary mechanism of practical reasoning. She thus takes responsibility for actions that issue from that mechanism. However, Judith did not take responsibility

---

33. Fischer and Ravizza, *Responsibility and Control*, 232.
34. Fischer and Ravizza, *Responsibility and Control*, 232–33.

for the mechanism implanted into her brain by the scientist (involving direct stimulation of the brain). In this case, the mechanism is moderately reasons-responsive. This is so because she would not act on the extremely strong desire if she knew that it would cause the deaths of a large number of people. There is a possible world in which this mechanism does not act because of a good moral reason. However, she has not taken responsibility for that mechanism and because of this, Fischer and Ravizza's account does not hold her responsible. The mechanism by which she acted is not her own.

It is possible that Judith could become responsible for acting on this extremely strong desire if she were to reflect and choose this mechanism. That is, she becomes aware that she is being manipulated, but upon becoming aware of this, she reflects and wants to have this mechanism as her own. This would make her responsible on Fischer and Ravizza's account:

> Now it is possible that Judith becomes aware of the stimulation of her brain by the scientist. She thus can understand the provenance of her previously inexplicable desire to punch. She now has two choices. Presumably, she will modify her desire so that she returns to her normal state (antecedent to the implantation of the desire). Alternatively, it is conceivable that she will decide to keep the new desire, upon reflection. (Perhaps she will have decided that she likes it). Either way, awareness and reflection returns Judith to the mechanism of ordinary practical reasoning, and she can subsequently be held morally responsible. Awareness and reflection of a certain sort returns Judith to a situation in which she is acting from her own mechanism.[35]

There is one final illustration given by Fischer and Ravizza. This illustration involves manipulation that gets the agent to take responsibility:

> But it is conceivable that a different sort of manipulation takes place, in which the agent's taking responsibility itself is somehow electronically implanted. That is, it is conceivable that the individual's view of himself as an agent and an apt candidate for the reactive attitudes be electronically implanted . . .
>
> Earlier, we specified the third condition on taking responsibility as follows: the agent's view of himself must be based on his evidence in an appropriate way. Obviously, this is abstract and schematic. This condition is intended (in part) to imply that an individual who has been electronically induced to have the relevant view of himself (and thus satisfy the first two conditions on taking responsibility) has *not* formed his view of himself in

---

35. Fischer and Ravizza, *Responsibility and Control*, 235.

the appropriate way. But the relevant notion of appropriateness must remain unanalyzed.[36]

As we saw, there is a third condition for taking responsibility: That is basing the agent's view of himself on evidence in an appropriate way. This condition is supposed to help with the manipulation cases that involve agents being manipulated into taking responsibility. However, Fischer and Ravizza do not elaborate on what it means to base the agent's view of himself on the evidence in an appropriate way.

Subjectivist View

At this point, it would be helpful to discuss two more issues and then summarize their account of taking responsibility. The first issue involves what Fischer and Ravizza call their "subjectivist" view. The second issue involves showing that their view of mechanism ownership is compatible with causal determinism. I will attend to these two issues before giving a summary.

Fischer and Ravizza call their view of mechanism ownership a subjectivist view. It is called this in the sense that:

> We require that an agent have a certain sort of view of himself in order to be morally responsible. That is, moral responsibility, on our view, is not simply a matter of having a set of "objective" features; in addition, one must (in the way we have specified) *view oneself* in a certain way.[37]

The reason for this is as follows:

> This is because the first two conditions for taking responsibility require that the individual see himself as an agent (in the sense specified earlier) and as a fair target of the reactive attitudes. (Of course, this subjectivity does not imply that there are not important "objective" elements of our accounts of taking responsibility and moral responsibility.) A theory of moral responsibility is supposed to give expression to (and more concrete content to) our inchoate, intuitive conceptions of ourselves as active and in control; and it is highly plausible to think that our having a certain sort of *view of ourselves* is required in order for us to be active and in control. In the absence of such a view, why wouldn't

---

36. Fischer and Ravizza, *Responsibility and Control*, 236–37.
37. Fischer and Ravizza, *Responsibility and Control*, 221.

we be like the sailor who is buffeted by the wind because he lacks a belief that his rudder is working?[38]

It is an important aspect of Fischer and Ravizza's view that the agent subjectively view himself as an agent and as an apt candidate for the reactive attitudes. As we have seen earlier, an agent that does not see himself in this way has something seriously wrong with him. If they do not see themselves as the cause of their actions, then they certainly do not see themselves as in control of their actions. This is something that we would associate with a mentally deranged person or even someone that is coerced. The same can be said about not seeing oneself as praiseworthy or blameworthy. Those who do not see themselves in this manner are regarded as lacking something important to humanity. This is why a crucial aspect of mechanism ownership is the subjective view of oneself as an agent and as an apt candidate for praise and blame.

The second thing to see is that Fischer and Ravizza believe that their account of taking responsibility is compatible with causal determinism. They begin by returning to the second condition, that the agent believes that he is an apt target for reactive attitudes. Previously they made a distinction between those agents who do not reflect on the compatibility of moral responsibility and causal determinism and those who do. They first consider the compatibility of causal determinism and taking responsibility for those who do not reflect on their compatibility:

> Here it seems straightforward that our three conditions are compatible with causal determinism. Clearly, causal determinism does not rule out an individual's believing that he is an agent (in our sense) and that the given social practices render him a fair target for the reactive attitudes in certain circumstances.... Finally, causal determinism does not rule out the fact that this picture of himself be produced in the agent by the evidence for it (in an appropriate way). Thus, in the nonreflective case, which is clearly the typical case—it is evident that taking responsibility (on our account) is compatible with causal determinism.[39]

Next Fischer and Ravizza examine the agent who does reflect on the compatibility of causal determinism and the fairness of the application of the reactive attitudes. This would be the kind of agent who immerses himself in the debates surrounding free will, moral responsibility, and determinism. He is more philosophically inclined. In light of this reflection, he

---

38. Fischer and Ravizza, *Responsibility and Control*, 223.
39. Fischer and Ravizza, *Responsibility and Control*, 225–26.

has called into question whether he is really responsible for his mechanisms. He knows that his society holds him responsible for actions flowing from his mechanisms, but he himself wonders if they should. He believes that to do so is metaphysically suspect, even if socially it is a given:

> It is important to distinguish a *social judgment* from what we might call a *metaphysical judgment*. A social judgment is simply a judgment about our given *social practices*. This is the sort of judgment involved in the nonreflective version of the second condition. But what is required in the reflective version is not simply a social judgment; here, the individual must make some sort of metaphysical judgment to the effect that, all things considered, it is appropriate to subject certain individuals—including himself—to the reactive attitudes in certain contexts.[40]

The idea is that causal determinism is true and the agent we are considering knows that it is true:

> Note that now the question is *not* simply about the given social practices; the question is whether these practices can be justified, all things considered.[41]

These people can be convinced that it is plausible to believe that causal determinism is compatible with the aptness of reactive attitudes. They can even be convinced to put aside their doubts for practical purposes. In light of this, Fischer and Ravizza say:

> This suggests the following version of the second condition on taking responsibility (the version pertinent to cases in which there is philosophical reflection on the relationship between causal determinism and the fairness, all things considered, of the reactive attitudes). An individual must view himself as, prima facie at least, an apt candidate for the application of the reactive attitudes, and be willing to put aside his residual doubts, for all practical purposes. In the context of explicit philosophical reflection, we contend that the satisfaction of this version of the condition is enough (in conjunction with the satisfaction of the other two conditions) for the agent to have taken responsibility.[42]

---

40. Fischer and Ravizza, *Responsibility and Control*, 226.
41. Fischer and Ravizza, *Responsibility and Control*, 226.
42. Fischer and Ravizza, *Responsibility and Control*, 227.

This may be the case, but why should anyone adopt this view of himself? Fischer and Ravizza believe that they have given good enough arguments in *Responsibility and Control* to move someone in that direction:

> First, we have sought to defend the idea that the sort of control that involves *alternative possibilities* is *not* required for moral responsibility. Thus, we have attempted to remove what is probably the most significant objection to the compatibility of causal determinism and the appropriateness of the reactive attitudes. This should move reflective, open-minded individuals towards adopting the stance we have specified.
>
> Further, we have contended that moral responsibility is grounded in a kind of control—guidance control—with two components. The first component is moderate reasons-responsiveness of the mechanism leading to the behavior in question. And we have argued that this sort of responsiveness is entirely compatible with causal determinism. Of course, the second component remains—the ownership condition. But we would suggest that the Frankfurt-type examples are also illuminating here.[43]

The Frankfurt examples make a distinction between the actual sequence and the alternative sequence. Fischer and Ravizza think that this helps out their view of mechanism ownership:

> But there is *another* important difference: the actual-sequence mechanism is, intuitively, the agent's *own*, whereas the alternative-scenario mechanism is *not*. But the Frankfurt-type cases are entirely consistent with causal determinism's being true. Another way of making the point is that causal determinism in itself does *not* imply that all sequences are relevantly similar to the alternative scenario of a Frankfurt-type case, in which there is, for example, significant direct manipulation of the brain (and thus the mechanism is not the agent's own).[44]

Fischer and Ravizza believe these considerations will move any open-minded person to adopt the stance associated with taking responsibility (in the reflective case). However, not everyone will be convinced. Fischer and Ravizza do not claim to advance knock down arguments:

> Such individuals will not deem themselves apt targets for the reactive attitudes, and thus they will not take responsibility

---

43. Fischer and Ravizza, *Responsibility and Control*, 227.
44. Fischer and Ravizza, *Responsibility and Control*, 228.

for the kinds of mechanisms that lead to their behavior. Thus, on our account, they will *not* be morally responsible for their behavior. But we do not take this to be a defect of our theory. Indeed, it follows straightforwardly from the fact (noted earlier) that we agree with Galen Strawson in embracing a "subjectivist" approach to moral responsibility. . . . In order to be morally responsible, a person must see himself as an agent who is an appropriate candidate for the reactive attitudes.[45]

It would seem that on their account a hard determinist is not morally responsible. This appears to be a problem with their theory. In chapter four, I will argue that reformed theology has the resources to affirm a subjectivist condition without this problem with hard determinism.

We have seen that Fischer and Ravizza's account is subjectivist and we have seen how it is that they regard their account as compatible with causal determinism. Now I will briefly summarize the three conditions on taking responsibility.

For Fischer and Ravizza there are three conditions necessary to take responsibility. The first one is that the agent must see himself as an agent. He cannot regard all his actions as chance occurrences or as coerced. Instead, he must acknowledge that he caused at least some of his actions and is thus an agent. The second condition was that he see himself as a fair target of the reactive attitudes. We have seen that these are attitudes that other people ascribe to the agent. They are attitudes surrounding praise and blame. They are attitudes such as admiration, pride, disgust, anger, etc. An agent must see himself as the fair target of these kinds of attitudes in at least some of his actions. The third condition was basing his view of himself, in the first and second conditions, as appropriately having a bearing on the evidence. Fischer and Ravizza leave this unanalyzed.

Summary

At this point, it would be helpful to summarize guidance control along the lines of the sourcehood condition, the alternative possibilities condition, reasons-responsiveness and the subjectivist condition. First, guidance control denies the sourcehood condition. It denies that freedom and moral responsibility require that the agent be the ultimate source of his actions. Instead, it holds that guidance control is sufficient to regard the agent as being the proper source of his actions. Second, guidance control also rejects the alternative possibilities condition. It is not necessary that the agent

45. Fischer and Ravizza, *Responsibility and Control*, 228–29.

have access to alternative possibilities in the actual sequence in order for the agent to be free and morally responsible. Third, guidance control affirms that reasons-responsiveness is necessary for freedom and moral responsibility. It advocates a type of reasons-responsive theory called moderate reasons-responsiveness. Finally, guidance control affirms a subjectivist condition as mechanism ownership. It holds that for an agent to be free and morally responsible, the agent must view himself in a certain manner. He must view himself as an agent that is properly subject to the reactive attitude and he must base this on the evidence.

It is important to summarize guidance control along these lines because reformed theology and Jonathan Edwards make the same denials and affirmations. Throughout the rest of this book, we will see that reformed theology and Jonathan Edwards deny the source and alternative possibilities conditions, they affirm reasons-responsiveness and they affirm a type of subjectivist condition similar to guidance control. Along the lines of these four categories we can see substantial compatibility between guidance control, reformed theology and Jonathan Edwards.

CHAPTER THREE

Decree, Foreknowledge, and Providence

Introduction

WE HAVE SEEN FISCHER and Ravizza's ideas regarding the sourcehood condition and the alternative possibilities condition. Now we need to ask if their ideas are compatible with reformed theology. We will see that reformed theology denies the sourcehood condition as ultimate sourcehood. The ultimate source of an agent's actions is God's decree, foreknowledge and providence. In addition, reformed theology denies the alternative possibilities condition. An agent cannot thwart God's decree, foreknowledge and providence. I plan to do this in five parts. The first part will ask the question: "What is reformed teaching on God's decree, providence, and foreknowledge?" The second part will clarify the Principle of Alternative Possibilities (PAP) in relation to God's decree, foreknowledge, and providence. The third part will discuss whether Fischer and Ravizza's thought on the sourcehood condition and the alternative possibilities condition falls within the bounds of the Westminster Standards. The fourth part will interact with the Utrecht School concerning their claims about synchronic contingency and determinism. The fifth part will draw parallels between Fischer and Ravizza's thought and reformed theology.

Reformed Teaching on Decree, Providence, and Foreknowledge

In order to answer the question whether or not Fischer and Ravizza's thought is compatible with reformed theology, we must first identify the reformed teachings on God's decree, providence, and foreknowledge. We can begin by identifying the reformed theological trajectory from the Reformation.

It is not my purpose to give a detailed account of the history of reformed theology. Instead, I intend to identify a brief trajectory from the Reformation to the formation of its authoritative creeds and confessions. Once this is done, we can better identify reformed theological teaching on decree, providence, and foreknowledge.

Herman Selderhuis tells us where we find the fountainhead of reformed theology. He writes:

> Reformed is understood as the tradition of the Reformers such as Zwingli, Bucer, Calvin and Bullinger, but also Luther, Melanchthon, Vermigli and Cranmer. This means that "Reformed" is broader than what is often called "Calvinistic," although in the period after Calvin much of what is defined as Reformed finds it basis in Calvin's theology.[1]

The reformed tradition has its foundation in these theologians.[2] Through the years there was a development of the insights of these theologians. This led to a long period of time known as reformed orthodoxy. Willem van Asselt writes:

> The term "Reformed Orthodoxy" refers to the period of institutionalization and codification following the Reformation. Beginning in the late sixteenth century and extending into the eighteenth, it would be the dominant form of Reformed theology for nearly two hundred years. Historically, this theology is identified as orthodox or confessional because it attempted to codify and systematize "right teaching" within the bounds created by the Reformed confessions of the sixteenth century. It was taught at the new protestant academies and universities with the

---

1. Selderhuis, "Introduction," 2. Richard Muller speaks of the orthodox Protestants as continuing the thought of the Reformers: "What the Reformation began in less than half a century, orthodox Protestantism defended, clarified, and codified over the course of a century and a half. The Reformation is incomplete without its confessional and doctrinal codification. What is more, Protestantism could hardly have survived if it had not developed, in the era of orthodoxy, a normative and defensible body of doctrine consisting of a confessional foundation and systematic elaboration" (Muller, *Prolegomena to Theology*, 27).

2. It is important to note that the theology of the Reformers does not originate in these theologians alone. It has roots in the early and medieval church. "Every major tenet of the Reformation had considerable support in the catholic tradition" (Pelikan, *Riddle of Roman Catholicism*, 49). It could be argued that the Reformation differed from their Roman Catholic opponents, not with regard to the doctrine of God, but in areas of soteriology and where the doctrine of God intersected with this. "The doctrine of God was not an area of significant theological debate, but Reformed theologians sharply disagreed with their Roman Catholic opponents where the doctrine of God intersects with soteriology" (Fesko, *Theology of the Westminster Standards*, 94).

help of the so-called scholastic method. Scholarship identifies roughly four phases: early orthodoxy (1565–1620), high orthodoxy (1620–1700), a transitional phase influenced by pietism (1700–1740), and, finally, the phase of late orthodoxy or supernaturalism (1740–1800). Throughout the nineteenth and even into the twentieth century, Reformed orthodoxy and Scholasticism have remained alive in the theological works of Heinrich Heppe, Charles Hodge, Herman Bavinck, and Louis Berkhof.[3]

This brief summary gives us an idea of the trajectory of reformed theology. Reformed theology was codified in the confessions and catechisms of the reformed churches. These catechisms and confessions define the theological content of reformed theology. R. Scott Clark writes concerning the word "reformed":

> I contend that the word denotes a confession, a theology, piety, and practice that are well known and well defined and summarized in ecclesiastically sanctioned and binding documents . . . By "confession" I mean narrowly the sixteenth and seventeenth-century Reformed confessions, which we might call the six forms of unity (i.e., Belgic Confession [BC], HC [Heidelberg Catechism], Canons of Dort [CD], Westminster Confession of Faith [WCF], Westminster Larger Catechism [WLC] and Westminster Shorter Catechism [WSC] . . . and more broadly, however, I mean the understanding of those confessions as articulated by the classical sixteenth and seventeenth-century Reformed theologians and by those who continued that tradition.[4]

Clark identifies reformed theology with the confessions and catechisms as the reformed tradition of the sixteenth and seventeenth centuries would have understood them. R. Michael Allen agrees with this, "Historically, Reformed theology is best identified by looking to confessions of the Reformed churches."[5]

---

3. Van Asselt, "Reformed Orthodoxy," 11. There are other slightly different ways of distinguishing the eras of Reformed orthodoxy. "Within the larger era of Reformed Orthodoxy, three periods can be distinguished: Early Orthodoxy (1565–1635), High Orthodoxy (1635–1700), and Late Orthodoxy (1700–1790). See te Velde, *Doctrine of God*, 21–22. "The post-Reformation development of Protestantism can be divided, for the sake of convenience, into three periods: early, high, and late orthodoxy. Early orthodoxy, in two fairly distinct phases (1565–1618–1640) . . . High orthodoxy (1640–1685–1725) . . . [and] Theology after 1725, in what can be called 'late orthodoxy'" (Muller, *Prolegomena to Theology*, 30–32).

4. Clark, *Recovering the Reformed Confessions*, 3.

5. Allen, *Reformed Theology*, 5.

We could divide these confessions and catechisms into two categories: First the Continental tradition and second the English tradition. Representative of the Continental tradition are the Three Forms of Unity; these consist of the Belgic Confession, the Heidelberg Catechism, and the Canons of Dort. Representative of the English tradition are the Westminster Confession and Catechisms. These consist of the Westminster Confession of Faith, the Westminster Larger Catechism, and the Westminster Shorter Catechism.

We identify reformed thought on the decree, providence, and foreknowledge by looking to the confessions and catechisms of the Reformed Churches, especially the Three Forms of Unity and the Westminster Confession and Catechisms. The Continental and English tradition are substantively identical on these issues. R. Scott Clark writes:

> Between 1523 and 1675, no fewer than twenty-five major confessions or catechisms appeared. In addition to these, there were too many regional, local, and minor confessions to mention here. Even if we consider only these twenty-five documents, nevertheless, in the space of 152 years, the Reformed churches published, on average, a major confession every six years. If we add just a few of the minor confessions, the frequency with which the Reformed churches published confessions becomes even greater. What is most important is that, despite the regional diversity and minor variations in expression, the doctrine was substantially the same in all the major documents.[6]

The Reformed Confessions and Catechisms teach substantially the same doctrine. This is especially true of the doctrines of God's decree, providence, and foreknowledge. Specifically, we could say that the reformed considered these to all be instances of hypothetical necessity. J. Martin Bac writes:

> The Reformed model of divine agency centers on the decision of God. This should not be interpreted as theological determinism, since it implies only a hypothetical necessity in its effects, which in themselves remain contingent.[7]

---

6. Clark, *Recovering the Reformed Confessions*, 28–29.

7. Bac, *Perfect Will Theology*, 395. We will deal with his claim that hypothetical necessity is not theological determinism later in this chapter. Briefly, the problem with this is that contemporary analytic philosophers define determinism as hypothetical necessity.

Bac identifies the reformed model as hypothetical necessity. Van Asselt, Bac, and te Velde also identify the reformed tradition on God's decree, providence, and foreknowledge as hypothetical necessities. They write:

> The application of the necessity of the consequence (with their belief in the effective will of God) shows in a nutshell the Reformed ontological convictions underlying their discussions of free choice:
>
> (17) N (M (GWp)→Mp)
>
> In this ontology, the contingency of the effect can be united with a hypothetical necessity of the effect . . . as we will see in the individual texts below, the distinction between absolute necessity (*simpliciter: necessitas consequentis*) and relative necessity (*secundum quid: necessitas consequentiae*) enabled the Reformed scholastics to point out how necessity and contingency/freedom are in certain respects compatible instead of squarely contradictory.[8]

From this we see that the reformed regarded God's decree, providence, and foreknowledge to be instances of hypothetical necessity. More specifically, the decree and providence were labeled "necessity of immutability" and foreknowledge was labeled "necessity of infallibility." Both of these were necessities of the consequence or hypothetical necessities. Van Asselt, Bac, and te Velde write:

> Necessity of immutability: a necessity on supposition of God's decree and providence that encompasses all that happens in the world. The Reformed scholastics make it clear that this is a necessity of the consequence (if God decrees a to happen, a will happen), which imposes no (absolute) necessity on the thing itself.
>
> Necessity of infallibility: a necessity on supposition of divine foreknowledge, which is again a necessity of the consequence which imposes no (absolute) necessity on the thing itself.[9]

The reformed tradition taught that God's decree, providence, and foreknowledge were not absolute necessities, but hypothetical necessities or necessities of the consequence. A hypothetical necessity does not state that an event or choice must occur absolutely, but that it must occur given the antecedent conditions. We could describe these teachings as follows:

---

8. Van Asselt et al., *Reformed Thought on Freedom*, 38.
9. Van Asselt et al., *Reformed Thought on Freedom*, 39.

[ ] (If God decrees x, then x)

[ ] (If God's providence governs x, then x)

[ ] (If God foreknows x, then x)

These hypothetical necessities are stated in a more or less detailed manner in the reformed confessions and catechisms. For example, Article 13 of the Belgic Confession: The Doctrine of God's Providence states:

> We believe that this good God, after he created all things, did not abandon them to chance or fortune but leads and governs them according to his holy will, in such a way that nothing happens in this world without his orderly arrangement.

This is an informal statement of hypothetical necessity or the necessity of immutability. God's holy will is the antecedent condition for nothing happening in this world without His orderly arrangement. Consider also WCF 5:2. This is a more precise statement of hypothetical necessity:

> Although, in relation to the foreknowledge and decree of God, the First Cause, all things come to pass immutably and infallibly.

The antecedent conditions are God's foreknowledge and decree. Given these conditions, all things come to pass immutably and infallibly. This language reflects what van Asselt, Bac, and te Velde called the necessity of immutability and the necessity of infallibility. These were necessities of the consequence or hypothetical necessities.

We have seen that the reformed theological trajectory began with certain theologians at the time of the Reformation. The insights of these theologians were developed and codified into Confessions and Catechisms of the Reformed Churches.[10] These Confessions and Catechisms taught substantially the same thing; the decree, providence, and foreknowledge were affirmed as hypothetical necessities. This is reflected less precisely in the Belgic Confession and more precisely in the Westminster Confession. The Westminster Confession and Catechisms give more precise and detailed teaching on these subjects, though they are substantially the same as in the Continental tradition. It is because of this greater detail that I will use the Westminster Confession and Catechisms as representative teaching of the reformed tradition of decree, providence, and foreknowledge.

The question we will seek to answer in this chapter will be whether or not Fischer and Ravizza's thought on PAP and sourcehood is compatible with

---

10. For a compilation of Reformed confessions, see Dennison, *Reformed Confessions*.

reformed theology, where reformed theology is defined by the Westminster Confession of Faith and the Westminster Larger and Shorter Catechisms.

Defining PAP More Precisely

In the previous chapters we have seen that Fischer and Ravizza reject the idea that PAP is necessary for moral responsibility. PAP has been defined as follows, "an agent S is morally responsible for it being the case that p only if S could have made it not the case that p." The basic idea is that moral responsibility requires that an agent be "able to do otherwise" or "can do otherwise" or "could have done otherwise" or "it is possible to do otherwise." These phrases communicate the same idea, namely that moral responsibility requires that an agent have accessible alternative possibilities.

Some reformed theologians appear to affirm this idea. For example, John Fesko writes the following:

> Without God decreeing to create creatures that have the freedom to choose among various options, there would be no freedom whatsoever because free creatures would not exist.[11]

Van Asselt, Bac, and te Velde write:

> A radical alternative was established by Duns Scotus around 1300. Central to his philosophy and theology is the concept of what we call "synchronic contingency." Synchronic contingency means that for one moment of time, there is an alternative for the state of affairs that actually occurs. It can be argued that only this synchronic contingency can account for real freedom of choice, both on God's part and on our part. The reason is that without synchronic contingency there is no structural alternativity in reality, so neither can there be alternativity in acting, which is a requirement of freedom.[12]

These theologians also appear to link alternative possibilities to moral responsibility. For example, Fesko writes:

> The point cannot be stressed enough: the divines believed that if human actions were not contingent (that is freely chosen), then God could in no way hold sinners accountable for their sin.[13]

---

11. Fesko, *Theology of the Westminster Standards*, 103.
12. Van Asselt et al., *Reformed Thought on Freedom*, 41.
13. Fesko, *Theology of the Westminster Standards*, 110.

As we saw in Fesko's previous quote, freedom means "to choose among various options." Van Asselt, Bac, and te Velde write:

> The natural freedom by which man's will can choose between opposites without being necessitated towards one of both, remains after the Fall. This natural freedom is essential to man, in the sense that without this freedom he would no longer be man as a rational and responsible creature.[14]

We see from these quotations that some contemporary reformed theologians appear to hold that alternative possibilities are required for freedom and moral responsibility.

Fischer and Ravizza deny that alternative possibilities are necessary for moral responsibility. For them, moral responsibility consists of guidance control. This does not require alternative possibilities in the actual sequence. However, this does not mean that all alternative possibilities have no role. Instead, Fischer and Ravizza uphold alternative possibilities in other possible worlds to test the mechanism. They write:

> Thus, we have associated moral responsibility with a dispositional or modal property. It is important to see that, whereas other possible worlds are relevant to ascertaining whether there is some actually operative dispositional feature (such as weak reasons-responsiveness), such worlds are *not* relevant in virtue of bearing on the question of whether some alternative sequence is *genuinely accessible* to the agent.
>
> On our approach to moral responsibility, then, other possible scenarios are relevant to the issue of whether the *actual sequence* has certain features (such as weak reasons-responsiveness). But it does *not* follow that our approach is committed to the claim that agents can have it in their power to *actualize* such scenarios—that is a quite different matter.[15]

Fischer and Ravizza are not saying that there is no sense in which the mechanism "could have done otherwise." In fact, other possible worlds are necessary to test the mechanism.

This leaves us with the need to make very specific what Fischer and Ravizza are denying. They are denying that alternative possibilities are necessary for moral responsibility in the actual sequence. In other words, the actual world could be causally determined or determined by God and yet humans remain morally responsible. Fischer writes:

---

14. Van Asselt et al., *Reformed Thought on Freedom*, 235.
15. Fischer and Ravizza, *Responsibility and Control*, 53.

This account goes some distance toward establishing semi-compatibilism: the doctrine that causal determinism (or God's existence) is compatible with moral responsibility, even if causal determinism (or God's existence) rules out freedom to do otherwise.[16]

Fischer sees causal determinism and God's existence not as metaphysically identical but as functionally similar. Casual determinism rules out man's ability to do otherwise in the actual sequence. So also, God's existence (in virtue of foreknowledge, the decree, foreordination, and/or providence) rules out man's ability to do otherwise in the actual sequence. However, neither would rule out man's moral responsibility. The reason for this is because moral responsibility consists of guidance control and this is compatible with causal determinism, God's decree, foreknowledge, and providence.

In light of this, we could formulate two versions of PAP. The first one has causal determinism as the metaphysical background and the second has God's existence as the metaphysical background. First causal determinism:

(1) An agent S morally responsibly does x only if S could have done otherwise than x given C (causal determinism).[17]

This principle is a little bit different from the version of PAP that I used in previous chapters. This formulation enables us to make it clear that there are different formulations of PAP in relation to various circumstances. In this first principle, we see that circumstance C equals causal determinism. Fischer and Ravizza are denying this principle.

The second principle takes circumstance C to be God's existence, more specifically God's decree, foreknowledge, and providence:

(2) An agent S morally responsibly does x only if S could have done otherwise than x given C (God's decree, foreknowledge and providence).

Fischer and Ravizza are also denying this principle. They do not believe that moral responsibility requires the ability to do otherwise than God's decree, foreknowledge, or providence in the actual sequence.

Understanding exactly what Fischer and Ravizza are denying is helpful because it prevents them from being misunderstood. They are not denying that an agent cannot do otherwise in every possible sense.[18] There are a

16. Fischer, *Metaphysics of Free Will*, 189.
17. Thanks to James Anderson for suggesting a formula similar to this one.
18. In a currently unpublished paper (February 2019) for a festschrift in honor of T. H. Irwin, Fischer makes this clear. He is responding to comments from Christopher Franklin: "I completely agree with Franklin that I do indeed believe that *various* kinds

variety of senses in which an agent could have done otherwise. It would be helpful to explore some of those senses.

John Frame discusses the various meanings of words like "ability," "possibility," "can," and related expressions. He writes, "These terms are important, not only for the discussion of human freedom, but also in many other theological debates."[19] It is also important for moral responsibility. Frame identifies various senses of the word 'possibility.' The first one is logical possibility. This refers to the "mere absence of inconsistency."[20] For an agent to have the possibility of doing otherwise in this sense means that there is no logical contradiction in doing otherwise. We could formulate PAP along these lines:

> An agent S morally responsibly does x only if S could have done otherwise than x given C (the law of non-contradiction).

This principle tells us that there is no logical contradiction involved in S doing otherwise than x. Fischer and Ravizza affirm this. If the laws of logic determine an agent's action, then it is not a morally responsible action.

It is helpful for us to see this type of formula because there are various other senses of the word 'possible' that Fischer and Ravizza could affirm. It is also the case that reformed theology can affirm most of these senses.

John Feinberg writes:

> There are various senses in which "can" and "could" may be used, and most are senses in which a soft determinist could say that the agent could do otherwise. Hence, if being able to do otherwise is a criterion for free action, compatibilistically done actions are free.[21]

---

of alternative possibilities are required for moral responsibility (although not for the 'grounding' or explanation of moral responsibility), and thus my repeated contention that alternative possibilities are not required for moral responsibility might well have caused confusion. Of course, in the Frankfurt-style Cases Jones does not lose his general ability to vote Republican (i.e., to do otherwise in the context), just as we do not lose various general abilities when we are asleep. One might say that we keep our general abilities in these contexts, although we do not have the opportunity to exercise them (immediately). Again: I do not lose my general ability to play the piano when there is no piano in my vicinity; I simply do not have the opportunity to exercise it" (Fischer, "Freedom Required for Moral Responsibility," 11).

19. Frame, *Doctrine of God*, 131.
20. Frame, *Doctrine of God*, 133.
21. Feinberg, *No One Like Him*, 722.

Feinberg goes on to list eight different senses of "can" and "could."[22] Of the eight that Feinberg lists, only one is contrary to what he calls soft compatibilism:

> Therefore, if an action counts as free only if the agent could have done otherwise, then in the first seven senses of "could have" the soft determinist has just as much right to claim that the agent could have done otherwise as does the indeterminist. And this means that soft determinism counts as freedom just as much as does libertarian freedom.
>
> The one area of disagreement between the soft determinist and indeterminist relates to the eighth sense. No one can, consistent with determinism, hold that an agent can do otherwise in that sense, for to do so adopts the libertarian free will, which contradicts compatibilistic free will. But is this failure on the part of compatibilism a critical problem? Not at all, and we should see this once we recognize that it is the eighth sense about which both determinists and indeterminists argue. This is so because the eighth sense incorporates the indeterminist's definition of free will, and that is something a soft determinist will not allow. If the indeterminist says that unless one says that the agent could have done otherwise in this eighth sense, one's

---

22. He writes, "An initial sense of 'can' is the a*bility* sense. To say that someone can do otherwise means he has the ability or power to do so. . . . A second sense of 'can' is the *opportunity* sense. 'Can' in this sense involves more than just physical or mental abilities. One must be in circumstances that allow him to do the act. . . . Third, there is what John Canfield calls a *rule consistent* sense of 'can.' Here what one proposes to do (or what one could do but doesn't) is consistent with all know rules. . . . Fourth, Canfield also delineates an *ill-consequence free* sense of can. In this sense, being able to do something means that one can do it without any harmful consequences. . . . We can also use 'can' or 'could' in other senses. One of them I would call the *authority* sense of can. In this case a person who can do something has the authority to do it, regardless of whether that authority is used or not. . . . A sixth sense of 'can' understands it to mean 'reasonable.' That is, to say that someone can do something means that there are good reasons for it, the person knows those reasons, and in light of them does the act. . . . A seventh sense of 'can' or 'could' is the *conditional* sense. . . . This must not be misunderstood. I am not saying that all the evidence presented against conditional analysis of 'can' and 'could' statements should be ignored. I agree with those objections. However, while the objections show that this is an unacceptable way of understanding *all* 'can' statements, that doesn't mean a conditional analysis is never what we mean when we say 'can' or 'could.' . . . Finally, there is what we may call the *contra-causal* or *libertarian* sense. To say that someone could have done otherwise in this sense means that though there were various causal factors playing on one's will at the time of decision making, none of those factors individually nor all of them conjointly were sufficient to incline the person's will decisively one way or the other. Though causes may have pointed to one choice, the agent still could just as easily have done the other" (Feinberg, *No One Like Him*, 722–24).

position is not "real" or "genuine" freedom, this is nothing more than question-begging by demanding that an indeterminist definition of freedom is correct without proving it so.[23]

These observations are very important for our discussion. They show us that denying PAP in a specific sense does not mean that an agent could not do otherwise in every sense. Feinberg identified one sense in which reformed theology would deny the ability to do otherwise. I have already specified this with principle 2:

> (2) An agent S morally responsibly does x only if S could have done otherwise than x given C (God's foreknowledge, decree and/or providence).

Denying this principle as necessary for moral responsibility is not denying every sense of the phrase "could have done otherwise." Being clear on the exact principle that is being denied enables us to more clearly ask whether the Westminster Confession and Catechisms require us to affirm principle 2. We will do this in the next section.

Within the Bounds of The Westminster Confession and Catechisms

It is the purpose of this section to examine whether a denial of principle 2 falls within the bounds of the Westminster Confession of Faith (WCF), the Westminster Larger Catechism (WLC), and the Westminster Shorter Catechism (WSC). We will examine this question in three parts. The first part is to engage with what Oliver Crisp calls libertarian Calvinism. Men like John Girardeau argued that the Westminster Confession requires libertarian free will. Libertarian free will requires an affirmation of principle 2. I will supplement this part with Oliver Crisp's contribution to this debate. The second part will deal with other sections of the Confession and Catechisms that might be used to argue that we must affirm libertarian free will or principle 2. The third part will be to argue that the Confession and Catechisms advocate for a type of theological determinism.

Libertarian Calvinism

In his book, *Deviant Calvinism: Broadening Reformed Theology*, Oliver Crisp explores a position he calls Libertarian Calvinism. I say explores

---

23. Feinberg, *No One Like Him*, 724–25.

because Crisp is not advocating this position. He is merely testing to see if it is a legitimate position for a reformed theologian to hold. He is asking if it is legitimate in the sense that it falls within the bounds of the Westminster Confession. Crisp writes:

> It seems to me that in what the Confession does say, there is the conceptual space, so to speak, to prescind from determinism touching all human choices and to affirm some limited version of libertarianism.[24]

Crisp identifies an historical example of libertarian Calvinism in the person of Girardeau. In another publication, Crisp defines what he means by libertarianism and identifies it with Girardeau:

> I use the term "libertarian" and "libertarian choice" in a more restricted sense to mean a choice that is free in the sense of originating with the agent, not God. A libertarian choice is one for which the agent is morally responsible at least in part because he has an alternative possibility he could actualize at the moment of choice. This is a term of art that is consistent with what John L. Girardeau says . . . although he doesn't use the term itself.[25]

We see two things from this definition. First, the source of the choice is not God. The source is solely in the creature. This is what we earlier called the sourcehood condition. One mark of a libertarian is that they do not allow the source of a choice to be anything outside of the agent. This is what Crisp is affirming. Second, there is the alternative possibilities condition. We read that man "has an alternative possibility he could actualize at the moment of choice." This means that man could have chosen otherwise than he did in the same exact circumstances. This aspect of Crisp's definition of libertarianism is committed to affirming principle:

> (2) An agent S morally responsibly does x only if S could have done otherwise than x given C (God's decree, foreknowledge and providence).

We can see that Crisp means this because his use of the phrase "moment of choice" communicates that the circumstances do not necessitate one action. Instead, we could have the same circumstances (God's decree) and yet the agent could actualize x or not x at the moment of choice.

It is important to realize that Crisp and Girardeau affirm this type of freedom only for a certain realm of human actions. Crisp writes:

---

24. Crisp, *Deviant Calvinism*, 74–75.
25. Crisp, "John Girardeau," 286.

> In short, according to libertarian Calvinism, fallen human beings have significant free will in all sorts of mundane choices, some of which are important and influential (such as choosing to become a presidential candidate, or choosing to become a research scientist working on vaccines to prevent a pandemic). However, fallen human beings are incapable of making free choices about salvation.[26]

This means that we need to draw a distinction within the class of all human choices. There are those that pertain to salvation and then all the rest. Libertarian Calvinism affirms libertarian free will only in the non-salvific choices of man.

The main burden of our treatment of Libertarian Calvinism will be to explore whether it is consistent with the Westminster Confession of Faith and the Westminster Larger and Shorter Catechisms. Before I begin, I need to point out two difficulties in Crisp's formulation of Libertarian Calvinism. I believe these difficulties logically push him to affirm theological determinism and thus undermine his project.

First, Libertarian Calvinism really does not deny the sourcehood condition. The language that Crisp used to define Libertarian Calvinism stated that "a choice is free in the sense of originating with the agent, not God."[27] This language seems to exclude God from being the originator of the agent's free choice. However, this is inconsistent with what Crisp affirms elsewhere. Crisp affirms that God does ordain the choice, but he does not determine or cause the choice. Crisp writes:

> Note that this libertarian Calvinism does not deny that God ordains whatsoever comes to pass. It denies that God *determines* or *causes* whatsoever comes to pass.... There are those actions which are determined by God, the supreme example of which is human salvation.... Then there are those actions which are not determined by God but are foreseen and permitted by God.[28]

Crisp affirms that God does ordain whatsoever comes to pass. He ordains the salvific choices of men by determining/causing them. He ordains all other actions by foreseeing and permitting them. Crisp identifies God's ordaining of all non-salvific acts with His foreseeing and permitting them. According to Crisp, we should not understand God foreseeing and permitting these acts in an Arminian manner. The Arminian view is that

---

26. Crisp, *Deviant Calvinism*, 85.
27. Crisp, "John Girardeau," 286.
28. Crisp, *Deviant Calvinism*, 87.

God ordains and decrees on the basis of what he foresees man first do. Crisp denies that this is what he means by God foreseeing and permitting a future act. This is clear from his response to Jerry Walls. Crisp writes:

> But this is an anti-Arminian statement, which teaches that God does not decree what God does on the basis of foreknown outcomes, though God certainly knows all future conditionals (more precisely, God knows the truth-value of propositions that are future conditionals *to us*). This does not mean God determines all things in the strictest sense, because it is not equivalent to causal determinism.[29]

In this passage, we see two things that are important for our discussion. First, we see that Crisp, along with the WCF, reject the Arminian view that God ordains/decrees on the basis of His foresight. In Crisp's words, "God does not decree what God does on the basis of foreknown outcomes."[30]

Second, we see that Crisp affirms that God knows the truth-value of all future conditional propositions. Our question is, "How does God know the truth-value of these propositions?" Having rejected the Arminian answer to this question, Crisp is left with only two other options. First, God could know them because he assigns them a truth-value independently of their foreknown outcomes. Second, he could know them by His middle knowledge. If Crisp is going to be consistent with the WCF, then he must reject that God knows these future propositions by His middle knowledge. This is because the WCF rejects this option:

> Although God knows whatsoever may or can come to pass upon all supposed conditions, yet he hath not decreed anything because he foresaw it as future, or as that which would come to pass upon such conditions. (WCF 3:2)

The WCF rejects that God ordains/decrees on the basis of middle knowledge. The last clause, "or as that which would come to pass upon such conditions," is a rejection of middle knowledge. Robert Letham points this out:

> Both Helm and Fesko correctly identify Molinism as the target of the final clause. Following Luis de Molina (1535–1600), this was the proposition that God's decrees were based on his knowledge of all possible future actions.[31]

---

29. Crisp, *Deviant Calvinism*, 94.
30. Crisp, *Deviant Calvinism*, 94.
31. Letham, *Westminster Assembly*, 184–85.

In order for Crisp to be consistent with the Confession, he also must reject that God ordains/decrees on the basis of His middle knowledge. This means that Crisp must affirm that God foreknows future conditional propositions because God assigned a truth-value to them independently of the creature's actions.

This is consistent with what Van Asselt, Bac, and te Velde say with regard to the sense in which the reformed scholastics used the word "determined." They write:

> It is perhaps useful to point out here that "to determine" in scholastic usage often simply means "to assign a truth-value to a proposition." For example, if a scholastic author claims that the truth of a future contingent proposition is determined, mostly all that is meant is that it has a truth-value, in distinction from lacking it (being neither true nor false).[32]

When God was said to "determine" or decree something, this meant that he assigned a truth-value to the proposition. Crisp claims that his Libertarian Calvinist position is similar to these authors. He writes:

> More recently, something similar to what I have been calling Libertarian Calvinism has been the subject of heated and ongoing discussion after the recent publication by Dutch scholars Willem J. van Asselt, J. Matin Bac, and Roelf T. te Velde of their book, *Reformed Thought on Freedom*.[33]

In light of this, it is reasonable to hold that Crisp holds that God knows future conditional propositions because he first assigned a truth-value to them.

Since this is the case, it follows that Crisp's definition of libertarian Calvinism is not consistent with what he advocates elsewhere. God does originate the free choice of men in the sense of assigning a truth-value. For example, the future proposition "Adam falls in the garden" has a truth-value; it is either true or false. How is this truth-value assigned? It cannot be true because Adam first falls and then God foresees this and assigns the truth-value of true. Both Crisp and the Westminster Confession reject this. God also could not assign it by middle knowledge because the Confession also rejects this position. The only other option available is that God assigns the truth-value of true to the proposition "Adam falls in the garden." But this means that God is the originator of the free choice Adam made to

---

32. Van Asselt et al., *Reformed Thought on Freedom*, 189.
33. Crisp, *Deviant Calvinism*, 96.

fall in the garden. He is the originator in the sense that he assigns a truth-value of true to that proposition.

This means that one aspect of Crisp's definition of Libertarian Calvinism is inconsistent with what he elsewhere advocates is the Libertarian Calvinist view of God's foreknowledge. More specifically, the notion that "a libertarianly free choice is one that originates with the agent, not God" is inconsistent with the notion that God assigns a truth-value to future conditional propositions. If God assigns truth-values to these propositions, then He is the originator of the agent's choice as these propositions expressed. In this way, Crisp must affirm that God is the ultimate source of the agent's actions. Therefore, he must deny the sourcehood condition.

The second difficulty with Crisp's formulation of libertarian Calvinism is that denying the sourcehood condition in this sense also conflicts with the alternative possibilities condition that Crisp affirms. In his definition of libertarian Calvinism, Crisp said:

> A libertarian choice is one for which the agent is morally responsible at least in part because he has an alternative possibility he could actualize at the moment of choice.[34]

This is the alternative possibilities condition or principle 2. It states that a choice is free and morally responsible if and only if the agent could have done otherwise given the same exact circumstances. This means that if God decreed Adam to fall in the garden by assigning the truth-value of true to the proposition "Adam falls in the garden," then Adam would only be free and morally responsible if he could actualize the alternative possibility of "not falling in the garden" at the moment of choice. More precisely, if God assigned the truth-value of true at t_1 to the future proposition "Adam falls in the garden at t_2," then for Adam to be free and morally responsible he would have to be able at t_2 to actualize the alternative possibility of "not falling in the garden at t_2."

This would mean that Adam could change a truth-value that God assigned from all eternity. God could assign a truth-value and a creature could change or thwart the assignment of that truth-value. This is problematic for three reasons.

First, if it is God's will/decree at t_1 to assign a truth-value of true to the proposition "Adam falls in the garden at t_2," and it is the case that that Adam could actualize the alternative possibility of the proposition "Adam does not fall in the garden at t_2," then this amounts to the affirmation that a creature can thwart the will/decree of God.

34. Crisp, "John Girardeau," 286.

Second, if God knows the truth-value of the future proposition "Adam falls in the garden at t_2," and Adam could actualize the alternative possibility of the proposition, "Adam does not fall in the garden at t_2," then God does not know the truth-value of all future propositions. This is so because Adam could change a previously assigned truth-value at the moment of choice. In other words, God could assign a truth-value of true to the proposition, "Adam falls in the garden at t_2," from eternity t_1, yet Adam could render this proposition false at the moment of choice. This means that God could be wrong and therefore not know the truth-value of this proposition.

Third, affirming that God assigns a truth-value to future conditional propositions forces Crisp into theological determinism. This is the case for two reasons. First, Crisp must deny the sourcehood condition. The origins of an agent's actions lie in God in the sense of assigning a truth-value to the proposition that expresses that action. Second, God assigning a truth-value to future conditional propositions is inconsistent with the alternative possibilities condition.

I find these to be insurmountable problems for Crisp's formulation of libertarian Calvinism. In spite of this, my main purpose is to examine whether libertarian Calvinism is consistent with the Westminster Confession and the Larger and Shorter Catechisms. For this, I will discuss the arguments from the Westminster Confession to which Crisp and Girardeau appeal.

As we begin our discussion of Libertarian Calvinism and the Westminster Confession and Catechisms, it is important to point out that Girardeau is arguing that the Confession teaches Libertarian Calvinism and Crisp is only arguing that the Confession might allow for it. Girardeau and Crisp appeal to basically the same portions of the Confession.[35] The reason why they use these articles is because they want to argue that they justify (Girardeau) or leave room open to (Crisp) libertarian freedom among our first parents. Crisp writes in reference to various Confessions, especially the Westminster Confession:

> In each case there appears to be good *prima facie* evidence for the view that these confessions, like Calvin, allow for libertarianism with respect to the primal sin of our first parents.[36]

Girardeau writes:

> To sum up the matter: the standards say that Adam in innocence had the power of otherwise determining than he did; the Determinist says that he had not the power. The two doctrines

---

35. See WCF 4:2; 9:2–3; 19:1.
36. Crisp, "John Girardeau," 297.

are contradictory and mutually exclusive. We must make our election; and as, when we found Calvin and Edwards opposed to each other, we went with Calvin, so now we go with the Calvinistic standards rather than with the deterministic philosophy.[37]

In light of this we should look at some of the statements in the Westminster Confession to understand how they are being used to justify libertarian Calvinism. In WCF 4:2, the Confession is addressing the issue of creation. The language Girardeau and Crisp have in mind is:

> Having the law of God written in their hearts, and power to fulfill it: and yet under the possibility of transgressing, being left to the liberty of their own will, which was subject to change.

God created Adam and Eve with the power to obey God's law or to transgress God's law. This would seem to teach that man had an actualizable alternative possibility at the moment of choice.[38] We know that Adam fell, but he could have not fallen. In Girardeau's words:

> The standards say that being left to the freedom of his will, he fell; that his power to fulfill, to keep, the law was possessed under a possibility of his transgressing, because he was left to the liberty of his own will, which was subject to change; that he had freedom and power to will and to do what was right, mutably, so that he might fall from it. He might stand, yet he might fall; he might will and do right; yet he might will and do wrong; he might choose holiness, yet he might choose sin. When then did he sin, might he have not done otherwise? If so, although the terms *power of contrary choice* are not used—and we care for the thing, not the words—the power itself is so plainly asserted that he who runs may read.[39]

From these passages, we see that Girardeau affirms that the Confession teaches, while Crisp affirms that the Confession allows (1) Adam's choice to sin in the garden did not originate with God and (2) at the moment of choice, Adam could have chosen to sin or not to sin. In the next section, I will provide two arguments against Crisp and Girardeau's use of the WCF 4:2—the context argument and the moral condition argument.

---

37. Girardeau, *Will and its Theological Relations*, 297. That Calvin taught libertarian Calvinism is highly disputable. For a good response to this idea see Waddell, "Re-examination of Dr. Girardeau's Views," 690–716.

38. "At the moment of choice" was the language Crisp identified and attributed to Girardeau.

39. Girardeau, *Will and its Theological Relations*, 176–77.

Arguments Against Crisp and Girardeau's Use of WCF 4:2

The Context Argument

The first argument against Crisp and Girardeau's interpretation of WCF 4:2 is that it contradicts the Confession's teaching that God's decree and providence has the necessity of immutability. I will first state the Confession's teaching "Of God's Eternal Decree" and then the Confession's teaching "Of Providence."

We begin with WCF 3 "Of God's Eternal Decree." In WCF 3:1, the Confession states that God "freely and unchangeably ordain whatsoever comes to pass." The reformed tradition ascribed a certain type of necessity to God's decree and providence. Van Asselt, Bac, and te Velde call this the necessity of immutability. They write:

> Necessity of immutability: a necessity on supposition of God's decree and providence that encompasses all that happens in the world. The Reformed scholastics make it clear that this is a necessity of the consequence (if God decrees a to happen, a will happen), which imposes no (absolute) necessity on the thing itself.[40]

This type of necessity is the background of the Confession's statement "Of God's Eternal Decree." This type of necessity renders whatever God has decreed to come to pass with certainty. Van Asselt, Bac, and te Velde make it clear that this is not an absolute necessity, but a necessity of the consequence. They state this because an absolute necessity would take away man's freedom and moral responsibility. They correctly argue that a necessity of the consequence preserves it.

The medieval and Protestant scholastics distinguished between the necessity of the consequent and the necessity of the consequence. We can symbolize this distinction as follows: The necessity of the consequence:

$[\,](p \to q)$

The necessity of the consequent:

$(p \to [\,]q)$

The necessity of the consequence applies to the implication. Van Asselt, Bac, and te Velde describe it:

---

40. Van Asselt et al., *Reformed Thought on Freedom*, 39.

> First, the implication itself can be necessary: if p, then q *is always implied*. . . . This kind of necessity was called the necessity of the consequence by the Reformed. It is important to note that this necessity applies to the implication between two states of affairs. . . . So, the relation of implication itself is necessary. Yet, neither p nor q have to be necessary; because p and q can be perfectly contingent.[41]

On the necessity of the consequence, p and q are contingent in and of themselves. However, when they are related to each other by the necessity of the consequence, q will always obtain when p obtains. Since it is the case that q will always obtain when p obtains, it follows that there is never a time when p obtains that q fails to obtain. This means that when p obtains, q could not fail to obtain.

The necessity of the consequence does not imply the necessity of the consequent. It is important to keep these two types of necessity distinct. On the necessity of the consequent, if p is true, then q is necessary *in itself*. As van Asselt, Bac, and te Velde put it, q "would be necessary *in every respect*."[42] Kenneth Konyndyk describes this distinction as follows,

> Remember that to assert the necessity of the consequence is to assert that it is broadly logically impossible for the antecedent of the conditional to be true while the consequence is false. Asserting the necessity of the consequent, on the other hand, is to claim that the antecedent implies the necessary truth of the consequent.[43]

Like van Asselt, Bac, and te Velde, Konyndyk affirms that on the necessity of the consequence, it is broadly logically impossible for p to obtain and q not obtain. In other words, it could not be the case that:

1. [ ] (p→q)

2. p

C. ~q

The necessity of the consequence means that whenever the antecedent and the consequent are joined together by the necessity of the implication, it follows that if p obtains, then q necessarily obtains.

---

41. Van Asselt et al., *Reformed Thought on Freedom*, 36 (emphasis mine).
42. Van Asselt et al., *Reformed Thought on Freedom*, 37 (emphasis mine).
43. Konyndyk, *Introduction to Modal Logic*, 23.

Konyndyk states that the necessity of the consequent is different. On the necessity of the consequence, both p and q are contingent in themselves. However, on the necessity of the consequent, q is a necessary truth.

The reformed understanding of God's decree and providence as a necessity of immutability is not a necessity of the consequent, but a necessity of the consequence. As van Asselt, Bac, and te Velde put it, "If God decrees a to happen, a will happen."[44] If we apply this to the fall of Adam it would say, "If God decreed Adam to fall, then Adam will fall." Or [ ] (if God decreed Adam to fall, then Adam will fall). The necessity applies to the connection between the antecedent and the consequent. This preserves contingency because God could have decreed Adam to not fall. If God decreed this, then Adam would not have fallen. This means that Adam could have done otherwise if God had decreed him to do otherwise. On the necessity of the consequence, both the antecedent and the consequent are contingent in and of themselves. This is why the Confession says:

> Yet so, as thereby neither is God the author of sin, nor is violence offered to the will of the creatures, nor is the liberty or contingency of second causes taken away, but rather established.

God's decree does not force Adam to sin; neither does it violate Adam's nature as a second cause nor does it take away his liberty or contingency. The reformed understood the necessity of immutability as rendering God's decree certain without violating man's freedom and moral responsibility.

We can see this more clearly by exploring other types of necessity that the reformed distinguished. The reformed taught that the necessity of immutability is not the type of necessity that conflicted with freedom and moral responsibility. Those types of necessity are called natural necessity and physical necessity. Van Asselt, Bac, and te Velde define these:

> Natural necessity: necessity inherent in the essential nature of a thing. For example, it is necessary for a stone to fall downward, at least in the physics of that time. Or, it is necessary for a lion to kill its prey.
>
> Physical necessity: necessity deriving from an outward cause that forces someone or something. This is often called *coercion*.[45]

Van Asselt, Bac, and te Velde go on to list four other types of necessity: rational necessity, moral necessity, necessity of immutability, and necessity of infallibility. They tell us that the reformed thought these four types of

---

44. Van Asselt et al., *Reformed Thought on Freedom*, 39.
45. Van Asselt et al., *Reformed Thought on Freedom*, 39.

necessity were consistent with freedom and moral responsibility, but natural and physical necessity were not:

> As the Reformed argue, of these six kinds of necessity only the first two are incompatible with contingency and freedom; the latter four, being examples of relative necessity, are fully consistent with contingency and rather enable the free agency of human beings.[46]

From this discussion we can see two things. First, God's decree and providence have a necessity of immutability which is a necessity of the consequence. This means that when p and q are united by the necessity of the consequence, whenever p obtains, q must obtain also and cannot be otherwise. Second, because it is a necessity of the consequence, p and q are both contingent. This means that they could be otherwise in themselves, when not related to each other by the necessity of the consequence. These two points are relevant for our discussion of Crisp and Girardeau's treatment of WCF 4:2.

In light of our discussion with Crisp and Girardeau concerning Adam in his created state, let us apply the necessity of immutability to the fall. As we have seen, the Confession teaches that God decrees "whatsoever comes to pass." The fall of Adam is part of whatsoever comes to pass. Therefore, God's decree that Adam fall has the necessity of immutability. The reformed would understand it as follows:

[ ] (if God decreed Adam to fall → then Adam will fall)

This does not teach that God necessarily had to decree Adam to fall. God was free to decree Adam to fall or Adam to not fall; the antecedent of this conditional is free and contingent. But once God decreed Adam to fall, then the necessity of immutability applies. Once God decreed Adam to fall, Adam's fall was certain or immutable. Yet the consequent of this conditional is not an absolute necessity. If God had decreed differently, then Adam would have behaved differently. The point is that if God decreed Adam to fall, then Adam could not resist or thwart this decree. WCF 3:1 is teaching that God's decree has the necessity of immutability.

Francis Turretin makes it clear how the orthodox regard this type of necessity. He asks the question "Does the decree necessitate future things? We affirm."[47] He goes on to describe how the Pelagians and semi-Pelagians deny this, but the reformed orthodox affirm it. He writes:

---

46. Van Asselt et al., *Reformed Thought on Freedom*, 39.
47. Turretin, *Institutes of Elenctic Theology*, 319.

> I. The question is agitated between us and the Pelagians and semi-Pelagians (old and new) who, to establish the more easily the idol of free will, deny the necessity of things from the decree and foreknowledge (which the orthodox constantly maintain).[48]

Turretin affirms that the reformed orthodox "constantly maintain" the necessity of things from the decree and foreknowledge. He goes on to describe this necessity:

> II. On the state of the question observe (1) that a thing is said to be necessary which *cannot be otherwise* (to me endechomenon allos echein).[49]

This means that when the necessity of the decree and foreknowledge are applied, it cannot be otherwise. Applying the necessity of the decree and foreknowledge to Adam's fall yields the result that Adam will fall and it cannot be otherwise. The language "cannot be otherwise" is not intended to apply in every sense. It only applies in relation to God's decree and foreknowledge. This is what was meant by the necessity of the consequence. Turretin goes on to describe necessity as it applies to God and then to the thing. For our purposes, the third item he mentions about the necessity applied to the thing is important. He writes:

> (3) hypothetical of the event or dependence through which a thing, although naturally mutable and contingent, *cannot but be* (on account of its dependence upon the ordination of God whose will cannot be changed nor his foreknowledge be deceived).[50]

Turretin teaches that if God decrees something to happen or if God foreknows something to happen, then it "cannot but be." If it could be otherwise, then God's will would be changed and his foreknowledge would be deceived. These are impossibilities for Turretin and the reformed orthodox. They are not impossibilities absolutely, but only in relation to God's decree and foreknowledge.

Returning to the discussion regarding Crisp and Girardeau, we conclude that the reformed taught that God's decree had a necessity of immutability. This necessity is a necessity of the consequence. This necessity rendered the decreed event or action to be certain. If God decreed Adam to fall, then Adam will fall with the necessity of immutability. WCF 3:1 is

---

48. Turretin, *Institutes of Elenctic Theology*, 319.
49. Turretin, *Institutes of Elenctic Theology*, 320 (emphasis mine).
50. Turretin, *Institutes of Elenctic Theology*, 320 (emphasis mine).

teaching this type of necessity and this means that the preceding context of WCF 4:2 contradicts Crisp and Girardeau's reading of WCF 4:2.

More precisely, Crisp defined Libertarian Calvinism as affirming that "A libertarian choice is one for which the agent is morally responsible at least in part because he has an alternative possibility he could actualize at the moment of choice."[51] This means that Adam, at the moment of choice, could choose to fall or not to fall. Adam could make this choice even if God decreed him to fall. This teaching contradicts WCF 3:1 as God's decree being a necessity of immutability.

Crisp and Girardeau have this same problem when it comes to God's providence. Following WCF 4 is the Confession's treatment of Providence in chapter 5. As we have seen, the reformed tradition regarded God's providence as having the necessity of immutability. This is problematic for Crisp and Girardeau because the Confession clearly teaches that God's providence covers all things including Adam's fall and all sins.

In article 1 we see that the Confession teaches that God's providence covers all things including human actions. It says, that God "doth uphold, direct, dispose, and govern all creatures, actions, and things . . . by . . . his most wise and holy providence." Since this is the case, then it follows that the necessity of immutability applies to the actions of all creatures.

In article 2 we see that the Confession reflects the type of necessity that applies to providence. It says, "in relation to the foreknowledge and decree of God, the First Cause, all things come to pass immutably, and infallibly." We see here the Confession reflecting the reformed orthodox concept of the necessity of immutability. It says that in relation to the decree and foreknowledge of God, all things come to pass with the necessity of immutability. In other words, God's providence applies to everything with the necessity of immutability. Like the article on God's decree, the divines are careful to state that this does not take away freedom and contingency. Article 2 goes on to say:

> Yet, by the same providence, he ordereth them to fall out according to the nature of second causes, either necessarily, freely, or contingently.

We saw that the necessity of immutability is a necessity of the consequence. Applying this to God's providence means that the actions that are governed by God's providence are contingent in themselves. However, on the supposition of God's providence, they have the necessity of immutability.

---

51. Crisp, "John Girardeau," 286.

Article 4 tells us that this providence extends to the fall of Adam. It says, "The almighty power, unsearchable wisdom, and infinite goodness of God so far manifests themselves in his providence, that it extendeth itself even to the first fall, and all other sins of angels and men." This means that the fall is rendered certain by the necessity of immutability which comes from God's decree and providence.

Like the decree, if God's providence extends to the fall, then the fall will happen with the necessity of immutability. We could state it as follows:

[ ] (God's providence extends to the Adam's fall → Adam will fall).

As we saw in the necessity of the consequence, the antecedent and the consequent are not necessary in themselves. Instead, they are contingent in themselves. However, when they are related by the necessity of immutability, then whenever the antecedent obtains, the consequent will always obtain.

As we saw with the decree, this necessity of immutability does not take away man's freedom and responsibility. God does not necessitate Adam's fall neither by natural necessity nor physical necessity. These were the only types of necessity the reformed saw as incompatible with freedom and moral responsibility. This is why the Confession goes on to say:

> Yet so as the sinfulness thereof proceedeth only from the creature, and not from God; who, being most holy and righteous, neither is nor can be the author or approver of sin.

WCF 5 teaches that God's providence extends to the fall with a necessity of immutability. As we have seen, this kind of necessity is consistent with freedom and moral responsibility, yet it renders the fall certain. Adam could not negate the necessity of immutability. Adam could not resist this necessity. Therefore, Adam did not have an alternative possibility he could have actualized at the moment of choice. The Confession's teaching on providence is inconsistent with libertarian free will. Therefore, Crisp and Girardeau's interpretation of WCF 4:2 contradicts with WCF 5.

We could more clearly state the difference between Crisp, Girardeau, and the Confession as follows. Let p= God's providence extends to the fall and q= Adam will fall. The Confession's teaching would look as follows:

1. [ ] (p→q)

2. p

C. q

Crisp and Girardeau affirm the following as an actualizable possibility:

DECREE, FOREKNOWLEDGE, AND PROVIDENCE   87

1. [ ] (p→q)

2. p

C. ~q

This is a denial of the necessity of immutability and thus a denial of the reformed understanding of providence.

Given this discussion from God's decree and providence, it follows that Crisp and Girardeau's interpretation of WCF 4:2 contradicts the Confession's teaching on the decree and providence. Their interpretation amounts to a denial of the decree and providence having the necessity of immutability. The reformed tradition clearly taught that the decree and providence had the necessity of immutability. Therefore, it is highly unlikely that the Westminster Divines intended WCF 4:2 to allow for libertarian free will.

The Moral Condition Argument

We have seen that Crisp and Girardeau's interpretation of WCF 4:2 contradicts WCF 3 and 5. Now we need to see what the Confession affirms in WCF 4:2. I will argue that the confession is teaching us about Adam's moral condition at creation. It is not teaching us that he could do otherwise than God's decree, foreknowledge, or providence. Instead, it is teaching us that Adam was created with the freedom from moral necessity. It would be helpful to restate the Confession's language:

> After God had made all other creatures, he created man, male and female, with reasonable souls, endued with knowledge, righteousness, and true holiness, after his own image, having the law of God written in their hearts, and power to fulfil it; and yet under a possibility of transgressing, being left to the liberty of their own will, which was subject to change.

A. A. Hodge says that this article is speaking about the moral condition of Adam before the fall. He explains this along the lines of the fourfold state of man. The four states are: (1) man at creation, (2) man after the fall, (3) man as regenerated, and (4) man glorified. In states 2 through 4, man is under a type of moral necessity. It is only in state 1 that man is free from moral necessity. Before we get to Hodge's comments, we need to define moral necessity. Van Asselt, Bac, and Te Velde write:

> Moral necessity: given someone's moral character (good or bad), it is necessary that she performs either good or bad acts.

The Reformed scholastics employ this type of necessity to account for the different states of man.[52]

Van Asselt, Bac, and te Velde point out that this category of moral necessity was common in the reformed tradition. Moral necessity is the background of the Confession's teaching regarding Adam's moral nature before the fall. In light of this, we will look at Hodge's exposition of the article. He writes:

> 5. That Adam, although created holy and capable of obedience, was at the same time capable of falling, is evident from the event. This appears to be the *moral condition* in which both angels and men were created. It evidently was never intended to be the permanent condition of any creature.[53]

Hodge is stating that this article is talking about the moral condition of Adam. It is a moral condition that is neither state 2, 3, nor 4, as listed above. Instead it corresponds to state 1. Adam was created holy, yet not confirmed in that holiness. This means that his moral condition was such that he was capable of falling. It was free from moral necessity. Hodge continues:

> God, angels, and saints in glory are free, but with natures certainly and infallibly prompting them to holiness.[54]

This corresponds to state 4: Man, as glorified. In this state, man has a moral condition such that his nature certainly and infallibly prompts him to holiness. There is a moral necessity to man in this state. It is a moral necessity to holiness. It would be impossible for man to sin in this moral condition. WCF 4:2 is teaching that Adam was not created in this moral condition. He was free from the moral necessity to holiness. He was created holy, but mutable. This means that nothing in his moral nature necessitated him to obey God. Hodge continues,

> Devils and fallen men are free, with natures infallibly prompting them to evil.[55]

This corresponds to state 2: Man, after the fall. In this state, fallen man has a moral condition such that his nature infallibly prompts him to evil. His nature is morally necessitated to prompt him to commit evil. This is what it means to be in bondage to sin. WCF 4:2 is teaching that Adam was

---

52. Van Asselt et al., *Reformed Thought On Freedom*, 39.
53. Hodge, *Westminster Confession*, 89 (emphasis mine).
54. Hodge, *Westminster Confession*, 89.
55. Hodge, *Westminster Confession*, 89.

not created in this moral condition. He was free from the moral necessity to evil. Hodge continues,

> The imperfectly sanctified Christian is the subject of two conflicting inherent tendencies, the law in the members and the law of the Spirit.[56]

This corresponds to state 3: Man, as regenerated. In this moral condition, Christians have two conflicting tendencies within them. The first is the regenerate tendency. This tendency prompts man to holiness. The second tendency is the sinful nature. This tendency prompts him to evil. WCF 4:2 is teaching that Adam was not created in this moral condition. He did not have a sinful nature, but a holy nature. Yet this holy nature was not confirmed in righteousness. It was mutable and capable of falling. The point Hodge is making is that WCF 4:2 is speaking about the moral condition of Adam at creation. He was created holy but capable of sinning. The article is not saying that Adam could defy God's decree, providence, and foreknowledge, only that his moral nature was such that it was free from moral necessity to good or evil. As we have seen from WCF 3 and 5, the reformed were clear that God's decree and providence cannot be resisted. Turretin writes about this as follows:

> VI. The liberty of Adam was not the liberty of independence (as if he was irresponsible [anypeuthynos] and absolutely his own master) because he ought always to be in subjection (as a creature to his Creator, as a second cause to the first and to depend upon his will). It was not the liberty of a will undetermined by the practical intellect; for this would have changed the will into an irrational appetite, so that he would have sought evil as evil. This would not have been so much liberty as an unbridled license, incompatible (asystatos) with the image of God. But there was in him another threefold liberty: (1) from coaction; (2) from physical necessity; (3) from slavery (both to sin and misery). The former two constituted his essential liberty. It belongs to man in whatever state constituted and has two characteristics; preference (to proairetikon) and will (to hekousion), so that what is done may be done by a previous judgment of the reason and spontaneously. But the latter was accidental because it comes in upon the essential liberty and can be separated from it (since true liberty exists where freedom from slavery does not exist, as in a state of sin).[57]

---

56. Hodge, *Westminster Confession*, 89.
57. Turretin, *Institutes of Elenctic Theology*, 570.

Turretin states that before the fall, Adam did not have the liberty of independence. He goes on to define what that means. It means that Adam was not absolutely his own master. He was in subjection to God as creature to Creator and as second cause to first cause. This means that Adam depended upon God's will. Turretin is affirming that in Adam's originally created state, he was not autonomous, but rather dependent upon God's will. This means that he was dependent upon God's decree and providence because this is God's will. So, Turretin is stating that Adam was not independent of God's decree and providence. He could not resist or thwart God's decree and providence but it comes to pass by the necessity of immutability.[58]

Though Adam was subject to God's decree and providence, Turretin goes on to say that he was free from being enslaved to sin and misery. In other words, he does not have the power or ability to resist God's decree and providence, but his moral nature was such that it was free from the moral necessity to sin. Turretin distinguishes between Adam's power to resist God's decree and providence and his power, residing in his moral condition, to resist sin.

In another place, he makes it clear that man is dependent upon God:

> First, as the necessity of dependence upon God, free will does not exclude, but supposes it (whether we understand the moral dependence of right reference to the divine law from which the rational creature can never be exempted; or the physical dependence of deed as to the concourse of providence, by which things so depend upon God, as the highest ruler and first cause in being, becoming and operating that they can neither be, nor do anything except in dependence upon him; or a dependence of futurition as to foreknowledge and the decree, from which arises the necessity of infallibility and of immutability). For however great may be the liberty of the creature in its operations, still they are necessary in these respect, otherwise the foreknowledge of God could be deceived and his decree changed.[59]

Turretin is very clear that the liberty of man cannot be thought of as having the ability to deceive God's foreknowledge or change his decree. In other words, man—even Adam in the Garden—could not do otherwise than

---

58. Turretin says again: "The third is the necessity of the creature's dependence on God, as much as to right and the law established by him as in reference to fact (to wit, the government of providence: [1] in the antecedent decree; [2] in the subsequent execution). This necessity is called hypothetical both of infallibility (with respect to prescience) and of immutability (with respect to the decree and actual concourse)" (Turretin, *Institutes of Elenctic Theology*, 570).

59. Turretin, *Institutes of Elenctic Theology*, 663.

God's decree, providence, and foreknowledge. Man does not have this ability or power; call it metaphysical power. This is standard reformed teaching.

Adam did, however, have a threefold liberty. That liberty consisted of liberty from coaction (or force), from physical necessity, and from slavery both to sin and misery. Liberty from coaction and physical necessity exist in man in every state. However, liberty from sin and misery exist only in Adam's original created state and in the saints in heaven. This is liberty from moral necessity to evil. WCF 4:2 affirms that Adam had this liberty.

Turretin is teaching that the reformed tradition did not teach that Adam had the liberty of independence but the liberty from sin and misery. He distinguishes the liberty of independence from the liberty from sin and misery which is a moral condition. Thus, 4:2 is merely affirming Adam's liberty from sin and misery not his liberty of independence. Adam had a nature such that he was neither confirmed in righteousness nor in bondage to sin. That is all 4:2 is affirming. Crisp and Girardeu go beyond what the Confession says in stating that 4:2 is affirming that Adam had libertarian free will. This would be for Adam to have the liberty of independence.

In light of this discussion, it is important to distinguish two things that Crisp and Girardeau confuse. It is the distinction between a moral ability and a metaphysical ability. Adam's moral ability is his ability to do good or evil because he is free from moral necessity. This was the state in which Adam was created and this is what 4:2 is affirming. Man's metaphysical ability is his ability to resist or do other than God's decree and providence. We have seen that reformed theology does not affirm that man has this ability. Man is not free from the necessity of immutability that attaches to God's decree and providence nor does he have the liberty of independence, as Turretin states.

This distinction is important because it enables us to pinpoint Crisp and Girardeau's misunderstanding of the Confession. They confuse moral ability with metaphysical ability. They read the Confession's statement about Adam's moral ability as a metaphysical ability. These two should be kept distinct. Turretin teaches that the reformed tradition keeps them distinct. Next, we will see Calvin and Witsius as further examples of this distinction. Calvin writes,

> In this integrity man by free will had the power, if he so willed, to attain eternal life. *Here it would be out of place to raise the questions of God's secret predestination because our present subject is not what can happen or not, but what man's nature was like.* Therefore Adam could have stood if he wished, seeing that he fell solely by his own will. But it was because his will was

capable of being bent to one side or the other, and was not given the constancy to persevere, that he fell so easily. Yet his choice of good and evil was free, and not that alone, but the highest rectitude was in his mind and will, and all the organic parts were rightly composed to obedience, until in destroying himself he corrupted his own blessings.[60]

We see here that Calvin distinguishes between Adam's moral nature before the fall and God's secret predestination. In talking about Adam's moral nature before the fall, Calvin does not consider God's decree to have Adam fall. He talks about Adam's moral nature abstracted from God's secret predestination. He does this in order to teach that Adam's moral nature at creation was free from moral necessity.

We know that Calvin rejected the idea that Adam had what we are calling a metaphysical ability to resist God's decree or providence. Calvin writes:

Let him, therefore, who would beware of this infidelity ever remember that there is no erratic power, or action, or motion in creatures, but that they are governed by God's secret plan in such a way that nothing happens except what is knowingly and willingly decreed by him.[61]

Calvin taught that even Adam's fall was under God's control. He begins book 3, chapter 23, section 7 of the Institutes with the heading "God has also predestined the fall into sin."[62] He goes on to say:

Again I ask: whence does it happen that Adam's fall irremediably involved so many peoples, together with their infant offspring, in eternal death unless because it so pleased God. . . . The decree is dreadful indeed, I confess. Yet no one can deny that God foreknew what end man was to have before he created him, and consequently foreknew because he so ordained by his decree.[63]

Calvin writes again:

For the first man fell because the Lord judged it to be expedient; why he so judged is hidden from us.[64]

---

60. Calvin, *Institutes of the Christian Religion*, 195 (emphasis mine).
61. Calvin, *Institutes of the Christian Religion*, 201.
62. Calvin, *Institutes of the Christian Religion*, 955.
63. Calvin, *Institutes of the Christian Religion*, 955.
64. Calvin, *Institutes of the Christian Religion*, 957.

From this we see that Calvin also makes this distinction between a metaphysical power and a moral power. He teaches that God decreed and foreknew Adam's fall, yet he is also able to teach about Adam's moral ability without consideration of the decree to fall.

Herman Witsius makes a similar distinction. First, he is clear that God's decree and providence govern Adam's fall and that Adam could not do otherwise:

> For if all creatures depend on God in acting: if he not only concurs with them, when they act, but also excites them to act; if that excitation be so powerful, as that upon supposing it, *the effect cannot but follow*; if God with the same efficacy influences vicious actions, so far as they are physical; if the creature cannot give its actions their due moral goodness without God; *it infallibly follows*, that Adam, God himself moving him to understand, will, and eat; and God not giving goodness to those actions, man could not understand and will in a right manner.[65]

Witsius affirms that God governs Adam's fall in such a manner that "the effect cannot but follow" and "it infallibly follows" that he falls. Witsius continues:

> But it does not follow, that man was obliged to what was simply impossible. For, it is only a consequential and eventual infallibility and necessity, which we have established. God bestowed sufficient powers on man, even such as were proper for a creature, by which he could have overcome the temptation. But then he could not proceed to action without presupposing divine concurrence. Who shall deny, that man has a locomotive faculty, so sufficient in its kind, that he requires no more? *For, will any affirm, that man, by that locomotive faculty, can actually move independently of God*, as the first cause, without discovering his ignorance both of the supremacy of God, and the subordination of man? *In like manner, we affirm, that, though God granted man such sufficient abilities to fulfill all righteousness*, that he had no need of any further grace, as it is called; *yet all this ability was given him in such a manner that he should act only dependently of the Creator, and his influence.*[66]

Witsius is very clear that Adam could not act apart from God's decree and providence. Yet at the same time, he says that Adam was given sufficient powers to overcome the temptation. He says that "God granted man such

---

65. Witsius, *Economy of the Covenants*, 145 (emphasis mine).
66. Witsius, *Economy of the Covenants*, 145 (emphasis mine).

sufficient abilities to fulfill all righteousness." Yet he could only act "dependently of the Creator, and his influence." We see Witsius distinguishing between Adam's moral powers (to fulfill all righteousness) and Adam's lack of metaphysical powers (to act independently of God's providence).

The distinction between moral and metaphysical powers is made in various ways. Turretin distinguishes between the liberty of independence (metaphysical ability) and the liberty from sin and misery (moral ability). Calvin distinguishes between God's secret predestination (metaphysical ability) and Adam's original moral nature (moral ability). Witsius distinguishes between Adam's ability to fulfill all righteousness (moral ability) and his lack of ability to act independent of God (metaphysical ability). Van Asselt, Bac, and te Velde tell us that the reformed scholastics distinguished between the necessity of immutability (metaphysical ability) and moral necessity (moral ability). The distinction is stated and nuanced in different ways, but the substance of it is in the reformed tradition.[67]

In conclusion, WCF 4:2 teaches that Adam was free from moral necessity. It teaches that his moral condition at creation was such that he had the power to fulfill God's law and yet the possibility of transgressing it. It focuses on Adam's freedom from moral necessity.

The article is not discussing nor affirming that Adam had the ability to do otherwise than God's decree and providence. Like Turretin, Calvin, Witsius, and the reformed tradition, it is teaching about Adam's moral nature at creation in distinction from God's decree and providence. WCF 3 and 5 clearly teach that God's decree and providence have the necessity of immutability. They also teach that Adam was not free from this necessity of immutability when in relation to God's decree and providence. This means that he did not have the metaphysical ability to do other than God's decree and providence. Therefore, it is illegitimate for Crisp and Girardeau to use WCF 4:2 in support of libertarian free will or to teach that Adam had this metaphysical ability.

---

67. Contemporary Reformed theologians also make this distinction. John Frame writes: "One can think of many other kinds of possibilities and abilities: legal, medical, musical, and so on. In the previous section, *we referred to moral ability and to the human ability to frustrate God's plan, which we might call 'metaphysical ability.'* Plainly an act or event can be possible in one sense, but not in other senses. Jesus' bones were physically breakable, but they could not be broken in violation of God's intention" (Frame, *Doctrine Of God*, 133–34 [emphasis mine]).

Arguments Against Crisp and Girardeau's Use of WCF 9:1 and 2

The next portions of the Confession that Crisp and Girardeau cite are WCF 9:1–2. These articles say:

1. God hath endued the will of man with that natural liberty, that it is neither forced, nor, by any absolute necessity of nature, determined to good or evil.

2. Man, in his state of innocency, had freedom, and power to will and to do that which was good and well pleasing to God, but yet mutably, so that he might fall from it.

Crisp writes of these articles:

> The issue was this: Was the primal sin of Adam and Eve freely entered into? Were they free to sin and free to refrain from sinning at the moment of choice? To this question, the libertarian Calvinist, in keeping with the symbols of Reformed theology like the Westminster Confession, can offer an affirmative response. They were free to act in this way.[68]

Crisp does not really make an argument here. He merely states that based on WCF 4 and 9, the libertarian Calvinist could affirm that Adam and Eve freely sinned in the libertarian sense. Notice the language, "Were they free to sin and free to refrain from sinning at the moment of choice?" to which he answers, "They were free to act in this way."

But the Confession never makes use of the language "at the moment of choice." Crisp is most likely reading the following language this way, "God hath endued the will of man with that natural liberty" not "determined to good, or evil." And that man had the freedom and power "to will and to do that which was good . . . but yet, mutably." This would be the same strategy we saw with Girardeau concerning WCF 4:2. They understand this language to mean that Adam had libertarian freedom or the metaphysical power to do other than God's decree, providence, and foreknowledge.[69]

---

68. Crisp, *Deviant Calvinism*, 83–84. That Crisp has WCF chapter 9 and WCF chapter 4 in view is made clear from his footnote: "In addition to the words of chapter 9 of the Confession cited earlier, chapter 4, on creation, says that Adam and Eve in their state of original righteousness had 'the law of God written in their hearts, and power to fulfil it.' Yet they were 'under a possibility of transgressing, being left to the liberty of their own will, which was subject unto change'" (Crisp, *Deviant Calvinism*, 84n11).

69. Girardeau uses this language from the Confession to attempt to make the same point that Crisp is making against the determinist or Jonathan Edwards. We can see a sampling of Girardeau stating what he thinks the Confession is advocating: "In the first

In response, we have already seen that this interpretation would contradict the Confession's teaching on the decree and providence. The decree and providence have the necessity of immutability. This means that if God wills A to happen, then A will happen. We saw how this was related to the fall of Adam. If Crisp and Girardeau are right about their interpretation of WCF 9:1–2, then there is a contradiction between WCF 3 and 5 with WCF 9.

Secondly, the type of liberty the Confession is affirming is not libertarian free will. It is not the ability to do other than God's decree and providence, but the liberty from coercion and moral necessity. We know this from the language of the Confession.

In WCF 9:1 it says that this natural liberty is not forced. This means that natural liberty is to be understood as a lack of coercion. G. I. Williamson comments on this as follows:

> By free will we mean that man's will is not coerced. We mean that man is not forced by some external force greater than himself to do something he does not want to do. We mean that man is free to do what he wants to do within the limits of his ability.[70]

Turretin calls this freedom from coaction. He writes:

> (2) Liberty of coaction by which man acts spontaneously and with freedom; this is opposed to the necessity of coaction seen in those who act through force.[71]

Van Asselt, Bac, and te Velde call this freedom from physical necessity. They write:

> Physical necessity: necessity deriving from an outward cause that forces someone or something. This is often called coercion.[72]

The Confession is teaching that one aspect of this natural liberty is man's ability to act in a non-coerced manner. The Confession is not teaching

---

place, these standards unmistakably declare that man at first had freedom of the will; that our first parents were left to the liberty or freedom of their own will; and that the will of man is endued with natural liberty. Here it is plainly asserted that freedom is a property of the will. . . . In the second place, the standards affirm that man in innocency had freedom to will and to do, etc. They assert the freedom of the man both in willing and in doing" (Girardeau, *Will and its Theological Relations*, 173–74).

Girardeau takes statements about the moral power of man before the fall and understands them to be advocating the power of contrary choice or libertarian free will.

70. Williamson, *Westminster Confession of Faith*, 112.
71. Turretin, *Institutes of Elenctic Theology*, 569.
72. Van Asselt et al., *Reformed Thought on Freedom*, 39.

that man has the ability to do other than God's decree or providence. Rowland Ward comments on this:

> The Bible does not envisage human freedom as freedom from all restrictions or a freedom to act autonomously, nor does it regard God's sovereignty as a threat to man's freedom or vice versa.[73]

In other words, man is genuinely free, but not in the sense that he can act autonomously from God. It is a freedom that is consistent with God's sovereignty, i.e., his decree and providence. Part of this natural liberty consists of freedom from force or coercion and this type of freedom is consistent with a lack of metaphysical power.

In WCF 9:1 the Confession states another aspect of this natural liberty, namely that it is not determined to good or evil by an absolute necessity of nature. Chad Van Dixhoorn makes clear that this article is talking about the moral realm. He writes:

> In the moral realm . . . we know that we are responsible for our actions. All of Scripture teaches us that we will answer for what we do and say. And that brings us to the second point of this opening section: there is no "absolute necessity of nature" that determines whether we shall choose "good or evil."
>
> That is to say, there is no action or decision of ours that can be reduced to some natural law, some kind of inevitable system of causation, some force of the universe, some biological inheritance from our parents.[74]

Van Dixhoorn is stating that the Confession teaches that there is nothing in creation that determines man to good or evil. Natural liberty consists in freedom from causal determinism, biological or genetic determinism, or anything in nature determining man to good or evil. He is not saying that the Confession excludes God's decree and providence from determining man to good or evil. Natural liberty is consistent with God's decree, providence, and foreknowledge.

Furthermore, WCF 9:2 is teaching about Adam's original moral state at creation. It is reaffirming what it affirmed in WCF 4:2, namely freedom from moral necessity. William Cunningham writes:

> And accordingly it must be noticed that the Confession does not here speak generally of its being determined, but only of its being determined to *good or evil*. These words, "to good or evil," are a constituent part of the only affirmation here put forth. It

---

73. Ward, *Westminster Confession of Faith*, 78.
74. Van Dixhoorn, *Confessing the Faith*, 136.

is not a statement about the grounds and causes of the ordinary determinations of the will, or of the volitions in general, but about *determinations to good or evil*—that is, about volitions which involve a choosing between good and evil, or a preference of the one of these to the other. The general object of the whole chapter was to unfold the different aspects which man has presented in his fourfold state, as to freedom or liberty of will in *choosing between good and evil*. To the freedom or bondage of man's will, with reference to choosing between good and evil, as possessed and exhibited in four different conditions, the four following sections of the chapter are devoted; and the first section was evidently intended to be introductory to the exposition of this general topic in its different stages. So that, viewed in its connection with what it introduces, it may be fairly regarded as amounting, in substance, to a statement to this effect—that though man at different stages of his history—unfallen, fallen, renewed, glorified—has had his will determined to good and also determined to evil, *this result* is not to be ascribed in *either* case to force, or to any absolute necessity of nature, as that would be inconsistent with natural liberty with which God has endowed the will. This was the aspect in which, principally—we might almost say exclusively—both the Reformers of the sixteenth and the great Calvinistic divines of the seventeenth century contemplated the subject of free will; and it is this sense alone, we are convinced, that the compliers of the Westminster Confession intended to expound it.[75]

Cunningham is saying that chapter 9 is talking about Adam's moral power. That is the general topic of the chapter. It is talking about his moral power in various stages. Article 1 is a general statement about moral freedom. In any one of the four stages, man was not forced by absolute necessity of nature to good or evil. The Confession is not teaching about man's freedom to do otherwise than God's decree and providence.

This means that Crisp and Girardeau's use of these articles once again confuses moral power with metaphysical power. Like WCF 4:2, WCF 9:2 is affirming man's moral power at creation. Crisp and Girardeau read this as

---

75. Cunningham, *Reformers*, 496–97. Van Dixhorn argues the same thing: "The following four paragraphs in this confession (9.2–9.5) look at the will of man through four different stages of redemptive history. Paragraph 2 considers Adam and Eve as they were created" (Van Dixhorn, *Confessing the Faith*, 139). A.A. Hodge makes the same point: "These sections briefly state and contrast the various conditions which characterize the free agency of man in his four different estates of innocency, hereditary sin, grace, and glory" (Hodge, *Westminster Confession*, 101).

a metaphysical power to do otherwise than God's decree, providence, and foreknowledge at the moment of choice.

Arguments Against Crisp and Girardeau's Use of WCF 19:1

The final article that Girardeau appeals to is WCF 19:1. The article reads as follows:

> God gave to Adam a law, as a covenant of works, by which he bound him and all his posterity to personal, entire, exact, and perpetual obedience, promised life upon the fulfilling, and threatened death upon the breach of it, and endued him with power and ability to keep it.
>
> Girardeau does not directly comment on this article, but he lists it among the others as justifying what he has already argued, namely that it supports the power of contrary choice or libertarian free will. Most likely, Girardeau would see the language "and endued him with power and ability to keep it" as affirming libertarian free will.[76]

This article is affirming what WCF 4:2 and 9:2 affirm. Adam, in his unfallen state, was free from moral necessity. It is affirming that Adam had this moral power. It is not affirming that Adam could do otherwise than God's decree and providence.

We have seen how Crisp and Girardeau interpret WCF 4, 9, and 19. We have seen that they consistently confuse moral power with metaphysical power. Interpreting the Confession in this manner entails a contradiction between these articles and WCF 3 and 5. It also fails to understand that WCF 4, 9, and 19 are affirming a moral power. For these reasons, we must reject their interpretation of these articles. In rejecting their interpretation of these articles, we are also undermining their Confessional evidence for Libertarian Calvinism. This means that they have failed to show that Libertarian Calvinism is consistent with the Westminster Confession of Faith and thus they have failed to show that the Confession requires us to affirm principle 2.

---

76. We have already seen him argue this in regard to chapter 4. He wrote: "That he had freedom and power to will and to do what was right, mutably, so that he might fall from it. He might stand, yet he might fall; he might will and do right; yet he might will and do wrong; he might choose holiness, yet he might choose sin. When then did he sin, might he have not done otherwise? If so, although the terms *power of contrary choice*" (Girardeau, *Will and its Theological Relations*, 177).

It is illuminating to see how Crisp regards their treatment of Libertarian Calvinism and the Confession. He writes:

> Manifestly, these statements are consistent with Girardeau's claims about prelapsarian human free will (I do not say they *require* it).[77]

Crisp is saying that these Confessional statements are consistent with libertarian Calvinism but they do not require libertarian Calvinism. We have disputed that they are consistent with libertarian Calvinism and we will further dispute this in the next section. However, Crisp's statement that they do not require it illustrates our point. Nothing in the Confession excludes Fischer and Ravizza's position of sourcehood and alternative possibilities conditions.

Other Confessional Statements

We have examined various articles in the Confession that Girardeau and Crisp appealed to in support of libertarian Calvinism. Now we must look at other articles that might be used to argue for principle 2 or libertarian Calvinism. These articles are WCF 3:1; 5:2, 4. Let us begin with WCF 3:1:

> God from all eternity, did, by the most wise and holy counsel of His own will, freely, and unchangeably ordain whatsoever comes to pass yet so, as thereby neither is God the author of sin nor is violence offered to the will of the creatures; nor is the liberty or contingency of second causes taken away, but rather established.[78]

The reformed believed that God decrees, foreknows and is providentially in control of everything, yet he is not the author of sin. By "author of sin" they meant that God is not the efficient cause of sin. Vermigli writes:

> Even though God rules over sins and evils, he may not be said strictly to be their efficient cause.[79]

Herman Bavinck says:

---

77. Crisp, "John Girardeau," 298.

78. We see similar language in WCF 5:2, where it says: "He ordereth them to fall out, according to the nature of second causes, either necessarily, freely or contingently" (WCF 5:2). The concepts of "second causes," "freely" (or "liberty" in WCF 3:1), and "contingently" will be the same as in WCF 3:1. Therefore we will not deal with WCF 5:2.

79. Vermigli, *Philosophical Works*, 230.

In the case of the good, God's providence must be understood as God himself by his Spirit working in the subject and positively enabling this subject to do good. In the case of sin, it may not be pictured that way. Sin is lawlessness, deformity, and does not have God as its efficient cause, but at most as its deficient cause.[80]

In speaking of the reformed view of evil, J. Martin Bac writes of Leydecker:

> Leydecker, however, expressly denies that divine providence concerns sin as sin, that is, the vitiosity of the act. In this respect, he notes that evil is nothing but the privation of the good, and therefore nothing positive, of which God can be the author. It is something privative that is founded in something positive, and therefore evil does not have an efficient cause, but only a deficient one.[81]

According to the reformed, for God to be the author of sin means that God efficiently causes the lawlessness or vitiosity of the sinful act. In order to explain this, we need to take account of the various distinctions that the reformed made regarding a sinful act. Heppe writes that the reformed make a distinction within the sinful act between the substance of the act and the badness of the act:

> God's decree is sheerly the efficient cause of everything good, the effectually permissive cause of evil. For it is God who effects that which in a sinful act bears the stamp of a real *res*, namely the substance of the act, in order even thereby to reveal his glory. The really bad in it, which has not true being at all, He merely permits.[82]

Bavinck puts this in terms of a material/formal distinction:

> This applies even more intensely to the sinful deed. Materially, certainly, this must be attributed to God, but formally it remains the responsibility of human beings. When a murderer kills somebody, all the planning ability and the power he needs for that purpose comes from God, but the act, from a formal point of view, is his, not God's. Indeed, the fact of homicide taken by itself is not yet a sin, for the same thing frequently occurs in war and on the scaffold. What makes homicide a sin is not the matter, the substrate, but the form, that is, the depravity, the

---

80. Bavinck, *Reformed Dogmatics*, 63.
81. Bac, *Perfect Will Theology*, 464.
82. Heppe, *Reformed Dogmatics*, 143.

lawlessness (anomia) of the deed; not the substance but the accident in the act.[83]

The point of this material/formal distinction is to distinguish the essence of the sinful act from the good material or substance of the action. An alternative formulation of this is found in Voetius. He distinguishes the sinful act into three parts: (1) the substratum, (2) the sinfulness, and (3) the end:

> In a 1643 disputation Voetius distinguished between an abstract and a concrete aspect of sin: taken abstractly sin is "lawlessness (anomia) or divergence from the law of God formally and as such." In the concrete sense three aspects of the sinful act can be distinguished. In the first place there is an act that, so to say, as a substratum carries the sin. Voetius here means, for instance, a human hand that is moving in order to steal something. Secondly, the sinful act includes the iniquity or the anomia. In the chosen example this would be the morally wrongful act of stealing that is accomplished by the physical act of someone's hand. In the third place, the sinful act can be directed to some good end. The first aspect—the basic act that is the substratum—is good, as is the third dimension also. The point of this distinction of three aspects is that it allows Voetius to argue that God's providence relates in different ways to the different aspects of the human sinful act.[84]

Turretin similarly writes:

> First, three things must be accurately distinguished in sin: (1) the entity itself of the act which has the relation of material; (2) the disorder (ataxia) and wickedness joined with it (or its concomitant) which puts on the notion of the formal; (3) the consequent judgment called the adjunct. God is occupied in different ways about these. As to the first, since an act as such is always good as to its entity, God concurs to it effectively and physically, not only by conserving the nature, but by exciting its motions and actions by physical motion, as being good naturally.... As to the third (which is related to the judgment of God) which is joined with sin, not of itself in relation to the sinner ... but accidentally in relation to God permitting sins and ordaining them to a good end beyond their own nature—God holds himself also

---

83. Bavinck, *Reformed Dogmatics*, 62.
84. Goudriaan, *Reformed Orthodoxy and Philosophy*, 189.

positively and efficaciously, since what as such has the relation of good must be from God . . .

As to the second, which is the lawlessness (anomia) itself, God can be called neither its physical cause (because he neither inspires nor infuses nor does it) nor its ethical cause (because he neither commands nor approves and persuades, but more severely forbids and punishes).[85]

The purpose of these types of distinctions is to show that God's decree and providence govern everything and yet God is not the author of sin. God has an asymmetrical relationship to the various parts of the sinful act. Given the material/formal distinction, God is the efficient cause of the material, but not the formal cause. Given the substratum/lawlessness/end distinction, God efficiently causes the substratum and end, but not the lawlessness. The reformed taught that God is not the author of sin because he does not efficiently cause the formal aspect or lawlessness of the sinful action.

In fact, the reformed argue that God could not be the efficient cause of evil because evil cannot have an efficient cause since it is a privation of the good. Evil or the lawlessness of sin is not something positive; it is a privation of the good. Evil can only exist as a deformity or lack of something good. Vermigli writes:

> I will say something about evil, the genus under which sin is included. Evil is a lack [privatio], I mean of goodness; not of all goodness but of such a good as is required for the perfection of the creature, which I say belongs to the perfection of the subject that is corrupted. If we take sight away from a stone, it receives no injury, for that quality of nature does not apply. As a privation, evil cannot exist without good, for it must have a subject. Since a subject is a substance [natura], it is good; so evil can exist only in some good—blindness is a deprivation of sight; it does not hang in the air, but stays in the eye . . . sin itself deprives human action of honor and obedience towards the word of God.[86]

As a privation, evil is not a positive substance and thus does not need an efficient cause. Since it does not need an efficient cause, God could not possibly be the efficient cause. Though God does not efficiently cause evil, he does permit it by a permissive decree and govern it by providence. He governs the substratum in which sin inheres and he governs the good end that he intends by this sinful action. However, it is impossible for God to be

---

85. Turretin, *Institutes of Elenctic Theology*, 515–16.
86. Vermigli, *Philosophical Works*, 223.

the efficient cause of the lawlessness. In speaking of Voetius and van Mastricht, Goudriaan writes:

> The characterization of sin as a privation has its second reason in the fact that "if it were something real, substantial and positive, it would necessarily require God as its author," for what is real is caused by Him.[87]

Vermigli writes:

> In the *City of God,* twelfth book and seventh chapter, Augustine speaks very well about the corrupt will: "An evil thing does not have an efficient cause, but a deficient one. And if anyone inquires into this efficient cause, it is as if he would see the darkness with his eyes, or apprehend silence with his ears. Since they are privations, they do not need efficient causes.[88]

We see from this that God is the efficient cause of the good but not of the evil. There is an asymmetrical relationship that God's decree and providence bear to good and evil. God is not the efficient cause of evil and thus not the author of sin.

Denying the sourcehood condition and the alternative possibilities condition does not make God the efficient cause of the formal aspect or lawlessness of the sinful act. We are not committed to causality from the decree or providence. Even if one were, we would not need to be committed to God efficiently causing the sinfulness of the sinful act.

Secondly, denying the sourcehood and alternative possibilities condition is compatible with holding to the idea that evil is a privation. Thus, we could make the same arguments in favor of the idea that evil cannot have a cause, let alone God being that cause.

The next phrase we will examine is "nor is violence offered to the will of the creature." I will argue that this does not support libertarian freedom. John Fesko writes:

> The human will is bound to sin, but our choices are free and not forced upon us. Even though God decrees whatsoever comes to pass, people freely make their own choices. God is not the author of sin and offers no violence to the will of creatures—they freely choose sin.[89]

---

87. Goudriaan, *Reformed Orthodoxy and Philosophy*, 192.
88. Vermigli, *Philosophical Works*, 230.
89. Fesko, *Theology of the Westminster Confession*, 111. G. I. Williamson makes this same point: "Freedom may be defined as 'the absence of external coercion.' If a man is not forced by any power outside himself to do that which is contrary to what he wants

Fesko identifies the phrase "nor is violence offered to the will of the creature" with the human will not being forced to choose. This understanding is compatible with God decreeing human choices. Reformed theologians have traditionally understood God's decree as not exercising coercion on man's will. We have already seen that the necessity of immutability, which is the necessity of God's decree and providence, does not coerce man's actions. Thus, we should conclude that the Confession is not here advocating that the human will can do other than God decreed at the moment of choice. It is merely advocating that the human will is not coerced.

Denying the sourcehood and alternative possibilities conditions do not commit us to holding that God forces the will of man to act. The necessity of immutability renders the act certain and unable to do otherwise, but does not coerce it.

The last part of the article says, "Nor is the liberty or contingency of second causes taken away." This statement is intended to affirm the reality of second causes and man's freedom. Fesko helps us to understand the Confession's definition of contingency. He writes:

> Contingency does not mean that something does not have a cause, as Jonathan Edwards argued. Rather, it means that something could be otherwise.[90]

The events of the universe, including man's free actions, could have been otherwise. This phrase "could have been otherwise" is ambiguous. As we have seen there are many ways to understand this and only one of them is incompatible with a denial of PAP given the decree or principle 2.

The Confession is not using contingency in the sense of an agent doing other than God decreed at the moment of choice. The basic sense of contingency does not require this. All it requires is that the universe could have been different. One sense in which it could have been different is if

---

to do, then we may properly say that he is free" (Williamson, *Westminster Confession of Faith*, 41). The point here is not so much to agree with Williamson's definition of freedom as it is to see that he regards the Confessions statement here to refer to a lack of force which is compatible with God decreeing the free act. Chad Van Dixhorn takes this statement to simply affirm man's freedom in some sense: "The second fence is almost as important as the first. And the point is that we need to remember that God's ordaining of whatsoever comes to pass does not do 'violence' to the will of men and women. . . . God is sovereign, but in a very real way we are free, and in every way we are responsible for our actions" (Van Dixhorn, *Confessing the Faith*, 45).

We see that all the Confession requires is that man is free and responsible. It does not require a particular definition of freedom and responsibility other than "not being forced." This is compatible with God decreeing the action and the agent not being able to do otherwise in the actual sequence at the moment of choice.

90. Fesko, *Theology of the Westminster Standards*, 103.

God had decreed it to be different. But this is consistent with the agent not being able to do other than God decreed in the actual sequence at the moment of choice. Also, as we will see in the next section, the Confession teaches that man cannot do otherwise than God's decree, foreknowledge, and providence at the moment of choice. So, the Confession contradicts any understanding of contingency along the lines of principle 2.

Furthermore, recall our treatment of the necessity of the consequence. This was distinguished from the necessity of the consequent. The necessity of the consequent did not allow the consequent to be contingent. However, the necessity of the consequence did allow the consequent to be contingent in itself. This is what the confession is saying. The consequent in itself could have been otherwise. However, when the consequent is related to the antecedent in the necessity of the consequence, then the consequent could not have been otherwise. This is what we are affirming.

Van Asselt, Bac, and te Velde show that the reformed orthodox distinguish the necessity of immutability in regards to the decree, providence, and necessity of infallibility with regard to foreknowledge. Both of these are a necessity of the consequence. The consequent is contingent in itself, but not when related to the decree, providence, and foreknowledge. This is what we are affirming. This is what Fisher and Ravizza mean by the actual sequence. The thing in itself is contingent, but when placed in the actual sequence (given God's decree, providence, and foreknowledge or the laws of physics), it could not be otherwise.

Van Asselt, Bac, and te Velde say the same:

> If God foreknows p, p shall surely happen, and in that sense *it is not possible that it does not happen*. Yet the Reformed were eager to show that this kind of necessity can be united with the contingency of p. This would only be impossible if we ignore the distinction between the necessity of the consequent and the necessity of the consequence: in that case there would be no difference between both kinds of necessity and p would be necessary in every respect.[91]

Here we see van Asselt, Bac, and te Velde affirm that given the necessity of the consequence, it is impossible that the consequent does not happen. This is just another way of saying that it could not be otherwise. However, apart from this necessity, the consequent is in itself contingent. They continue with regard to God's will:

---

91. Van Asselt et al., *Reformed Thought on Freedom*, 37 (emphasis mine).

The same holds for God's will. In contrast to the will of the creatures, God's will is always effective and is never frustrated. Again, the reformed distinguish between

(13) N (GWp→p) (it is necessary that if God wills p, then p occurs)

And

(14) GWp→Np (if God wills that p, p is necessary itself)[92]

They are affirming that God's will cannot be frustrated. In other words, if God wills or decrees p, then p occurs. It is impossible that p frustrates God's will. This is another way of saying that given God's will, it is impossible for p to be otherwise. Yet p is not necessary in itself.

This understanding of contingency is precisely what Fischer and Ravizza affirm. They are not affirming an absolute necessity or a necessity of the thing in itself. Instead, they are saying that given the laws of physics and the current state of the universe, it is impossible for p to be otherwise in the actual sequence. This type of necessity and contingency is compatible with what the Confession is saying.

This article of the Confession also affirms the reality of second causes. Robert Letham writes,

> In short, if something happens, it happens because God ordained it happen. In the case of free agents, the things that happen is of our own choosing. In the case of events in the natural world, the thing that happens is in accordance with the laws of nature. If it rains, God ordained it so. Yet it rains due to the atmospheric circumstances prevailing. In other words, God has so created the universe as to maintain its own contingent freedom within the scope of his unchangeable purpose. God and man are not competitors.[93]

The affirmation of man as a genuine second cause does not mean that the Confession is advocating libertarian free will. Compatibilist views of human freedom also affirm that man is a genuine second cause.

---

92. Van Asselt et al., *Reformed Thought on Freedom*, 37.

93. Letham, *Westminster Assembly*, 184. Chad Van Dixhorn also writes, "The third protective fence is that God's plan still employs real secondary causes. In other words, God has decided the end from the beginning, but the middle still matters. . . . The important thing to remember now is that the liberty or freedom of these causes is real: the contingency or possibility of these events is not taken away, a point that is effectively identical with that made before" (Van Dixhorn, *Confessing the Faith*, 184).

We have seen that both Crisp's and Girardeau's arguments for libertarian free will from the Confession fail to prove their point. We have also seen that other passages from the Confession that might be used to argue for libertarian free will fall short. Next, I want to argue that the Confession teaches a form of theological determinism. This means that it excludes libertarian freedom as specified in the sourcehood and the alternative possibilities conditions.

Confession Affirms Theological Determinism

We have seen that the Confession does not require that we affirm libertarian freedom. Now we need to see that the Confession excludes libertarian freedom. In order to do this, let us return to Crisp's definition of libertarianism. He writes:

> I use the term "libertarian" and "libertarian choice" in a more restricted sense to mean a choice that is free in the sense of originating with the agent, not God. A libertarian choice is one for which the agent is morally responsible at least in part because he has an alternative possibility he could actualize at the moment of choice.[94]

Libertarian freedom consists of two conditions. First is the sourcehood condition. A libertarian choice does not have its origin in God, but in man. The second is the alternative possibilities condition. At the moment of choice, the agent could have actualized either x or not x. With these two conditions in mind, we need to ask two questions. First, "Does the Westminster Confession exclude the sourcehood condition?" and second, "Does the Westminster Confession exclude the alternative possibilities condition?" I will argue that the Confession excludes both.

First, let us look at the sourcehood condition. Crisp refers to this when he says that a libertarian choice originates not with God, but with the agent. We could make this clearer by using an illustration from Robert Kane:

> *Free Will,* in the traditional sense I want to retrieve . . . is *the power of agents to be the ultimate creators (or originators) and sustainers of their own ends or purposes* . . . such a notion of *ultimate* creation is obscure . . . its meaning can be captured initially by an image: when we trace the causal or explanatory chains of action back to their sources in the purposes of free agents, these causal chains must come to an end or terminate in

---

94. Crisp, "John Girardeau," 286.

the willings (choices, decisions, or efforts) of the agents, which cause or bring about their purposes. If these willings were in turn caused by something else, so that the explanatory chains could be traced back further to heredity or environment, to God, or fate, then the ultimacy would not lie with the agents but with something else.[95]

In light of this understanding of the sourcehood condition, we need to ask if the Confession teaches that man's choices trace back either to man or to God.

It seems clear that the Confession teaches that man is not the ultimate originator of his actions, but they trace back to God's decree. WCF 3:1 says:

> God, from all eternity, did, by the most wise and holy counsel of his own will, freely, and unchangeably ordain whatsoever comes to pass: yet so, as thereby neither is God the author of sin, nor is violence offered to the will of the creatures; nor is the liberty or contingency of second causes taken away, but rather established.

This article teaches that God, and not man, is the ultimate source of man's actions. We could state the argument this way:

1. "Whatsoever comes to pass" traces back to God's decree (WCF 3:1)

2. Man's choices and actions are part of "whatsoever comes to pass." (Implied by WCF 3:1)

C. Man's choices and actions trace back to God's decree (From WCF 1 and 2)

The first premise is clear from WCF 3:1 when it states "God, from all eternity, did, by the most wise and holy counsel of his own will, freely, and unchangeably ordain whatsoever comes to pass." This statement is teaching that God is the ultimate source or originator of everything that happens in the universe. Premise two is implied by the meaning of "whatsoever comes to pass," which is intended to cover everything that happens in the universe, including man's choices and actions. From these two premises, it follows that man's choices and actions trace back to God's decree. This means that man

---

95. Kane, *Significance of Free Will*, 4. J. P. Moreland and William Lane Craig define this source condition as follows: "He is the absolute originator of his own actions. . . . When an agent acts freely, he is a first or unmoved mover; no event or efficient cause causes him to act. His desires or beliefs may influence his choice or play an important role in his deliberations, but free acts are not determined or caused by prior events or states in the agent; rather, they are spontaneously done by the agent himself acting as a first mover" (Moreland and Craig, *Philosophical Foundations*, 270).

is not the ultimate source or originator or creator of his choices and actions. Thus, the sourcehood condition is not compatible with the Confession.

As we have seen, this does not mean that man is not free and morally responsible. It also does not mean that man is not a genuine agent. As the Confession says, he is a "second cause." This means that he has a will, a mind, and other faculties that are necessary for human agency. However, what man does with that free and responsible agency ultimately traces back to God's decree. This is the salient point for our current discussion because it shows that the Confession excludes the sourcehood condition. God is the ultimate source or origin of man's free and responsible choices.

The Confession makes this even clearer in article 2. It says:

> Although God knows whatsoever may or can come to pass upon all supposed conditions, yet hath he not decreed anything because he foresaw it as future, or as that which would come to pass upon such conditions.

This article is teaching us that God's decree is not based on anything outside of himself. Letham identifies three positions that this article excludes:

> God's foreknowledge is utterly comprehensive, contrary to the Socinian heresy that had reared its head at the time. However, his decree is not based upon his foreknowledge, as Arminius had held. . . . Both Helm and Fesko correctly identify Molinism as the target of the final clause. Following Luis de Molina (1535–1600), this was the proposition that God's decrees were based on his knowledge of all possible future actions.[96]

This means that God's decree is not based upon anything in creation. The Socinians taught that God could not decree or foreknow human free actions. This is because libertarian free will is incompatible with God's decree and foreknowledge. If man is the ultimate originator of his actions, then God's decree is not. The Confession rejects this view.

Arminianism was another school of thought that held to libertarian free will. They taught that man is the ultimate originator of his choices, even though God's decree and foreknowledge is all encompassing. This is possible because God's decree and foreknowledge is based on what he foresees. The Confession rejects this position as well.

Molinism also teaches that man is the ultimate originator of his choices and actions. Man possesses libertarian free will and God decrees and foreknows everything that comes to pass. God is able to decree and foreknow

---

96. Letham, *Westminster Assembly*, 185.

man's libertarian actions because he has middle knowledge. This type of knowledge consists of God knowing what a creature will libertarianly do in every possible circumstance. God decrees a world in which he has organized all the various circumstances he wants that will produce the libertarian actions that he wants. Though God decrees and foreknows all things, man is the ultimate originator. The Confession rejects this position as well.

With the Confession rejecting these three positions, it is clearly affirming that God, not man, is the ultimate originator of man's choices and actions. This means that the Confession excludes the sourcehood condition. It is clear that God bases his decree upon the counsel of His will and nothing else.

We could make a similar argument from the Confession and Catechism's treatment of providence. The Larger Catechism makes clear the relationship between the decree and providence. In question 14 it says:

> Q. How does God execute his decrees? A. God executeth his decrees in the works of creation and providence, according to his infallible foreknowledge, and the free and immutable counsel of his will.

The Larger Catechism teaches us that God's providence is based on His decree. Whatever God executes via his providence is entirely in accord with His decree. Since it is the case that God's decree depends on nothing outside of himself, it follows that God's providence is executed by and according to nothing outside of himself. Therefore, whatsoever comes to pass, including human actions, originates in God's decree; creation and providence actualize it.

WCF 5:1 states that God's providence covers everything.

> God the Creator of all things doth uphold, direct, dispose, and govern all creatures, actions, and things, from the greatest even to the last, by his most wise and holy providence, according to his infallible foreknowledge, and the free and immutable counsel of his own will, to the praise of the glory of his wisdom, power, justice, goodness, and mercy.

The Confession is teaching us that God's providence governs everything, including men's actions. This even extends to the fall of Adam and all the sins of men and angels. WCF 5:4 says:

> The almighty power, unsearchable wisdom, and infinite goodness of God so far manifest themselves in his providence, that it extendeth itself even to the first fall, and all other sins of angels and men; and that not by a bare permission, but such as hath joined with it a most wise and powerful bounding, and otherwise

ordering, and governing of them, in a manifold dispensation to his holy ends; yet so, as the sinfulness thereof proceedeth only from the creature, and not from God, who, being most holy and righteous, neither is not can be the author or approver of sin.

Article 4 makes clear that God even decreed the first fall and humans' sins; they are actualized under His providence. From these statements of the Confession and Catechism, it seems clear that all human actions, good or evil, have their origin in God's decree and providence. Therefore, the Confession excluded the sourcehood aspect of libertarian Calvinism.

What about the alternative possibilities condition? This was the view that an agent could actualize x or not x at the moment of choice. This is what we have been referring to as principle 2 or PAP. The Confession excludes this condition as well. Drawing on the language of the Confession, I will give two arguments that entail that man cannot do otherwise than God decreed or foreknew. The first argument consists of language from WCF 3:1; 5:4; and WLC 12 and 14.

1. Unpreventably (If God decrees Adam to fall, then Adam will fall) (WCF 3:1; WLC 12)

2. Unpreventably (God decreed Adam to fall) (WCF 5:4; WLC 12)

C. Unpreventably (Adam falls) (1, 2 and transfer principle)[97]

Premise 1 is stating what WCF 3:1 and WLC 12 state. In WCF 3:1 it says, "God . . . [did] ordain whatsoever comes to pass." This is stating that what God ordains will come to pass. The WLC 12 says something similar. It says God "hath foreordained whatsoever comes to pass in time, especially concerning angels and men." This again states that whatever God decrees/foreordains comes to pass. This has special reference to men and angels, which includes their free actions. There is nothing that man can do to prevent God from decreeing/ordaining as he does. The fall of Adam is included under "whatsoever comes to pass." Therefore, Adam could not prevent "if God decrees Adam to fall, then Adam will fall."

Premise 2 is justified from the language of WCF 5:4 and WLC 14. WLC 14 tells us that God's providence is based on his decree. It says, "God executeth his decrees in the works of creation and providence, according to his infallible foreknowledge and the free and immutable counsel of his own will." This is teaching us that God's providence is based upon his foreknowledge and decree or the counsel of His own will. This means that by whatever means God works, His providence was first foreknown and decreed. We saw

---

97. I am grateful to Paul Manata for help with this argument.

previously that His foreknowledge is based in His decree. So really this is teaching us that God's providence is based on His decree.

WCF 5:4 teaches us that God's providence extends to Adam's fall. It says, "The almighty power, unsearchable wisdom, and infinite goodness of God so far manifest themselves in his providence, that it extendeth itself to the first fall." Since God's providence extends to the first fall and God's providence is based on His decree, it follows that God decreed Adam to fall. Adam could not prevent God from decreeing him to fall.

The conclusion follows from premise 1 and premise 2 and the transfer principle. The transfer principle states that $[] (p \rightarrow q) \rightarrow [] (p) [] (q)$.[98] This principle says that the necessity of p→q transfer to p and to q. In our case, the unpreventability of "if God decrees Adam to fall, then Adam will fall" and the unpreventability of "God decrees Adam to fall" transfers to "Adam will fall."[99] So it follows that Adam could not prevent his fall. In other words, Adam could not do otherwise than God's decree for him to fall at the moment of choice. This means that the Confession excludes principle 2. In other words, this shows that the Confession rejects the alternative possibilities condition. We are justified in saying this because God decrees all human choices and actions. Therefore, it is unpreventable for any human being to do otherwise than God has decreed him to do at the moment of choice.

A similar argument could be formulated from the Confession's material on providence. This second argument is based on the language of WCF 5:1 and 4.

1. Unpreventably (If God foreknows that Adam will fall, then Adam will fall) (WCF 2:2)

2. Unpreventably (God foreknows that Adam will fall) (WCF 5:1, 4)

C. Unpreventably (Adam will fall) (1, 2 and transfer principle)

This argument is similar to the previous one except it is concerning God's foreknowledge. WCF 2:2 justified premise 1. This says, "His knowledge is infinite, infallible and independent upon the creature, so as nothing to him is contingent or uncertain." Since God's knowledge is infallible, it follows that whatever He foreknows must come to pass. It is also important to see that his knowledge is "independent upon the creature." This means that His foreknowledge that Adam will fall is independent of Adam. God did not foresee that Adam would fall and then foreknow that he would fall; He foreknew it because he decreed it to happen.

98. Konyndyk, *Introductory Modal Logic*, 32.

99. William Lane Craig acknowledges this "for from two necessary premises, a necessary conclusion follows" (Craig, *Only Wise God*, 75).

WCF 5:1 and 4 justified premise 1. In 5:1, we see that his providence is "according to His foreknowledge" and in 5:4 we read that His providence extends "to the first fall." As we saw in the previous argument, this means that God's providence is based on His foreknowledge, which is based on His decree. Since Adam could not prevent God from decreeing him to fall, it follows that Adam could not prevent God foreknowing that he would fall.

The conclusion follows from premise 1, premise 2, and the transfer principle stated above. This means that Adam could not do otherwise (he could not prevent) his fall. Thus, the alternative possibilities condition is false. We are justified in saying this because God foreknows all human choices and actions. This means that it is unpreventable for any person to do otherwise than God foreknew him to do at the moment of choice.

Of course, affirming that man cannot do other than what God's decree and foreknowledge dictate does not mean that man is not free and morally responsible. It only means that he is not free and morally responsible in the libertarian sense. Man is free and morally responsible in a compatibilist sense. God decrees or determines everything and man is free and morally responsible in a sense that is compatible with God's decree. The Confession does not mandate a particular theory of compatibilist freedom and moral responsibility. Many different theories fall within the bounds of the Confession. Fischer and Ravizza's is but one of them.

Our discussion of the Westminster Confession and Catechisms in relation to Libertarian Calvinism has shown that the Confession and Catechisms reject Libertarian Calvinism. The Confession teaches that the sourcehood condition is false as well as the alternative possibilities condition. This means that the Confession is committed to a form of theological determinism and a form of compatibilistic freedom and moral responsibility for man. This also means that Fischer and Ravizza's view on sourcehood and alternative possibilities are compatible with the Westminster Confession and Catechisms. This provides the context for us to ask whether guidance control is a form of compatibilist freedom and moral responsibility that is compatible with reformed thought. This is the subject of the next chapter. Before we move on to the next chapter, we need to discuss another potential objection to our thesis that Fischer and Ravizza's thought on sourcehood and alternative possibilities is compatible with reformed theology. This objection comes from the Utrecht School.

The Utrecht School

My thesis has been that Fischer and Ravizza's thoughts on the sourcehood and alternative possibilities condition are consistent with reformed theology as expressed in the Westminster Confession and Catechisms. I now want to turn to another debate within reformed theology that is somewhat related. There is a group of reformed theologians and philosophers associated with the University of Utrecht who argue that the reformed orthodox affirmed the alternative possibilities condition. Historian Richard Muller also argues this point.

The claims of the Utrecht School and Muller are not determinative of our thesis because they do not make the argument that the Westminster Standards affirmed the alternative possibilities condition. However, they are making the claim about the early history of reformed theology so it is important for us to see how Fischer and Ravizza's thought compares with this claim. There is much to discuss regarding their work. I will not be able to deal with all of it. However, I will discuss those aspects of their work that relate to Fischer and Ravizza's thought as we have been examining it, namely regarding the sourcehood and alternative possibilities condition.

Using these two conditions, we could state their position as follows: The reformed orthodox denied the sourcehood condition but affirmed the alternative possibilities condition. This is different from the Libertarian Calvinist. The Libertarian Calvinist affirmed both the sourcehood and alternative possibilities condition whereas Muller and the Utrecht School only affirm the alternative possibilities condition. We could state their position in the words of Muller:

> Reformed orthodox theologians of the early modern era argued positive divine determination of events, full and certain divine foreknowledge of future contingency, but also freedom of will and free choice, grounded in multiple potencies of will and understood in terms of liberty of contradiction and contrariety. In a given moment, the past being unaltered, human beings have potencies to more than one effect and can do otherwise.[100]

We can see from this quotation that Muller affirms that the reformed orthodox denied the sourcehood condition. They taught that God is the ultimate source of all human actions. However, Muller argues that the reformed orthodox affirm the alternative possibilities condition. Given the same past, man can do otherwise. Muller and the Utrecht School affirm the same position concerning the reformed orthodox regarding the sourcehood

---

100. Muller, "Jonathan Edwards and Francis Turretin," 284.

and alternative possibilities conditions. Muller, however, disagrees with some of the Utrecht Schools claims regarding the reformed orthodox. In particular, he disagrees that the reformed orthodox were Scotists. Instead, he argues that they were eclectic. Since the Utrecht School has written detailed and specialized works on this topic, I will primarily be interacting with them in this chapter. Muller's views will be considered in the following two chapters. We will find that, despite appearances, the Utrecht School and Muller are really not denying theological determinism.

I will be discussing three topics. First, that the reformed orthodox were Scotists, especially with regard to synchronic contingency. Second, I will discuss their thesis that the reformed orthodox were not determinists. Third, I will discuss the textual evidence that the Utrecht School uses to justify that the reformed orthodox taught synchronic contingency.

(1) The Reformed Orthodox Were Scotists

The Utrecht School[101] claims that the reformed orthodox were Scotists, especially with regard to Scotus's doctrine of synchronic contingency.[102] The question we are asking is, "Did the early reformed orthodox adopt the Scotistic conception of synchronic contingency?" This is the claim of the Utrecht School. Antonie Vos states it as follows:

> This basic structure of theological contingency thought conquers the academic scene of the *Ecclesia Reformata* at the beginning of the seventeenth century at a great pace. It will almost

---

101. For a helpful overview of the work of the Utrecht School, see te Velde, *Doctrine of God in Reformed Orthodoxy*, 481–692, esp. the section on synchronic contingency for an overview of the history of debate on this issue (670–76).

102. Paul Helm has argued against the idea that the reformed scholastics adopted Scotus's doctrine of synchronic contingency. See Helm, "Synchronic Contingency in Reformed Scholasticism," 207–23; "Synchronic Contingency Again," 234–38; "Reformed Thought on Freedom," 184–206; "'Structural Indifference' and Compatibilism," 184–205; "Necessity, Contingency," 243–62. From the Utrecht School, see Beck and Vos, "Conceptual Patterns to Reformed Scholasticism," 224–33; Van Asselt and Dekker, *Reformation And Scholasticism*; Van Asselt et al., *Reformed Thought on Freedom*; Vos, "Paul Helm On Medieval Scholasticism," 263–83.

Richard Muller does not agree with the Utrecht school thesis that the reformed orthodox were Scotists, however, he advances a thesis that the reformed tradition departed from the reformed orthodox with Jonathan Edwards. As mentioned, he comes to similar conclusions as the Utrecht School with regards to the reformed orthodox on freedom. Paul Helm disputes his conclusions. For that discussion see Muller, "Jonathan Edwards and the Absence," 42–60; Helm, "Jonathan Edwards," 42–60; Muller, "Johnathan Edwards and Francis Turretin," 266–85; Helm, "Turretin and Edwards Once More," 286–96.

completely dominate her theology of reformed scholasticism during the next two centuries.[103]

Van Asselt, Bac, and te Velde also write:

> There is enough evidence to argue that Reformed theology and anthropology participated in a tradition articulating an overarching theory of synchronic contingency developed by Duns Scotus, in which the radical dependence and freedom of all creaturely beings was formulated.[104]

The argument is not that the reformed orthodox used the terminology of synchronic contingency or that they explicitly made use of the concept. Instead, the argument is that they presupposed it as a logical framework. Beck and Vos write:

> We only claim that synchronic contingency is the presupposed logical framework of a truly non-necessitarian ontology.[105]

By this they mean that the reformed orthodox made use of concepts that presupposed synchronic contingency. They write:

> The ontological analysis by logical distinctions like the necessity of the consequence/consequent, the volitional analysis by logical distinctions like first and second act or divided and compound sense and the analysis of freedom by the distinctions

---

103. Vos, "Scholasticism and Reformation," 114. J Martin Bac writes: "Vos sketches Scotus as the mediator, who acknowledged the necessary existence of divine essence and the contingent actions of divine will. This view became the dominant Christian position but was forgotten because it was either interpreted in either an essentialist manner (the Thomist way) or a voluntarist manner (the Nominalist way). In this respect, the three medieval *viae* of Thomism, Scotism, and Nominalism can be sketched roughly by modal interpretations of divine being and agency. Thomism views both as necessary; Scotism advocates God's necessary being and his contingent agency, whereas Nominalism reckons both contingent.

The Reformed model of divine agency is a proper criterion to review the traditional historical background of Reformed scholasticism. It is a central aspect of the doctrine of God that is worked out differently along Thomist, Scotist, or Nominalist lines. In this study, I will try to show that a Scotist interpretation best fits the present evidence" (Bac, *Perfect Will Theology*, 34).

104. Van Asselt et al., *Reformed Thought on Freedom*, 22. They also write: "On this point we differ from Richard Muller, who discerns 'eclectic tendencies' towards the medieval schools of Thomism, Scotism and Nominalism and 'Christian Aristotelianism.' . . . To be sure, Reformed authors cite various sources to prove their case, but we propose they interpret these passages from one coherent systematic undercurrent [which of course is Scotism]" (Van Asselt et al., *Reformed Thought on Freedom*, 26n35).

105. Beck and Vos, "Conceptual Patterns," 224.

of freedom of contrariety and contradiction all seem to suggest an ontology of synchronic contingency. These distinctions all presuppose that contingency is not a matter of temporal change, but of simultaneous logical alternatives.[106]

The reformed orthodox use of these concepts, according to the Utrecht School, is evidence that they presupposed synchronic contingency.

Synchronic contingency is first argued in relation to God. Beck defines it as follows:

> 2. God does *p*, and he has simultaneously the possibility of not-doing *p*. In this sense the statement is true. Applying this distinction, Voetius in fact follows Scotus's innovative concept of synchronic contingency showing that a contingent state of affairs (for instance, "God's doing *p*") does not exclude the synchronic *possibility* of the opposite state of affairs ("God's not-doing *p*").[107]

Beck is arguing that Voetius followed Scotus in teaching that God had alternative possibilities. He could do *p* or not *p*.

Furthermore, the Utrecht School claims that man also has this type of freedom. Van Asselt, Bac, and te Velde write:

> In the classic triad of natural, moral and spiritual freedom, the Fall causes damage or loss of moral and spiritual freedom (man can no longer do the good of love God): the natural freedom by which man's will can choose between opposites without being necessitated towards one of both, remains after the fall. This natural freedom is essential to man, in the sense that without this freedom he would no longer be man as a rational and responsible creature.[108]

---

106. Van Asselt et al., *Reformed Thought on Freedom*, 47. This claim is disputed by Paul Helm. His objection is that the presence of these distinction in the writings of the reformed orthodox do not in themselves provide evidence of a presupposed synchronic contingency. He writes: "It is hard to see how these various distinctions taken by themselves, suggest an ontology of synchronic contingency, or presuppose a particular view of contingency, synchronic contingency, as claimed. And even when the examples considered are those of human actions, it does not follow that a writer in using them has synchronic contingency in mind. For instance, he may simply be disambiguating certain expressions to avoid possible misunderstandings. These various distinctions cannot be the criteria of the presence of the freedom of synchronic contingency" (Helm, "Reformed Thought on Freedom," 191).

107. Beck, "Gisbertus Voetius (1589–1676)," 216.

108. Van Asselt et al., *Reformed Thought on Freedom*, 235. J. Martin Bac argues that because we are created in God's image, man also has freedom like God's to choose from alternatives at the same time. He writes: "Since human persons are created in the

DECREE, FOREKNOWLEDGE, AND PROVIDENCE

This would appear to be an affirmation of principle 2. However, it will become apparent that the Utrecht School is really not affirming principle 2. Beck and Vos state their claim even more clearly:

> Moreover, it is still true according to this definition that "the entire history of the universe, up to the point of our choice, is consistent either with our performing of that action or with our refraining from it." This "sense of freedom" that Helm himself considers as being "incompatible with determinism," is surely not rejected by Voetius.[109]

Beck and Vos are making the argument that the reformed orthodox, and Voetius in particular here, advocated this type of freedom. We can see how this appears to match principle 2. Principle 2 stated, "An agent S does X freely only if S could have done otherwise than X given C, (God's decree, providence, and foreknowledge)." In Beck and Vos's words, "The entire history of the universe up to the point of our choice" includes everything in the past including God's decree, providence, and foreknowledge. Our performing or not performing an action is consistent with this entire history of the universe. In other words, we could have the same past (God's decree, providence, and foreknowledge) but a different future. We will see towards the end of this section that the Utrecht School has stated its claim ambiguously. It turns out that they really do not affirm principle 2.

At this stage, we have been dealing only with the historical claim that the reformed orthodox followed Scotus's doctrine of synchronic contingency. In response to this, we need to point out that many scholars disagree with the Utrecht School that the reformed orthodox were generally Scotists and that they presupposed synchronic contingency. This fact casts doubt on the historical claim made by the Utrecht School. Muller argues that the reformed orthodox were not Scotists, generally speaking, but eclectic:

> The large number of reformed denials of univocity of being calls into question both the positive and the negative readings of the Reformation as foundationally Scotist in its philosophical directions. Against the positive approach of Vos, Beck, Bac, and others, we must offer a partial verdict, inasmuch as the absence of one key Scotist theme, although it undermines their unqualified identification of Reformed theology as Scotist, does

---

image of God, their finite and created freedom reflects the infinite and uncreated divine freedom. Just like divine freedom, human freedom elicits possibilities to be actualized" (Bac, *Perfect Will Theology*, 420).

109. Beck and Vos, "Conceptual Patterns," 228. Notice also that this is a very similar claim to that of Richard Muller at the beginning of this section.

not demonstrate the absence of other Scotisms. Rather it points toward the generally eclectic reception of mediaeval materials on the part of the early modern reformed.[110]

Muller makes it even more clear:

> Reformed theology of the orthodox era reflects primarily the later medieval and Renaissance modifications of Christian philosophy (again, Thomist, Scotist, and nominalist) and only secondarily a classic Aristotelianism. It is certainly more useful to characterize many of the Reformed orthodox as holding a form of modified (sometimes highly modified) Thomism often with Scotistic or nominalistic accents, sometimes with strong affinities for the philosophies of the day, whether that of Suarez or of Descartes, than to speak of them as simply Aristotelian.[111]

So, we see that the reformed orthodox were not Scotist, but eclectic. In fact, some scholars argue that they were eclectic but leaned in the Thomist direction, as Muller mentioned above. John Patrick Donnelly writes:

> The theology of Vermigli and Zanchi, together with parallel developments within Lutheranism, show that when Protestants came to recast their theology into a scholastic form, they rather consistently avoided nominalism as a base. Insofar as the roots of Protestant scholasticism go back to the Middle Ages, they tend to go back to the *via antiqua* and Thomism. Protestant fruit grows quite well on the Thomist tree, even better than on the bad nominalist tree.[112]

---

110. Muller, "Not Scotist," 146. Muller also writes: "Reformed theology was not, after all, definitively attached to a particular version of the Aristotelian tradition, nor was it (as Roman Catholic theology) attached to the thought and the major teaching traditions of the monastic and mendicant orders. Citation of older theological and philosophical materials by the Reformed thinkers of the early orthodox era manifests both a broad interest in such as Aquinas, Durandus, Scotus, Gregory of Rimini, Thomas of Strasborg, and William of Ockham and highly eclectic appropriation of materials. The same can be said the use of contemporary Roman Catholic thinkers like Suarez or Banez. These observations concerning an eclectic rootedness in the past are applicable also to the other theological and philosophical movements of the seventeenth century" (Muller, "Reformation, Orthodoxy," 319).

111. Muller, "Reformation, Orthodoxy," 323.

112. Donnelly, "Calvinist Thomism," 454. Donnelley writes again: "In fact Zanchi's "summa" gives the impression of his being closer to Thomas than he really was. The first three tomes of his "summa" deal with the Trinity, the nature of God and creation. While their methodologies were very different, Thomas and Calvin were largely in agreement on these subjects. Mainly Thomas took up many questions that Calvin avoided. In most of this vast area of theology there was no sharp conflict between Thomism and Calvinist orthodoxy" (Donnelly, "Calvinist Thomism," 451).

We are to conclude from these statements that generally speaking, it is doubtful that the reformed orthodox were Scotists. Muller seems to be right in arguing that they were eclectic, even modified, Thomists.

The Utrecht School makes the further claim that the reformed orthodox followed Scotus with his doctrine of synchronic contingency. As we did above, we need to point out that this is highly disputed. When it comes to the idea of contingency, scholars disagree that the reformed orthodox were Scotist. John Fesko writes:

> There is debate in the secondary literature over two issues: (1) whether Reformed orthodoxy taught contingency; and (2) to what degree the Reformed were influenced by Duns Scotus. . . . For the second issue, the influence of Duns Scotus seems to be a bit overstated, as Twisse, for example, appeals both to Aquinas and to Duns Scotus on matters of contingency. As others have argued, the Reformed were quite eclectic.[113]

---

113. Fesko, *Theology of the Westminster Standards*, 103n20. Carl Trueman writes on this matter: "Prominent among those in this field has been Utrecht philosopher-theologian, Antonie Vos, who . . . has done significant work in demonstrating the dependence of Reformed theology upon medieval metaphysics right from its inception in the work of men such as John Calvin. Vos has argued consistently for a strong Scotist dimension to Reformed thought, particularly as this manifests itself in a commitment to what he has called *synchronic contingency,* a way of construing the relation between God and creation which allows for divine sovereignty and yet avoids both the Scylla of determinism and the Charybdis of human autonomy. While Vos's work has proved to be of immense value in opening up discussion of Reformed theology in a manner not tainted at the outset with the anti-metaphysical prejudices of modern thought, my own view is that his case for the absolute fundamental importance of Scotism, almost to the exclusion of other options, needs to be balanced by acknowledgment of other influences and issues. . . . For this reason, I myself am convinced that, whatever the undoubted contemporary systematic gains to be made by emphasizing Scotist contingency in such a vigorous fashion, the historian needs to be open to a more flexible, eclectic model of metaphysical influence when approaching the Reformed Orthodox in order to produce a proper contextual and historical account. . . . A nuanced historical approach which is properly sympathetic to the work of Vos but which also seeks to do justice to the eclectic nature of Reformed Orthodoxy is thus offered by Sebastian Rehnman, the Swedish scholar, in his study of John Owen's theological prolegomena. He helpfully characterizes his subject as holding to a Scotistically modified Thomism. While this Thomistic dimension does not mark Owen out as distinctive, being typical of theological discourse which was sensitive to the revitalized Thomism of the Renaissance" (Trueman, *John Owen*, 57–58).

In fact, Trueman goes on to talk about how Owen's Thomism is determinism. He writes: "The continuation and development of medieval metaphysical discussion, along with its technical conceptual vocabulary, was to prove a most useful phenomenon for the Reformed Orthodox, and Owen's own exposure to this at Oxford was to bear significant fruit in his own theology. For example, take the issue of contingency. Owen's use of an established Thomisitc argument from the nature of being to the necessity of

Of course, this debate cannot be settled here. The point to take away is that the Utrecht School's claim that the reformed orthodox were Scotists, and in particular adopted his view of synchronic contingency, is highly disputed. In fact, Sebastian Rehnman considers it the minority view. He writes:

> In recent years a small group of scholars has attempted to make a questionable interpretation of John Duns Scotus into a central dogma of the Reformed orthodox doctrine of God.[114]

In light of this, we conclude that the Utrecht School's claim that the reformed orthodox held to Scotus's doctrine of synchronic contingency is suspect. This means that we cannot simply assume that when the reformed orthodox speak about contingency, they mean synchronic contingency.

(2) The Reformed Orthodox Were Not Determinists

The second claim that the Utrecht School makes is that the reformed orthodox were not determinists. Let's begin by asking what they mean by determinism. Beck and Vos write:

> We mean by the term "determinism" absolute or "hard" determinism in the sense of necessitarianism.[115]

Bac understands determinism as emanationism. He writes,

---

all created being deriving its reality from one supreme entity, points clearly towards a basic determinism, one which is most conducive to what he sees as the Bible's teaching about the sovereignty of God, and for which he is happy to offer exegetical justifications. Yet uses of specifically metaphysical argumentation and medieval distinctions enables Owen to nuance this determinism in a way which represents a clear advance on the somewhat bald statements of earlier generations of Protestants" (Trueman, *John Owen*, 59–60). Thus, according to Trueman, the reformed orthodox, like Owen, generally thought of 'contingency' along the lines of Thomas. In personal correspondence, he wrote, "I think the Westminster divines are by and large Thomists (albeit Scotistically modified at point) and that contingency is a matter of secondary causality a la Thomas." This is different from the synchronic contingency advocated by Vos. Trueman makes this clear in the following: "The difference between the absolute necessity of God's existence and the contingent necessity of the existence of any given creation. And this distinction fulfils a similar purpose within Owen's Reformed Orthodox construction of the creator-creature relationship: created entities are contingent precisely because they do not have to exist in the way that God, the one *necessary* being has to exist" (Trueman, *John Owen*, 60). Thus "contingency" is not understood by Owen and other Reformed orthodox as synchronic contingency.

114. Rehnman, "Doctrine of God," 353n1.
115. Beck and Vos, "Conceptual Patterns," 225.

DECREE, FOREKNOWLEDGE, AND PROVIDENCE 123

> Vos elaborates on some of de Rijk's interpretations of medieval scholasticism as developing a Christian philosophy that radically departed from ancient philosophy. Inspired by their Christian faith they wished to overcome the necessitarian philosophy of Aristotle by developing new terminist logic, which enabled a logical and semantic analysis of language, scholasticism being the first kind of conceptual analysis. Hereby, ancient emanative philosophy was transformed into a metaphysic of radical contingency in all created being.[116]

They also seem to understand it in terms of stoic fate:

> The Reformed account of predestination and providence was held to imply "Stoic fate." Ever since, a deterministic interpretation of Reformed thought seemed obvious.[117]

They also seem to understand determinism in the sense that the universe could not be other than it is. They write:

> Here we can also distinguish the second consequence, namely, that the principle of plentitude leads to determinism. According to Aristotle's principle of plentitude, the history of the eternal world cannot develop except in the way it has developed. This too, is denied in Christian thought. God created the world according to the determination of His will, and that determination is free. He also could have created another world. God disposes of more possibilities than those that are actually realized. There is more potential than that which is finally actualized.[118]

They also seem to understand determinism as a denial of PAP, or principle 2, as we have been denying it. They write:

> De Moor emphasizes that *rational* spontaneity should not be confounded with spontaneity as such (called *natural* spontaneity by others). Spontaneity as such refers to acts which originate from an internal principle (they are not externally coacted), but still it is possible that the agents do not have any choice (for instance, animals that are driven by their own instinct to eat, but do not have the choice to do otherwise). When the Reformed position is interpreted in this way, it could easily be integrated

---

116. Bac, *Perfect Will Theology*, 11.

117. Van Asselt et al., *Reformed Thought on Freedom*, 15. They write again, "The concept of determinism was denoted by other terms like 'Stoic fate'" (Van Asselt et al., *Reformed Thought on Freedom*, 31).

118. Van Asselt, *Introduction to Reformed Scholasticism*, 38.

in a deterministic system. Then man can be determined (e.g., by God's providence and predestination) and have no real possibility to do otherwise, but still act spontaneously. However, rational spontaneity requires not only an internal principle which is not coacted upon but a *rational* internal principle, which acts on (grounds of) both the judgment of reason and the "pleasure/compliance" of the will. Hereby, man always has free choice, so this possibility to choose whichever he like. Thus rational spontaneity grants real freedom to man and provides him with the opportunity of a real choice.[119]

By determinism they mean five things: First, absolute or hard determinism; second, emanationism; third, stoic fate; fourth that the universe could not have developed otherwise; and fifth, a denial of PAP or principle 2. I have argued that the Westminster Confession and Catechisms are deterministic, but it is important to say that I do not mean this in senses one through four. I only mean this in sense five. I have argued that the Westminster Standards exclude PAP or principle 2.

Yet, this should not be problematic since there is a common definition of determinism to which the Westminster Confession and Catechisms line up. In addition to this, many reformed theologians have understood reformed theology to be deterministic in this sense. Hence, the Utrecht School is not correct to claim that reformed theology is not deterministic in this sense.

It would be helpful to understand what I mean by reformed theology being deterministic. Robert Kane points out that doctrines of determinism have historically taken different forms. However, he identifies a core idea that unites them all:

> An event (such as a choice or action) is *determined* when there are conditions obtaining earlier (such as the decrees of fate or the foreordaining acts of God or antecedent causes plus laws of nature) whose occurrence is a sufficient condition for the occurrence of the event. In other words, it must be the case that, *if* these earlier determining conditions obtain, then the determined event will occur.[120]

---

119. Van Asselt et al., *Reformed Thought on Freedom*, 221–22.

120. Kane, *Contemporary Introduction to Free Will*, 5–6. John Frame also notes the variety of types of determinism: "Determinists believe that every event (or every event in a certain category) has a cause that makes it happen exactly as it happens. Among the varieties of determinism are the views of (1) Plato, who holds that one's ethical choices are determined by his view of the good; (2) B. F. Skinner, who believes that stimuli, dispositions and motives govern all human behavior; (3) Democritus, Hobbes,

As we have seen, the Westminster Standards fall into this category. They teach that God decrees whatsoever comes to pass. This is the "earlier determining condition." Once God decrees something to come to pass, it comes to pass or "the determined event will occur." Thus, the Westminster Confession and Catechisms qualify as deterministic on this definition of determinism. This definition of determinism is the hypothetical necessity that the reformed tradition also taught.

Kane is clearer that determinism is conditional or hypothetical necessity. He writes:

> Determinism is thus a kind of necessity, but it is a conditional necessity. A determined event does not have to occur, no matter what else happens (it need not be *absolutely* necessary). But it must occur when the determining conditions have occurred.[121]

As we have seen, reformed teaching on the decree, providence, and foreknowledge is hypothetical necessity. With regard to the decree and providence, the reformed tradition taught that these had the necessity of immutability. With regard to foreknowledge, the reformed tradition taught that this had the necessity of infallibility. This means that the reformed tradition held to a type of determinism, namely theological determinism.

The *Cambridge Dictionary of Philosophy* defines theological determinism:

> But there is also *theological determinism,* which holds that God determines everything that happens or that, since God has perfect knowledge about the universe, only the course of events that he knows will happen, will happen.[122]

The Westminster Confession and Catechisms teach that God both decrees and foreknows everything that happens. This is why Frame argues that the Westminster Confession advocates a type of theological determinism:

> This seems to be the position of the *Westminster Confession of Faith*, which says that "God did . . . ordain whatsoever comes to

---

Spinoza, and many others, who hold that every event in the universe is determined by a physical cause. Of special interest to us are (4) theological determinists, who hold that all events occur exactly as God had foreordained them. Note that it is possible to be a determinist in sense (4) without being a determinist in any of the previous senses" (Frame, "Determinism, Chance, and Freedom," 218).

121. Kane, *Contemporary Introduction to Free Will*, 6.
122. Audi, *Cambridge Dictionary of Philosophy*, 198.

pass," but also says that man's will is neither forced, nor, by any absolute necessity of nature, determined to good or evil.[123]

They also teach that God knows everything and therefore he knows what will happen. Crisp also notes that reformed theology is deterministic and compatibilistic:

> According to the Reformed, human beings are free only in the compatibilist sense, that is, in a way that is consistent with divine determinism. God determines all human actions according to his divine decree. But all human acts are also free insofar as (1) they are the actions of the creaturely agent, not God, and (2) they are actions chosen by the creaturely agent without any coercion or interference from other agents. It is no part of this account of creaturely freedom that the agent in question could have refrained from acting as she did. All that is required is that if the agent were to have chosen differently, she would have had the power to choose differently, provided the alternative in question was one that the agent would have had the power to choose had she so chosen. In this way the conjunction of (1) and (2) is commensurate with God's absolute predestination of all that comes to pass.[124]

We see from this discussion that there are different definitions of the word determinism. The Westminster Confession, Catechisms, and the reformed tradition fall into the category of determinism as hypothetical necessity. Thus, there is a legitimate sense in which we should call reformed theology deterministic. However, the Utrecht School argues that reformed theology is not deterministic. We have seen that this is largely a terminological difference. One can affirm determinism as outlined by Kane, Frame, Crisp, and *The Cambridge Dictionary of Philosophy* without affirming absolute determinism, emanationism, Stoic fate, and the impossibility of the universe developing other than it has.

The only understanding of determinism that would conflict with what has been argued is the affirmation of PAP or principle 2. The Utrecht School seems to define determinism as also a denial of PAP. Given their claim that the reformed orthodox affirmed synchronic contingency, one can understand why they would say reformed theology is not deterministic. They appear to think that the reformed orthodox affirm principle 2.

In response to this, we should point out that we have seen that it is not the case that the Westminster Standards affirm synchronic contingency or

123. Frame, "Determinism, Chance, and Freedom," 218.
124. Crisp, *Jonathan Edwards On God and Creation*, 58.

principle 2. Also, it is disputable that the reformed orthodox affirm synchronic contingency. It is also not the case that they affirm principle 2. Furthermore, when we examine the Utrecht School's position, we will find that they also do not affirm principle 2. Thus, we are not compelled to think that reformed theology is not determinism in the fifth sense identified by the Utrecht School.

For example, Turretin represents the reformed tradition as teaching theological determinism. He affirms hypothetical necessity. He writes, "Does the decree necessitate future things? We affirm."[125] He continues:

> On the state of the question, observe: (1) that a thing is said to be necessary which cannot be otherwise. . . . Now this can be viewed in two ways: either in God or in the things themselves. In God, a twofold necessity is commonly remarked: the one absolute, the opposite of which is simply impossible to God (as when God is said to be incorruptible and incapable of denying himself); another hypothetical, arising from the hypothesis of the divine decree which, being made the effect itself willed, must necessarily follow. . . . This last is again twofold: one of immutability from the immutable decree; another of infallibility from his infallible foreknowledge.[126]

Turretin is affirming hypothetical necessity and thus theological determinism. He is saying that whatever God decrees must come to pass necessarily. He is clearer:

> The reasons are: (1) All things were decreed of God by an eternal and unchangeable counsel; hence they cannot but take place in the appointed time; otherwise the counsel of God would be changed, which the Scriptures declare to be impossible.[127]

---

125. Turretin, *Institutes of Elenctic Theology*, 319.

126. Turretin, *Institutes of Elenctic Theology*, 320. Carl Trueman also mentions a basic determinism that was inherited in the reformed tradition through Thomas Aquinas: "The continuation and development of medieval metaphysical discussion, along with its technical vocabulary, was to prove a most useful phenomenon for the Reformed Orthodox, and Owen's exposure to this at Oxford was to bear significant fruit in his own theology. For example, take the issue of contingency. Owen's use of an established Thomistic argument from the nature of being to the necessity of all created being deriving its reality from one supreme entity, points clearly towards a basic determinism, one which is most conducive to what he sees as the Bible's teaching about the sovereignty of God, and for which he is happy to offer exegetical justification. Yet use of specifically metaphysical argumentation and medieval distinctions enable Owen to nuance this determinism in a way which represents a clear advance on the somewhat bald statements of earlier generations of Protestants" (Trueman, *John Owen*, 59–60).

127. Turretin, *Institutes of Elenctic Theology*, 320. Aza Goudriaan argues that

Turretin also denies PAP or principle 2 when he says "hence they cannot but take place." This is another way of saying that given God's decree, the agent could not do otherwise. This is theological determinism as taught by one of the foremost reformed orthodox. Turretin also affirms this via foreknowledge:

> (4) As all things are foreseen by an infallible foreknowledge (Acts 15:18; Heb 4:13), so they must necessarily happen infallibly. (5) They are certainly predicted as future so that the word of God cannot fail, nor can Scripture be broken. Therefore they must happen necessarily, if not as to the mode of production (which is often contingent), still as to the certainty of the event (which cannot be otherwise).[128]

Turretin denies PAP or principle 2 in relation to God's foreknowledge when he says "which cannot be otherwise." In other words, man cannot do other than God foreknows. He also denies libertarian freedom. He writes:

> We contend here against the Jesuits, Socinians, and Remonstrants who (following Pelagius) place the essence of free will in indifference (*adiaphoria*) and are wont to define it as "the faculty by which all things requisite for acting being posited, the will can act or not act." Now those are called requisites to action without which the action cannot be performed (such as the decree of God and his concourse; the judgment of the mind; and other circumstances which belong here).[129]

Paul Helm identifies the view that Turretin is denying as libertarian free will:

Gisbertus Voetius also affirm theological determinism. He writes: "Events in the created world, such as the end of a person's life, are necessary in the sense of this fourth kind of necessity, that is to say, they are necessary not in themselves, but for a reason that is external to created beings, namely by a necessity 'of *infallibility* because of God's prescience, and of *immutability* because of God's will or decree.' It is *necessary* that a particular person dies at a particular hour, in the sense that it is infallibly known by God and immutably decreed by Him. Voetius thus clearly endorses what could be called the theological determinism of Reformed theology or, in a formulation of Norman S. Fiering, 'the divine determinism of the Protestants': everything is ultimately determined by God and thus necessary with a 'not absolute, intrinsic, but only hypothetical, extrinsic, and respective necessity.' . . . Yet he rejects the view of God as the sole cause of everything, and accordingly he defends not only the theological necessity of events, but also their simultaneous contingency" (Goudriaan, *Reformed Orthodoxy and Philosophy*, 150–51).

128. Turretin, *Institutes of Elenctic Theology*, 320.
129. Turretin, *Institutes of Elenctic Theology*, 665.

This view is very similar to versions of what in modern philosophy is referred to as libertarian freedom, or perhaps better as "contra-causal freedom" and which in the eighteenth century was referred to (by David Hume and others) as the "liberty of indifference."[130]

From this discussion, we see that the Westminster Confession and Catechisms teach theological determinism. We also see that the reformed tradition is committed to theological determinism as a hypothetical necessity. In addition to this, Turretin represents the reformed orthodox as denying PAP or principle 2. This means that the Utrecht School's claims that the reformed orthodox were not determinists are false.

(3) Textual Evidence Used By The Utrecht School

The third claim of the Utrecht School is that the texts of the reformed orthodox presuppose synchronic contingency. Let us remind ourselves of what synchronic contingency means. Beck and Vos define it clearly:

> Moreover, it is still true according to this definition that "the entire history of the universe, up to the point of our choice, is consistent either with our performance of that action or with our refraining from it."[131]

Van Asselt, Bac, and te Velde define it similarly:

---

130. Helm, "Reformed Thoughts on Freedom," 193n8. Martinus Vitringa also notes: "The view of most Reformed theologians concerning the formal character of freedom amounts to this. In the negative sense it consists in immunity from coercion, [natural] force and natural necessity, and positively [it consists] in rational freedom by which it acts spontaneously on the basis of the practical judgment of reason. The papists, however, and in particular Jesuits, Socinians and Arminians, want the nature of freedom to be located in indifference toward both opposites [i.e., alternatives], and they describe it as a power that is active by its intrinsic force and as an indifferent nature so that, when all requisites for acting are met, it nevertheless can act or act not, or [can] do this or that" (Vitringa quoted in Goudriaan, *Reformed Orthodoxy and Philosophy*, 174). Thus, we see that most early Reformed theologians denied the alternative possibilities condition also.

Aza Goudriaan also notes that the early reformed orthodox were compatibilists: "Voetuis, Van Mastricht, and Driessen all represent what in modern terminology has been termed 'soft determinism' or 'compatibilism,' by claiming 'that freedom and determinism are compatible with each other, and thus the truth of determinism does not eliminate freedom'" (Goudriaan, *Reformed Orthodoxy and Philosophy*, 187).

131. Beck and Vos, "Conceptual Patterns," 228.

> Synchronic contingency means that for one moment of time, there is a true alternative for the state of affairs that actually occurs.[132]

Helm also defines it as:

> The agent is free in the synchronically contingent sense if at the moment that the agent chooses A (when the world is in state S) it is possible that at that very moment (the world being in state S) the agent chooses not-A instead.[133]

Moving back to Beck and Vos's, definition we could clarify it as follows: suppose that P = the entire history of the world. P includes things such as God's decree, providence, foreknowledge, and the actual course of the world up to the moment of choice. Beck and Vos define synchronic contingency as given P and agent can do X or not X. Given God's decree, providence, and foreknowledge, the agent could choose X or not X. This is what we have been referring to as PAP or principle 2.

There are two lines of evidence in the texts of the reformed orthodox to which the Utrecht School appealed. They are (1) texts that make use of certain logical and syntactical distinctions and (2) texts that appeal to the notion of indifference. We see their affirmation of (1) when Van Asselt, Bac, and te Velde write:

> The ontological analysis by logical distinctions like the necessity of the consequence/consequent, the volitional analysis by logical distinctions like first and second act or divided and compound sense and the analysis of freedom by the distinctions of freedom of contrariety and contradiction all seem to suggest an ontology of synchronic contingency. These distinctions all presuppose that contingency is not a matter of temporal change, but of simultaneous logical alternatives. Among other things, the subsequent chapters will test in which respects this initial hypothesis is confirmed or questioned by textual evidence.[134]

It is neither claimed that the reformed orthodox used the terminology of synchronic contingency, nor is it claimed that they explicitly advocated the doctrine of synchronic contingency. Instead, it is claimed that they presupposed it. The evidence for this presupposition is found in the use of the reformed orthodoxy's above-mentioned distinction.

---

132. Van Asselt et al., *Reformed Thought on Freedom*, 41.
133. Helm, "'Structural Indifference' and Compatibilism," 185.
134. Van Asselt et al., *Reformed Thought on Freedom*, 47.

DECREE, FOREKNOWLEDGE, AND PROVIDENCE

In response, Helm argues that the use of these distinctions is not evidence of a presupposed synchronic contingency. He writes:

> It is hard to see how these various distinctions, taken by themselves, suggest an ontology of synchronic contingency, or presuppose a particular view of contingency, synchronic contingency, as it is claimed. And even when the examples considered are those of human action, it does not follow that a writer in using them has synchronic contingency in mind. For instance, he may simply be disambiguating certain expressions to avoid possible misunderstanding. These various distinctions cannot be the criteria of the presence of the freedom of synchronic contingency.[135]

Helm's argument is that the use of these types of distinctions in themselves do not necessarily indicate a presupposed synchronic contingency. The reason is that the use of these distinctions has many purposes, none of which must be taken as evidence of synchronic contingency.

For example, he takes the distinction between the necessity of the consequence and the necessity of the consequent and applies it to an apple:

> Yet the distinction itself is purely logical or syntactical, and covers many different kinds of examples. The apple's being on the plate does not make any reference to human actions, any more than does Calvin's example of the physical make-up of bones. The use of the distinction is not a presupposition of the freedom of synchronic contingency or only applicable to such cases of contingency.[136]

Helm's argument is that this distinction can be applied to many things that have nothing to do with human action or the question of free will or synchronic contingency. Since this is the case, the mere appearance of this distinction is not evidence of a presupposed synchronic contingency. This is not sufficient evidence to establish the Utrecht School's conclusion.

Another example Helm uses is with the distinction between the divided and the compound sense. This distinction is used to clarify ambiguous sentences. For example, "Socrates sits and runs." This could be interpreted in two ways:

> First, one could interpret the sentence diachronically: Socrates sits at t0 and runs at t1. However, our authors prefer an interpretation in terms of modality. A valid interpretation is in the

---

135. Helm, "Reformed Thought on Freedom," 191.
136. Helm, "Reformed Thought on Freedom," 188.

divided sense: Socrates sits at to and it is *possible* that he runs at to. The same is invalid in the compound sense: it is not possible that (Socrates sits at to and Socrates runs at to).[137]

Helm's response is that "the same options are open in the case of states of affairs where the nature of freedom is not an issue."[138] The distinction could also be applied to inanimate objects such as apples. This causes Helm to conclude:

> Once again, these examples and the resolution of their ambiguity seem to have nothing necessarily to do with human action. So their deployment by a writer is not in and of itself an indication that the writer thinks of human freedom in terms of synchronic rather than diachronic contingency. These are general logical and syntactical distinctions with universal application.[139]

Helm's argument is convincing. The mere presence of these logical and syntactical distinctions does not necessarily indicate the presupposition of synchronic contingency. The Utrecht School's reasoning along these lines is not sufficient to demonstrate their conclusion that the reformed orthodox presupposed synchronic contingency. Helm's counterargument is strengthened when we take into consideration that it is doubtful that the reformed orthodox taught synchronic contingency and the fact that the reformed tradition is theological determinism. In light of these facts, there appears to be little to no evidence for a presupposed synchronic contingency.

The second line of evidence that the Utrecht School uses is in reformed orthodox texts that appeal to indifference. Helm says that this is the most promising line of reasoning for their position. He writes:

> By far the most promising sign of the presence of the freedom of synchronic contingency present in the writings of the Reformed Scholastics is the term "indifference," (*indifferentia*) used in discussion of the human will and of human freedom. We shall find later on that there are such favourable uses, but as the term itself is somewhat ambiguous, as between the will and the freedom of the will, the presence of the word as such is not decisive. It may be used in such a way as not to commit the writer to freedom in the synchronic sense, for the use of the

---

137. Van Asselt et al., *Reformed Thought on Freedom*, 47.
138. Helm, "Reformed Thought on Freedom," 189.
139. Helm, "Reformed Thought on Freedom," 189.

term may be consistent with compatibilism and so inconsistent with the freedom of indifference.[140]

Helm agrees that there are uses of the term indifference in the reformed orthodox tradition; however, he disagrees that this usage is evidence of synchronic contingency. We can see a standard reformed orthodox usage of indifference in Turretin. He writes:

> Hence it is evident that it is not inquired here concerning indifference in the first act or in the divided sense, as to simultaneity of power which is called passive and objective (to wit, whether the will considered absolutely from its natural constitution, the requisites to action being withdrawn, is determinable to various objects and holds itself indifferently towards them). We do not deny that the will of itself is so prepared that it can either elicit or suspend the act (which is the liberty of exercise and of contradiction) or be carried to both of opposite things (which is the liberty of contrariety and of specification). We also confess that the will is indifferent as long as the intellect remains doubtful and uncertain whither to turn itself. But concerning indifference in the second act and in the compound sense (as to simultaneity of power called active and subjective)—whether the will (all requisites to acting being posited; for example the decree of God and his concourse; the judgment of the practical intellect, etc.) is always so indifferent and undeterminable that it can act or not act. This our opponents pretend in order that its own liberty may be left to the will. We deny it.[141]

Turretin argues that the reformed orthodox affirm indifference in the divided sense, but deny indifference in the compound sense. The divided sense is speaking about the will in itself. It is the will in the abstract with the requisites for action being withdrawn. Turretin understands the requisites for action that are withdrawn as follows:

> Now those are called requisites to action without which the action cannot be performed (such as the decree of God and his concourse; the judgment of the mind; and other circumstances which belong here).[142]

Turretin affirms that the will is indifferent in the divided sense and the divided sense means that the will is abstracted from certain conditions. It

---

140. Helm, "Reformed Thought on Freedom," 191.
141. Turretin, *Institutes of Elenctic Theology*, 665–66.
142. Turretin, *Institutes of Elenctic Theology*, 665.

means the will is considered apart from God's decree, providence (concourse), judgment of the mind, and other circumstances (or past history of the world). It is important to see that Turretin seems to clearly deny synchronic contingency as defined by the Utrecht School. They defined it as follows:

> Moreover, it is still true according to this definition that "the entire history of the universe, up to the point of our choice, is consistent either with our performance of that action or with our refraining from it."[143]

This is teaching that the will has the freedom of indifference given the entire history of the world up to the point of choice. This means that the Utrecht School seems to affirm that the will has the freedom of indifference even when the requisites for action are in place. Turretin affirmed indifference only when these requisites were withdrawn. These two positions appear to be substantially different. Turretin argues that the reformed orthodox are denying what the Utrecht School appears to affirm.

Turretin goes on to define the compound sense. He argues that the reformed orthodox deny indifference in this compound sense. As we read in the above quotation from Turretin, he understands the compound sense to be the will with the requisites for action being posited. The difference between the divided sense and the compound sense is that in the divided sense, the will is considered with the requisites for action withdrawn. In the compound sense, the requisites for action are present. When the will is thought of in the compound sense, the will is considered with God's decree, providence, judgment of the intellect, and other circumstances being present. In this sense, Turretin clearly says that the reformed orthodox deny indifference. This compound sense appears to be indistinguishable from the Utrecht School's notion of synchronic contingency. Turretin clearly says that the reformed orthodox deny this sense.

The reformed orthodox deny indifference in the compound sense but affirm it in the divided sense. Andreas Beck, however, wants to deny that synchronic contingency is similar to the compound sense. In order to show this, he provides a unique interpretation of the divided sense which he argues affirms synchronic contingency. He writes:

> The will decides to select B [from A, B, and C], **and it is possible that the will decides to select A or** C (divided sense).[144]

---

143. Beck and Vos, "Conceptual Patterns," 228.
144. Helm, "'Structural Indifference' and Compatibilism," 197.

Beck claims that this is an interpretation of the divided sense that distinguishes it from the compound sense but also affirms synchronic contingency.

Helm responds by arguing that this is not an accurate interpretation of the reformed orthodox. He writes:

> For such an interpretation does not make it clear that Turretin, Voetius, and the RO in general have in mind the will *in itself*, in the divided sense, and not what is true once all the requisites for the action are in place, the compound sense.[145]

Helm is correct that this interpretation of the divided sense looks very much like the compound sense. If the will decides to select B, then this means that the requisites for action were in place. Otherwise, the will could not decide. However, Beck goes on to say "and it is possible that the will decides to select A or C (divided sense)."[146] This sounds like a reiteration of the compound sense, which the reformed orthodox deny.

Beck wants to deny that this is the compound sense. In order to further distinguish his divided sense from the compound sense, he clarifies what he means by the word 'possible' in his divided sense formulation. It is this clarification that will ultimately show that the Utrecht School really does not affirm principle 2. He writes:

> True: in every possible world in which RA is true A is true as well. But still A is contingently true in these possible worlds, as RA is contingent, that is, there is at least one close pw (possible world) in which A is not true (nor RA, of course) . . . to say that A, which is true in pw1 at time t1 is contingent, is equivalent to saying that there is at least one pw X in which A is not true at time t1.[147]

Beck is arguing that the word 'possible' in his formulation of the divided sense does not mean possible in the same world in which "if RA, then A" is true. The compound sense would affirm that the word 'possible' means possible in the same world in which "if RA, then A" was true. Beck clearly denies this and shows that his formulation of the divided sense is not the same as the compound sense. Perhaps we could clarify his meaning by providing an alternative formulation of his divided sense. It would read as follows:

---

145. Helm, "'Structural Indifference' and Compatibilism," 200.
146. Helm, "'Structural Indifference' and Compatibilism," 200.
147. Helm, "'Structural Indifference' and Compatibilism," 198.

The will decides to select B [from A, B, and C] **and there exists a different, close possible world in which the will decides to select A or C (divided sense).**

The advantage of this formulation is that it distinguishes it from the compound sense and it clarifies that Beck's use of the word 'possible' refers to a different possible world. This formulation would enable him to affirm,

(1) [ ] (If RA then, A)

(2) RA

(C) not A

He could do this because there is at least one close possible world where not A is true. The exact sense of the word 'possible' in his divided sense is not with reference to the world "if RA, then A," but in a close possible world. In this way, he hopes to secure the contingency of A, even if it is true that "if RA, then A."

Helm responds that this is a misunderstanding. He writes:

> However, there appears to be some misunderstanding here. The contingency of *If RA then A* is due solely to the fact that *If RA then A* is true in only some possible worlds. The contingent truth *If RA then A* is secured if *If RA then A* is true in the actual world alone, and (more generally) if it is true in at least one possible world.[148]

Helm is arguing that the contingency of A is secured because "If RA then A" is true in some possible worlds.

Furthermore, Helm points out that Beck affirms truths that undermine synchronic contingency. Helm writes:

> Beck correctly maintains that for Voetius RA "strictly implies" A. . . . So, in all possible worlds in which RA, then A. For how could it be that there is at least one possible world in which RA strictly implies A, and not-A obtain, given that in any possible world in in which RA is true A must be true?[149]

Helm is arguing that Beck's formulation of the divided sense misses the point at issue. The question is not whether or not "not-A" is true in a different possible world. The issue is whether or not it is possible for "not-A" to be true in the world where "if RA strictly implies A" is true. If it is not possible that "not-A" be true in that world, then the will cannot

---

148. Helm, "'Structural Indifference' and Compatibilism," 198.
149. Helm, "'Structural Indifference' and Compatibilism," 197.

have alternative possibilities in that world. This is precisely what Helm and Fischer and Ravizza affirm. It is also something that Beck and the Utrecht School ought to clearly affirm.

Since Beck maintains that RA strictly implies A, this means that whenever RA is true then A must be true. Given the world *RA strictly implies A*, there is no possibility of *not-A*, otherwise RA would not strictly imply A. This is a denial of PAP or principle 2. Beck affirms this, but tries to give a different interpretation of the divided sense to secure a different sense of contingency for A. Helm argues that this misses the point.

Beck's affirmation that RA strictly implies A ends the argument. He has agreed to a proposition that excludes alternative possibilities in every world in which "if RA, then A" is true and this is a denial of PAP or principle 2. Furthermore, Beck's interpretation of the divided sense and my further clarification of that formulation do not accurately represent the reformed orthodox understanding of the divided sense. As we have seen, the divided sense for the reformed orthodox merely affirms that the will in the abstract is indifferent. Beck's formulation does not make this clear. Helm argues that a better way to formulate it is as follows:

> (3) The will of itself has the power to choose A or not-A, or to choose either A or B.[150]

In conclusion, the evidence that the Utrecht School uses to support synchronic contingency is weak. It is doubtful that the reformed orthodox were Scotists. It is not true that the reformed orthodox were not determinists and the evidence from the texts of the reformed orthodox do not show that they presupposed synchronic contingency. First, the logical and syntactical distinctions that the reformed orthodox used do not necessarily demonstrate a presupposition of synchronic contingency. Second, their use of the word indifference is not affirming synchronic contingency. It merely affirms the will's indifference in the abstract only.

Furthermore, as we have seen from the interaction between Beck and Helm, the Utrecht School does not really affirm principle 2. This means that they are theological determinists in the sense that I have argued. They use language that appears to affirm principle 2, but when pressed, they actually deny this. In the next chapter, we will see that the same is true of Muller.

---

150. Helm, "'Structural Indifference' and Compatibilism," 199.

Similarities between the Reformed Orthodox and Fischer and Ravizza

In summary, I would like to point out areas of formal similarities between Fischer and Ravizza and the reformed orthodox. The first area of formal similarity is that both deny the sourcehood and alternative possibilities conditions. Like Fischer and Ravizza, the reformed orthodox deny that an agent must be the ultimate source of his choice or actions in order to be free and morally responsible. The reformed orthodox ultimately trace the source of an agent's choice and action to God's decree, providence, and foreknowledge. In addition to this, the reformed orthodox also deny the alternative possibilities condition. God's decree, providence, and foreknowledge have a hypothetical necessity. This means that in relation to God's decree, providence, and foreknowledge, the agent's action is certain and cannot be otherwise. As we have seen, this is not an absolute necessity, but a hypothetical necessity. Therefore, the agent's choice and action remain contingent in itself.

In addition to the similarities between Fischer and Ravizza and the reformed orthodox on the sourcehood and alternative possibilities condition, we could point out another important similarity. It is regarding the indifference of the will. As we have seen, the reformed orthodox distinguish between the divided and the compound sense and the first act and the second act. Van Asselt, Bac, and te Velde write concerning this distinction:

> In the first act (*in actu primo*)/in the second act (*in actu secundo*): This distinction (used by Turettini and de Moor) parallels the anthropological distinction between potency (*facultas*) and act (*actus*). Abstracted from a concrete volition, the will is capable of willing opposite acts (*in actu primo*); involved in a concrete act, the will cannot simultaneously will opposite things.
>
> In the divided sense (*in sensu diviso/divisionis*)/in the compound sense (*in sensu composito/compositionis*). This distinction explains how two opposite acts are possible. A standard example is "Socrates sits and runs." As it stands this proposition contains an apparent contradiction (sitting and running). Several solutions for this difficulty are possible. First, one could interpret the sentence diachronically: Socrates sits at t0 and runs at t1. However, our authors prefer an interpretation in terms of modality. A valid interpretation in the divided sense: Socrates sits at t0 and it is *possible* that he runs at t0. The same is invalid in the compound sense: it is not possible that (Socrates sits at t0 & Socrates runs at t0).[151]

---

151. Van Asselt et al., *Reformed Thought on Freedom*, 47.

The divided sense and the first act are speaking about the will in the abstract. The reformed orthodox communicated this by saying that it is the will with the requisites for action being withdrawn. The compound sense and the second act are speaking about the will in concrete acts. The reformed orthodox communicated this by saying that this is the will with the requisites for action being present. The reformed orthodox distinguish between the will in the abstract or in itself and the will in the concrete instances of willing. In the former, the will is indifferent. In the latter, the will is not indifferent.

This distinction is formally similar to Fischer and Ravizza's contention that the agent's mechanism has alternative possibilities outside the actual sequence, but not in the actual sequence. Outside of the actual sequence is equivalent to the will in the divided sense or the first act. Outside of the actual sequence, the mechanism is considered in the abstract. It is abstracted from the actual sequence in order to explore other possible worlds in which the mechanism exists for the purpose of discovering its properties. Outside of the actual sequence, the mechanism is indifferent. This means that it could choose from a number of alternative possibilities.

The actual sequence is equivalent to the compound sense or the second act. The actual sequence is the mechanism in actual instances of willing. It is the mechanism with the requisites present. In this case, the mechanism is not indifferent. It cannot choose alternative possibilities.

This is formally similar to the reformed orthodox because there is the distinction between the will/mechanism in the abstract and the will/mechanism in the concrete. It is also formally similar because they both hold that in the abstract, the will/mechanism is indifferent and it can choose from alternative possibilities. In the concrete, the will/mechanism is not indifferent and it cannot choose from alternative possibilities. The difference is in the content of what the reformed orthodox would call the requisites. For the reformed orthodox, the requisites are God's decree, concursus, judgment of the intellect, and other circumstances. For Fischer and Ravizza, the requisites are the laws of physics and the current state of the universe at the moment of choice.

These formal similarities show a compatibility between Fischer and Ravizza and the reformed orthodox. Like Fischer and Ravizza, this means that the reformed orthodox could not consistently affirm libertarian freedom. Instead, they must adopt a view of freedom and moral responsibility that is consistent with the denial of the sourcehood and alternative possibilities conditions. For Fischer and Ravizza this is guidance control. In the next chapter, we will explore these formal similarities as they relate to the compatibility of guidance control with reformed theology.

CHAPTER FOUR

Rational Spontaneity and The *Sensus Divinitatis*

Introduction

I HAVE ARGUED THAT the reformed doctrines of the decree, foreknowledge, and providence are instances of hypothetical necessity. As such, they are a form of theological determinism. This means that they deny both the source and alternative possibilities conditions. By denying these two conditions, these reformed doctrines are broadly compatible with guidance control.[1]

In this chapter, we ask whether reformed theology is more specifically compatible with the two elements of guidance control: moderate reasons-responsiveness and mechanism ownership. I will argue that reformed theology is compatible with these two elements and thus with guidance control. I will argue this in six parts. In the first section, I will argue that reformed theology is a type of compatibilism. In the second section, I will identify the type of compatibilism. In the third section, I will argue that the reformed doctrine of rational spontaneity is a type of reasons-responsive theory and is thus compatible with moderate reasons-responsiveness. In the fourth section, I will argue that reformed theology has a similar subjectivist view as that of mechanism ownership. In the fifth section, I will address how reformed theology has the resources to address the problem of hard determinism that guidance control, as articulated by Fischer and Ravizza, does not. In the sixth section, I will address the problem of original sin and guidance control.

---

1. This also means that they are broadly compatible with a number of other compatibilist theories. However, our purpose is to compare them with guidance control and therefore, we will not pursue these other theories.

A Type of Compatibilism

I have argued that reformed theology denies both the source and alternative possibilities conditions. In this manner, Fischer and Ravizza's position is the same as reformed theology. They have two propositions in common: (1) that it is not necessary for an agent to be the ultimate source of his actions in order for him to be free and morally responsible and (2) that it is not necessary for an agent to have genuine access to alternative possibilities in the actual sequence in order for him to be free and morally responsible.

The affirmation of these two propositions means that reformed theology is some type of compatibilism. It would be helpful to give a basic definition of compatibilism that analytic philosophers use in order to see this. As I have argued, reformed theology is theological determinism. In light of this, we need to define the positions of compatibilism and incompatibilism. McKenna and Pereboom define them as follows:

> *Compatibilism* is the thesis that it is metaphysically possible that determinism is true and some person has free will.
>
> *Incompatibilism* is the thesis that it is not metaphysically possible that determinism is true and some person has free will.[2]

These positions can also be defined in terms of moral responsibility. McKenna and Pereboom write:

> On these versions, compatibilism is the thesis that moral responsibility is compatible with determinism, and incompatibilism is the thesis that moral responsibility is not compatible with determinism.[3]

In light of this we could define compatibilism as follows:

---

2. McKenna and Pereboom, *Free Will*, 30. Others define 'compatibilism' similarly. Manuel Vargas writes: "*Compatibilism* about free will . . . is the view that free will is compatible with determinism. . . . 'Compatibilism' and 'Incompatibilism,' as I will use them, are simply labels for whether or not one thinks free will could exist in a deterministic world: the incompatibilist says 'no' and the compatibilist, 'yes'" (Vargas, *Building Better Beings*, 12). Meghan Griffith writes, "Compatibilism: in free will, the theory that determinism does not rule out the kind of free will required for moral responsibility. Compatibilism is a view about the relationship between determinism and free will and does not necessarily involve a belief in determinism" (Griffith, *Free Will*, 127). Peter Van Inwagen defines 'compatibilism' as "the thesis that free will and determinism are compatible" (Van Inwagen, *Essay On Free Will*, 13).

3. McKenna and Pereboom, *Free Will*, 30.

Compatibilism is the thesis that it is metaphysically possible that determinism is true and some person has free will and moral responsibility.[4]

I have argued that reformed theology's doctrines of the decree, providence, and foreknowledge amount to theological determinism. In addition, reformed theology affirms that man has free will and is morally responsible for his actions. This means that reformed theology clearly falls within the category of compatibilism, but not all are convinced. Muller objects to labeling reformed theology as compatibilism. I will survey his reasons.

Muller argues that the term compatibilism is anachronistic and does not fit what reformed theology has taught. He writes:

> I fully recognize, as Helm points out, that quite a few scholars have used the terms "libertarianism" and "compatibilism" to describe ancient, medieval, and early modern views on the subject of freedom and determination, but I maintain that the terms, particularly compatibilism, as typically used, are not only anachronistic but do not actually fit the case of early modern Reformed thought on the subject. By all accounts, classic compatibilism argues the compatibility of freedom, understood as the spontaneous and uncoerced ability of an agent to do as he pleases, does not conflict with determinism: this spontaneous and uncoerced ability is viewed as consistent with human responsibility and allows the ascription of praise and blame. In the Hobbesian form of compatibilism, the agent cannot will otherwise, but is in no way coerced by an external power.[5]

According to Muller, compatibilism is to be identified with the classical compatibilist definition of freedom. He equates compatibilist freedom with the "spontaneous and uncoerced ability of an agent to do as he pleases."[6] He further goes on to equate compatibilism with Hobbesian compatibilism with regard to the ability to do otherwise. He writes, "In the Hobbesian form of compatibilism, the agent cannot will otherwise, but is in no way coerced by an external power."[7] According to Muller, this concept of human freedom does not fit reformed theology and it is anachronistic to argue so.

---

4. Ishitayaque Haji defines it similarly: "*Incompatibilism* is the thesis that free actions and moral responsibility are incompatible with determinism. *Compatibilism* is the denial of incompatibilism in both domains: it is the thesis that determinism and moral responsibility, and determinism and free actions, can co-exist" (Haji, *Incompatibilism's Allure*, 19).

5. Muller, "Jonathan Edwards and Francis Turretin," 283.

6. Muller, "Jonathan Edwards and Francis Turretin," 283.

7. Muller, "Jonathan Edwards and Francis Turretin," 283.

Muller states that reformed theology does not hold to this compatibilist definition of freedom. In light of this, it would be helpful to understand more clearly what Muller regards to be the reformed view of freedom, in particular, as it applies to the ability to do otherwise. In describing the reformed view, he writes:

> Reformed orthodox theologians of the early modern era argued positive divine determination of events, full and certain divine foreknowledge of future contingency, but also freedom of will and free choice, grounded in multiple *potencies of will* and understood in terms of liberty of contradiction and contrariety. In a given moment, the past being unaltered, human beings *have potencies* to more than one effect and can do otherwise.[8]

According to Muller, the reformed differed from the classical compatibilist conception of freedom in that they held to "multiple *potencies of will* . . . understood in terms of liberty of contradiction and contrariety."[9] This means that the will of the agent has the power to do A or not-A (the liberty of contradiction) as well as the power to do A or B or C, etc. (the liberty of contrariety). In this way, the agent has the power or ability to do otherwise. Muller regards this to be different from classical compatibilism. According to him, classical compatibilism taught that the agent could not do otherwise.

In another place, Muller further describes these multiple potencies of will. He writes:

> But as a logical necessity, the act or event y does not remove or cancel the potency or capability of the individual to do not-A, which remains in the will according to its essential nature or primary actuality (*in actu primo*). Thus, A is the case at t_2, but in view of the resident potencies of the human agent, it could be otherwise-not in the very moment that it is doing A, but in the capabilities of the agent at t_1 to do either A or not-A, in the potency to do not-A that does not disappear when A is actualized, and in the capability at t_3 to do otherwise, namely not-A, as Aristotle indicated against the Megarists, a builder does not cease to be a builder when he is not engaged in building.[10]

According to Muller, these multiple potencies of will reside in the essential nature of the will, or *in actu primo*. As we saw in the last chapter, the

---

8. Muller, "Jonathan Edwards and Francis Turretin," 284.
9. Muller, "Jonathan Edwards and Francis Turretin," 284.
10. Muller, "Jonathan Edwards and Francis Turretin," 275.

will *in actu primo* is the will in itself without the requisites for action being in place. It is the will abstracted from God's decree, foreknowledge, rational necessity, etc. The will does not lose its essential nature when it acts. Thus, even if the agent chooses to do A, in virtue of the will's essential nature to the liberty of contradiction and contrariety, it could have done not-A, or B or C, etc. Muller illustrates this with an example from Aristotle, "a builder does not cease to be a builder when he is not engaged in building." That is, the builder has the power or ability of building even when he is not in the act of building. Likewise, an agent, in virtue of the essential nature of the will, has the ability or power to do not-A even when he does A.

However, it is important that Muller says, "Thus, A is the case at t_2, but in view of the resident potencies of the human agent, it could be otherwise-*not in the very moment that it is doing A*."[11] This means that at the moment the agent is performing the act, it is not possible for him to do otherwise. The very moment the agent is performing A is the actual world. Thus, Muller is saying that an agent S performs an action A at t_1 and it is not possible for the agent S to perform an action -A at t_1 (the very moment that he is doing A). This is the precise sense in which Fischer and Ravizza say that an agent cannot do otherwise. An agent cannot do otherwise in the actual sequence or, as Muller puts it, "in the very moment that it is doing A."[12]

Muller makes this point clearer:

> In his place in order of finite things, namely, within the realm of secondary causality, *A* can will either *p* or not-*p*; and God, in his place beyond and supportive of this order of finite things can will either that *A* wills *p* or that *A* wills not-*p*. Of course, given also the law of non-contradiction *A* cannot both will and not will *p* in the same way, at the same place, or at the same time as he will not-*p*; and given the divine *concursus* (whether construed in a Thomist, Scotist, or one or another Reformed manner), it also cannot be the case that God actually wills that *A* wills *p* and *A* actually wills not-*p* or that God actually wills not-*p* and *A* wills *p*![13]

Muller is clearly arguing that the reformed deny PAP or principle 2 in the actual sequence. In this passage, he uses the stronger language of "cannot." For example, he writes, "*A cannot* both will and not will *p* in the same way, at the same place, or at the same time as he will not-*p*."[14] In other words,

---

11. Muller, "Jonathan Edwards and Francis Turretin," 275 (emphasis mine).
12. Muller, "Jonathan Edwards and Francis Turretin," 275.
13. Muller, *Divine and Human Choice*, 314.
14. Muller, *Divine and Human Choice*, 314.

it is impossible (cannot) for an agent *A* to will not-*p* in the same way, at the same place, or at the same time as he wills p. That is, in the actual world or the actual sequence, when *A* wills *p*, he cannot do otherwise.

Muller also affirms that the reformed orthodox denied PAP in relation to divine providence or *concursus*. He writes:

> and given the divine *concursus* (whether construed in a Thomist, Scotist, or one or another Reformed manner), it also cannot be the case that God actually wills that *A* wills *p* and *A* actually wills not-*p* or that God actually wills not-*p* and *A* wills *p*![15]

In the actual world or the actual sequence that God wills, it cannot be the case that an agent *A* wills otherwise than what God willed that agent to do. This is about as clear a denial of PAP as can be stated.[16]

Muller further clarifies this potency and the sense in which the agent could not do otherwise by invoking the language of possible worlds. In this way, he is saying exactly what we noted Beck said in the last chapter. He writes:

> Whereas Edwards has an unbreakable single-level causal chain lacking contingencies (or hypothetical necessities), Turretin has a multi-level causal chain that presumes contingencies (or hypothetical necessities). In both cases, the future will not be otherwise, but in Turretin's case, albeit only in potency, it could be otherwise—pushed back into the divine mind, the otherwise is resident in a possible world that God does not will to actualize, but there is also a sense, in the simultaneity of potencies, that the "otherwise" does exist as pure potency, albeit unactualized in this world.[17]

Muller is comparing his view of Jonathan Edwards with his view of Turretin. Turretin is representative of the reformed orthodox position. He says that for both of them "the future will not be otherwise."[18] This means that the future God decreed and foreknew will come to pass and it will not

---

15. Muller, *Divine and Human Choice*, 314.

16. Muller further argues: "Still this synchronic contingency does not (and clearly cannot) indicate the synchronous actualization of contraries *in a given existent world or universe*, nor does it indicate that a human being has the ability to exercise a potency that is not in accord with the divine willing" (Muller, *Divine and Human Choice*, 314 [emphasis mine]). Again, Muller is clearly teaching that the Reformed Orthodox denied PAP. The synchronic actualization of contraries (PAP) in "a given existent world or universe" (the actual world or actual sequence) cannot happen.

17. Muller, "Jonathan Edwards And Francis Turretin," 276.

18. Muller, "Jonathan Edwards And Francis Turretin," 276.

be otherwise than God decreed and foreknew. Muller uses the language of "will not be otherwise" instead of "cannot be otherwise." However, in light of his previous comments, the "will not be otherwise" is equivalent to "cannot be otherwise in the very moment that it is doing A." As we saw earlier, if an agent S does A at t_1, then according to Muller the agent could not also perform not-A at t_1. This is what he previously meant when he said "Thus, A is the case at t_2, but in view of the resident potencies of the human agent, it could be otherwise-*not in the very moment that it is doing A*."[19] Thus, in the actual world, the world where the agent does A at t_1, the agent could not do otherwise at t_1. Fischer and Ravizza hold the same view as the reformed orthodox on this point.

However, Muller does identify two senses in which it could be otherwise. With regard to the first sense he writes, "In Turretin's case, albeit only in potency, it could be otherwise." Muller identifies this potency as a possibility in another possible world that God wills to not actualize. He writes, "pushed back into the divine mind, the otherwise is resident in a possible world that God does not will to actualize."[20] We see from this that the "power to do otherwise" does not reside in the actual world, but in another possible world. We have seen that Fischer and Ravizza affirm this.

With regard to the second sense he writes, "but there is also a sense, in the simultaneity of potencies, that the "otherwise" does exist as pure potency, albeit unactualized in this world."[21] The simultaneity of potencies or *potentia simultatis* is "The possibility of opposite acts at one moment."[22] Muller says that this exists as a pure potency. He means that the will in itself, without the requisites for action being in place, has this pure potency *in actu primo*. The agent has this pure potency as an essential part of the will. This pure potency does not go away in the actual world. It remains, though it lies dormant because it is "unactualized in this world."[23] This could be illustrated with the example from Aristotle that Muller previously presented. A builder does not cease to be a builder when he is not engaged in building. The builder retains his powers and abilities to build even when he is sleeping. Though during sleep his builder powers are not actualized, he still retains them. Likewise, when an agent does A, he retains his pure potency to do not-A, though this potency to do not-A is unactualized in this world. Again, we have seen that this is also the position of Fischer and Ravizza. In

19. Muller, "Jonathan Edwards And Francis Turretin," 275 (emphasis mine).
20. Muller, "Jonathan Edwards And Francis Turretin," 276.
21. Muller, "Jonathan Edwards And Francis Turretin," 276.
22. Van Asselt et al., *Reformed Thought on Freedom*, 47.
23. Muller, "Jonathan Edwards And Francis Turretin," 276.

alternative sequences, the agent or mechanism could do otherwise but in the actual sequence the agent could not.

We could illuminate the exact sense in which the agent could not do otherwise by referring back to a distinction that Fischer made between general ability and a specific ability. We will use the example of Fischer's piano player. The piano player has the power or ability to play the piano even when he is sleeping. Suppose we are in the actual world and we are at time slice t_1. At t_1 the piano player is sleeping in a hotel room in a hotel that does not have a piano. At t_1 the piano player still has the general power or ability to play the piano. However he does not have the specific ability to play the piano because he lacks the opportunity to do so. By "lacking the opportunity to do so," I mean that the actual world is such that (1) the piano player is sleeping and (2) the piano player is nowhere near a piano.

I think this example illuminates what Muller means by having a pure potency to do otherwise. The will in itself, *in actu primo*, has the power of the simultaneity of potencies. This is a general power to do A or not-A. This general power resides in the agent in the actual world. Now suppose that the agent does A at t_1 in the actual world. The agent still has the pure potency of the simultaneity of potencies to do not-A. This is a general power that resides in the agent even at t_1 when the agent is doing A. However, the agent does not have the specific power or ability to do not-A at t_1. The reason why is that given the state of the actual world at t_1, the agent lacks the opportunity to do not-A. He lacks the opportunity because the decree, foreknowledge, and providence of God hypothetically necessitate the agent to do A at t_1.

Let us now summarize Muller's view of the reformed orthodox. Muller objects to labeling reformed theology as compatibilism because (1) it is anachronistic and (2) it does not fit with what reformed theologians actually taught. This second objection is further clarified to mean that the label of compatibilism does not fit with the fact that reformed theologians taught (a) that the agent has a potency, *in actu primo* of contradiction and contrariety, to do otherwise in another possible world that God has not actualized and (b) that the agent also has a potency or power in the actual world as a general ability. In light of this exposition of Muller's position, there are four things to say in response.

First, let us deal with Muller's claim that using the term compatibilism, with regard to the reformed orthodox, is anachronistic. Though it is certainly true that the word compatibilism was not in use when the reformed orthodox wrote, it is also certainly true that the compatibilist project was present. That is, though the term was not there, the concept was. A compatibilist is basically attempting to show that determinism does not exclude free will and moral responsibility. The reformed orthodox were engaged in this very project, but they used different terms. They were trying to show that free will and moral responsibility were compatible with necessity, in particular hypothetical necessity.

For example, Turretin distinguished various senses of the word necessity for the purpose of showing that some senses of necessity do not exclude human freedom and moral responsibility. Turretin writes:

> The providence of God neither takes away the contingency of things (because it always remains indifferent with respect to the second cause, what become necessary by providence with respect to the first cause); nor overthrows the liberty of the will (because the hypothetical necessity of the decree brings no coaction to the will, but permits it to exercise its own movements most freely, although inevitably); nor does away with the use of means (because the certainty of the end does not take away, but supposes the necessity of the means) . . . nor does it abolish the relation of punishment and rewards because the necessity which providence brings is not absolute, physical and compulsory (which does not destroy liberty), but relative (from the hypothesis of the decree of immutability, which indeed renders man dependent and accountable [*hypeuthynon*], but always leaves him rational and free, and so worthy of reward or punishment in good and evil deeds).[24]

In this passage, we see Turretin engaged in the compatibilist project. He is arguing that the necessity of divine providence does not take away neither the liberty of the will nor moral responsibility. It does not take away the liberty of the will because providence is a hypothetical necessity in distinction from the necessity of coaction, nor does it take away punishment and rewards or moral responsibility because it is not an absolute necessity nor a physical nor compulsory necessity. Instead, it is a relative or hypothetical necessity.

By making these distinctions, Turretin is showing that hypothetical necessity (what analytic philosophers call determinism) is compatible with free will and moral responsibility. It should not matter that the word compatibilism is absent. Very clearly, Turretin is engaged in the compatibilist project and very clearly, he is advocating the concept of compatibilism.

We see this also with Voetius. In discussing the Jesuit view, Voetius writes:

---

24. Turretin, *Institutes of Elenctic Theology*, 492–93.

> Now these authors claim an indifference of the free potency to both components not only in a divided sense, but also in a compound sense, which implies a contradiction in terms. Likewise, they ask regarding the essence (*quidditas*) and integrity of a free nature for a twofold immunity, that is from coercion and from necessity, and indeed not only from intrinsic, absolute and natural necessity (to which we agree), but also from extrinsic, hypothetical necessity, which we deny. Thus, we need to deal with these two issues: We have to investigate the concept of the essence (*quidditas*) of freedom, *and we have to demonstrate its compatibility with necessity.*[25]

Voetuis's project was to show the compatibility of freedom with necessity, in particular hypothetical necessity. This is the same as the modern-day compatibilist project.

We also see this in de Moor. In his discussion of freedom, he also distinguishes between various senses of necessity. He aims to demonstrate that freedom conflicts with certain forms of necessity but not others. He writes:

> Positively, therefore, freedom is to be constituted in rational willingness [*lubentia rationalis*], by which man does what he wills, through a previous judgment of reason. . . . This rational willingness does not conflict (1) with the necessity of dependence on the divine will, which rather as a first cause excites and precedes the will to act freely; (2) nor does it conflict with the rational necessity of following the judgment of practical intellect, unless the will were to remove rationality; (3) therefore, it does not conflict with moral necessity either, which in man in the Fallen state, unable to do good, removes also the possible appetite of this, even so that fallen man cannot naturally produce any spiritual good, gracious to God. . . . But this moral necessity to sin and the impotence . . . of fallen man towards good does not conflict with rational willingness. This willingness, in which the essence of freedom consists, is so natural for man, that it can in no case or state be lost by man, unless together with rationality itself. . . . It can thus be affirmed in truth, that every man always has free choice, also in the Fallen state.[26]

De Moor is clearly engaged in the project of showing the compatibility of freedom (rational willingness) with various types of necessity. Given the fact that the reformed orthodox were engaged in the compatibilist project

---

25. Van Asselt et al., *Reformed Thought on Freedom*, 148–49 (emphasis mine).
26. Van Asselt et al., *Reformed Thought on Freedom*, 207–9.

without using that word, Muller should not object that applying the term compatibilism to the reformed orthodox is anachronistic.

Secondly, we need to respond to Muller's claim that the reformed orthodox do not fit the category of compatibilism. More specifically, he has in mind what he calls "classical compatibilism." He defines it as "the spontaneous and uncoerced ability of an agent to do as he pleases, does not conflict with determinism."[27] Yet as we have seen, the category of compatibilism is not committed to a specific understanding or theory of freedom. Analytic philosophers define it as:

> *Compatibilism* is the thesis that it is metaphysically possible that determinism is true and some person has free will.[28]

Compatibilism is not committed to any one particular view of human freedom. As we will see in the next section, compatibilists hold a variety of positions on freedom. There are mesh theories of human freedom, reasons-responsive theories, the new dispositionalists, and even classical compatibilists as Muller understands it. Compatibilism simply holds that determinism is compatible with free will and moral responsibility. Therefore, Muller should not object that compatibilism does not fit with the reformed orthodox teaching. It does fit with this common definition of compatibilism.

For example, Muller agrees that the reformed orthodox taught hypothetical necessity. He writes:

> Where Edwards has an unbreakable single-level causal chain lacking contingencies (or hypothetical necessities), Turretin has a multi-level causal chain that presumes contingencies (or hypothetical necessities). In both cases, the future will not be otherwise, but in Turretin's case, albeit in potency, it could be otherwise—pushed back into the divine mind, the otherwise is resident in a possible world that God does not will to actualize.[29]

This means that Muller regards the reformed orthodox as teaching hypothetical necessity or what analytic philosophers call determinism. He also regards them as teaching free will and moral responsibility. He writes:

> Reformed orthodox theologians of the early modern era argued positive divine determination of events, full and certain divine foreknowledge of future contingency, but also freedom of will and free choice, grounded in multiple potencies of will.

---

27. Muller, "Jonathan Edwards and Francis Turretin," 283.
28. McKenna and Pereboom, *Free Will*, 30.
29. Muller, "Jonathan Edwards and Francis Turretin," 276.

This is exactly what analytic philosophers define as compatibilism. Muller even hesitantly concedes this when he writes:

> If (conceding the term momentarily) the Reformed are identified as compatibilists, given their assumption that a divine determination of all things is logically and ontologically compatible with human free choice, they remain compatibilists of a rather different sort than Edwards.[30]

Though hesitant, he does agree with the point I am making at least for the sake of argument. His preference would be to not use the label compatibilism but if it is used, we must distinguish the reformed orthodox compatibilism from that of Edwards, though Helm disagrees with the judgement that it is a substantially different position.[31] We will examine that claim in the next chapter.

Muller need not shy away from the term compatibilism. It does accurately describe the reformed orthodox position broadly speaking. Of course, we may want to go further and distinguish the reformed orthodox position from other compatibilist positions.

Third, Muller does not want to use the term compatibilism because he thinks it does not fit with the reformed orthodox teachings on the potency of the will. He argues that for the reformed orthodox, the will in itself has the potency to do otherwise. It is the potency to do otherwise in another possible world that God has not actualized and a potency to do otherwise which remains in the abstract will even though it is not actualized.

However, most, if not all, contemporary compatibilists argue that an agent could have done otherwise than he did in a different possible world. McKenna and Pereboom write concerning the classical compatibilists on this point:

> First, determinism is a thesis about what future will unfold *given a specific past*, for example, given specific past wants. Determinism does not deny that, with a different past, a different future would unfold. Hence, it does not deny that, along with other conditions of the state of the world at a time, different wants would causally determine an agent to act other than the way she acted in the actual world.[32]

---

30. Muller, "Jonathan Edwards and Francis Turretin," 284.

31. Helm, "Johnathan Edwards and the Parting of Ways?," 42–60; "Turretin and Edwards Once More," 286–96.

32. McKenna and Pereboom, *Free Will*, 58.

Classical compatibilists substantially affirmed that there exist other possible worlds in which the agent does otherwise. Muller is wrong to suggest that classical compatibilists have no sense in which they believe an agent could have done otherwise.

More pertinent to our thesis, the compatibilist/semi-compatibilist John Martin Fischer affirms this as well. In a currently unpublished paper (February 2019) for a festschrift in honor of T. H. Irwin, Fischer makes this clear. He is responding to comments from Christopher Franklin:

> I completely agree with Franklin that I do indeed believe that *various* kinds of alternative possibilities are required for moral responsibility (although not for the "grounding" or explanation of moral responsibility), and thus my repeated contention that alternative possibilities are not required for moral responsibility might well have caused confusion. Of course, in the Frankfurt-Style Cases Jones does not lose his general ability to vote Republican (i.e., to do otherwise in the context), just as we do not lose various general abilities when we are asleep. One might say that we keep our general abilities in these contexts, although we do not have the opportunity to exercise them (immediately). Again: I do not lose my general ability to play the piano when there is no piano in my vicinity; I simply do not have the opportunity to exercise it.[33]

Fischer is arguing that his compatibilist (or semi-compatibilist) position affirms a general ability or power to do otherwise. Muller also affirms this of the reformed orthodox. Muller's example from Aristotle used to affirm this says, "As Aristotle indicated against the Megarists, a builder does not cease to be a builder when he is not engaged in building."[34] The ability or power to build does not go away when the builder is not engaged in building. So also, for Fischer, "I do not lose my general ability to play the piano when there is no piano in my vicinity."[35] In other words, a compatibilist (semi-compatibilist) such as Fischer fits in the category of compatibilism even though his position teaches that a general power remains in the agent even when it is not being actualized. In light of this, Muller ought not be concerned about the label compatibilist applied to the reformed orthodox.

Fourthly, not using the term compatibilism as a label for the reformed orthodox position causes unnecessary confusion. If the position conceptually falls under the definition of compatibilism, then it should be labeled so.

---

33. Fischer, "Freedom Required for Moral Responsibility," 11.
34. Muller, "Johnathan Edwards and Francis Turretin," 275.
35. Fischer, "Freedom Required for Moral Responsibility," 11.

Otherwise, it makes it difficult for non-reformed philosophers to understand the reformed position. This makes it unnecessarily more difficult to engage in fruitful philosophical dialogue.

When all is said and done, like the Utrecht School, Muller is not in substantial disagreement with what we have argued throughout this book. He affirms that the reformed orthodox taught hypothetical necessity (what analytic philosophers call determinism), freedom, and moral responsibility. He affirms that there is a sense in which the agent could do otherwise, i.e., in a different possible world and with regard to a general ability. Yet he also affirms that there is a sense in which the agent could not do otherwise, i.e., "not in the very moment that it is doing A"[36] or in the actual sequence of events. All of this means that with regard to the reformed orthodox, the question should not be whether we should use the term compatibilism, but rather what type of compatibilism is it? This is to what we now turn our attention.

What Type of Compatibilism?

In surveying the different compatibilist views we can identify five basic categories: (1) classical compatibilism, (2) mesh theories, (3) Strawsonian reactive attitude theories, (4) leeway theories, and (5) reasons-responsive theories. These are all compatibilist views in contemporary philosophy. However, they have different conceptions of freedom.

The first compatibilist theory is classical compatibilism. This is the view that Hobbes, Locke, Hume, and various others in the twentieth century held. McKenna defines it:

> According to the classical compatibilist, the free will at issue in the debate is an agent's ability to act and to refrain from acting unencumbered, that is, free from impediments that would stand in her way. The core idea is that free will consists in the absence of impediments both to making a choice and to refraining from doing so.[37]

This conception of freedom is certainly part of what reformed theology wants to affirm. As we will see, the notion of rational spontaneity includes within it a lack of coercion. However, rational spontaneity requires more. It also includes rational necessity. For an agent to be free, he must not merely lack impediments. He must also have the ability to respond to reasons in an appropriate manner, such that the will follows the intellect.

36. Muller, "Johnathan Edwards and Francis Turretin," 275.
37. McKenna and Pereboom, *Free Will*, 50.

A second type of compatibilism are mesh theories. McKenna and Pereboom characterize mesh theories as follows:

> A theory of action should be able to identify various psychological processes of agents that uniquely figure into the intentional actions of which normally functioning persons are capable. When the ingredients mesh in a harmonious way, then the agent acts unimpeded; her actions and the desires or intentions causing them are a free outcome of her own agency. Call any such theory a *mesh theory*.[38]

Harry Frankfurt's theory is a good example of a mesh theory. He defines freedom as follows: "It is in securing the conformity of his will to his second-order volitions, then, that a person exercises freedom of the will."[39] Frankfurt argues that this account is compatible with determinism.

Frankfurt's theory is interesting and valuable as a possible compatibilist option. However, reformed theology does not locate freedom in the proper mesh of desires or psychological states. Reformed theology locates freedom in rational spontaneity.[40]

A third type of compatibilist theory is the reactive attitude theory. The philosopher Peter F. Strawson offers this type of theory.[41] He makes the argument that freedom and responsibility revolve around the conditions upon which we hold people responsible. Strawson is attempting to analyze our ordinary practices of holding people responsible. In doing so he is shedding valuable light on the reasons why we hold people responsible. According to Strawson, when people behave in a certain way that we deem bad, we hold certain attitudes towards them. When bad behavior occurs, we resent, blame, hold anger towards, etc. the person that behaved badly. When a person behaves in a manner that we regard as good, we hold certain attitudes towards him. For example, we may praise him, show gratitude towards him, etc. The idea is that holding someone responsible means adopting certain attitudes towards them in reaction to their behavior. Strawson calls these attitudes "reactive attitudes." According to Strawson, being a free

---

38. McKenna and Pereboom, *Free Will*, 208.
39. Frankfurt, "Freedom of the Will," 331.
40. Michael McKenna and Chad Van Schoelandt offer the suggestion that mesh theories could be united with reasons-responsive theories. This could be a very fruitful and interesting combination for the reformed theologian. It would take the two best compatibilist theories and unite their insights thus making an even stronger compatibilism if successful. McKenna and Van Schoelandt, "Crossing Mesh Theory," 44–64.
41. Strawson, "Freedom and Resentment," 1–25.

and responsible person is being the fit subject of reactive attitudes. Strawson holds that this practice is compatible with determinism.

Reformed theology certainly holds that a person with genuine freedom is the proper subject of the reactive attitudes. However, this is not where it locates the essence of freedom. That resides in rational spontaneity. Though this theory could supplement reformed theology, it is not the essence of what they meant by freedom.

The fourth type of compatibilism are the leeway theories. A leeway theorist seeks to establish the compatibility of determinism with leeway freedom. Leeway freedom, in part, understands freedom to include the ability to do otherwise. An example of this is found in the work of Kadri Vihvelin.[42] McKenna and Pereboom write:

> Vihvelin develops a sophisticated compatibilist theory of free will that revives a conception that had largely been set aside for half a century, one that attempts to reconcile causal determinism with our being able to do otherwise from how we in fact act.[43]

The classical compatibilists previously attempted this with the conditional analysis of "could have done otherwise." Yet Vihvelin avoids the difficulties associated with that analysis by characterizing free will in terms of intrinsic dispositions:

> Vihvelin criticizes these kinds of objections using her core positive idea: that abilities to do otherwise are to be characterized in terms of intrinsic dispositions, that is, dispositions of agents that consist in intrinsic properties—by contrast with extrinsic or relational properties—that agents have. Because the essential features of such intrinsic dispositions are not analyzed conditionally, her view gains immunity to the assault on conditional analyses.[44]

The key idea is that leeway freedom is identified as a disposition or dispositions. In other words, an agent is free if the agent has the ability to do otherwise than the agent in fact did as characterized by a dispositional analysis of the "ability to do otherwise." The details of this view need to be left to the side for our purposes. The point is that freedom is characterized dispositonally.

Reformed theology could benefit from this view. As we have seen, Muller understands the reformed view of freedom to consist, in part, as

---

42. Vihvelin, *Causes, Laws, and Free Will*.
43. McKenna and Pereboom, *Free Will*, 225.
44. McKenna and Pereboom, *Free Will*, 226.

a simultaneity of potencies to act otherwise *in actu primo*. It is this potency or power that accounts for alternativity. Vihvelin is saying something similar and reformed theology could benefit from this type of dispositional analysis. Yet this account is still not where the reformed locate freedom and moral responsibility. They locate it in rational spontaneity and the ability to respond to reasons in an appropriate manner.

The fifth type of compatibilism are reasons-responsive theories. Meghan Griffith writes concerning these theories:

> The last kind of compatibilist view we will look at characterizes free will in terms of the ability to respond to reasons. The basic intuition here is that we are free in the sense required for moral responsibility when we are able to act according to reasons and when we are sensitive to reasons in the right way. . . . It just means that we must be *capable*, in a certain sense, of responding appropriately to reasons, whether we in fact do appropriately respond to them. We are not free if reasons are ineffective—that is, when we are *not able* to respond to them.[45]

Reasons-responsive theories teach that free will and moral responsibility are accounted for by the ability to respond to reasons in a certain way. This is at the heart of the class of reasons-responsive theories. From this core idea, philosophers develop various accounts of what exactly it looks like to respond to reasons in the proper way. Guidance control is a type of reasons-responsive theory. I will argue that the reformed doctrine of rational spontaneity is also a type of reasons-responsive theory.

At this point, it would be helpful to address the issue of semi-compatibilism and reformed theology. In chapter one, I noted that guidance control is considered a type of semi-compatibilism. This is a sub-category of compatibilism in contemporary philosophy. McKenna defines it as follows:

> Semi-compatibilism holds that determinism is incompatible with the freedom to do otherwise but compatible with moral responsibility.[46]

"Freedom to do otherwise" is understood as regulative control or the ability to do otherwise in the actual sequence. It is an affirmation of PAP or principle 2. It is this specific conception of freedom that is incompatible with determinism. However, freedom is not limited to this specific definition. With regard to this sense of freedom, reformed theology is semi-compatibilist.

45. Griffith, *Free Will*, 61.
46. McKenna, "Assessing Reasons-Responsive Compatibilism," 91.

As we have seen, reformed theology denies PAP. Furthermore, it holds that this concept of freedom is incompatible with hypothetical necessity or determinism. For example, Turretin, writing against the libertarianism of the Pelagians and semi-Pelagians, argues that the decree implies the necessity of the event. He writes:

> The reasons are (1) All things were decreed of God by an eternal and unchangeable counsel; hence they cannot but take place in the appointed time; otherwise the counsel of God would be changed, which the Scriptures declare to be impossible.[47]

Turretin argues that the Pelagian and semi-Pelagian concept of free will, as the ability to do otherwise with all the requisites for action being present, is incompatible with the hypothetical necessity of God's decree. So also, semi-compatibilism holds that PAP is incompatible with determinism.

In my opinion, the issue of semi-compatibilism is largely terminological. It all comes down to how one defines freedom. Nonetheless, in order to communicate reformed theology to the audience of analytic philosophers, we could say that it fits under the category of semi-compatibilism.

In the remainder of this chapter, I am going to argue that Fischer and Ravizza's doctrine of moderate reasons-responsiveness is substantially the same as the reformed doctrine of rational spontaneity. In addition, I am going to argue that Fischer and Ravizza's subjectivist view of mechanism ownership has basic similarities to the reformed doctrine of the *sensus divinitatis*. In making these comparisons, we will see that guidance control is substantially compatible with reformed teachings on freedom and moral responsibility.

Rational Spontaneity as a Reasons-Responsive Theory

The first aspect of guidance control is moderate reasons-responsiveness. This is a type of reasons-responsive theory. It is the view that freedom and moral responsibility are rooted in the agent's ability to respond to reasons appropriately, namely somewhere in between strong and weak reasons-responsiveness. We examined the details of moderate reasons-responsiveness in chapter one, so we will not rehearse those details. Instead, I want to highlight that it is a reasons-responsive theory and argue that this is the fundamental continuity it has with rational spontaneity. In order to argue this, we need to understand the reformed doctrine of rational spontaneity.

---

47. Turretin, *Institutes of Elenctic Theology*, 320.

There are two ways in which we can illuminate the reformed notion of freedom and moral responsibility as rational spontaneity. The first comes from the Westminster Confession of Faith and the second comes from the reformed tradition more broadly. I will first look at the Westminster Confession of Faith.

WCF 9:1 defines free will as follows:

> God hath endued the will of man with that natural liberty, that it is neither forced, nor, by any absolute necessity of nature, determined to good, or evil.

In commenting on this article, John Murray identifies it as a statement of rational spontaneity. He writes:

> Freedom is thus defined negatively and affirmatively, as the absence of compulsion and *self*-determination respectively. A man is responsible for his acts because they are due to *his* volitions. He is responsible for his volitions because they are self-propelled, exercised without compulsion, and expressive of what he is in the innermost bent, bias, and disposition of heart and mind. Understood thus, *freedom is rational spontaneity*.[48]

Murray tells us that the Confession is identifying human freedom with rational spontaneity. He then goes on to define this concept's two basic elements. First, "the absence of compulsion."[49] An agent is free, in part, if his actions come about with a lack of external coercion. Second, rational spontaneity is an expression of the "disposition of heart and mind."[50] This is the rational part of rational spontaneity. An agent that has rational spontaneity acts based upon how he is in his heart and mind; in other words, when he expresses his thoughts, beliefs, character, etc. in an uncoerced manner. We will see that, generally speaking, the reformed tradition affirms these two elements of rational spontaneity.

Francis R. Beattie also identifies WCF 9:1 as affirming rational spontaneity or rational self-determination. He writes:

> According to this view, the will is the faculty of rational self-determination. . . . It is in this limited sense that the term is used in the Standards, and care must be taken to keep this in mind in the exposition of their doctrine on the subject. The nature of the will, as a faculty of the constitution of man, denotes the power of choice, in the sense of free rational

---

48. Murray, *Collected Writings of John Murray*, 63 (emphasis mine).
49. Murray, *Collected Writings of John Murray*, 63.
50. Murray, *Collected Writings of John Murray*, 63.

self-determination. In his very constitution, this endowment belongs to man. The will is not something apart from or other than the man; but it is just the man choosing or determining himself by means of free rational volition. . . . The fact that the Standards clearly teach that man is a free rational agent is emphasized, and this simply means that there is in his nature a power of free rational self-determination, and that this is the adequate basis of his moral responsibility.[51]

Beattie identifies two features of rational spontaneity. First, an agent is uncoerced or as Beattie puts it, "it is just the man choosing or determining himself."[52] The agent is free if he is self-determined; that is, not externally coerced to perform the action he performs. Second, the agent is free if he also performs the action "by means of free rational volition."[53] In other words, he must be rational or respond to reasons appropriately. This is the basis of moral responsibility. Beattie writes:

> The fact that the Standards clearly teach that man is a free rational agent is emphasized, and this simply means that there is in his nature a power of free rational self-determination, and that this is the adequate basis of his moral responsibility.[54]

From these two expositions of the Confession we can see that the Confession identifies human freedom with rational spontaneity or rational self-determination. This consists of two basic elements, (1) lack of coercion and (2) rationality or the ability to respond to reasons appropriately. The reformed tradition at large shared this concept of freedom as rational spontaneity.

Van Asselt, Bac, and te Velde characterize the reformed view of freedom as rational spontaneity. They write:

> The character of freedom as consisting of rational spontaneity instead of indifference. Our authors characterize freedom as "rational spontaneity": the will acts out of itself (*sua sponte*), not being driven by an inward or outward determining cause. This spontaneity is called "rational" inasmuch as the will is informed by the intellect and thus is not blind or whimsical in acting. The definition of freedom in terms of indifference was advocated by Jesuit and Arminian adversaries of the Reformed: they

---

51. Beattie, *Presbyterian Standards*, 172–73.
52. Beattie, *Presbyterian Standards*, 172–73.
53. Beattie, *Presbyterian Standards*, 172–73.
54. Beattie, *Presbyterian Standards*, 172–73.

state that, if all the requisites for acting were posited (rational judgement of the goodness of an action, God's decree), the will was still indifferent towards acting or not acting. The Reformed argued that this destroys man's dependence on God and even makes impossible all reasonable action. While most authors extensively argue for the untenability of conceiving of freedom by indifference, some authors argue explicitly for a structural indifference or alternativity and make clear that this is factual contingency, which is also supposed in their conception of freedom as rational spontaneity.[55]

Van Asselt, Bac, and te Velde argue that rational spontaneity is the reformed concept of human freedom. The reformed affirmed this in contrast to the Jesuit and Arminian notion of indifference. Indifference is defined as:

> if all the requisites for acting were posited (rational judgement of the goodness of an action, God's decree), the will was still indifferent towards acting or not acting.[56]

We saw in the last chapter that this is libertarian freedom and that the reformed rejected this concept of freedom.

Van Asselt, Bac, and te Velde identify three elements of rational spontaneity. First, "the will acts out of itself (*sua sponte*), not being driven by an inward or outward determining cause."[57] This is the lack of coercion element of rational spontaneity. Second, it is rational in that "the will is informed by the intellect and thus not blind or whimsical in acting."[58] The intellect responds to reasons and determines which reason is best. The will follows this judgment of the intellect and acts. This element of rational spontaneity is the ability to respond to reasons appropriately. Third, they add a structural indifference or alternativity. We saw in the last chapter that this is indifference

---

55. Van Asselt et al., *Reformed Thought on Freedom*, 46. J. Martin Bac also says: "The Reformed scholastics unanimously accepted power to the contrary (*indifferentia*) in the first structural moment, granting the will a real choice between various options. . . . In the second structural moment, the will freely determines itself to a certain act or object. Turretin precisely defines the essential structure of freedom in terms of: Rational spontaneity, by which a free person does what he pleases, a rational judgement preceding.

The main aspect is the desire or pleasure of the will. The will being an intentional faculty that longs for the good, its decision must be both rational and spontaneous according to the Reformed. Accordingly, the power by which the will acts is called 'free choice' (*liberum arbitrium*), reflecting both voluntative and intellective components" (Bac, *Perfect Will Theology*, 421–22).

56. Van Asselt et al., *Reformed Thought on Freedom*, 46.

57. Van Asselt et al., *Reformed Thought on Freedom*, 46.

58. Van Asselt et al., *Reformed Thought on Freedom*, 46.

in the first act and the divided sense. It is an indifference in the will as it is in itself. It is an indifference that is different from the Jesuit sense. It is not an indifference with all the requisites for action being present. Rather, it is an indifference without the requisites for action being present.

Aza Goudriaan quotes Martinus Vitringa, identifying the reformed view of freedom as rational spontaneity. He writes,

> The view of most Reformed theologians concerning the formal character of freedom amounts to this. In the negative sense it consists in immunity to coercion, [natural] force and natural necessity, and positively [it consists] in rational freedom by which it acts spontaneously on the basis of the practical judgment of reason.[59]

We see again two elements of rational spontaneity: First, "immunity to coercion" and second, "rational freedom by which it acts spontaneously on the basis of the practical judgment of reason."[60]

Turretin identifies the two elements of rational spontaneity that we have been discussing as freedom. He writes,

> There are two principal characteristics of free will in which its formal nature consists: (1) the choice (*he proairesis*), so that what is done is done by a previous judgement of reason; (2) the willingness (*to hekousion*), so that what is done is done voluntarily and without compulsion.[61]

Turretin clearly identifies the two elements of rational spontaneity as the reformed view of freedom.

De Moor identifies freedom as rational willingness, which is another name for rational spontaneity. He writes:

---

59. Goudriaan, *Reformed Orthodoxy and Philosophy*, 174.
60. Goudriaan, *Reformed Orthodoxy and Philosophy*, 174.
61. Turretin, *Institutes of Elenctic Theology*, 662. Richard Muller further describes Turretin's view: "Turretin divides the act into an intellective choosing or determining of an object and a free willing of the object that the intellect has chosen. With objects in view, prior to the determination of the intellect, the will is prepared to accept them or reject them, namely to will or to nil (liberty of exercise and contradiction) or to accept either one or the other (liberty of contrariety or specification). Without the act of the intellect, there could be no determination of an object to be willed; without the act of the will, there could be no movement toward the object. The willing is free because it is a matter of rational willingness or spontaneity in following the determination of the intellect" (Muller, "Jonathan Edwards and Francis Turretin," 281).

> Positively, therefore, freedom is to be constituted in rational willingness (*lubentia rationalis*), by which man does what he wills, through a previous judgment of reason.[62]

We can see from this discussion that the Westminster standards and the reformed tradition identify freedom as rational spontaneity. This consists of two parts: (1) a lack of coercion and (2) the will follows the intellect or rational necessity. Van Asselt, Bac, and te Velde added a third component to this, namely structural indifference or alternativity. As we will see, Muller also adds a similar third part. Thus, there appears to be a disagreement in the tradition as to what constitutes rational spontaneity. I will argue that there is no substantial difference. First, I would like to further clarify the second element of rational spontaneity, namely rational necessity.

According to Van Asselt, Bac, and te Velde, the reformed tradition understood rational necessity as:

> Rational necessity: if the intellect judges an act to be good, it is rationally necessary that the will assents.[63]

There is a necessary relationship between the intellect and the will. The intellect responds to moral reasons; it judges an act to be good, then the will assents or follows this judgement. We can see from this understanding that the core idea of rational necessity is the ability to respond to reasons. Carl F. Gobelman further clarifies rational necessity:

> What about the relationship between the will and the intellect? In this sense, the will cannot be said to determine itself; rather, it is determined "by the intellect whose last judgment of practical intellect it must follow." What is in view here is the internal deliberations that we all make-whether consciously or unconsciously. The intellect weighs the pros and cons of a given choice, and once that choice is made the will acts upon it. Therefore, the will is rightly determined by the judgment of the intellect while at the same time we are choosing and acting freely without constraint.[64]

Gobelman points out that the intellect responds to reasons. It weighs the pros and cons of a given choice. When the intellect decides which reason to choose, then the will follows the intellect. The intellect has the ability to

---

62. Van Asselt et al., *Reformed Thought on Freedom*, 205.
63. Van Asselt et al., *Reformed Thought on Freedom*, 39.
64. Gobelman, "To Be Free," 137.

respond to reasons and the will necessarily follows this judgment. This means that the reformed concept of freedom is fundamentally reason based.

Furthermore, Gobelman describes Turretin's view of necessity and highlights that free will and moral responsibility are located in reason. He writes:

> Turretin makes a distinction between extrinsic necessity (that which comes from the outside) and intrinsic necessity (that which comes from the inside), and in both cases (extrinsic and intrinsic) there is a necessity that impedes liberty and a necessity that enhances liberty. The necessity of coaction (which is extrinsic) and the necessity of instinct (which is intrinsic) are both incompatible with human liberty. In the former case, the action is not flowing freely and spontaneously, and in the latter case, the action is not flowing from rational understanding.[65]

Gobelman uses Turretin's distinction to further clarify rational necessity. He says that Turretin distinguishes between extrinsic and intrinsic necessity. Extrinsic necessity is the necessity of coaction or coercion. The intrinsic necessity is that of instinct. He says that both of these are incompatible with freedom but for different reasons. The necessity of coaction is incompatible with freedom because it "is not flowing freely and spontaneously" and intrinsic necessity is not compatible because "the action is not flowing from *rational understanding*."[66] Gobelman is identifying freedom with lack of coercion and rational understanding or the ability to respond to reasons appropriately.

He further highlights rational necessity:

> The intellect is free in the sense of determining whether or not something is good. The will is free in that once a determination is made, it moves to desire that which is good and avoid that which is bad.[67]

In other words, the will is free even though it is under rational necessity.

We should see from this that rational necessity is the ability to respond to reasons in the appropriate manner with the will following the intellect. It is here that we locate reformed theology as a type of reasons-responsive theory. It is also here that we see a fundamental compatibility with the first

---

65. Gobelman, "To Be Free," 131. It is interesting that Fischer would say something similar about someone acting from an addiction or compulsion or being electronically stimulated. These mechanisms of action bypass rationality. They are not the result of responding to reasons in the appropriate way.

66. Gobelman, "To Be Free," 131 (emphasis mine).

67. Gobelman, "To Be Free," 134.

component of guidance control, moderate reasons-responsiveness. We could view this compatibility on two levels. The first level is the foundation. The one thing all reason responsive theories share in common is that they locate freedom and moral responsibility in the ability to respond to reasons in the appropriate manner. Reformed theology affirms this in its conception of rational spontaneity; more particularly, rational necessity.

The second level is that of elaboration. There are various types of reasons-responsive theories. All of them are elaborating, in various ways, upon the foundation that freedom and moral responsibility are located in the ability to respond to reasons in the appropriate manner. Reformed theology did not elaborate on this second level. Instead, they were content to leave it at the foundational level. It is at the second level, that of elaboration, where moderate reasons-responsiveness could supplement the reformed view of rational spontaneity.

At this point, it is important for us to go back and discuss what some proposed to be a third element of rational spontaneity. We have seen that the Utrecht School believes that rational spontaneity contains a structural indifference or alternativity. Therefore, rational spontaneity ought to include this alternativity in its definition. Likewise, Muller holds to a third element in rational spontaneity. Let us look at the concerns of the Utrecht School and Muller.

Van Asselt, Bac, and te Velde write:

> While most authors extensively argue for the untenability of conceiving of freedom by indifference, some authors argue explicitly for a structural indifference or alternativity and make clear that this is factual contingency, which is also supposed in their conception of freedom as rational spontaneity.[68]

We saw in the last chapter that this structural indifference or alternativity is *in actu primo*. As Andreas Beck pointed out in his discussion with Helm, it is the ability to do otherwise in another possible world. As we saw, this is exactly what Fischer and Ravizza affirm. Thus, this concern does not harm our thesis.

Muller states his concern as follows:

> De Moor would later clarify the point, there is a formal distinction between the intellect and will and a compound act of judging and willing. The willing could have been otherwise, because either the initial appetite for the object or the intellective determination could have been otherwise—and the will's potency

---

68. Van Asselt et al., *Reformed Thought on Freedom*, 46.

to act otherwise remains *in actu primo*, namely, in the essential constitution of the will, albeit unactualized and unactualizable in the present moment.[69]

Like the Utrecht School, Muller affirms the will's potency to act otherwise or alternativity *in actu primo*. Furthermore, Muller writes:

> Both place the alternativity involved in free choice in the judgement of the intellect, with the will following freely the last determinate judgment of the practical intellect. What is important to recognize here is that they both affirm alternativity. Others among the reformed argue differently, placing alternativity in both intellect and the will, identifying the freedom as the free agreement of the will with the judgment of the intellect, others argue that the will, as a rational faculty, can in its freedom will or not will the object presented by the intellect placing the alternativity primarily in the will, and at least one writer posits an initial act of the will that induces to intellect to deliberate followed by the act of freely accepting the determinate judgment.[70]

Muller wants to affirm this alternativity as essential to rational spontaneity. He locates this alternativity in the first act and the divided sense.

He continues:

> First, although there is a movement from primary to secondary actuality identified in the act of willing, given that the movement is from the natural constitution of the will prior to its operation to the operation, it is not as if the natural constitution disappears as the operation begins—rather it remains as the underlying nature of the will that continues to define the operation. In other words, the indifferent *actus primus* of the will with its potencies to more than one effect belongs permanently to the will, and serves to identify the freedom and contingency of the *actus secundus* as an act that could be otherwise. Thus, in the divided sense, in case of a different judgment of the practical intellect (also recognized as defined *in sensu diviso*) it is possible that, an individual willing A could have willed not-A.[71]

The alternativity is located in the essential nature of the will. This is different from the Jesuit concept of indifference in the second act and the compound sense.

---

69. Muller, "Jonathan Edwards and Francis Turretin," 282.
70. Muller, "Jonathan Edwards and Francis Turretin," 280–81.
71. Muller, "Jonathan Edwards and Francis Turretin," 282–83.

He further writes that the reformed orthodox identified freedom with more than a lack of coercion and rational necessity. He writes:

> There, Turretin is quite clear that the will, considered absolutely or simply, in its primary actuality, is free not merely because it is spontaneous and uncoerced but also because it has a root indifference prior to its act of willing and, given that root indifference, it has both freedom of contrariety and freedom of contradiction.[72]

In other words, rational spontaneity consists of more than the two elements of which we have discussed. A third element must be added, namely indifference or alternativity *in actu primo*.

Muller further elaborates on the alternativity of rational spontaneity:

> Their point is that Turretin, very much like Voetius, stresses the movement of the will from indifference *in actu primo* to a determination of its object *in actu secondo*. Turretin, moreover, explains this movement in terms of the distinction between the simultaneity of potencies and the potency of simultaneity: the will can have, simultaneous, potencies to opposite or contradictory effects—what it cannot do is simultaneously act on opposite or contradictory potencies. In its primary actuality (*in actu primo*) or most fundamental existence, apart from any operation and prior to any determination of an object, the will can be identified as indifferent inasmuch as it possesses simultaneously potencies to different effects. In its secondary actuality (*in actu secondo*) or operation as determined toward a particular object, the will is no longer indifferent and, having acted upon one of its potencies, has excluded the opposites from its present operation.[73]

Muller describes this alternativity as simultaneous potencies to opposite or contradictory effects. This alternativity is *in actu primo*.

In summary, Muller, like the Utrecht School, views rational spontaneity as consisting of three parts: first, lack of coercion; second, rational necessity; and third, alternativity or indifference *in actu primo*.

---

72. Muller, "Jonathan Edwards and Francis Turretin," 14. He writes again: "The older tradition understood that there had to be a root indifference prior to the engagement of will and intellect, defined by the potency of the will to multiple effects and characterized by freedom of contradiction and contrariety, in order for there to be freedom of choice" (Muller, "Jonathan Edwards and Francis Turretin," 15).

73. Muller, *Divine Choice and Human Choice*, 256–57.

Helm also places indifference or alternativity in rational spontaneity. He writes:

> Indifference in some sense is clearly an ingredient of what the Orthodox call the freedom of rational spontaneity. It follows that a good part of the controversy between the Orthodox and the Jesuits is concerned with different senses and roles of "indifference."[74]

The reformed orthodox placed indifference in the first act and the divided sense. The Jesuits placed indifference in the second act and the compound sense. This is clearly different, but Helm affirms indifference in the first act and the divided sense. He writes:

> So Turretin, Voetius, and the Reformed Orthodox in general, by upholding indifference in the divided sense, have in mind the will *in itself*. They deny that once the requisites for an action A are in place the will remains free to do B, which is freedom in the compound sense. That's the heart of the controversy with the Jesuits.[75]

From this discussion, we can conclude that the reformed orthodox identified freedom and moral responsibility with rational spontaneity. Rational spontaneity consists of three elements:

1. Lack of coercion
2. Rational necessity
3. Alternativity or indifference *in actu primo*

This is substantially the same as Fischer and Ravizza's moderate reasons-responsiveness. In the actual sequence of events, the mechanism is moderately reasons-responsive if it issues in an action uncoerced and responsive to reason in a moderate reasons-responsive manner. Yet the mechanism could have been otherwise. In the alternative sequence, the mechanism has the power or ability to issue in numerous other actions.

Translating this into the language of the reformed orthodox, we could say that rational spontaneity in the actual sequence equals the will with the requisites for action being present. This level consists of:

1. Lack of coercion
2. Rational necessity

---

74. Helm, "Johnathan Edwards and the Parting of Ways?," 46.
75. Helm, "Johnathan Edwards and the Parting of Ways?," 49.

Rational spontaneity in the alternative sequence equals the will without the requisites for action being present. It consists of:

3. *In actu primo* alternativity, which consists of the liberty of contradiction, the liberty of contrariety, and the simultaneity of potencies.

We conclude that there is a fundamental compatibility between moderate reasons-responsiveness and rational spontaneity. This compatibility is located in the fact that both root freedom and moral responsibility in man's ability to respond to reasons. They are both types of reasons-responsive theories. Therefore, rational spontaneity is compatible with moderate reasons-responsiveness.[76]

Mechanism Ownership and The *Sensus Divinitatis*

In this section, we ask if reformed theology is compatible with the second aspect of guidance control, mechanism ownership. I will argue that mechanism ownership, as a subjectivist view, is similar to and compatible with the *sensus divinitatis*.

In chapter 2, we examined Fischer and Ravizza's theory of mechanism ownership. In this section, I will briefly summarize it and then present the problem of hard determinism. Fischer and Ravizza's doctrine of mechanism ownership consists of three parts. First, the agent must see himself as the source of his behavior. Second, the agent must see himself as a fair target

---

76. One area of difference among the reformed orthodox is with regard to the exact relationship between the will and the intellect. Muller writes: "The Reformed do differ concerning how these two liberties are understood in relation to the interaction of intellect and will. According to Turretin and Maresius, these liberties in the will and its basic indifference in its natural constitution, persist 'as long as the intellect remains doubtful and uncertain where to turn itself.' Both place the alternativity involved in free choice in the judgement of the intellect, with the will following freely the last determinate judgment of the practical intellect. What is important to recognize here is that they both affirm alternativity. Others among the Reformed argue differently, placing alternativity in both intellect and will, identifying freedom as the free agreement of the will with the judgment of the intellect, others argue that the will, as a rational faculty, can in its freedom will or not will the object presented by the intellect, placing the alternativity primarily in the will, and at least one writer posits an initial act of will that induces the intellect to deliberate followed by the act freely accepting the determinate judgement" (Muller, "Johnathan Edwards and Francis Turretin," 281–82).

However, this debate does not affect the compatibility of rational spontaneity and moderate reasons-responsiveness. The reason for this is that all agree that freedom and moral responsibility are fundamentally reason based, regardless of where the alternativity is placed.

of the reactive attitudes. Third, this view of himself must be based on the evidence in an appropriate way.

Fischer and Ravizza's view of mechanism ownership is subjectivist. This means that there are certain beliefs that the agent must have about himself in order to qualify as morally responsible. However, these beliefs need not be conscious. Fischer and Ravizza write:

> This process may involve conscious and deliberative reflection, but it need *not*. Just as a person who acts for a reason need not explicitly formulate the reason or consciously invoke it as an action guide, so a person can take responsibility in an implicit, nondeliberative way.[77]

Furthermore, they regard their view as coming to have a cluster of beliefs. They write:

> Indeed, on our view, taking responsibility is not even an *action*; rather, it is (roughly) *coming to have a certain cluster of beliefs (in a certain way)*.[78]

These beliefs are non-voluntary and dispositional. They write:

> Alternatively, one might say that whereas it may be in one's control which "occurrent beliefs" one has, it is not similarly in one's control which "dispositional beliefs" one has. And of course our account of taking responsibility specifies a set of *dispositional* beliefs.[79]

Mechanism ownership is a subjectivist view in that it requires the agent to have certain beliefs about himself. These beliefs need not be conscious and they consist of clusters of dispositional beliefs.

Fischer and Ravizza's subjectivist view do not reject objective elements:

> We require that an agent have a certain sort of view of himself in order to be morally responsible. That is, moral responsibility, on our view, is not simply a matter of having a set of "objective" features; in addition, one must (in the way we have specified) *view oneself* in a certain way.[80]

More clearly, they write:

---

77. Fischer and Ravizza, *Responsibility and Control*, 214.
78. Fischer and Ravizza, *Responsibility and Control*, 217.
79. Fischer and Ravizza, *Responsibility and Control*, 217–18.
80. Fischer and Ravizza, *Responsibility and Control*, 221.

Of course, this subjectivity does not imply that there are not important "objective" elements of our account of taking responsibility and moral responsibility.[81]

In summary, Fischer and Ravizza's view of mechanism ownership is subjectivist. The agent must view himself in a certain way. This does not deny objective features of moral responsibility. The certain way in which the agent must view himself consists of a cluster of dispositional beliefs that need not be conscious. At the heart of these dispositional beliefs are the beliefs that (1) the agent sees himself as the source of his behavior, (2) the agent sees himself as the fair target of the reactive attitudes, and (3) the agent bases these beliefs on the evidence.

Michael McKenna raises a serious objection to this view. I also noted Fischer and Ravizza's identification of this problem in chapter 2. McKenna put it this way:

> According to Fischer and Ravizza, ownership requires that one adopt certain attitudes towards herself. This exposes them to the possibility that a person might not adopt the relevant attitudes, in particular, that the person might not come to think that she is an appropriate object of others' moral demands and expectations as manifested in the reactive attitudes.[82]

An example of this type of person would be a hard determinist. This person has concluded that determinism and free will/moral responsibility are incompatible and determinism is true. Therefore, they are not morally responsible. They do not see themselves as a fair target of the reactive attitudes. In Fischer and Ravizza's theory, the hard determinist is not morally responsible. Fischer and Ravizza admit that they have no knock down argument against this.

My argument is that reformed theology has a similar subjectivist view and this subjectivist view has the resources to avoid the problem of hard determinism. This is evident in the doctrine of the *sensus divinitatis*. The *sensus divinitatis* consists of three aspects. First, there exists in all men an implanted knowledge of God. Second, there exists in all men an implanted knowledge of God's Law. Third, this implanted knowledge is ineradicable from man. Implicit in this *sensus divinitatis* is a subjectivist view similar to Fischer and Ravizza's. In order to see this, I will examine the Westminster Confession of Faith and the reformed tradition more broadly with regard to the *sensus divinitatis*.

---

81. Fischer and Ravizza, *Responsibility and Control*, 223.
82. McKenna, "Contemporary Compatibilism," 194.

We begin our discussion with the Westminster Confession of Faith. WCF 1:1 says:

> Although the light of nature, and the works of creation and providence, do so far manifest the goodness, wisdom, and power of God, as to leave men inexcusable, yet they are not sufficient to give that knowledge of God, and of his will, which is necessary unto salvation.[83]

This article addresses natural revelation. God has revealed himself in "the light of nature" and in "creation and providence." Natural revelation renders all mankind "inexcusable" or morally responsible before God.

By the phrase "light of nature," the Confession means an implanted sense of divinity. J. V. Fesko and Guy M. Richard write:

> The phrase "the light of nature" occurs five times in the Confession (1.1; 1.6; 10.4; 20.4; 21.1) and three times in the larger Catechism (qq. 2, 60, 151) and refers primarily to an internal and natural or inborn testimony concerning God, a *sensus divinitatis*. In WLC q.2, the "light of nature" is depicted as being "in man" and, in both WLC 2 and WCF 1.1, it is clearly distinguished from the external works of creation. The Scripture proof texts, in particular Romans 1:19–20 and 2:14, along with the proof texts for 1.6, further demonstrate that the light of nature resides within the individual and includes the conscience, among other faculties, as a judge within us and a means for distinguishing right from wrong.[84]

The "light of nature" is a *sensus divinitatis*. This is an implanted knowledge of God, which includes our conscience and enables us to distinguish right from wrong. In WCF 21:1, we read about the content of the light of nature:

> The light of nature sheweth that there is a God, who hath lordship and sovereignty over all; is good, and doeth good unto all; and is therefore to be feared, loved, praised, called upon, trusted in, and served, with all the heart, and with all the soul, and with all the might.

---

83. The Canons of Dort also say this: "There remains, however, in man since the fall, the glimmerings of natural light, whereby he retains some knowledge of God, of natural things, and of the difference between good and evil, and shows some regard for virtue and for good outward behavior" (Dennison Jr., *Reformed Confessions*, 135).

84. Fesko and Richard, "Natural Theology," 252.

The "light of nature" consists of the knowledge that there is a God and of the knowledge that man has certain responsibilities to this God, namely that he is feared, loved, praised, called upon, trusted, and served.

Fesko and Richard write concerning this article:

> The thought in 21.1 should not be limited to merely the idea that the light of nature only "shows" these things (i.e., natural revelation), but it should clearly also include that these things are perceived and received by the individual (i.e., natural theology) to such an extent that he knows them and is thus rendered inexcusable for not worshipping God.[85]

In speaking of the "light of nature" Hodge writes:

> The same is disproved from the fact that conscience, which is a universal and indestructible element of human nature, necessarily implies our accountability to a personal moral Governor, and as a matter of fact has uniformly led men to a recognition of his existence and of their relation to him.[86]

---

85. Van Dixhoorn writes: "Instead, this historic statement of doctrine begins by reminding us that God has revealed to all people, even those without a Bible. The confession mentions that this general revelation comes to us in two forms. There is the 'light of nature,' by which is meant the divine imprint which is left on each of us by our Maker. That is, we are made in God's image and even though we are fallen creatures, God's image remains stamped upon us. And there are 'the works of creation and providence.' The world that we see and the world about which we read tell us of our creator and provider, the one who made and now upholds all things.... Here, unmistakably, the confession is following the trail laid down by the Apostle Paul in Romans 1–2.... In those chapters the apostle both reminds us of this general revelation and tells us that it leaves every person without an excuse before God" (Van Dixhoorn, *Confessing the Faith*, 4).

86. Hodge, *Westminster Confession*, 27. R. C. Sproul writes: "Paul talks about God's revealing his law inwardly through the human heart, so that every person is born with a conscience (Rom 2:14–15). God plants a sense of himself immediately in the soul of his creatures. John Calvin calls this the *sensus divinitatis*, 'the sense of the divine.' As fallen creatures we suppress the knowledge of right and wrong that God plants within us. But try as we may, we can never extinguish it. It is still present in the soul" (Sproul, *Truths We Confess*, 6). Leith writes: "The authors of the Confession were sure that God had revealed himself through the 'light of nature.' By 'light of nature' the members of the Assembly meant, according to Jack Bartlett Rodgers, 'a direct revelation of God implanted in the heart of man, a *sensus divinitatis*, which remains, by God's common grace, even after the Fall, though defaced and dimmed.' They were also sure that God revealed himself through his works of creation and providence. They did not denigrate this revelation. It was enough to leave man without excuse, but it was not sufficient for man's salvation" (Leith, *Assembly at Westminster*, 76).

Hodge argues that the *sensus divinitatis* is a universal and indestructible element of man. By it, we know of God's existence, our relationship to Him, and our accountability to Him.

From this discussion of the Westminster Confession of Faith we can conclude that it teaches that all men have a "light of nature" or *sensus divinitatis*. This *sensus divinitatis* consists of the knowledge that God exists and that we are morally responsible to Him. This *sensus divinitatis* is part of man's constitution. He is unable to eradicate it from his person. This means that man always has this knowledge of God and this knowledge that he is morally responsible to Him.[87]

More broadly, the reformed tradition also teaches that all men have a *sensus divinitatis*. John Calvin writes concerning the *sensus divinitatis*:

> There is within the human mind, and indeed by natural instinct, an awareness of divinity. This we take to be beyond controversy. To prevent anyone from taking refuge in the pretense of ignorance, God himself has implanted in all men a certain understanding of his divine majesty. Ever renewing its memory, he repeatedly sheds fresh drops. Since, therefore, men one and all perceive that there is a God and that he is their maker, they are condemned by their own testimony because they have failed to honor him and to consecrate their lives to his will.[88]

Calvin regards this sense of divinity to be implanted in all men by God. By this, men perceive that there is a God and He is their maker. This *sensus divinitatis* renders man responsible to God.

Calvin views this sense of divinity as permanent. He writes:

> Men of sound judgement will always be sure that a sense of divinity which can never be effaced is engraved upon men's minds. Indeed, the perversity of the impious, who though they struggle furiously are unable to extricate themselves from the fear of God, is abundant testimony that this conviction, namely,

---

87. These truths are reinforced by other statements in the Confession. For example, in WCF 4:2, the Confession speaks about man "having the law of God written in their hearts." A statement like this implies that man has knowledge of the Lawgiver and His will for us. It also implies that man sees himself as subject to God's evaluation or reactive attitudes.

The Confession says: "God gave to Adam a law, as a covenant of works, by which he bound him and all his posterity to personal, entire, exact, and perpetual obedience, promised life upon the fulfilling, and threatened death upon the breach of it, and endued him with power and ability to keep it" (WCF 19:1). This also implies the knowledge of God and that man views himself as subject to God's reactive attitudes.

88. Calvin, *Institutes of the Christian Religion*, 1:44.

that there is some God, is naturally inborn in all, and it is fixed deep within, as it were in the very marrow.[89]

This sense of divinity "can never be effaced" from man because it "is engraved upon men's hearts." Even the impious or fallen mankind "are unable to extricate themselves from the fear of God." Calvin's comments on the *sensus divinitatis* teach that all men have an implanted knowledge of God, that they have an implanted knowledge of their responsibility to God, and that this implanted knowledge cannot be removed from man.

Francis Turretin also teaches a *sensus divinitatis*. He writes:

> We find in man a natural law written upon each one's conscience excusing and accusing them in good and bad actions, which therefore necessarily implies the knowledge of God, the legislator, by whose authority it binds men to obedience and proposes rewards or punishments. "The Gentiles, which have not the law" (i.e., the law of Moses) "do by nature the things contained in the law, these, having not the law, are a law unto themselves: which show the work of the law written in their hearts, their conscience also bearing witness, and their thoughts the meanwhile accusing or else excusing one another (Rom 2:14–15). This could not be said if conscience did not dictate to each one that there is a deity who approves of good actions and disapproves and punishes evil deeds.[90]

Turretin argues that man has a knowledge of God's Law written upon their hearts. This knowledge implies a knowledge of God as the legislator. This knowledge functions as a basis of our responsibility before God.

Wilhelmus á Brakel writes:

> That man possesses such innate knowledge of God is evident in the following passage, "For when the Gentiles, which have not the law, do by nature the things contained in the law, these, having not

---

89. Calvin, *Institutes of the Christian Religion*, 46. B. B. Warfield elaborates on Calvin's teaching: "That the knowledge of God is innate (I. iii.3), naturally engraved on the hearts of men (I. iv. 1), and so a part of their very constitution as men (I. iii. 1), that it is a matter of instinct (I. iii. 1, I. iv. 2), and every man is self-taught it from his birth (I. iii. 3), Calvin is thoroughly assured. He lays it down as incontrovertible fact that 'the human mind, by natural instinct itself, possesses some sense of a deity' . . . and defends the corollaries which flow from this fact, that the knowledge of God is universal and indelible. All men know there is a God, who has made them, and to whom they are responsible. No savage is sunk so low as to have lost this sense of deity, which is wrought into his very constitution: and the degradation of men's worship is a proof of its ineradicableness" (Warfield, *Calvin And Augustine*, 34).

90. Turretin, *Institutes of Elenctic Theology*, 7.

the law ... shew the work of the law written in their hearts, their conscience also bearing witness, and their thoughts the mean while accusing or else excusing one another" (Rom 2:14–15).

Here the apostle refers to people who do not possess the Holy Scriptures. He states that the law is written in their hearts and that they know by nature that they must live according to this law.... The knowledge of the Lawgiver is proportionate to the knowledge of the law. This knowledge obligates them to obedience, and teaches that the Lawgiver will justly reward the obedient and punish the disobedient. This Lawgiver, not being a man, is therefore acknowledged to be God.[91]

A Brakel also teaches that man has an implanted knowledge of God and His Law and that this knowledge is the basis of man's responsibility to God.

He continues:

Fifthly, if this knowledge of God in man were not innate and he lacked the ability by way of the visible to ascend to the invisible God, then the heathen would be without sin. In the absence of a lawgiver there is also no law, and wherever there is no law there is no transgression; therefore, they could not be condemned. To hold to the latter is absurd, and thus it is certain that the heathen have knowledge of God.[92]

He argues that without this knowledge of the lawgiver and the knowledge that they must live according to the law, man is not responsible.

Herman Bavinck writes:

The laws of thought are the same for all; the theory of numbers is everywhere the same; the difference between good and evil is known by all. Similarly, there is no people without religion and knowledge of God. This is explicable only on the assumption of self-evident principles, ideas common to all, "eternal verities," which have been instilled in the human mind by nature. In religion, whether we want to or not, we always have to go back to a "seed of religion," a "sense of divinity," a "divine instinct," an "innate knowledge." Scripture itself sets an example in this. While it binds us as powerfully as possible to God's objective revelation in nature and grace, it at the same time attests that humanity is God's image and offspring, that humans possess in their minds a capacity to see God in his works and have the

---

91. á Brakel, *Christian's Reasonable Service*, 8.
92. á Brakel, *Christian's Reasonable Service*, 10.

requirements of the law written in their hearts (Gen 1:26; Acts 17:27; Rom 1:19; 2:15).[93]

Bavinck describes the *sensus divinitatis* as consisting of a capacity in man's mind to "see God in His works" and also that man has "the requirements of the law written in their hearts."

W. T. Shedd writes:

> Second, the pagan, though having an imperfect, yet has a valid and trustworthy knowledge of God. . . . It is sufficient to constitute a foundation for responsibility and the imputation of sin. Idolatry is charged against the pagan as guilt, because in practicing it he is acting against his better knowledge (1:20). Sensuality is guilt for the same reason (1:32). Unthankfulness is guilt (1:21). Failure to worship the true God is guilt (1:21). Accordingly, Westminster Confession 1.1 affirms that "the light of nature and the works of creation and providence do so far manifest the goodness, wisdom, and power of God, as to leave man inexcusable."[94]

According to Shedd, the pagan has knowledge of God and this knowledge is a foundation for responsibility.

He continues:

> There must always be something innate and subjective, in order that the objective may be efficient. The objects of sense themselves would make no conscious impression if there were not five senses in man upon which to impress themselves. In like manner, the order, design, and unity of external nature would not suggest the idea of a Supreme being if that idea were not subjective to man.[95]

He argues that this knowledge is innate and subjective.

From this discussion, we see that the reformed tradition and the Westminster Confession of Faith affirm three things: (1) man has an implanted knowledge of God, (2) man has an implanted knowledge of God's law, and (3) this knowledge of God and His Law is ineradicable. My argument is that these three propositions implicitly contain a subjectivist view similar to and compatible with mechanism ownership. We can see this by more closely considering these three propositions.

---

93. Bavinck, *Reformed Dogmatics*, 71.
94. Shedd, *Dogmatic Theology*, 186.
95. Shedd, *Dogmatic Theology*, 187.

First, let us consider the proposition that man has an implanted knowledge of God. Our purpose is not to give an analysis concerning the exact nature of this knowledge.[96] Rather, our concern regards what this knowledge implies. It seems reasonable to infer that this first proposition implies that man knows he is distinct from God. The reformed tradition regards this knowledge of God to be substantially in line with their doctrine of God. Though this knowledge of God may or may not yield knowledge of something like the doctrine of the Trinity, it seems reasonable to hold that it yields knowledge that man is not God, that he is distinct from God. This means that man views God as distinct from himself, which implies that man views himself as distinct from God. In the language of the Westminster standards, man views God as the first cause and he views himself as a second cause. Viewing himself as a second cause implies that man views himself as a genuine second cause of at least some of his actions. We can see from this that Fischer and Ravizza's first condition of taking responsibility is reasonably inferred from the implanted knowledge of God. Man views himself as the source of his behavior.

Second, let us further consider the proposition that man has an implanted knowledge of God as well as the proposition that man has an implanted knowledge of God's law in relation to the reactive attitudes. As we have seen, the reformed tradition regards the implanted knowledge of God as a basis for man's moral responsibility. This knowledge made man aware, at some level, that he is morally responsible to God. Man thus views himself as morally responsible to God. This implies that man views himself as the apt target of God's reactive attitudes. Man views himself as legitimately subject to God's reactive attitudes of praise and blame. In this way, we see that Fischer and Ravizza's second condition of taking responsibility is reasonably inferred from the implanted knowledge of God, namely that the agent must view himself as a fair target of the reactive attitudes.

This is further strengthened by considering the proposition that man has the implanted knowledge of God's law. The Westminster Confession of Faith describes this implanted knowledge of God's law as the Ten Commandments. WCF 4:2 says that God created man "having the law of God written in their hearts." WCF 19:1 elaborates on this, "God gave to Adam a law as a covenant of works." WCF 19:2 identifies this law as the Ten Commandments, "This law, after his fall, continued to be a perfect rule of righteousness, and,

---

96. Contemporary philosophers differ on this. Alvin Plantinga holds that it is a disposition to form belief in God (see Plantinga, *Warranted Christian Belief*, 167–98); Paul Helm views it as the knowledge of a proposition that God exists (see Helm, *John Calvin's Ideas*, 209–45); and Cornelius Van Til views it as a presupposition by which man's knowledge is possible (see Van Til, *Introduction to Systematic Theology*).

as such, was delivered by God upon Mount Sinai, in ten commandments." The implanted knowledge of the Ten Commandments also implies that man views himself as a fair target of God's reactive attitudes. Furthermore, it implies that man views himself as a fair target of God's reactive attitudes for specific things, namely the Ten Commandments.

This is important because it implies that man also views himself as the fair target of the reactive attitudes of other people. WCF 19:2 goes on to say that the Ten Commandments were "written on two tables, the first four commandments containing our duty towards God, and the other six, our duty towards man." The law of God written in our hearts causes man to view himself as having a duty towards God as well as other people. This implies that man views himself as the fair target of the reactive attitudes of God as well as other people. Man views himself as the fair target of the praise of God and man when he fulfils his duty towards them and he views himself as the fair target of the blame of both God and man when he does not fulfill his duty towards them. In this way, we can reasonably infer that the implanted knowledge of God's law implies the second condition of Fischer and Ravizza's subjectivist view of taking responsibility.

Third, Fischer and Ravizza's view of taking responsibility requires that the agent base the first two conditions on the evidence. They had left it unclear as to exactly what this means. Yet from a reformed perspective, we can see how these first two conditions are based upon the evidence of the *sensus divinitatis*. Man's view of himself as a genuine second cause and man's view of himself as the fair target of the reactive attitudes of God and others are based upon the implanted knowledge of God and His law. This implanted knowledge is genuine knowledge and thus the highest quality of evidence. It is also ineradicable knowledge. This means that man will always have the highest quality of evidence on which to base his view of himself as a genuine cause of some of his actions as well as the fair target of the reactive attitudes of God and others.

From this discussion, we conclude that reformed theology and guidance control have very similar subjectivist conditions on moral responsibility. This means that the second aspect of guidance control is compatible with reformed theology. We must now briefly address two objections.

The Problem of Hard Determinism

We saw that Fischer and Ravizza encountered a problem with the hard determinist. This person had convinced himself that determinism and moral responsibility are incompatible and that determinism is true. Give these beliefs, the hard determinist does not view himself as the proper target of the reactive attitudes. According to Fischer and Ravizza, this means that he is not morally responsible.

The reformed subjectivist view does not encounter this problem. The *sensus divinitatis* is an essential part of man that cannot be eradicated. Though man can convince himself of many false beliefs, including hard determinism, he can never eradicate the *sensus divinitatis*. This means that in some sense, man will always view himself as the source of his actions and the proper subject of the reactive attitudes. Man can suppress these truths but he can never eliminate them. They will always be at least dispositional beliefs that make up the background of man's psychology, even if they are not conscious. This means that reformed theology has the resources to hold a subjectivist view while also avoiding the problem of hard determinism.

The Problem of Original Sin

A final problem to discuss is original sin. If guidance control is necessary for freedom and moral responsibility, then we cannot be held responsible for something done without our guidance control. This would appear to imply that we cannot be responsible for original sin. Yet reformed theology clearly teaches that we are guilty of Adam's sin. Does this mean that guidance control is not compatible with reformed theology after all? This concern can be answered by the reformed doctrine of original sin, in particular the federal headship of Adam.

The idea that mankind in some sense sinned in Adam goes all the way back to the early church. However, the way in which the reformed conceived of the transmission of Adam's guilt was unique. Louis Berkhof writes:

> They gave a more exact definition of the relation of Adam's sin to that of his descendants. By substituting for the realistic theory of Tertullian, Augustine and Anselm, the covenant idea. It is true that they did not fully develop this idea; yet they utilized it in defining the relation between Adam and his descendants. Beza especially emphasized the fact that Adam was not only the natural head of the human race, but also its federal representative; and that consequently his first sin is imputed as guilt to all his descendants.[97]

As Berkhof notes, the reformed utilized the covenant idea to describe the way in which Adam's guilt was transmitted to mankind. Adam was in

---

97. Berkhof, *History of Christian Doctrines*, 147.

a covenant with God and he was the legal or federal representative of all mankind. Mankind was "in Adam" in the sense that we were represented by Adam in a covenant. Since Adam was our representative, his guilt was imputed or credited to our account.

Donald McLeod notes that federalism was not the only view held in the reformed tradition, but it came to be the dominant view. He writes:

> This federal understanding of the relationship between Adam and his posterity became the standard Reformed position. There was, however, one exception: W. G. T. Shedd. . . . Shedd maintains the realist view that the whole of human nature, and indeed every human being, was present in Adam and acted in him, in the moment of his fall. . . . Contrary to the opinion of Shedd, however, the overall Reformed consensus has been that the union between ourselves and Adam was not real but federal. Yet, as we have seen, this federal headship is justified by his biological connection with the human species, and it receives further justification from the fact that Adam, our "root," was asked to complete his probation under ideal conditions.[98]

The view that came to dominate reformed theology consisted of three basic elements. First, Adam was in an original covenant of works with God. Second, Adam was the legal or federal representative of mankind in this covenant. Third, when Adam sinned, the guilt of that sin was imputed to all mankind. In this way, all mankind sinned in Adam.

We see these basic elements in the Westminster Confession and catechisms. In WCF 7:2 we read:

> The first covenant made with man was a covenant of works, wherein life was promised to Adam; and in him to his posterity, upon condition of perfect and personal obedience.

The Confession affirms that Adam was in a "covenant of works." This establishes a legal or federal relationship between Adam and "his posterity."

WCF 6:3 teaches that the guilt of Adam's first sin was imputed to all mankind:

> They being the root of all mankind, the guilt of this sin was imputed, and the same death in sin and corrupted nature conveyed to all posterity, descending from them by ordinary generation.

God legally credited or imputed the guilt of Adam's sin to all mankind because we all sinned representatively in Adam.

---

98. Macleod, "Original Sin in Reformed Theology," 138.

Original sin consists of more than the imputation of the guilt of Adam's sin. We see this in WLC 25:

> Q. Wherein consisteth the sinfulness of that estate whereunto man fell? A. The sinfulness of that estate whereunto man fell, consisteth in the guilt of Adam's first sin, the want of that righteousness wherein he was created, and the corruption of his nature, whereby he is utterly indisposed, disabled, and made opposite unto all that is spiritually good, and wholly inclined to all evil, and that continually; which is commonly called Original Sin, and from which do proceed all actual transgressions.

The Catechism defines original sin to consist of three parts: (1) the guilt of Adam's first sin, (2) the want of original righteousness, and (3) the corruption of his nature and then adds, "which is commonly called original sin." For our purposes, we are concerned more specifically with how mankind could be guilty of Adam's first sin without making use of their individual guidance control. We will see that the reformed tradition has the resources to answer this question in federalism.[99] We can tell a brief explanatory story combining the resources of federalism with guidance control.

Adam was created perfectly good and in a covenant of works with God as mankind's federal representative. God endowed Adam with genuine free will conceived of as guidance control. This meant that Adam had the ability to respond to reasons in a moderately reasons-responsive sense. It also meant that Adam viewed himself in a certain manner; as a genuine agent or second cause of his actions. He viewed himself as an apt target of God's reactive attitudes and he based both of these on the *sensus divinitatis*; that is, on the implanted knowledge of God and God's law.

Adam was in the garden with his wife Eve and the serpent approached them. The serpent spoke with Adam and Eve giving them reasons why they should eat from the tree of the knowledge of good and evil. Adam was neither under coercion nor was he as an agent unable to respond to reasons appropriately. Having witnessed his wife eat the fruit, Adam decided to eat the fruit knowing full well that God had forbidden it, that he was the genuine second cause of this action, and that he was the apt target of God's reactive attitudes, basing this, in part, on the *sensus divinitatis*.[100] Thus, Adam committed this sin using his individual guidance control.

---

99. For an interesting federal view without relying on a covenant of works, see McGowan, *Adam, Christ, and Covenant*.

100. It would also have been based on the special command that God gave them in the garden to not eat of the tree.

As our federal representative, we sinned in Adam. When Adam used his guidance control to sin, he and his guidance control functioned in our place. In a representative sense, Adam's individual guidance control was our individual guidance control. This is why it was just for God to impute the guilt of Adam's sin to all mankind. God is not imputing the guilt of Adam apart from the exercise of mankind's individual guidance control. Mankind did utilize their individual guidance control representatively in Adam.

Summary

In this chapter, we have seen five things. First, we have seen that the reformed view of free will and moral responsibility is a type of compatibilism. Second, we have seen rational spontaneity is a type of reasons-responsive compatibilism. This establishes compatibility between reformed theology and the first part of guidance control, moderate reasons-responsiveness. Third, we have seen that the *sensus divinitatis* implies a similar subjectivist view to that of guidance control. This establishes compatibility between reformed theology and the second part of guidance control, mechanism ownership. Fourth, we have seen that the ineradicable nature of the *sensus divinitatis* provides the resources to adopt a subjectivist view without the problem of hard determinism that Fischer and Ravizza face. Fifth, we have seen that the guilt of Adam's sin is justly imputed to mankind because Adam, using his guidance control, represented mankind.

CHAPTER FIVE

Jonathan Edwards and the Reformed Tradition

Introduction

IN THE PREVIOUS TWO chapters, we saw that reformed theology is compatibilism. God's decree, foreknowledge and providence are consistent with man's freedom and moral responsibility. We have also seen that reformed theology is a type of reasons-responsive theory and has a type of subjectivist condition. We saw this by surveying the teachings of the reformed confessions and the reformed orthodox on these matters. Now we need to take up the thinking of Jonathan Edwards. Edwards stands within the reformed tradition and has written the most complete treatment of these issues the tradition has known, namely *The Freedom of the Will*.

Yet, it has been recently argued that Edwards departed from the tradition.[1] Richard Muller argues for a "parting of the ways" between the reformed orthodox and Edwards. Paul Helm has challenged this point.[2] This chapter will have a twofold purpose. I will seek to demonstrate that Edwards thinking on these issues is compatible with guidance control and I will seek to establish substantial continuity between Edwards and the reformed orthodox.

I will do this in seven parts. First, I will argue that Edwards denies the sourcehood condition. Second, I will argue that Edwards denies the alternative possibilities condition. This provides substantial continuity between guidance control, the reformed orthodox and Edwards. It clearly places all of them in the compatibilist camp. Third, I will give a brief description of Edwards view of freedom. Fourth, I will argue that Edwards affirms a type

---

1. See Muller, "Jonathan Edwards and the Absence," 42–60; "Jonathan Edwards and Francis Turretin," 268–85.

2. See Helm, "Jonathan Edwards and the Parting of Ways?," 42–60; "Turretin and Edwards Once More," 286–96; "Turretin and Edwards Compatibilism," 335–55.

of reasons-responsive theory. Fifth, I will argue that Edwards has a similar type of subjectivist condition. Affirming these two shows more continuity between guidance control, the reformed orthodox and Edwards. Sixth, I will survey the Muller/Helm debate. This survey will argue that there are differences between Edwards and the reformed orthodox. However, these differences are not sufficient to place them in different categories. In other words, Edwards and the reformed orthodox are reasons-responsive compatibilists, yet with some differences. Seventh, I will make a couple concluding points of my own regarding the Muller/Helm debate.

Let us begin by noticing how the reformed orthodox and Edwards had similar projects. In the conclusion to *Freedom of the Will*, Edwards summarizes his project. He writes:

> Hereby it becomes manifest, that God's moral government over mankind, his treating them as moral agents, making them the objects of his commands, counsels, calls, warnings, expostulations, promises, threatening, rewards and punishments, is not inconsistent with a determining disposal of all events, of every kind, throughout the universe, in his providence; either by positive efficacy, or permission. Indeed such an *universal determining providence*, infers some kind of necessity of all events; such a necessity as implies an infallible previous fixedness of the futurity of the event; but no other necessity of moral events, or volitions of intelligent agents, is needful in order to this, than *moral* necessity; which does as much ascertain the futurity of the event, as any other necessity.[3]

In light of this passage, we can state that Edward's thinks he has justified a version of compatibilism. He writes that "God's moral government over mankind . . . is not inconsistent with a determining disposal of all events."[4] He writes that God's "treating them as moral agents, making them objects of his commands, . . . rewards and punishments, is not inconsistent with . . . *universal determining providence*."[5] This "infers some kind of necessity of all events."[6] Though the word 'compatibilism' is not used, Edwards clearly has a compatibilist project. His compatibilism reminds us of what we saw in the reformed orthodox. Like Edward's, they were demonstrating that necessity is compatible with freedom and moral responsibility.

---

3. Edwards, *Freedom of the Will*, 431.
4. Edwards, *Freedom of the Will*, 431.
5. Edwards, *Freedom of the Will*, 431.
6. Edwards, *Freedom of the Will*, 431.

I have previously articulated the compatibilism of the reformed orthodox in terms of the denial of the sourcehood and alternative possibilities conditions and the affirmation of a type of reason-responsive theory and subjectivist condition. I now wish to articulate Edwards's view in these terms as well. The result will be a substantial continuity between guidance control, the reformed orthodox and Edwards.

Sourcehood Condition

That Edward's denied the sourcehood condition is abundantly clear from many of his comments on God's foreknowledge, decree and providence. Let us first recall the sourcehood condition and then see examples of Edward's denial. The sourcehood condition stated, "It is necessary for an agent to be the ultimate source of his actions in order for him to be free and morally responsible." Edward's comments on God's decree, foreknowledge, and providence show that he regarded God as the ultimate source of man's actions, thus denying this condition.

We have already seen, from the introductory quote, that Edwards affirms "God's moral government over mankind." He affirms God's "disposal of all events" and His "universal determining providence."[7] Clearly, the source of man's actions does not terminate in man, but traces back to God's providence. This is a clear denial of the sourcehood condition.

In addition to this, Edwards affirms that God's decree is the ultimate source of man's actions. He writes:

> From what has been observed it is evident, that the absolute *decrees* of God are no more inconsistent with human liberty, on account of any necessity of the event which follows from such decrees, then the absolute *foreknowledge* of God. Because the connection between the event and certain foreknowledge, is as infallible and indissoluble, as between the event and an absolute decree. That is, 'tis no more impossible that the event and decree should not agree together, than that the event and absolute knowledge should disagree.[8]

In this passage, Edwards asserts that "the absolute *decrees* of God are no more inconsistent with human liberty." Again, we see his compatibilism. There is a "necessity of the event" that "follows from such decrees." The decrees are the source of the event since the event "follows from such decrees."

---

7. Edwards, *Freedom of the Will*, 431.
8. Edwards, *Freedom of the Will*, 261.

God's decrees bring about the event with necessity. Among the events that follow from the decrees are the actions of man. Thus, man is not the ultimate source of his actions. God's absolute decrees are the ultimate source.

Edwards argues again that human actions terminate in God's decree. He writes:

> And the certain truth of these doctrines, concerning God's eternal purposes, will follow from what was just now observed concerning God's universal providence; how it infallibly follows from what has been proved, that God orders all events, and the volitions of moral agents amongst others, by such a decisive disposal, that the events are infallibly connected with his disposal. For if God disposes all events, so that the infallible existence of the events is decided by his providence, then he doubtless thus orders and decides things *knowingly,* and *on design.* God don't do what he does, nor order what he orders, accidentally and unawares; either *without,* or *beside* his intention. And if there be a foregoing *design* of doing and ordering as he does, this is the same with a purpose or *decree.*[9]

Here we see that "God orders all events, and the volitions of moral agents . . . by his providence." Yet this providence does not occur blindly, "but knowingly, and on design." This 'knowingly" and "on design" is God's decree. Edward's writes, "And if there be a foregoing design . . . this is the same with a purpose or decree." Edwards, clearly teaches that God's decree is the ultimate source of the volitions of moral agents.

In another passage, Edwards asserts that God's foreknowledge presupposes His decree:

> I might also shew, how God's certain foreknowledge must suppose an absolute decree, and how such a decree can be proved to a demonstration from it; but that this discourse mayn't be lengthened out too much, that must be omitted for the present.[10]

Edwards tells us that God's foreknowledge "supposes an absolute decree." God knows all things because he has decreed all things. As we have seen, God decrees the actions of men. Thus, the ultimate source of men's actions is God's foreknowledge based on his decree. In line with the reformed orthodox, Edwards teaches that all things, including the free and morally responsible actions of men, trace back to God's decree, foreknowledge and providence. Thus, Edwards clearly denies the sourcehood condition.

---

9. Edwards, *Freedom of the Will*, 434.
10. Edwards, *Freedom of the Will*, 435.

Alternative Possibilities Condition

In addition to denying the sourcehood condition, Edwards also denied the alternative possibilities condition. Let me restate the alternative possibilities condition or principle (2):

> (2) An agent freely and morally responsibly does x only if S could have done otherwise than x given C (God's foreknowledge, decree and/or providence).

Edwards clearly denies that things could have been otherwise in regard to God's foreknowledge. He writes,

> So that it is perfectly demonstrable, that if there be any infallible knowledge of future volitions, the event is *necessary;* or, in other words, that it is *impossible* but the event should come to pass. For if it ben't impossible but that it may be otherwise, then it is not impossible but that the proposition which affirms its future coming to pass, may not now be true. But how absurd is that, on the supposition that there is now an infallible knowledge (i.e knowledge which it is impossible should fail) that it is true. There is this absurdity in it, that it is not impossible but that there now should be no truth in that proposition, which is now infallibly known to be true.[11]

Edwards teaches that infallible foreknowledge renders the event as necessary. This means "that it is *impossible* but the event should come to pass. For if it ben't impossible but that it may be otherwise." In other words, if God foreknows x, it is impossible for x to be otherwise. Edwards started this paragraph by speaking of future volitions, "if there be any infallible knowledge of future volitions." These future volitions or choices are infallibly known by God. Thus, they cannot be otherwise given God's foreknowledge. This is a clear denial of principle (2) or the alternative possibilities condition.

Edwards writes again:

> 'Tis as evident, as 'tis possible anything should be, that it is impossible a thing which is infallibly known to be true, should prove not to be true; therefore there is a necessity that it should [not] be otherwise; whether the knowledge be the cause of this necessity, or the necessity the cause of the knowledge.
>
> All certain knowledge, whether it be foreknowledge or after-knowledge, or concomitant knowledge, proves the thing

---

11. Edwards, *Freedom of the Will*, 258.

> known now to be necessary, by some means or other; or proves that it is impossible it should now be otherwise than true.[12]

Edwards teaches not only that God's foreknowledge renders the thing known necessary, but any knowledge. If something is known, then it is necessary and if it is necessary, then it cannot be otherwise. As we have seen, man's actions are known by God. Therefore, they cannot be otherwise given God's foreknowledge.

We should observe at this point that Edwards regards God's foreknowledge to "suppose an absolute decree."[13] Thus, since man's actions cannot be otherwise given God's foreknowledge, they also cannot be otherwise given God's absolute decree.

Another way we can see Edward's denial of the alternative possibilities condition is by his treatment of necessity. Edwards writes:

> Philosophical necessity is really nothing else than the full and fixed connection between the things signified by the subject and predicate of a proposition, which affirms something to be true. When there is such a connection, then the thing affirmed in the proposition is necessary, in a philosophical sense; whether any opposition, or contrary effort be supposed, or supposable in the case, or no. When the subject and predicate of the proposition, which affirms the existence of anything, either substance, quality, act or circumstance, have a full and certain connection, then the existence or being of that thing is said to be necessary in a metaphysical sense. And in this sense I use the word "necessity," in the following discourse, when I endeavor to prove that necessity is not inconsistent with liberty.[14]

Necessity is just certainty. The connection between subject and predicate. But if something is certain, then it could not be otherwise.

Helm agrees that Edwards denied the alternative possibilities condition. In speaking of the combined or compound sense, he writes:

> If we understand indifference as a reference to the power of choice, then Edwards would have nothing to do with the second sense because he has strong exceptions to contingency as a categorical alternativity, a choice which, in a given situation, may

---

12. Edwards, *Freedom of the Will*, 264.
13. Edwards, *Freedom of the Will*, 435.
14. Edwards, *Freedom of the Will*, 152.

be equally a choice of A or B. Such a choice would be causeless and irrational.[15]

As Helm notes, Edwards denies "a categorical alternativity." He denies that "a choice which in a given situation, may be equally a choice of A or B."

Though Edwards clearly denies the alternative possibilities condition, we should observe that he does have a conditional sense of "could have been otherwise." Edwards writes:

> It can't be truly said, according to the ordinary sense of language, that a malicious man, let him be never so malicious, can't hold his hand from striking, or that he is not able to shew his neighbor kindness; or that a drunkard, let his appetite be never so strong, can't keep the cup from his mouth. In the strictest propriety of speech, a man has a thing in his power, if he has it in his choice, or at his election: and a man can't be truly said to be unable to do a thing, when he can do it if he will. 'Tis improperly said, that a person can't perform those external actions, which are dependent on the act of the will, and which would be easily performed, if the act of the will were present.[16]

Edward's teaches that there is a sense in which the agent could do otherwise. He could do otherwise if he willed to do otherwise. As we saw with guidance control and the reformed orthodox, there are various senses in which an agent "could do otherwise." Here, Edwards identifies a sense in which he believes an agent could do otherwise. Yet, the relevant sense, for our purposes, is principle (2). Guidance control, the reformed orthodox and Edwards deny this sense.

I want to end this section with an observation Oliver Crisp makes about Edwards theological opponents. It reinforces what I have been arguing. Crisp writes,

> In his crosshairs were theological libertarians, who maintained that a human being is free and morally responsible for the choices she makes provided that (1) at the moment of choice the person choosing is not determined or otherwise caused to choose one thing over another—his choice is "self-determined" in Edward's language—and (2) the person choosing has a real alternative to the choice he makes—an alternative possibility that he might have realized had he chosen differently, where he was free and able to choose differently at the moment of choice.[17]

15. Helm, *Human Nature*, 215.
16. Edwards, *Freedom of the Will*, 162.
17. Crisp, *Jonathan Edwards*, 64.

Crisp notes that Edwards was arguing against the libertarians. The libertarians held two basic propositions. First, the sourcehood condition. Crisp and Edwards call this "self-determined" choice. Second, the alternative possibilities condition. Crisp identifies this as the agent being "free and able to choose differently at the moment of choice." Crisp does not use the same language I have, but his point is the same. Edwards project was to refute the libertarians. The libertarians affirmed the sourcehood and the alternative possibilities conditions. Edwards denied both. In fact, he thought that the libertarian position was incoherent.

Like guidance control and the reformed orthodox, Edwards denies the sourcehood condition and the alternative possibilities condition. This demonstrates substantial continuity between them. It places them in the compatibilist camp. As we saw in the last chapter, compatibilism's basic thesis is that determinism or necessity is compatible with freedom and moral responsibility.

Edward's View of Freedom

The denial of the sourcehood and alternative possibilities condition does not exhaust Edwards's view of the freedom of the will. There are other elements of his view which we will explore in this section. Edwards is seeking to understand the ordinary sense of the word 'will.' Thus, he does not make use of the traditional scholastic language. He writes:

> And therefore I observe, that the will (without any metaphysical refining) is plainly, that by which the mind chooses anything. The faculty of the will is that faculty or power or principle of mind by which it is capable of choosing: an act of the will is the same as an act of choosing or choice.[18]

Edwards views the will as a power of the mind. It is necessarily tied to the mind in that it is the mind choosing. However, Edwards can distinguish between the mind proper and the will or the mind choosing. He does not hold to the traditional faculty psychology, but he nonetheless has a distinction between the mind and the will. Edwards understands the will to be simply the mind choosing. This understanding is "without metaphysical refinement." It is the ordinary, common sense, understanding of the will.

Edwards goes on to discuss the determination of the will. He writes:

> By "determining the will," if the phrase be used with any meaning, must be intended, causing that the act of the will or choice

18. Edwards, *Freedom of the Will*, 137.

should be thus, and not otherwise: and the will is said to be determined, when, in consequence of some action, or influence, its choice is directed to, and fixed upon a particular object.

For Edwards, the will is determined or caused by something other than itself. The will is caused or determined to a particular object. This means that the will cannot do otherwise than what it is determined or caused to do. If the will is determined to do P, then it cannot do not-P or Q or R or S, etc.

It would also be helpful here to discuss Edwards's view of causation. Edwards writes:

> Before I enter on any argument on this subject, I would explain how I would be understood, when I use the word "cause" in this discourse: since, for want of a better word, I shall have occasion to use it in a sense which is more extensive, than that in which it is sometimes used. The word is often used in so restrained a sense as to signify only that which has a positive efficiency or influence to produce a thing, or bring it to pass. But there are many things which have no such positive productive influence, which yet are causes in that respect, that they have truly the nature of a ground or reason why things are, rather than others; or why they are as they are rather than otherwise.[19]

Edwards is basically making the distinction between efficient causality and counterfactual causality. An efficient cause is a cause that positively energizes or brings about something. A counterfactual cause does not do this. Rather it is merely an antecedent of the effect or consequent. Edwards calls this the ground or reason. It does not follow from this type of causation that the antecedent positively brings about the consequent. This shows that Edwards's view of the determination of the will is not some mechanical view of purely efficient causes.

Edwards goes on to say:

> Therefore I sometimes use the word "cause" in this inquiry, to signify any antecedent, either natural or moral, positive or negative, on which an event, either a thing, or the manner and circumstance of a thing, so depends, that it is the ground and reason, either in whole, or in part, why it is, rather than not; or why, it is as it is, rather than otherwise; or, in other words, any antecedent with which a consequent event is so connected, that it truly belongs to the reason why the proposition which affirms that event, is true; whether it has any positive influence, or, not. And in an agreeableness to this, I sometimes use the word

19. Edwards, *Freedom of the Will*, 180.

"effect" for the consequence of another thing, which is perhaps rather an occasion than a cause, most properly speaking.[20]

Thus, Edwards has a broader conception of 'cause' than efficient cause. This means that the determination of the will cannot be simplistically thought of as the efficient cause of the will.

If the will is determined, then it must have a determiner. Edwards argues that the will is determined by the strongest motive at the time of choice. He writes:

> It is sufficient to my present purpose to say, it is that motive, which, as it stands in the view of the mind, is the strongest, that determines the will.[21]

It is the strongest motive, as it stands in the mind which determines or causes the will. Notice the key role of the mind. The mind will judge which is the strongest motive.

An agent's motive inclines him or has a tendency to draw him towards something. It is that which moves the mind to choose. The strongest motive is that motive which has the strongest tendency at the moment. It is this strongest motive that determines the will to choose what it does.

The mind or understanding presents things and the motive, as it stands in the mind, either excite or move the will or they do not. Edwards writes:

> The previous tendency of the motive is what I call the "strength" of the motive. That motive which has a less degree of previous advantage or tendency to move the will, or appears less inviting, as it stands in the view of the mind, is what I call a "weaker motive." On the contrary, that which appears most inviting, and has, by what appears concerning it to the understanding or apprehension, the greatest degree of previous tendency to excite and induce the choice, is what I call the "strongest motive." And in this sense, I suppose the will is always determined by the strongest motive.[22]

Edwards acknowledges differing strengths in motives. Motives can also compete with one another. An agent may have a motive to choose P and a motive to choose Q. The strongest motive will ultimately win out. This strongest motive is characterized as "that which appears most inviting . . .

---

20. Edwards, *Freedom of the Will*, 180–81.
21. Edwards, *Freedom of the Will*, 141.
22. Edwards, *Freedom of the Will*, 142.

to the understanding or apprehension." The understanding will judge what appears most inviting and that is what the agent will choose.

It is important to point out here that Edwards is affirming a type of intellectualism. The will follows the judgement of the understanding. I will have more to say on this in the next section. The strongest motive is that motive with the greatest tendency to move the will. It is the most appealing to the understanding or the mind. We see here a relationship between the mind or understanding and the will. The mind or understanding perceives or judges something. That perception or judgement causes the strongest motive to move the will. In this way, Edwards has a type of reasons-responsive view of the will.

Thus far we have seen that Edwards defines the will as the mind choosing. He explains a bit of the functioning between the mind, the motives and the will. He argues that what is most appealing in the mind's eye moves the will to act because the strongest motive at the time determines the will.

In light of this, Edwards goes on to define 'freedom' or 'liberty.' Again, he believes that he is elucidating the common notion. He writes:

> The plain and obvious meaning of the words "freedom" and "liberty," in common speech, is power, opportunity, or advantage, that anyone has, to do as he pleases. Or in other words, his being free from hinderance or impediment in the way of doing, or conducting in any respect, as he will.

Liberty or freedom is defined as an agent doing as he pleases unhindered. I am free when I am able to do what I want without coercion. Edwards regards this as the common sense meaning of the word. At the same time, we cannot understand Edward's view of liberty apart from his view of the relation between understanding and will. Edward's view of freedom is not simply doing as one pleases unhindered. The role of the understanding is crucial. The understanding is presented with different things. The mind makes the judgement as to which is the strongest motive or the greatest apparent good. This then moves the will to act. When the will acts unhindered, this is liberty. Yet the will acting unhindered is tied to the judgement of the understanding. Thus, Edwards holds to rational spontaneity. We saw, in the last chapter, that this is what the reformed orthodox defined as free will. Edwards is in agreement.

In light of what we have seen, it would be helpful to summarize Edwards view thus far. First, the understanding is presented with an object or objects. Second, the mind judges which of the objects is the greatest apparent good. Third, the strongest motive at the time will be judged by the mind to be the greatest apparent good. This is because the strongest motive at the time appears most inviting to the understanding. Fourth, when the understanding judges the strongest motive to be the greatest apparent good, the strongest motive causes the will to choose that object. Fifth, the agent acts freely when he is able to translate this strongest motive into action unhindered. Sixth, at the same time, the make-up of the soul or the make-up of an agent's character will determine what is most inviting to the understanding. I will have more to say on this sixth point in the next section.

Edwards view of freedom is pretty simple. However, he adds important nuances to his view. He distinguishes between natural necessity and moral necessity. He defines moral necessity as follows:

> And sometimes by "moral necessity" is meant that necessity of connection and consequence, which arises from such *moral causes,* as the strength of inclination, or motives, and the connection which there is in many cases between these, and such certain volitions and actions. And it is in this sense, that I use the phrase "moral necessity" in the following discourse.[23]

Moral necessity is internal. Thus, it is consistent with liberty or freedom. The drunkard, because his character is so formed to be a drunkard, is morally necessitated to drink. Yet, this is a free and morally responsible act because he does as he pleases unhindered. Taking a drink is what appears to be the greatest good to the understanding at the time. This kind of necessity arises from moral causes. It arises from an agent's habits, dispositions or character.

Edwards defines natural necessity as follows:

> By "natural necessity," as applied to men, I mean such necessity as men are under through the force of natural causes: as distinguished from what are called moral causes, such as habits and dispositions of the heart, and moral motives and inducements.[24]

Natural necessity is external. Thus, it is inconsistent with liberty or freedom. An agent who is coerced to drink with a gun to his head, is not free and morally responsible. He wanted to refrain from drinking, but was forced to drink by an external source. He did not do as he pleases unhindered. Natural necessity arises from an agent being forced to do something or externally.

Moral and natural necessity have the corollaries of moral and natural inability. Edwards defines natural inability as follows:

---

23. Edwards, *Freedom of the Will*, 156.
24. Edwards, *Freedom of the Will*, 156–57.

> We are said to be *naturally* unable to do a thing, when we can't do it if we will, because what is commonly called nature don't allow of it, or because of some impeding defect or obstacle that is extrinsic to the will; either in the faculty of the understanding, constitution of body, or external objects.[25]

An agent is naturally unable to do something when he is being coerced to do it or when natural causes prevent him from doing it.

He defines moral inability as follows:

> *Moral* inability consists not in any of these things; but either in the want of inclination; or the strength of a contrary inclination; or the want of sufficient motives in view, to induce and excite the act of the will, or the strength of apparent motives to the contrary.[26]

An agent is morally unable to do something when his habits, dispositions or character do not give rise to the motives that cause our will to act. The distinctions between moral/natural necessity and moral/natural inability help Edwards to nuance his view of freedom and deal with potential objections.

Reasons-Responsiveness

We have seen that Edwards denies the sourcehood and alternative possibilities conditions. We have also seen his basic view of the freedom of the will. Now, we will see that Edwards also affirms a type of reasons-responsive theory.

We should recall that a reasons-responsive theory essentially teaches that freedom and moral responsibility are rooted in the agent's ability to respond to reasons appropriately. We saw a sophisticated reasons-responsive theory in guidance control. We saw a less sophisticated reasons-responsive theory in the reformed orthodox notion of rational spontaneity. In Edwards, we will also see a type of reasons-responsive theory that is continuous with the reformed orthodox notion of rational spontaneity.

Let us first recall how the reformed orthodox defined rational spontaneity. Turretin writes:

> There are two principle characteristics of free will in which its formal nature consists: (1) the choice (he proairesis), so that what is done is done by a previous judgement of reason; (2) the

---

25. Edwards, *Freedom of the Will*, 159.
26. Edwards, *Freedom of the Will*, 159.

willingness (to hekousion), so that what is done is done voluntarily and without coercion.[27]

The essential nature of free will consists in the intellect, or reason making a judgement and the action being done without coercion. It is the "rational" part of rational spontaneity that links it to a type of reasons-responsive theory. The reformed orthodox understood this "rational" part as "rational necessity." Van Asselt, Bac and te Velde define this as, "Rational necessity: if the intellect judges an act to be good, it is rationally necessary that the will assents."[28]

The basic idea here is that the intellect or understanding judges an act to be good or not. Gobleman elaborates on rational necessity. He writes:

> What is in view here is the internal deliberations that we all make-whether consciously or unconsciously. The intellect weighs the pros and cons of a given choice, and once that choice is made the will acts upon it.[29]

Thus, the intellect or understanding weighs the reasons for thinking an act is good or not. Once it decides that it is good, the will acts. As we will see, Edwards holds this kind of rational necessity and thus a type of reasons-responsive theory. We see it in his language that the will follows the last dictate of the understanding or that the will follows the greatest apparent good as it stands in the mind or that the will is determined by the strongest motive as it stands in the mind.

There are many statements in *Freedom of the Will* that speak of this connection between the mind and the will. For example, Edwards writes:

> It is sufficient to my present purpose to say, it is that motive, which, as it stands in the view of the mind, is the strongest, that determines the will.[30]

Edwards first points to the motive "as it stands in the view of the mind." The mind is crucial for Edwards understanding of the working of the will. The mind must judge according to what it determines are the best reasons. Those best reasons include what the mind finds most appealing or the greatest apparent good. Thus, the mind has a kind of priority over the will. It is the mind's judgement of the strongest motive that "determines the will." This is what the reformed orthodox called rational necessity.

27. Turretin, *Institutes of Elenctic Theology*, 662.
28. Van Asselt et al., *Reformed Thought on Freedom*, 39.
29. Gobelman, "To Be Free," 137.
30. Edwards, *Freedom of the Will*, 141.

Edwards writes again:

> On the contrary, that which appears most inviting, and has, by what appears concerning it to the understanding or apprehension, the greatest degree of previous tendency to excite and induce the choice, is what I call the "strongest motive." And in this sense, I suppose the will is always determined by the strongest motive.[31]

It is that which appears or is judged by the understanding to be "most inviting" that is the strongest motive. This in turn determines the will. The mind must judge what is most inviting then the will is caused to move. Edwards notes that this is the way things "always" happen, "and in this sense, I suppose the will is always determined by the strongest motive."

Edwards writes again:

> It must be observed in what sense I use the term "good": namely, as of the same import with "agreeable." To appear good to the mind, as I use the phrase, is the same as to appear agreeable, or seem pleasing to the mind. Certainly, nothing appears inviting, and eligible to the mind, or tending to engage its inclination and choice, considered as evil or disagreeable. But if it tends to draw the inclination, and move the will, it must be under the notion of that which *suits* the mind. And therefore that must have the greatest tendency to attract and engage it, which, as it stands in the mind's view, suits it best, and pleases it most; and in that sense, is the greatest apparent good: to say otherwise, is little, if anything, short of a direct and plain contradiction.[32]

Again, it is what the mind judges to be good, agreeable or pleasing that "engages its inclination and choice." It is that which "in the mind's view, suits it best, and pleases it most" that is "the greatest apparent good." This greatest apparent good is the strongest motive which moves the will. It will only move the will if the mind first judges it to be the greatest apparent good.

Edwards writes again:

> It is manifest, that the acts of the will are none of them contingent in such a sense as to be without all necessity, or so as not to be necessary with the necessity of the consequence and connection; because every act of the will is some way connected with the understanding, and is as the greatest apparent good is, in the manner which has already been explained: namely, that

---

31. Edwards, *Freedom of the Will*, 142.
32. Edwards, *Freedom of the Will*, 143.

the soul always wills or chooses that which, in the present view of the mind, considered in the whole of that view, and all that belongs to it, appears most agreeable.[33]

Here Edwards describes a kind of necessity of the will. The "acts of the will are none of them contingent." Rather, they are necessary with "the necessity of the consequence and connection." This necessity is described in the terms the reformed orthodox called rational necessity. Edwards writes, "every act of the will is some way connected with the understanding." This connection is "that the soul always wills or chooses that which, in the present view of the mind, considered in the whole of that view, and all that belongs to it, appears most agreeable." This is rational necessity.

Edwards writes again:

> It appears from these things, that in some sense, the will always follows the last dictate of the understanding. But then the understanding must be taken in a large sense, as including the whole faculty of perception or apprehension, and not merely what is called reason or judgement. If by the dictate of the understanding is meant what reason declares to be best or most for the person's happiness, taking in the whole of his duration, it is not true, that the will always follows the last dictate of the understanding.[34]

Here we have the clear language of the intellectualist position "the will always follows the last dictate of the understanding." However, Edwards defines the understanding to be more than reason. He then denies that the will always follows reason.

Yet it is important to point out that this is still an intellectualist position. It is still rational necessity. Steven Studebaker writes, "Intellectualism affirms that the will follows the intellectual power of the soul."[35] It need not be the case that the will follows reason. It only needs to be the case that the will follows the intellectual power of the soul. This is basically what Edwards means by the understanding.

Many scholars place Edwards outside the intellectualist camp. Instead, they place him in the Augustinian voluntarist camp. Studebaker defines this tradition as follows,

---

33. Edwards, *Freedom of the Will*, 217.
34. Edwards, *Freedom of the Will*, 148.
35. Studebaker, *Jonathan Edwards's Social Augustinian Trinitarianism*, 145.

Augustinian voluntarism underscores the bent of the soul and its determinate influence on all the faculties of the soul.[36]

It is the bent of the soul that governs the understanding and the will. The way in which the soul is bent determines what will appear as the greatest apparent good to the mind, which in turn will move the will. The functional relationship between the understanding and the will is not the whole story to Edwards view of freedom.

We can see this from the following passage from *Freedom of the Will*:

> I might further observe, the state of the mind that views a proposed object of choice, is another thing that contributes to the agreeableness or disagreeableness of that object; the particular temper which the mind has by nature, or that has been introduced and established by education, example, custom, or some other means; or the frame or state that the mind is in on a particular occasion. That object which appears agreeable to one, does not to another. And the same object don't always appear alike agreeable to the same person, at different times. It is most agreeable to some men, to follow their reason; and to others, to follow their appetites: to some men, it is more agreeable to deny a vicious inclination, than to gratify it: others it suits best to gratify the vilest appetites. 'Tis more disagreeable to some men than others, to counteract a former resolution. In these respects, and many others which might be mentioned, different things will be most agreeable to different persons; and not only so, but to the same person at different times.[37]

Here we see Edwards describing certain things about the agent that would contribute to what his mind finds agreeable or disagreeable concerning an object. He identifies some of these as "the particular temper which the mind has by nature, or that has been introduced and established by education, example, custom, or some other means; or the frame or state that the mind is in on a particular occasion."[38]

The temper of the mind contributes to what the mind finds agreeable. This temper of mind is affected by education, example, custom, etc. In other words, the agent's upbringing, education, character, etc. form the way in which the mind will perceive the greatest apparent good.

We can see this more clearly in Edwards's *Religious Affections*. Edwards defines the affections as "the more vigorous and sensible exercises of the

---

36. Studebaker, *Jonathan Edwards's Social Augustinian Trinitarianism*, 145.
37. Edwards, *Freedom of the Will*, 146–47.
38. Edwards, *Freedom of the Will*, 146–47.

inclination and will of the soul."[39] By the word 'soul' he meant the understanding and the will.[40] McDermont and McClymond write, "For Edwards, the affections move the soul, which means they move the mind as well as the will."[41] Thus, we see that the affections govern the mind and will. Studebaker understands the distinguishing mark of the Augustinian voluntarist tradition to be that "a fundamental orientation directs the human soul toward God or evil. The will is unfettered from the faculty of the intellect, but determined by the soul's innate disposition toward sin or its reorientation toward God by the infusion of grace."[42]

In light of this, it would seem that Edwards has both intellectualist and Augustinian voluntarist elements in his view. How can these elements be brought together? It seems wrong to classify him as a pure intellectualist. He teaches that the affections govern the understanding and the will. Yet it also seems wrong to consider him a pure Augustinian voluntarist. There is a strong relationship between the understanding and the will. I think the best way to make sense out of Edwards is to view him under Studebaker's intellectualist, Augustinian voluntarist label. Studebaker writes:

> Edwards's dispositional psychology is a synthesis of intellectualism and Augustinian voluntarism. As previously noted, Fiering correctly identifies Edwards with Augustinian voluntarism, but he assumes that Augustinian voluntarism necessarily excludes an intellectualist theory of the relationship between the understanding and the will. However, Augustinian voluntarism is not primarily concerned with maintaining the indeterminacy of the will relative to the understanding, but affirming the disposition of the soul governs the orientation and operation of both understanding and will.
>
> Augustinian voluntarism is voluntarist in that the will does not always follow the dictate of *reason*. But, as Edwards notes, the faculty of understanding refers to the comprehensive ability of the soul to perceive objects and not simply reason. A person may choose a course of action that is contrary to the counsel of reason, but nonetheless perceived as the good by the power of the soul denominated understanding. In this sense, while the act may not be rational, it seems reasonable and makes sense to the person. Moreover, because the object of the will is determined

---

39. Edwards, *Religious Affections*, 96.
40. McClymond and McDermott, *Theology of Jonathan Edwards*, 312.
41. McClymond and McDermott, *Theology of Jonathan Edwards*, 312.
42. Studebaker, *Jonathan Edwards's Social Augustinian Trinitarianism*, 144.

by the understanding's apprehension of and judgement of the good, Edwards's theory is a form of intellectualism ...

Although Edwards conceived the relationship between the understanding and the will in intellectualist terms, he is fundamentally an Augustinian voluntarist because the underlying disposition or inclination of the soul determines the perception of the understanding.[43]

Studebaker views Edwards as a synthesis of intellectualism and Augustinian voluntarism. He is intellectualist "because the object of the will is determined by the understanding's apprehension and judgement of the good." He is Augustinian voluntarist because "the underlying disposition or inclination of the soul determines the perception of the understanding."

Edwards's view of the understanding is wider than the counsel of reason. Thus, the understanding can go against "reason." In doing this it still has its reasons. The object "seems reasonable and makes sense to the person." The understanding still judges the greatest apparent good according to its reasons, even though they may be poor reasons. The understanding is still responding to reasons.

In my view, Studebaker's category of intellectualist, Augustinian voluntarist best accounts for the various statements in Edwards regarding the understanding and the will. There is a functional relationship between the understanding and the will. The will always follows the understanding. The understanding has its reasons, even though they may be false reasons. Helm agrees that Edwards assigns priority to the understanding. He writes: "The power of the understanding and will are ordered. With the Scholastics, both Locke and Edwards assign priority to the understanding."[44] And again, "For Edwards, the will is a reasoned or reason-informed power (*potentia*), the power to choose, which is exercised on sufficient reasons or grounds."[45] Nonetheless, what the understanding finds to be the greatest apparent good is controlled by the fundamental disposition of the soul.

Thus, Edwards can be considered to have a type of reasons-responsive theory. This can be found in the functional link between the understanding and the will. This link is what the reformed orthodox called rational necessity. The understanding must judge what is the greatest apparent good. There will be various kinds of reasons why the understanding does this. Nonetheless, it is the understand that does this judging. Once the judgement is made, then the will is moved to choose.

43. Studebaker, *Jonathan Edwards's Social Augustinian Trinitarianism*, 153–54.
44. Helm, *Human Nature*, 221.
45. Helm, *Human Nature*, 215.

Subjectivist Condition

We have seen that Edwards denies the sourcehood and alternative possibilities conditions. We have seen that he affirms a form of reasons-responsive theory. Now we will see that he also affirms a type of subjectivist condition. Recall from last chapter that the subjectivist condition consisted of three parts. First, an agent must see himself as the source of his behavior. Second, the agent must see himself as the fair target of the reactive attitudes. Third, this view of himself must be based on the evidence in an appropriate way.

That Edwards taught a type of subjectivist condition should be unsurprising. He was a reformed theologian and agreed with the scholastics on the implanted knowledge of God in man. McDermott writes:

> Now it is important to note at this point that Edwards believed not only in an inborn principle of causation which reason can use to prove God's existence but also in an innate, pre-reflexive awareness of God.[46]

Darren M. Polluck agrees:

> Even now the unregenerate can, by God's common providence and the "light of nature," experience true impressions of God externally through nature and internally through conscience. The awareness of the divine attainable through these avenues is, however, nonsalvific, sufficing only to render the reprobate inexcusable for their sin.[47]

Polluck also points out that Edwards view of natural revelation was in accord with that of the Reformed Scholastics: "Edwards's conception of natural revelation fits soundly within the mainstream of Reformed thought."[48]

We should view Edwards understanding of natural revelation as continuous with the reformed orthodox. Thus, like them, he taught a type of subjectivist condition. One place we see this in in his discussion of natural conscience.

In *Miscellany 533*, we read:

> In order to men's having the law of God made known to them by the light of nature, two things are necessary. The light of nature must not [only] discover to them that these and those things are their duty, i.e., that they are right, that there is a justice and equality in them, and the contrary unjust; but it must discover

---

46. McDermott, *Jonathan Edwards Confronts the Gods*, 57.
47. Polluck, "Natural Revelation," 393.
48. Polluck, "Natural Revelation," 393.

to 'em also, that 'tis the will of God that they should be done, and that they shall incur his displeasure by the contrary. For a law is a signification of the will of a lawgiver, with the danger of the effects of his displeasure, in case of the breach of that law.

The Gentiles had both these. Their natural consciences testified to the latter after this manner: natural conscience suggests to every man the relation and agreement there is, between that which is wrong or unjust, and punishment; this naturally disposes men to expect it.[49]

In this miscellany, we see the elements of a subjectivist condition. The first thing to see is that God makes his law known to man, "In order to men's having the law of God made known to them by the light of nature." God has made his law known to all through the light of nature. This means two things. First, all men know the content of God's law through the light of nature: "The light of nature must not only discover to them that these and those *are* their duty." The light of nature shows men that these and those things are their duty. Second, the light of nature shows them that they are responsible agents to God, "but it must discover to 'em, that 'tis the will of God that they should be done, and that they shall incur his displeasure by the contrary." Finally, the light of nature is given to all in natural conscience, "The gentiles had both of these. Their natural conscience testified."

We see from this that the criteria of the subjectivist condition are fulfilled. First, an agent must see himself as the source of his behavior. We see that this is implied in the notion that God's Law is made known to man. The implication is that man is distinct from God and thus a distinct moral agent. As such, man has a view of himself as the source of his behavior. Of course, he is not the ultimate source, but a genuine source nonetheless. Second, the agent must see himself as the fair target of the reactive attitudes. We see that man views himself in this manner because it is built into natural conscience. Edwards makes it clear that natural conscience shows man God's displeasure for going against His Law. This means that man views himself as the fair target of God's reactive attitudes. It also implies that man is the fair target of other peoples' reactive attitudes. God's law, after all, shows man how to behave toward God and towards other people. Third, this view of himself must be based on the evidence. Man's view of himself as a genuine source of his behavior and his view of himself as the fair target of the reactive attitudes is based upon the knowledge of God and his law in natural conscience. This natural conscience is common to all human beings and thus this knowledge of God and his law is ineradicable.

49. Edwards, *"Miscellanies" 501–832*, 77.

In *the Nature of True Virtue*, Edwards expands on the natural conscience. He writes that the natural conscience consists in two things. First:

> In that which has now been spoken of: that disposition to approve or disapprove the moral treatment which passes between us and others, from a determination of the mind to be easy, or uneasy, in a consciousness of our being consistent or inconsistent with ourselves.[50]

This is what McClymond and McDermont call the golden rule: "In other words, God has implanted into all human beings an awareness of the Golden Rule, and conscience uses that to direct every human being."[51] The golden rule is a summary of the law of God. It is implanted in all human beings. From this we see that man has an awareness that he is the source of his behavior and that he is subject to the reactive attitudes of others. This is the first and second parts of the subjectivist condition.

Edwards states the second component of natural conscience:

> The other thing which belongs to the approbation or disapprobation of natural conscience is the sense of desert, which was spoken of before: consisting, as was observed, in a natural agreement, proportion and harmony between malevolence or injury and resentment and punishment; or between loving and being loved, between showing kindness and being rewarded, etc.[52]

Edwards connects the natural conscience to the law of God:

> Thus, natural conscience, if the understanding be properly enlightened, and errors and blinding stupefying prejudices are removed, concurs with the law of God, and is of equal extent with it, and joins its voice with it in every article.[53]

We see here again the substance of a subjectivist view. First the agent views himself as the source of his actions in that there is a sense of desert. This sense of desert means that the agent really is the source of his actions and thus morally responsible. Second, the agent views himself as the fair target of the reactive attitudes. That he has a sense of desert shows that he regards himself as the fair subject of God's and man's reactive attitudes. We see this in the functioning of the natural conscience, consisting, as was observed, in a natural agreement, proportion and harmony between malevolence or

---

50. Edwards, "Nature of True Virtue," 529.
51. McClymond and McDermott, *Theology of Jonathan Edwards*, 541.
52. Edwards, "Nature of True Virtue," 593.
53. Edwards, "Nature of True Virtue," 594.

injury and resentment and punishment; or between loving and being loved, between showing kindness and being rewarded, etc.

By natural conscience, the agent see himself and others as with a sense of desert. Third, this is based on the evidence of the knowledge of God and his law implanted in the natural conscience. This knowledge is ineradicable. Thus, like the reformed orthodox and guidance control, Edwards has a similar type of subjectivist condition.

Muller/Helm Debate

Given the previous discussion, I maintain that there is substantial continuity between guidance control, the reformed orthodox and Jonathan Edwards. All denied the sourcehood and alternative possibilities conditions. All affirm a type of reasons-responsive theory and all affirm a subjectivist condition. I maintain that this demonstrates that all fall into the compatibilist category. However, Richard Muller see a "parting of the ways" between the reformed orthodox and Jonathan Edwards. He argues that Edwards departed from the reformed orthodox in his view of freedom. As such, Edwards and the reformed orthodox cannot be seen as falling into the same category. For Muller, as we have seen, the reformed orthodox are neither compatibilists nor libertarians, but some kind of third thing. In the last chapter, I argued that this is false. The reformed orthodox are compatibilists.

In this section, I wish to dispute that there was a substantial "parting of the ways" between Edwards and the reformed orthodox. I have already pointed out substantial continuity between them. Now, I wish to address some of Muller's reasons for thinking that there was a parting of the ways. To accomplish this, I will make use of the debate between Muller and Helm. I will state some of Muller's reasons for a parting of the ways and then Helm's response. I will argue that there are differences between Edwards and the reformed orthodox. However, they are not sufficient to place them in different categories. They are differences within the same category, namely compatibilism.

I want to preface this discussion with the caveat that I am not attempting a thorough survey of the debate. Rather, I am attempting to do two things. First, I am attempting to show that in almost every instance where Muller charges a parting of ways, Helm adequately responds that Edwards is doing the same as the reformed orthodox in different language. Second, I want to show that the "crux of the matter," namely multiple potencies, need not be viewed as a parting of the ways. Even if the reformed orthodox taught multiple potencies in Muller's sense, Edwards can be seen as teaching something substantially similar. Thus, there is no parting of the ways on this either.

First, Muller states that the reformed orthodox held "free choice to consist not merely in spontaneity but also in freedom of contrariety and contradiction."[54] Muller charges that Edwards view is not as rich as the reformed orthodox. He merely identifies freedom with spontaneity or acting as one pleases unhindered. In this way, Edwards departs from the Reformed orthodox.

We have already seen that Edwards does not teach a mere spontaneity. He teaches a rational spontaneity. The understanding responds to reasons and the will follows unhindered. Helm adds to this that Edwards also has a place for free choice as freedom of contrariety and contradiction. He writes,

> But Edwards also cites examples of contrariety. "If it be now, on the whole of what at present appear to him, most agreeable to speak, then he chooses to speak: if it suits him to keep silence, then he chooses to keep silence." . . . And he cites examples of the liberty of contradiction, "So whatever names we call the act of the will by-choosing, refusing, approving, disapproving, liking, disliking, embracing, rejecting . . . all may be reduced to this of choosing." We note again that the classification of actions into types of choices cannot be a sufficient reason for concluding that the choices are libertarian.[55]

Edwards does in fact teach that a free agent can choose A or B (freedom of contrariety) and he can choose A or not-A (freedom of contradiction). Clearly there is a sense in which Edwards teaches a freedom of contrariety and contradiction. Muller would argue that the reformed orthodox held to a resident potency to contrariety and contradiction at the moment of choice. Thus, Edwards departs from the reformed orthodox in that sense.

In response, it should be pointed out that it is debatable that the reformed orthodox held this position. Even if they did, Edwards can be seen as holding something similar. He held that an agent always has a natural ability to do otherwise if he willed. I will explore this more fully later. For now, it is worth pointing out that even if Muller is correct in his interpretation of the reformed orthodox here, it is not sufficient to justify the claim of a parting of the ways by Edwards.

Second, Muller accuses Edwards of denying contingency as "could be otherwise." Thus, he departs from the reformed orthodox on contingency. He writes:

54. Muller, "Jonathan Edwards and the Absence," 7.
55. Helm, "Turretin and Edwards Compatibilism," 344.

JONATHAN EDWARDS AND THE REFORMED TRADITION 207

> As might be inferred from his views on God, substance, and finite beings, Edwards did not leave room for contingency in the world order, viewing it as a necessary sequence of causes and also denied contingency in acts of the human will.... Since nothing can occur without a cause and since there must be a fixed connection between cause and effect, Edwards rules out contingency—specifically as if contingency were to be defined as something lacking a cause or reason for existing. The argumentation is very different from the approach of the older Reformed tradition where contingencies were defined not as things lacking cause but as things that could be otherwise.[56]

Muller sees a parting of the ways in that Edwards leaves no room for contingency in the world order and in human choices.

Helm responds by citing how Edwards uses 'contingency' and that he does have a place for "could have been otherwise." He writes:

> Edwards distinguishes two senses of contingency. An event is said to be contingent in one sense "when its connection with its cause or antecedents, according to the established course of things, is not discerned, and so is what we have no means of the foresight of."[57]

Helm points out the second sense of contingency in Edwards:

> But for something which has absolutely no previous ground or reason, with which its existence has any fixed, and certain connection.[58]

Helm agrees that Edwards does not use contingency as "could be otherwise." However, this does not mean that Edwards has no place for "could be otherwise." Helm writes:

> Edwards also has a place for a person deciding to do act A when his choice could have been otherwise [i.e., when he could have decided to do B]. The critical question to ask ... when a person chose A, could he in exactly those circumstances and in the same state of mind have rather chosen B? The Jesuits, as understood by the Reformed Orthodox, answered this question in the affirmative. Edwards ridiculed it.[59]

---

56. Muller, "Jonathan Edwards and the Absence," 8–9.
57. Helm, "Jonathan Edwards and the Parting of Ways?," 58–59.
58. Helm, "Jonathan Edwards and the Parting of Ways?," 58–59.
59. Helm, "Turretin and Edwards Once More," 59.

As we have seen, Edwards has a conditional analysis of "could have done otherwise." If an agent had a prevailing reason to do otherwise, he could have done otherwise. Thus, it is not accurate to say that Edwards has no place for "could have been otherwise." Muller is right that Edwards does not use 'contingency' as "could have been otherwise," but Edwards clearly had a place for it without labeling it 'contingency.' I will also argue later that the reformed orthodox were committed to a conditional sense of "could be otherwise." In this way, despite Muller's objection, there was no parting of ways.

Of course, Muller would respond that Edwards does depart from the reformed orthodox in that he did not hold to a resident potency to do otherwise at the moment of choice. Again, this interpretation is disputable, but, even if it were correct, Edwards can be seen as holding to something similar.

Third, Muller charges Edwards with losing the important language of causality that the reformed orthodox used. He writes:

> What has been lost is a language of causality that extends beyond efficiency and materiality to formality and finality and, in concert with that language, the assumption of levels of causality, namely primary and secondary, each operating and interrelating in terms of their own efficiencies, formalities and finalities.[60]

Helm, responds by pointing out that Edwards does abandon scholastic language, but answers these four why questions in his own ways as well as affirms the substance of the primary/secondary causes. He writes:

> Muller says that Edwards . . . abandons the scholastic understanding of action in terms of four-fold causation—material, efficient, formal and final—and then that this has serious consequences for his view of freedom. But Edwards can be thought of as providing answers to the four "Why?" questions posed by the fours scholastic terms in ways of his own.[61]

Furthermore, Helm writes:

> While it is certain that Edwards abandoned Aristotelian causality, he did not confine his account to efficient causality, for he held that intelligent beings have intentional ends, God has ends and his creatures have different, creaturely ends. The system is teleological, not mechanical. And though as far as I can tell, Edwards does not use the distinction between primary and secondary causes[62] he ascribes causal powers both to God and to

---

60. Muller, "Jonathan Edwards and the Absence," 11.
61. Helm, "Jonathan Edwards and the Parting of Ways?," 288.
62. In personal correspondence, Helm nuanced this with the words "very often

his creatures; indeed it may be that, as part of his occasionalism, he ascribes to God alone the power of efficient causality.[63]

In light of this, we can see Edwards as doing the same work as the reformed orthodox with regard to these issues, but using different language. Thus, there is no substantial parting of the ways. Even if Edwards did not answer these why questions and did not substantially make a primary/secondary cause distinction, that isn't enough to place him in the compatibilist camp and the reformed orthodox outside of it.

Fourth, Muller argues that Edwards confuses the distinction between necessity of consequence and the necessity of the consequent. He writes:

> Edwards appears, therefore to confuse necessity of the consequence with necessity of the consequent, assuming that a necessity of the consequence entails an "infallible connection with [some] thing foregoing."[64]

Helm, responds by pointing out that Edwards does not confuse the distinction, he rejects it. Helm argues that this is a difference between the reformed orthodox and Edwards:

> Muller thinks that Edwards has misunderstood the distinction. But an alternative view is that Edwards refuses to accept the distinction and deliberately disregards its language. Why would this be? I suggest that it is because God, according to Edwards, does not have the freedom of alternativity and the distinction cannot be applied in respect of God's action, anymore (he thinks) it can be deployed in respect of human choice. . . . So here there is an undoubted difference between the two theologians, but not because of their anthropology pure and simple, but because of their anthropology when understood in relation to their doctrine of God.[65]

In my view, Edwards's denial of alternativity in God is the most substantial parting of the ways between him and the reformed orthodox. Yet we must ask, does this alone place the reformed orthodox outside the compatibilist camp? I cannot see how it would. They still denied the sourcehood and alternative possibilities conditions. This alone makes them compatibilists.

(there are some instances where he does)." Helm, email to the author, December 4, 2018.

63. Helm, "Turretin and Edwards Once More," 55.
64. Muller, "Jonathan Edwards and Francis Turretin," 273.
65 Helm, "Turretin and Edwards Once More," 292.

Muller needs to spell out more clearly how this would place them outside the compatibilist camp.

Fifth, Muller argues that the reformed orthodox held to a root indifference that Edwards rejects. He writes:

> The older tradition understood that there had to be a root indifference prior to the engagement of will and intellect, defined by the potency of the will to multiple effects and characterized by freedom of contradiction and contrariety, in order for there to be free choice.[66]

As we have seen previously, the reformed orthodox placed this indifference in the first act and the divided sense, not the second act and the compound sense. Edwards can be seen as holding to something similar.

Helm writes:

> It is clear to any reader of his *Freedom of the Will* that the prospect of future pleasure (an 'end') has degrees, a point emphasized in a passage such as the following:
>
>> If several future enjoyments are presented together, as competitors for the choice of the mind, some of them judged to be greater, and others less; the mind also having a greater sense and more lively idea of the good of some of them, and of others a less; and some are viewed as of greater certainty and probability than others; and those enjoyments that appear most agreeable in one of these respects, appear less so in others . . .
>
> Such a way of thinking is perfectly consistent with recognizing there are situations in which the will hesitates because the mind is not yet made up.[67]

In this passage, Helm identifies Edwards as teaching something similar to Turretin's divided sense. The will hesitates or is indifferent until the mind makes up its mind. Edwards covers the same ground as Turretin here without using his language.

Regarding the compound sense Helm writes:

> In the case of indifference *in sensu composito* . . . the *Freedom of the Will* may be said to present an at-length critique of this notion favored by the Jesuits and Arminians.[68]

---

66. Muller, "Jonathan Edwards and the Absence," 15.
67. Helm, "Turretin and Edwards Compatibilism," 343.
68. Helm, "Turretin and Edwards Compatibilism," 343.

JONATHAN EDWARDS AND THE REFORMED TRADITION   211

The reformed orthodox and Edwards reject indifference in the compound sense. However, Muller would respond, the reformed orthodox still held to a resident potency at the moment of choice. In light of this potency, the agent had the liberty of contrariety and contradiction. Again, this interpretation is disputed. But even if it were correct, Edwards can be seen as holding something similar. I will explain this shortly.

Sixth, Muller disagrees with Helm that the phrase "could have been otherwise" is vague.

> I disagree with Helm that the phrase "could be otherwise" is unclear.[69]

Helm responds by distinguishing a conditional and unconditional sense.

> In this connection it is necessary to say a word about Muller's remark that he thinks that the expression "could be otherwise" is clear, despite my suggestion that it is ambiguous. It is ambiguous because a choice could be otherwise in either a conditional or unconditional sense. If the first then it could be other otherwise [sic.] only if there was a reason or ground for it to be so. If in the unconditional sense it could have been different even if the world inside and outside the agent have been unchanged.[70]

This distinction by Helm is common and well known in the literature on free will and moral responsibility. Muller fails to see this.

Yet, we must ask, does Muller think that the reformed orthodox affirm a conditional sense or an absolute sense? I think that he is logically forced to conclude that the reformed orthodox affirm a conditional sense. This is because we have shown that the reformed orthodox reject the alternative possibilities condition or principle (2).[71]

Let us recall principle (2):

> (2) An agent S freely and morally responsibly does x only if S could have done otherwise than x given C (God's foreknowledge, decree, and/or providence).

This principle affirms an absolute sense of "could have done otherwise." It does so because God could decree that S do x at t_1 and S actually does not-x at t_1. The ability of the agent is not conditioned on God's decree but is absolute in that it can thwart God's decree and render it false.

---

69. Muller, "Jonathan Edwards and Francis Turretin," 274.
70. Muller, "Jonathan Edwards and Francis Turretin," 289.
71. See chapter 3.

As we saw in the previous chapter, Muller says that the reformed orthodox reject this. He writes:

> In his place in the order of finite things, namely, within the realm of secondary causality, A can will either p or not-p; and God, in his place beyond and supportive of this order of finite things can will either that A wills p or that A will not-p. Of course, given the law of non-contradiction A cannot both will and not will p in the same way, at the same place, or at the same time as he wills not-p: and given the divine *concursus* (whether construed in a Thomist, Scotist, or one or another Reformed manner), it also cannot be the case that God actually wills that A wills p and A actually wills not-p or that God actually wills not-p and A wills p.[72]

We can see from this quote that Muller believes the reformed orthodox must be committed to denying an absolute sense of "could have done otherwise." This is very clear in the following section of the quote:

> it also cannot be the case that God actually wills that A wills p and A actually wills not-p or that God actually wills not-p and A wills p.

God cannot will or decree that A wills p and then A actually wills not-p. In other words, A cannot do otherwise than what God wills or decrees. This is a denial of principle (2) and thus the absolute sense of "could have done otherwise."

Muller is committed to a conditional sense of "could have done otherwise." Minimally he must affirm the following:

> An agent A at time t_1 does x and A could have done other than x (not-x) at t_1 only if God willed or decreed for A to do not-x at t_1.

This is a type of the conditional sense that Edwards would affirm given his view of God's absolute decree.

I think that we can make Muller's view of the reformed orthodox and Edwards even closer. As we saw, Edwards held to a conditional analysis of "could do other" that invoked the will of the agent. He affirmed: "An agent A at time t_1 does x and A could have done other than x (not-x) at t_1 only if the A willed or wanted to do not-x at t_1."

Given Muller's language he would seem to be committed to the same view. Notice how he invokes the will of the agent as well: "It also cannot be the case that God actually wills that *A* wills p and *A* actually wills not-p or that God actually wills not-p and *A* wills p."

---

72. Muller, *Divine and Human Choice*, 314.

God wills that A *wills* p. It cannot be the case that A actually *wills* not-p. That is, A's willing of p is dependent upon God's willing that A wills that p. This means that A cannot will not-p unless God wills that A wills not-p. This is but a more extended version of Edwards view, but it is something that Edwards would agree with in its extended form.

I think that we can conclude from this that Muller's view of the reformed orthodox with regard to the agent's ability to do otherwise is the same as Edwards. They both affirm a conditional sense. This is important because it shows, first, that there is no parting of the ways here between Edwards and the reformed orthodox. Second, I am going to argue that Muller's multiple potencies is not substantially different from Edwards natural ability.

Finally, I want to argue that Muller's multiple potencies are indistinguishable from Edward's natural ability. Let us first look at a statement of Muller on multiple potencies. He writes: "In a given moment, the past being unaltered, human beings have potencies to more than one effect and can do otherwise."[73]

There are a number of questions of clarification we could ask about such as what is meant by "the past?," "What does it mean for the past to be unaltered?," etc. I want to focus in on what the phrase "can do otherwise" means here. As we saw in the previous section, Muller must affirm a conditional sense of this phrase. A human being can only do otherwise if God wills that he wills to do otherwise. Let me unpack this more clearly

1. God wills that A wills x at t_1
2. A has potencies to do not-x, y or z at t_1
3. Potency not-x can only be actualized at t_1 if God wills that A wills not-x at t_1
4. Potency y can only be actualized at t_1 if God wills that A wills y at t_1
5. Potency z can only be actualized at t_1 if God wills that A wills z at t_1
6. Apart from God willing that A wills to actualize one of these potencies, these potencies are unactualizable.
7. A cannot do otherwise in the absolute sense even though A has potencies to do otherwise.

I believe that this position is indistinguishable from Edward's natural ability. Let us turn to an examination of Edwards's natural ability.

As we have seen, Edwards held to a conditional analysis and makes a distinction between moral inability and natural inability. A drunkard is

73. Muller, "Jonathan Edwards and Francis Turretin," 284.

morally necessitated to drink the beer. However, he has the natural ability to not drink the beer (liberty of contradiction) and the natural ability to drink milk (liberty of contrariety). The drunkard can only not drink the beer if he willed to not drink the beer. He can only drink the milk if he willed to drink the milk.

Edwards ties this conditional analysis to his notion of natural inability. He writes:

> We are said to be naturally unable to do a thing, when we can't do it *if we will*, because what is commonly called nature don't allow of it, or because of some impeding defect or obstacle that is extrinsic to the will, ether in the faculty of the understanding, constitution of the body, or external objects.[74]

This natural inability implies a natural ability. One is naturally able to do something if nature allows it, even though one does not will it. Edwards writes:

> It can't be truly said, according to the ordinary use of language, that a malicious man, let him be never so malicious, *can't* hold his hand from striking. Or that he *is not able* to shew his neighbor kindness; or that a drunkard, let his appetite be never so strong, *can't* keep the cup from his mouth. In the strictest propriety of speech, a man has a thing *in his power*, if he has it in his choice, or at his election; and a man can't be truly said to be unable to do a thing, when he can do it if he will. 'Tis improperly said, that a person can't perform those external actions, which are dependent on the act of the will and which would be easily performed, if the act of the will were present.[75]

An agent has a power or ability to do other than he has done. The drunkard has the power or ability to "keep the cup from his mouth," even while he brings the cup to his mouth. The malicious man has the power or ability to "hold his hand from striking," even as his hand is striking. What is lacking is not the power or ability, but the will. This power or ability is Edwards natural ability.

Edwards further clarifies this. He writes:

> In this case, not only is it true, that it is easy for a man to do the thing if he will, but the very willing is the doing; when once he has willed, the thing is performed; and nothing else remains to be done. Therefore, in these things to ascribe a nonperformance

---

74. Edwards, *Freedom of the Will*, 159 (emphasis mine).
75. Edwards, *Freedom of the Will*, 162 (emphasis mine).

to the want of power or ability, is not just; because the thing wanting is not a being *able*, but a being *willing*. There are faculties of mind, and capacity of nature, and everything else, sufficient, but a disposition: nothing is wanting but a will.[76]

An agent has the power or ability to do otherwise if he will. That is, there is something resident in the nature of the drunkard, to be able to keep the cup from his mouth. There is something resident in the malicious man to hold his hand from striking. Edwards calls this a power or ability, a natural ability. I ask, what is the difference between this natural ability and Muller's multiple potencies? It can't be that these potencies have an unconditional ability to do otherwise. We saw that this must be a conditional ability just like Edwards. So, what is the difference?

Helm rightly calls this issue of multiple potencies "the crux of the matter."[77] He does not believe that the reformed orthodox taught multiple potencies. Whatever position one takes on this exegetical issue, we can grant Muller's point for the sake of argument. Muller thinks this is a substantial parting of the ways with Edwards, such that it renders the reformed orthodox not compatibilists. My question is "how is this a parting of the ways?" In light of Edwards natural ability, how has he parted from the reformed orthodox on this point? I believe Muller needs to spell out the difference before he can conclude a parting of the ways.

Conclusion

We have seen that Edwards denied the sourcehood and alternative possibilities conditions. We have seen that Edwards affirms a type of reasons-responsive theory and a type of subjectivist condition. This makes his thinking about free will and moral responsibility substantially continuous with guidance control and the reformed orthodox. They are all some sort of reasons-responsive compatibilists. In this way, there has been no parting of the ways between Edwards and the reformed orthodox.

We have also surveyed the Muller/Helm debate. In this survey we saw that Muller failed to present evidence that there has been a parting of the ways. Though Edwards used different language and categories, he covered the same ground and gave substantially the same answers as the reformed orthodox. The main discontinuity was located in Edwards denial of hypothetical necessity.

76. Edwards, *Freedom of the Will*, 162.
77. Helm, "Turretin and Edwards Compatibilism," 350.

We ended our discussion by noting that even if we granted Muller the multiple potencies, this still does not establish a parting of the ways. These multiple potencies would still have to be conditional abilities to do otherwise and Muller's potencies would be indistinguishable from Edwards's natural ability.

Conclusion

IN THIS STUDY, WE have asked the question, "Is reformed theology compatible with guidance control?" This question was answered in the affirmative. Guidance control and reformed theology reject the sourcehood and alternative possibilities conditions. Guidance control and reformed theology affirm a type of reasons-responsive theory and a type of subjectivist condition.

In the course of this study, we have affirmed a number of other propositions that have been in dispute lately. First, we have affirmed that the reformed view of God's decree, foreknowledge and providence is theological determinism. We have seen that contemporary analytic philosophers regard determinism to be hypothetical necessity. Clearly the reformed orthodox affirmed that God's decree, foreknowledge and providence are instances of hypothetical necessity and therefore theological determinism. This is an important finding in light of the denials from the Utrecht school and Richard Muller that reformed theology is theological determinism. It is also an important finding in light of Oliver Crisp's libertarian Calvinism. It shows that his project cannot succeed because libertarian free will is excluded by theological determinism.

Second, we have affirmed that reformed theology is compatibilism or semi-compatibilism. The project of the reformed orthodox with regard to freedom and moral responsibility was to show that hypothetical necessity is compatible with freedom and moral responsibility. This is precisely the same project as contemporary compatibilists. This is a significant finding in light of the denials from the Utrecht school and Richard Muller that reformed theology is not compatibilism.

Third, we have affirmed that Jonathan Edwards has not parted ways with the reformed orthodox on the issues of freedom and moral responsibility. We saw substantial continuity between them on the issues of sourcehood, alternative possibilities, rational spontaneity/reasons-responsiveness and the subjectivist condition. This is a significant finding in light of Richard Muller's claim that Edwards in fact departed from the reformed tradition. Furthermore, we have seen that Muller's claim that the reformed orthodox held to multiple potencies is substantially indistinguishable from Edwards teaching on natural ability. This is highly significant because this is the heart of Muller's claim that Edwards parted ways with the reformed orthodox. If it cannot be demonstrated that multiple potencies are substantially different from natural ability, then Muller's claim of a parting of the ways fails.

It is my hope that a study such as this one will serve as a catalyst for reformed theologians and philosophers to mine the resources of contemporary analytic philosophy on the issues of free will and moral responsibility. I believe that there is a wealth of material that could aid reformed theologians and philosophers in articulating a sophisticated and rigorous view of a reformed doctrine of free will and moral responsibility. This could aid us greatly in answering challenges from our opponents.

APPENDIX

Criticisms of Fischer and Ravizza

Introduction

I COMPLETED MY EXPOSITION of guidance control. Though the theory has received high acclaim, it has also received its share of criticisms. This appendix will explore some of those criticisms. We will see that some of the criticisms do not ultimately work. Others point out correctable weak spots making the theory better; in particular, the criticisms from Michael McKenna with regards to mechanism individuation and manipulation cases. I will argue that Fischer and Ravizza adequately answer their critics, but McKenna's additions are very helpful and make the theory better. This is not intended to be an exhaustive defense of guidance control. Rather, it is intended to give the reader a good idea of how one might philosophically defend guidance control.

This appendix will be divided into two main parts. First, an analysis of Frankfurt Style Cases and second, an analysis of guidance control. This second section will further break down into three parts: First, an analysis of mechanism individuation, second, some brief comments on mechanism ownership, and third, an analysis of manipulation cases.

Frankfurt Examples

Frankfurt Style Cases (FSC) form an important part of Fischer and Ravizza's case for the compatibility of determinism and moral responsibility. One main challenge to this compatibility is called the Principle of Alternative Possibilities (PAP). This principle states that for an agent to be morally responsible, he must be able to do other than what he did. If the agent has murdered someone, then he must have been able to refrain from murdering that person. If he was not able to refrain from murdering that person, then he cannot be held morally responsible. It is argued that PAP is highly intuitive and implies that determinism is incompatible with moral responsibility. FSCs challenge this intuition.

A garden of forking paths can illustrate the main work that FSCs perform. If you imagine a garden that branches out into many forking paths, then you can see a good illustration of the Principle of Alternative Possibilities. According to the PAP view, a morally responsible agent will have access to numerous forking paths (or possibilities). The work that FSCs perform is to question this view and offer the alternative illustration that there is really only one physically possible path.[1] If a case can be made for the success of FSCs, then one major objection to the compatibility of moral responsibility and determinism has been removed.

To begin, let me state an example of an FSC in Fischer's words:

> Because he dares to hope that the Democrats finally have a good chance of winning the White House, the benevolent but elderly neurosurgeon, Black, has come out of retirement to participate in yet another philosophical example . . . he has secretly inserted a chip in Jones's brain that enables Black to monitor and control Jones's activities. Black can exercise this control through a sophisticated computer that he had programmed so that, among other things, it monitors Jones's voting behavior. If Jones were to show any inclination[2] to vote for McCain (or, let us say, anyone other than Obama), then the computer, through the chip in Jones's brain, would intervene to assure that he actually decides to vote for Obama (as Black, the old progressive, would prefer), the computer does nothing but continue to monitor—without affecting—the goings-on in Jones's head.
>
> Now suppose that Jones decides to vote for Obama on his own, just as he would have if Black had not inserted the chip in his head. It seems, upon first thinking about this case, that Jones can be held morally responsible for his choice and act of voting for Obama, although he could not have chosen otherwise and he could not have done otherwise.[3]

In this example, the intuition that Jones is morally responsible is elicited. However, the existence of Black as the counterfactual intervener

---

1. It is important to keep in mind that there are various senses of the word 'possibility.' Fischer and Ravizza are not arguing that there is only one *logically* possible path, but only one *physically* possible path.

2. In Frankfurt style cases of various sorts, the phrase "show any inclination" will take various forms. This is typically referred to as "prior signs." These prior signs could include, a blush, a twitch, a furrowing of the eyebrow, a neurological pattern, etc.

3. Fischer, "Frankfurt Cases," 34.

eliminates Jones's ability to do otherwise. Therefore, the intuition behind PAP is called into question.

It is important to see that FSCs not only question the intuition that PAP is necessary for moral responsibility, but they also point us in the direction that we should look for an analysis of the concept of moral responsibility. They point us away from analyzing the concept of moral responsibility in terms of alternative possibilities and point us towards analyzing it in the actual sequence of events. In an FSC there are two sequences. The first is the alternative sequence. In this sequence, Black intervenes and forces Jones to vote for Obama. The second is the actual sequence. In this sequence, Black does not intervene and Jones votes for Obama on his own. It is by analyzing the actual sequence that Fischer and Ravizza come to their concept of moral responsibility.

It is also important to note that if the Frankfurt examples are not successful, this would not dampen the adequacy of Fischer and Ravizza's account of moral responsibility. This is why they do not provide a defense of Frankfurt cases in *Responsibility and Control*. Frankfurt cases are helpful in questioning the necessity of PAP, but they are not the only way to do this. Other ways may be successful even if FSCs fail. So, we should not view the success of Fischer and Ravizza's account of moral responsibility as necessarily dependent upon the success of FSCs.

Given the above considerations, it would be helpful to evaluate the success of FSCs. I will look at some of the major objections that have been given against them in the literature. The conclusion will be that FSCs do not eliminate all alternative possibilities. However, they do eliminate what Fischer calls, all "robust" alternative possibilities.

Many philosophers are not convinced that FSCs uncontroversially refute PAP. Fischer believes that they do show to a reasonable degree that PAP is false. In addition to this, he believes that they are also part of a larger argument for the compatibility of causal determinism and moral responsibility. He writes,

> More specifically, I have argued that the FSCs provide a plausibility argument for the (preliminary) conclusion that if the agent in the example is not morally responsible, it is not because he lacks freedom to do otherwise. I have further argued that causal determinism in the actual sequence does not in itself and apart from ruling out alternative possibilities constitute a responsibility undermining factor. . . . Thus, I hold that the FSCs are an

important part of a two-step argument to the conclusion that causal determinism is compatible with moral responsibility.[4]

Fischer is not arguing that FSCs refute PAP in such a way that every rational person must yield to them; this is too high a bar to establish. This is also not something that we would require of any position. Instead, they not only show that PAP is false to a reasonable degree, but they also contribute significantly to an account that shows the compatibility of causal determinism and moral responsibility. This is important because not everything rides on the success of FSCs. In order to see that they reasonably refute PAP, we need to look at the arguments that have been raised against them.

Arguments Against FSCs

Many philosophers do not accept that FSCs refute PAP. The following worry is characteristic of many of these philosophers:

> (PAP) is deeply ingrained both in common sense and in our more reflective theorizing both in philosophy and the criminal law. It is indeed highly intuitive as well as almost universally accepted. Given this, it would take—or should take—a lot to persuade us to overturn and reject it. Further, the arguments against it seem to be "close calls"; they are highly contentious, in any case, and even if some argument or other is persuasive to some, it will not be so clearly compelling that any fair and open-minded philosopher (not already committed to a view about [PAP]) would need to accept it. Indeed, the arguments are either extremely "close calls" or are so complex that, even if one is inclined to accept them, one should not be very confident that one has really grasped all of the relevant issues. Given all of this, it just doesn't seem philosophically prudent or sensible to give up such a deeply plausible and central philosophical principle, such as (PAP).[5]

Fischer and Ravizza realize that they do not have a knockdown argument. They also realize that practically no one has a knockdown argument for anything. So, this should not dissuade us into thinking that FSCs do not work. However, many philosophers share the intuition concerning PAP expressed above. Thus, if the FSCs are going to provide a reasonable case, they must hold up under the various criticisms that philosophers have given.

---

4. Fischer, "Frankfurt-Style Cases," 44.
5. Fischer, "Frankfurt-Style Cases," 44–45.

The Flicker of Freedom Strategy

One strategy utilized to rebut FSCs is known as the flicker of freedom strategy. The basic idea is that FSCs do not remove all alternative possibilities. This is because in the FSCs themselves, there are alternative possibilities called flickers of freedom. Since they do not remove all alternative possibilities, it follows that FSCs are not analogous to deterministic worlds where there are no alternative possibilities. A proponent of PAP could argue that these alternative possibilities in the FSCs are the basis for moral responsibility. This accounts for why we have the intuition in FSCs that makes Jones morally responsible. Thus, it turns out that Jones has alternative possibilities after all.

In order to prime our intuitions about flickers of freedom, let us first look at an example in which Fischer and Ravizza grant alternative possibilities. Let us consider a man driving a car. Suppose that the man guides the car to the right in the normal manner. Now suppose that unbeknownst to him, the car's steering apparatus was broken in such a way that it would not steer in any other way than to the right. In other words, the driver had no alternative possibility other than steering to the right, which he happily did. Does this example eliminate all alternative possibilitieis? No, Fischer writes,

> But certainly I possessed *some* alternative possibilities: for example, apart from any special assumptions, there is no reason to deny that I could have formed the intention to guide the car in some *other* direction than right, and I could have attempted to steer the car in this other direction, and so forth. Thus I had *some* alternative possibilities, even if I could not change the path of the car.[6]

The "intention to guide the car in some other direction" and the "attempt to steer the car in the other direction" are alternative possibilities. The counterfactual intervener cannot eliminate these possibilities in FSCs. Thus, FSCs do not eliminate all alternative possibilities.

In light of examples like this, Fischer constructs FSCs that seek to eliminate these alternative possibilities. He does this by returning to the case of Jones and Black. Recall that in this case Jones could at least begin to choose to vote for Bush. He could be said to have at least this power. A reconstructed FSC would eliminate this from Jones. Fischer writes,

> But now it seems we can imagine another case in which Jones has a propensity to show some *sign* which reliably indicates his

---

6. Fischer, *Metaphysics of Free Will*, 135.

voting behavior prior even to his beginning to make a choice or form an intention. Suppose, that is, that Jones would blush red (or show some other sign that is readable by Black—perhaps a furrowed brow or raised eyebrow or even a complex and arcane neurophysiological pattern) prior to initiating any process of decision-making if and only if he were about to choose to vote for Bush. If Jones is like this, then Black could (by reading the sign) prevent him from even *beginning* to make the relevant choice or decision.[7]

This strategy of reconstructing the FSC to eliminate these alternative possibilities is important. In order to show that moral responsibility is compatible with a denial of PAP, all that needs to be done is to show one logically possible scenario where an agent is morally responsible and the agent did not have an alternative possibility. So, it is legitimate to reconstruct FSCs because in doing so we are looking for that one logically possible scenario where this happens.

However, there is a problem with these reconstructed FSCs. The problem is that they also do not eliminate all alternative possibilities. Fischer writes,

> But again a flicker emerges, for even here Jones has the power to show the relevant sign—to blush red or display the complex neurophysiological pattern, and so forth. And it is hard to see how a Frankfurt type example could be constructed which would have absolutely *no* such flicker.[8]

Thus, the flicker of freedom strategy has shown that we cannot eliminate all alternative possibilities from FSCs.

In response to the flicker of freedom strategy, it is important to point out that the mere presence of an alternative possibility does not adequately rebut FSCs.[9] Fischer argues that reconstructing FSCs may not eliminate all

---

7. Fischer, *Metaphysics of Free Will*, 136.
8. Fischer, *Metaphysics of Free Will*, 136.
9. It is important to note that some philosophers have come up with FSCs in which it is claimed that there are no alternative possibilities. These cases are referred to as blockage cases. For examples of blockage cases see Mele and Robb, "Rescuing Frankfurt-Style Cases." See also Mele and Robb, "Bbs, Magnets, and Seesaws."
One advocate of blockage cases is David P Hunt. See Hunt, "Moral Responsibility and Unavoidable Action." He elaborates on them in Hunt, "Freedom, Foreknowledge and Frankfurt."
Hunt summarizes the basic strategy, "Imagine then a mechanism that blocks neural pathways.... The mechanism blocks alternatives in advance, but owing to a fantastic coincidence the pathways it blocks just happen to be all the ones that will be unactualized

alternative possibilities, but the ones that are left are too exiguous to ground moral responsibility. For example, Jones blushing red is not an alternative possibility that could ground moral responsibility. Fischer calls these types of alternative possibilities "mere flickers of freedom." These mere flickers of freedom are irrelevant because they cannot ground moral responsibility. Thus, we can conclude that FSCs do eliminate all alternative possibilities capable of grounding moral responsibility, or as Fischer puts it, all "robust alternative possibilities."[10]

This is a significant point and it merits elaboration. Here is what Fischer says,

> I am willing to grant to the flicker theorist the claim that there exists an alternative possibility here; but my basic worry is that this alternative possibility is not sufficiently *robust* to ground the relevant attributions of moral responsibility. . . . I suggest that it is not enough for the flicker theorist to analyze the relevant range of cases in such a way as to identify an alternative possibility. Although this is surely a first step, it is not enough to establish the flicker of freedom view, because what needs also to be shown is that these alternative possibilities *play a certain role* in the appropriate understanding of the cases. That is, it needs to be shown that these alternative possibilities *ground* our

---

in any case, while the single pathway that remains unblocked is precisely the route the man's thoughts would be following anyway (if all neutral pathways were unblocked). Under these conditions, the man appears to remain responsible for his thoughts and actions" (Hunt, "Moral Responsibility and Unavoidable Action," 218).

Hunt himself doubts the success of these cases. He writes, "Unfortunately, while blockage cases have much to recommend them, they come with their own set of difficulties, and recent discussions of my proposal by John Fischer, Derk Pereboom, Robert Kane, and David Widerker (among others) confirms my own reticence about pushing them too strongly as definitive counter examples to PAP, at least in their present form. The central difficulty is that the conditions barring Jones's access to alternative pathways and guaranteeing his decision to kill Smith must be distinguished, in some non-ad-hoc way, from the sorts of conditions that would beg the question against incompatibilism by *causally determining* Jones's decision. . . . So blockage is probably not the magic bullet for which PAP's critics are looking" (Hunt, "Moral Responsibility and Buffered Alternatives," 131–32).

10. Even incompatibilists such as David Widerker recognize the need for a robust alternative. He calls them "morally significant alternatives." He writes, "It is important to note that Frankfurt's case against PAP would be just as strong if, instead of establishing the possibility of a situation in which Jones had no actionally accessible alternative to his decision not to keep his promise (IRR-situation), he would be able to come up with a situation in which Jones had no *morally significant alternative* to that decision" (Widerker, "Frankfurt-Friendly Libertarianism," 273). In other words, Widerker is saying that a lack of a robust alternatives renders Frankfurt's argument just as strong as if the argument had eliminated all alternative possibilities.

attributions of moral responsibility. And this is what I find puzzling and implausible.[11]

The basic idea in Fischer's response is that not just any alternative possibility helps the defender of PAP. It must be a certain kind of alternative possibility. It must be a robust kind, the kind that grounds moral responsibility.[12] It would be helpful to explore in more detail what the term robust means in this context.

What does robustness amount to? It has to be more than simply "a blush" or "power to show the relevant sign." After all, these "mere flickers of freedom" are not voluntary. They must be more robust than this. In a more recent publication, Fischer borrows Derk Pereboom's definition of *robustness*:

> For an alternative possibility to be relevant to explaining why an agent is morally responsible for an action, it must satisfy the following characterization: she could have willed something different from what she actually willed such that she understood that by willing it she would thereby be precluded from moral responsibility.[13]

This definition of robustness has been challenged. For example, Dana Nelkin thinks that this is too strong and Pereboom agrees:

---

11. Fischer, *Metaphysics of Free Will*, 140

12. It is helpful to see the necessity of a "robustness" condition by exploring the traditional account of control that is associated with an alternative possibilities model. Fischer writes, "On the traditional alternative-possibilities picture, it is envisaged that an agent has a choice between two (or more) scenarios *of a certain sort*. In one scenario, he deliberates and forms an intention to perform an act of a certain kind and then carries out this intention in an appropriate way. In at least one other possible scenario, he deliberates and forms an intention to perform a different kind of act (or no act at all) and carries out this intention in an appropriate way. This is what is involved in having robust alternative-possibilities, and certainly this is the natural way to think about the sort of alternatives that allegedly ground moral responsibility.

But it is evident that in Frankfurt-type examples these conditions do *not* obtain: the alternative scenarios are not of the requisite kind. In the case of Jones and Black, in the alternative scenario Jones does *not* deliberate and then form an intention to vote for Bush (and then act on this intention in an appropriate way). Thus, even if there is a flicker of freedom in these cases, it does not seem to be *robust* enough to ground moral responsibility ascriptions. The traditional alternative-possibilities model links moral responsibility with *control* of a certain kind (regulative control); but for this kind of control to exist, surely the alternative possibilities which are invoked to ground the attributions of responsibility must be robust" (Fischer, *Metaphysics of Free Will*, 142).

13. Fischer, *Deep Control*, 82

As a result, Nelkin thinks that Robustness (A) is too strong, and I believe she is right. She suggests that understanding isn't required, but only some lower level of cognitive sensitivity to the fact that the alternative possibility would have precluded him from the responsibility she actually has.[14]

A few others have raised objections that Pereboom mentions. Jonathan Vance raises an objection about the epistemic requirement also via a coffee cup example:

> In the coffee-cup example, is having a non-occurrent or even occurrent belief that taking a sip from the coffee cup *might* result in his being blameless enough for robustness? It seems not. For, if asked, Joe might well agree that the probability of this connection is non-zero—he might admit, for instance, that it's at least .000001, and if he's taken a class in epistemology or probability, something like this might well be his response. But, intuitively, this is not sufficient to generate robustness. Should it be required for robustness that Joe understood that taking the sip of coffee would, with a probability of 1.0, result in his being blameless? This is clearly too strong, for it would intuitively be enough for robustness if he understood that the probability was, say, 0.95. But the threshold probability, as one would expect, is difficult or impossible to determine.[15]

In light of these criticisms, Pereboom has refined his definition of robustness as follows:

> Robustness (B): For an agent to have a robust alternative to her immoral action A, that is, an alternative relevant per se to explaining why she is blameworthy for performing A, it must be that

---

14. Pereboom, "Frankfurt Examples," 300. The following example motivates Nelkin's point, "Huck Fin sincerely expresses the view that allowing Jim, the slave, to go free, is morally wrong, but nonetheless allows him to go free instead of returning him to his owner. We imagine that Huck has some cognitive and affective sensitivity to the moral rightness of letting Jim go free. Suppose that he instead, holding that moral psychology fixed, did return him to his owner, and that this is in fact morally wrong. Does Huck have a robust alternative possibility that can ground his moral responsibility—his allowing Jim to go free?" (Pereboom, "Frankfurt Examples," 300).

15. Pereboom, "Frankfurt Examples," 300–301. In the same paper, Pereboom identifies a criticism from J. Hobbs that there should be a specification of voluntariness in refraining or avoiding the action. He also mentions Dana Nelkin stating an asymmetry. "As Nelkin (2011) emphasizes, the requirement of an alternative that precludes actual responsibility is clearer and is more intuitive from immoral and blameworthy actions than for morally exemplary and praiseworthy actions."

> (i) She instead could have voluntarily acted or refrained from acting as a result of which she would be blameless, and
>
> (ii) For at least one such exempting acting or refraining, she was cognitively sensitive to the fact that she could so voluntarily act or refrain, and to the fact that if she voluntarily so acted or refrained she would be, or would likely be, blameless.[16]

From this definition, we can see why "mere flickers of freedom" are not robust. Pereboom's account identifies "voluntariness" as essential to robustness. A "mere flicker of freedom," such as a blush, is not voluntary. Therefore, it is not robust. Given this, Fischer's strategy is successful; he has created FSCs in which all that remains is a non-robust alternative possibility.

However, Pereboom's new definition has also been challenged. Carlos Moya challenges it in response to Pereboom's buffer zone case, Tax Evasion 2, as follows,

> Suppose that someone is walking along a street and she suddenly witnesses an accident: a pedestrian is run over by a car and lies on the ground, with quite serious injuries; suppose further that the car driver absconds and that she is the only person who has witnesses the accident; she has the moral duty to help the victim; as it happens, she is a doctor, with a long experience in treating traumas, and has got a first aid case; what she does, however, is take her mobile, dial an emergency number and ask for an ambulance; she could additionally have examined the injured person in order to determine his condition and see how she could start helping him with his injuries before the ambulance arrives, but she just feels tired and not in the mood to do that.[17]

In this example, Moya thinks that our intuitions make us blame this doctor. The reason is because she could have done more. She could have helped the victim and if she did, then we would not hold her blameworthy at all. The helping of the victim constitutes what Moya calls and "exempting alternative." What is interesting is if we apply the same exempting alternative to a slightly different example:

> But think of the following counterfactual variation of the story: things happen as in the original example, but now the witness is not a doctor, but a lay person, with no medical knowledge or training at all. In this counterfactual story, the witness of the

---

16. Pereboom, *Free Will*, 13
17. Moya, "On the Very Idea," 13.

accident would not have been blameworthy; the alternative she chose (to dial an emergency number and ask for an ambulance) exempted her from blame, for there was nothing she could additionally do to help the victim.[18]

There is obviously a difference here. In the first case, our intuitions seem to hold the doctor partially blameworthy. We would completely exempt her if she offered help. However, in the second case, our intuitions seem to exempt the layperson entirely. Moya thinks that the difference lies in the circumstances. The doctor could do more, but the layperson could not. In light of this, Moya lays down the following principle:

> (C) If someone cannot reasonably do more than she actually does in order to fulfill her moral duties, she is not morally obliged to do more, and so she is not morally blameworthy for not doing more.[19]

This principle is supposed to challenge Pereboom's definition of robustness. It yields the idea that "doing the next best action" is a robust alternative. In the context of an FSC like Tax Evasion 2, that "next best thing" would be "trying to decide not to evade taxes."[20] Moya writes,

> And this is also the case with Joe in Tax Evasion: he does not believe that simply becoming attentive to moral reasons against evading taxes would exempt him from blame, for this is everything he could reasonably have done, in the context he was in, in order to fulfill his moral duty not to (decide to) evade taxes. This is what trying to decide not to evade taxes would actually

---

18. Moya, "On the Very Idea," 13.

19. Moya, "On the Very Idea," 14. In light of this principle, Moya goes on to lay down a couple more that are relevant to robustness, especially in Pereboom's Tax Evasion 2. "(NBA-ign) If, unbeknownst to her, an agent cannot do something A such that, if she did it, she would fulfil her duty and would be precluded from blame (and she knows that she would), then, in order to be so precluded, she should perform the next best action that reasonably was in her power to perform in order to fulfil her duty, where 'the next best action' may be characterized, in general terms as trying to attempt to A" (Moya, "On the Very Idea," 15).

He also lays down the following principle, "(NBA-kn) If an agent knows (or justifiably believes) that she cannot do something A such that, if she did it, she would fulfil her moral duty and be precluded from blame, then, in order to be so precluded, she should perform the next best action that reasonably is in her power in order to fulfil her moral duty" (Moya, "On the Very Idea," 16).

20. Moya, "On the Very Idea," 16.

amount to in these circumstances and what Joe should, and could, have done.[21]

In light of Moya's argument, it would seem like robustness includes alternatives like "trying to decide" or "trying to do." These can be "robust alternatives" if they are the next best thing that an agent can do in a certain situation. Thus, robustness would seem to include some of what Fischer and Pereboom would call flickers of freedom.

In response, Pereboom does not think that Moya's argument really gets at the issue properly. He agrees that in the tax evasion case, Joe is blameworthy for not "becoming more attentive to moral reasons." For this he would have a robust alternative possibility, namely "becoming more attentive to moral reasons." Pereboom even agrees that "becoming more attentive to moral reasons" is the next best thing to evading taxes. But Moya's point does not provide a robust alternative for evading taxes and this is the whole point. Pereboom writes,

> True, under the supposition that without the availability of a robust alternative to an action an agent cannot be blameworthy for performing it, it's natural to hold that if what would ordinarily count as a robust alternative is unavailable she would be blameless in her situation if she does the best she can. But the supposition is part of what's being challenged by the Frankfurt defender.[22]

Moya wants us to lower the standards of robustness in FSCs so that "doing the next best thing" counts as a robust alternative. The reason he wants to do this is because in FSCs there is not an available alternative to get one "off the hook." So, Jones does not have the option of not killing Smith or Jones does not have the option of not evading taxes. In these situations, Moya thinks that "doing the next best thing" amounts to fulfilling one's moral duties and that this should count as a robust and exempting alternative.[23]

21. Moya, "On the Very Idea," 18.
22. Pereboom, *Free Will*, 17.
23. Moya writes, "In normal circumstances, with no device lurking the standards for exempting alternatives would have risen to deciding not to evade taxes and not evading them: merely attending to moral reasons would not have been enough; but, since Joe could not have decided and acted that way, the standards lower to the next best action he could perform in order to fulfil his moral duties, which so becomes an exempting alternative.

So, on this plausible interpretation of the notion of an exempting alternative, *Tax Evasion* and structurally similar examples do not refute PAP: the agent is morally blameworthy, but, against appearances, he has robust, even exempting alternatives after

Pereboom responds as follows,

> The feature of the context that Moya claims to alter the standard from the usual one is the unavailability of what would under normal circumstances be an exempting alternative. However, this claim is itself fueled by the robust alternative possibilities requirement, which is what's at issue. If Moya's proposal for altering the usual standard could be justified by considerations independent of this requirement, then perhaps it should sway the Frankfurt defender. But the justification he sets out, while not implausible, is not independent of this requirement, and so his proposal is not a dialectically satisfying response.[24]

Moya is motivated to alter the standard of robustness because there is no "normal" exempting alternative in FSCs. Pereboom argues that this is correct. There is no "normal" exempting alternative, but this is the whole point. FSCs do not have what would normally be exempting alternatives. But Moya wants to use this fact to change what should count as a robust alternative. Pereboom basically argues that you cannot just change the standard to suit your purposes. Thus, Moya's argument really misses the point.

The first objection to FSCs is the Flicker of Freedom objection. It tries to undermine FSCs by pointing to alternative possibilities in FSCs. It is argued that these alternative possibilities account for our intuition that the agent is morally responsible in FSCs. Fischer responds by constructing FSCs in which only "mere flickers of freedom" remain. These "mere flickers of freedom" cannot ground moral responsibility because they are not robust. In order to defend the necessity of robust alternative possibilities, Fischer appeals to Pereboom's definition of robustness which Pereboom defends against objections.

The Dilemma Defense

Another objection to FSCs is what has come to be known as the Dilemma Defense. In Harry Frankfurt's original example, he did not specify how

---

all" (Moya, "On the Very Idea," 17).

It is interesting to note that Moya does concede here that "in normal circumstances" an exempting alternative in Tax Evasion would only be "deciding to not evade taxes and not evading them." This is basically what people like Fischer and Pereboom have always said would amount to a robust alternative in FSCs. The problem was that these are not available in FSCs and thus the agent has no robust alternative. Moya tries to get around this by arguing that FSCs are not normal circumstances and thus a lower standard ought to apply.

24. Pereboom, *Free Will*, 17

Black knew that Jones would do something other than what Black wanted. Instead he merely said, "Black is an excellent judge of such things."[25] Later FSCs were designed to fill in how Black could know.[26] They made use of a prior sign such as blushing, a furrowed brow, or a neural sequence. The idea is that the blush or other prior sign is part of a causal chain that leads to the action. So, if Jones blushes, then Black knows that Jones will not do the action Black wants. If Jones does not blush, then Black knows that Jones will do the action that Black wants. So, Black just needs to watch for the blush or some other prior sign.

The Dilemma Defense focuses on the relationship between the prior sign (blush) and the action.[27] According to proponents of the Dilemma Defense, this relationship can only take one of two forms. Either the relationship between the prior sign and the action is deterministic or it is indeterministic. Either option is problematic. If the relationship is deterministic, then this begs the question against incompatibilists because they do not think that moral responsibility and determinism are compatible. Thus, they will not grant that Jones is morally responsible in a deterministic FSC. If the FSC is indeterministic, then Jones will have alternative possibilities and the FSC will have failed to refute PAP. Fischer states the indeterministic horn of the dilemma,

> Does the mere presence of Black, together with his dispositions and technology, really make it the case that Jones cannot at just prior to the time of his choosing to vote for Obama (say time T2) do (i.e., choose) otherwise at T2? On the first horn of the dilemma, we suppose that causal indeterminism obtains, and that it obtains specifically in the relationship between Jones's mental states prior to T2 and his choice at T2. Now it would seem that, no matter what occurs along the sequence to T2, Jones can still at least begin to choose to vote for someone other than Obama (or not at all) right at T2. So under the assumption of causal indeterminism (underwritten or made true by lack of

---

25. Frankfurt, "Alternative Possibilities and Moral Responsibility," 172.

26. Fischer, *Metaphysics of Free Will*, 135. Fischer writes, "Now this sort of worry is part of the motivation for the elaborate set-up of the case of Jones and Black. In this case, should Jones show any indication that he is about to choose to vote for Bush, Black will intervene to assure that he does not even *choose* to vote for Bush." It is the indication or prior sign that enables Black to know what Jones will choose.

27. For formulations of the Dilemma Defense, see Kane, *Free Will and Values*, 51n25; *Significance of Free Will*, 142; Widerker, "Libertarianism and Frankfurt's Attack," 248; Ginet, "In Defense of the Principle," 403–17. I will be relying on the way Fischer states the dilemma.

determination in the appropriate location) Jones would seem to have at least *an* alternative possibility, truncated as it would be.[28]

The idea behind the Dilemma Defense is that we must either assume that determinism or indetermininsm obtains in the FSC. If indeterminism obtains, then it appears that Jones has an alternative possibility. He could begin to choose to vote for someone other than Obama. Without Black's intervention, he would carry out this choice into the action of not voting for Obama. Of course, Black would detect Jones beginning to choose and intervene, resulting in Jones actually voting for Obama. However, he would be able to begin to choose to vote against Obama and this is an alternative possibility. In other words, FSCs do not establish that no alternative possibilities exist. On the assumption of indeterminism, Jones can always "begin to choose" to vote against Obama. Therefore, so the argument goes, on indeterminism, FSCs fail to refute PAP.

What would happen if we do not assume indeterminism, but we assume determinism? The assumption of determinism is the other horn of the Dilemma Defense. Fischer says,

> On the other horn of the dilemma, we assume a causally deterministic relationship between Jones's prior mental states and his choice at T2 to vote for Obama. Now the proponent of the so-called "Dilemma Defense" will contend that it would be question-begging to extract the conclusion that Jones is morally responsible for choosing at T2 to vote for Obama. After all, the proper conceptualization of the relationship between causal determinism and moral responsibility is precisely what is at issue in the context in which FSCs are invoked. So the very resources used to secure the claim that the relevant agent lacks freedom to do otherwise seem to call into question whether he can legitimately be deemed morally responsible for the behavior in question.[29]

The problem with assuming determinism in an FSC is that it begs the question. The Dilemma Defense seeks to defend PAP against FSCs by putting the proponent of FSCs on the horns of a seemingly irresolvable dilemma. We must either assume that FSCs take place in an indeterministic world or in a deterministic world. On the indeterminism horn, all alternative possibilities have not been eliminated. Jones can still "begin to choose" to do otherwise. Thus, FSCs fail to refute PAP. On the determinism horn of the dilemma, FSCs beg the question against the proponent of PAP. What is

28. Fischer, "Frankfurt-Style Cases," 45.
29. Fischer, "Frankfurt-Style Cases," 46.

at issue is whether or not determinism is compatible with moral responsibility. If FSCs assume determinism and then declare that FSCs show that Jones is morally responsible, then this is clearly question-begging. It would appear that the Dilemma Defense is strong evidence against FSCs.

Response to the Dilemma Defense

There are a number of approaches to the Dilemma Defense.[30] I will be following Fischer's approach in this section as supplemented by Pereboom. Fischer first responds to the indeterministic horn of the dilemma. This response seeks to construct FSCs on the assumption of indeterminism. The second type of response targets the deterministic horn of the dilemma. This type of response seeks to show why the assumption of determinism does not illicitly beg the question against the incompatibilist.

---

30. One approach to the indeterministic horn is to construct FSCs that assume indeterminism but rule out alternative possibilities or robust alternative possibilities. This is the approach Fischer hints at and is developed by Pereboom that we will be pursuing. For other similar approaches, see Mele and Robb, "Rescuing Frankfurt-style Cases"; Pereboom, "Source Incompatibilism and Alternative Possibilities."

One approach to the deterministic horn is to argue that the Dilemma Defence focuses on something accidental to FSCs, namely the prior sign. Other FSCs can be given that do not have prior signs and thus avoid the dilemma altogether. For this approach, see Timpe, "Trumping Frankfurt," 485–99; *Free Will*, 81–98. Timpe writes, "Nevertheless, I think that the Dilemma Defense fails regardless insofar as it depends on an element of existing FSCs which is merely accidental—namely the relationship between the prior sign and the action. This feature is not essential to FSCs because one can develop an FSC that does not contain a prior sign at all and, as such, need not illicitly presuppose determinism in order for the agent to lack the ability to do otherwise" (Timpe, *Free Will*, 90).

Another approach to the deterministic horn is by Helen Beebee. She argues that we should not be concerned if we beg the question against the incompatibilist, "If your interest is in defending compatibilism, however, you might be inclined to reply: *So what?* We can grant that if we think of the nefarious neurosurgeon case as an attack on incompatibilism, then it fails for just the reason given by the dilemma defence. But if we think of it as a *defence of compatibilism* against CA (Consequence Argument), why should we care if we beg the question against the incompatibilist? After all, the question we are addressing here is whether CA constitutes a *good argument for* incompatibilism. So, let's agree that the incompatibilist—or at least the kind who has *already* assumed that (PAP1) is true—is going to be unmoved by Frankfurt's argument because of the dilemma defence. But then, what business do they have being an incompatibilist in the first place? What, exactly, is their *argument* for that position? If the incompatibilist's answer to that question is: 'The Consequence Argument,' then it looks like it is the incompatibilist, and not Frankfurt, who is begging the question.... But in invoking the dilemma defence, the incompatibilist has *already* committed himself to a principle—(PAP1)—which, without CA to justify it, is simply an unargued assumption that the compatibilist should see no need to accept" (BeeBee, *Free Will*, 150).

APPENDIX: CRITICISMS OF FISCHER AND RAVIZZA

Fischer does not develop an FSC that assumes indeterminism, but he believes that they can be constructed. He writes,

> I find it plausible that an indeterministic Frankfurt-style case can be constructed in which the *only* remaining alternative possibilities are "mere flickers of freedom" and thus not sufficiently robust to ground attributions of moral responsibility.[31]

One such example of this type of indeterministic FSCs was developed by Derk Pereboom. He calls it "Tax Evasion" and it is in the category of what have been called "buffer zone" cases.[32] Pereboom's most recent iteration of this is Tax Evasion 2:

> Tax Evasion (2): Joe is considering claiming a tax deduction for the registration fee that he paid when he bought a house. He knows that claiming this deduction is illegal, but that he probably won't be caught, and that if he were, he could convincingly plead ignorance. Suppose he has a strong but not always overriding desire to advance his self-interest regardless of its cost to others and even if it involves illegal activity. In addition, the only way that in this situation he could fail to choose to evade taxes is for moral reasons, of which he is aware. He could not, for example, fail to make this choice for no reason or simply on a whim. Moreover, it is causally necessary for his failing to choose to evade taxes in this situation that he attain a certain level of attentiveness to moral reasons. Joe can secure this level of attentiveness voluntarily. However, his attaining this level of attentiveness is not causally sufficient for his failing to choose to evade taxes. If he were to attain this level of attentiveness, he could, exercising his libertarian free will, either choose to evade taxes or refrain from so choosing (without the intervener's device in place). However, to ensure that he will choose to evade taxes, a neuroscientist has, unbeknownst to Joe, implanted a device in his brain, which were it to sense the requisite level of attentiveness, would electronically stimulate the right neural centers so as to inevitably result in his making this choice. As it happens, Joe does not attain this level of attentiveness to his moral reasons, and he chooses to evade taxes on his own, while the device remains idle.[33]

---

31. Fischer, "Frankfurt-Style Cases," 47.
32. Fischer, "Frankfurt-Type Examples," 253.
33. Pereboom, *Free Will*, 15.

Pereboom highlights three distinguishing features of Tax Evasion 2. First, "the cue for intervention is a necessary condition for the agent's availing herself of any robust alternative possibility (without the intervener's device in place)."[34] In this case, the cue for intervention is "Joe attaining a certain level of attentiveness to moral reasons." This cue is not causally sufficient for Joe to refrain from evading taxes, but it is necessary. This cue functions as a "buffer zone" that Joe must cross if he is to have access to the relevant alternative possibility of refraining from evading taxes. The existence of this buffer zone renders Joe indeterministic. He can still choose either to evade taxes or not to evade taxes. However, our neuroscientist can know when he is in the buffer zone and this enables him to use his device to get him to evade taxes. This solves the problem that the indeterministic horn of the Dilemma Defense raises. That problem was the inability to predict what Joe would do in indeterministic contexts.

Pereboom identifies another feature of Tax Evasion 2. He writes, "the cue for intervention itself is not a robust alternative possibility."[35] This is important because Joe can reach a certain level of attentiveness to moral reasons or not. This means that he has alternative possibilities to do either. However, this alternative possibility cannot account for why he is responsible for evading taxes. It is not robust.

Pereboom identifies a third feature of Tax Evasion 2. The absence at any specific time of the cue for intervention in no sense causally determines the action the agent actually performs."[36] This means that Joe is in an indeterministic context whereas in other FSCs, the cue or prior sign does causally determine the action. In Tax Evasion 2, the cue does not.

This type of FSC attempts to answer the indeterministic horn of the dilemma by assuming indeterminism. There is also a buffer zone which consists of "a requisite level of attentiveness to moral reasons." If Joe enters this buffer zone, then our neuroscientist would detect it. However, entering this buffer zone does not determine Joe's choice. It is not causally sufficient for his failing to choose to evade taxes. Also, Joe could both choose to evade taxes or refrain from evading taxes in a libertarian manner. Hence, indeterminism is explicitly affirmed; however, the neuroscientist could detect that Joe has entered the buffer zone and put his device into action. Thus, Joe does not have a robust alternative possibility and yet he is in an indeterministic situation. This type of example is helpful in answering the indeterministic horn of the Dilemma Defense.

---

34. Pereboom, *Free Will*, 14.
35. Pereboom, *Free Will*, 14.
36. Pereboom, *Free Will*, 14–15.

I cannot deal with all the objections given to Tax Evasion 2, but I will deal with three that Pereboom highlights in his discussion.

The first objection comes from David Widerker. Widerker wants to make a distinction between derivative and non-derivative responsibility. Widerker writes,

> A problem with Pereboom's example is that, in it, the agent is *derivatively* blameworthy for the decision he made, because he has not done his reasonable best (or has not made a reasonable effort) to avoid making it. He should have been more attentive to the moral reasons than he in fact was—something he could have done. And in that case, he would not be blameworthy for deciding to evade taxes, as then he would be forced by the neuroscientist so to decide. If this is correct, then Pereboom's example is a case of derivative culpability, and hence is irrelevant to PAP, which . . . concerns itself only with direct or non-derivative culpability.[37]

The idea is to place a derivative/non-derivative schema on Tax Evasion 2. This schema is supposed to point out that the agent in Tax Evasion 2 is only derivatively responsible. This renders it not a counterexample to PAP because PAP only deals with non-derivative responsibility.

The paradigm example of this schema concerns someone that gets drunk. Pereboom explains,

> Biff decides to get drunk, understanding that when he is intoxicated he will no longer be able to avoid being abusive to his companions, and then when he is drunk he assaults one of them. In this example, Biff satisfies paradigmatic general conditions on moral responsibility at the time he decides to get drunk, but not when he is drunk and abusive. If he is morally responsible for the assault, it is only derivatively so—derivative, in particular, of his being non-derivatively morally responsible for deciding to get drunk, and foreseeing that when he is drunk he is likely to be abusive.[38]

This schema is supposed to be applied to Tax Evasion 2, but Pereboom argues that Joe and Biff's situations are very different. Therefore, this schema does not apply to Tax Evasion 2. Pereboom writes,

---

37. Pereboom, *Free Will*, 19. See Widerker, "Libertarianism and the Philosophical Significance," 163–87. Pereboom points out that this objection was anticipated by Carl Ginet (see Ginet, "In Defense of the Principle," 403–17).

38. Pereboom, *Free Will*, 18.

> In this example, while some of the uncontroversial general conditions on non-derivative moral responsibility fail to be satisfied when Biff gets drunk, they are all met at the time he decides to get drunk. But Biff's situation differs significantly from Joe's. Biff has knowingly placed himself in a position in which some of the uncontroversial general conditions on non-derivative moral responsibility will fail to be satisfied at relevant subsequent times. This is not true for Joe.[39]

Biff crosses over into a point of no return when he gets drunk. This makes him unable not to be abusive. However, this is not the case with Joe. Joe is able to become more attentive to moral reasons at any time. If at any time Joe is not more attentive to moral reasons, he knows that he can be at any other time. This is not so with Biff. Once Biff crosses the line of drunkenness, he is not able to cross back. This means that the comparison of Joe in Tax Evasion 2 and Biff is not appropriate. Since Widerker's objection depends on legitimately comparing Biff with Joe, his objection fails.

The second objection comes from Robert Kane. Pereboom describes Kane's objection as follows,

> Kane's reply to Tax Evasion crucially features the claim that the controller "is not going to let Joe make the undetermined choice between A and B," where A is the choice to evade taxes, and B is doing otherwise, and from this Kane concludes that Joe will not be (non-derivatively) morally responsible for the choice to evade taxes. His argument is this: if the cue for intervention, Joe's attaining the requisite level of attentiveness to moral reasons, does not occur, and he thus chooses A since the necessary condition for choosing B is not in place, Joe's decision "will not be a 'will-setting' SFA (self-forming action) ... because he'll only have reasons to 'set his will' on A and he won't have attended to any good reasons to set his will on B." If he does achieve the level of attentiveness, the controller will intervene and force him to choose A, and so Joe will not get a chance to make a true SFA *either way* once the controller is in the picture.[40]

Kane's objection is that Joe is not in a situation where he actually does have the undetermined choice between A and B. This is necessary for an agent to be able to set his own will and thus be non-derivatively responsible. What is needed for Kane is that Joe be in a situation where he has conflict

---

39. Pereboom, *Free Will*, 19

40. Pereboom, *Free Will*, 20. Kane's objection is found in Kane, "Libertarianism," 5–43; "Response to Fischer, Pereboom, and Vargas," 166–83.

of motivations where it is possible for him to choose to evade taxes or not to choose to evade taxes. Only in this situation is it possible to have non-derivative responsibility.

Pereboom disagrees. He writes,

> True, while Joe is aware of the moral reasons that conflict with his reasons for evading taxes, he won't be motivated by them in a way that makes it psychologically possible for him not to decide to evade taxes unless he attains a higher level of attentiveness to them than he actually does. But solely by way an exercise of his libertarian free will he could have become sufficiently more attentive to the moral reasons, as a result of which both choosing to evade taxes or not would have been psychologically possible for him. No feature of his situation prevents him from realizing this degree of attentiveness by means of his free agency.[41]

Pereboom is making the argument that since Joe has libertarian free will, he could have chosen to reach the requisite level of moral attentiveness and thus had a genuine libertarian choice to evade or not evade taxes. Thus, Kane is not right to argue that Joe did not have a genuine SFA situation.

The third objection comes from Carl Ginet. Ginet's objection goes like this,

> At t1, the precise time Joe makes the decision to evade taxes, he might have instead have been attending to the moral reasons, and that this alternative possibility is robust. . . . One might fail, he thinks, to distinguish Jones's doing B by t3 because they are morally equivalent in the sense that Jones would be blameworthy for the first as he would be for the second had Black's mechanism not been present. . . . What explains Jones's blameworthiness, in the correct analysis, is his having an alternative to doing B at t1, and what he is really blameworthy for is doing B at t1.[42]

According to Ginet, we must distinguish between doing B at two different times t1 and t3. In an FSC, Jones cannot do B at t3 because Black makes doing B at t3 unavoidable. However, Jones could have done B at t1, which would be a time earlier than t3. In this case, Jones could have avoided doing B at t1. Given the fact that B is the same action at t1 and t3, Ginet's argument is that in Pereboom's FSC, Jones is responsible because he could have done B at

---

41. Pereboom, *Free Will*, 21.
42. Pereboom, *Free Will*, 22. Ginet's argument is found in Ginet, "Review of *Living*," 305–9. For others that raise this concern, see Palmer, "Pereboom on the Frankfurt Cases" 261–72; Franklin, "Neo-Frankfurtians," 189–207.

t1. In other words, there is a robust alternative possibility here: That is doing B at a time prior to t3, which would be t1. Black's device would not work at t1, only at t3. This is why Jones is responsible in this FSC.

Pereboom responds to this by disputing "the claim that our sense that Jones is blameworthy for doing B at t3, or blameworthy at all, can be explained by his having an alternative possibility to deciding at t1."[43] He does this by providing another FSC that fits Ginet's schema. He calls this FSC Tax Cut:

> Jones can vote for or against a modest tax cut for those in his high income group by pushing either the "yes" or the "no" button in the voting booth. Once he has entered the voting booth, he has exactly two minutes to vote, and a downward-to-zero ticking timer is prominently displayed. If he does not vote, he will have to pay a fine, substantial enough so that in his situation he is committed with certainty to voting (either for or against), and this is underlain by the fact that the prospect of the fine, together with background conditions, causally determines him to vote. Jones has concluded that voting for the tax cut is barely on balance morally wrong, since he believes it would not stimulate the economy appreciably, while adding wealth to the already wealthy without helping the less well off, despite how it has been advertised. He is receptive and reactive to these general sorts of moral reasons: he would vote against a substantially larger tax cut for his income group on account of reasons of this sort, and has actually done so in the past. He spends some time in the voting booth rehearsing the relevant moral and self-interested reasons. But what would be required for him to decide to vote against the tax cut is for him to vividly imagine that his boss would find out, whereupon due to her political leanings she would punish him by not promoting him to a better position. In this situation it is causally necessary for his not deciding to vote for the tax cut, and to vote against it instead, that he vividly imagine her finding out and not being promoted, which can occur to him involuntarily or else voluntarily by his libertarian free will. Jones understands that imagining the punishment scenario will put him in a motivational position to vote against. But so imagining is not causally sufficient for him to decide to vote against the tax cut, for even then he could still, by his libertarian free will, either decide to vote for or against (without the intervener's device in place). However, a neuroscientist has, unbeknownst to him, implanted a device in his brain, which, were it to sense his vividly

---

43. Pereboom, *Free Will*, 22.

imagining the punishment scenarios, would stimulate his brain so as to causally determine the decision to vote for the tax cut. Jones's imagination is not exercised in this way, and he decides to vote in favor while the device remains idle.[44]

This FSC handles a concern for Tax Evasion 2. In Tax Evasion 2, Jones can avoid responsibility at any specific time into the indefinite future by being attentive to moral reasons. The objector to Tax Evasion argues that this is a robust alternative possibility. Tax Cut eliminates this by placing a time restriction on Jones. Jones is committed with certainty to voting by t_3. Pereboom writes,

> With this new provision in place, it is still true that at any specific time prior to t_3 he understands that by vividly imagining the punishment scenario he can avoid responsibility at that instant for deciding to vote in favor, which relative to those specific times would count as alternative possibilities. But it is not the case that relative to the entire interval up to and including t_3 he has a robust alternative possibility. In particular, it is ruled out by Jones's commitment to deciding to vote by t_3 that he not make a decision to vote at all during this interval by way of vividly imagining the punishment scenario.[45]

The first horn of the Dilemma Defense assumes indeterminism. The objection is that Jones necessarily has alternative possibilities given the assumption of indeterminism. Fischer responds by stating his confidence that an indeterministic FSC can be constructed in which there are no robust alternative possibilities. I pointed to Pereboom's Tax Evasion 2 as an example of such an FSC. From this discussion, we can conclude that Tax Evasion 2 provides a reasonable response to the indeterministic horn of the dilemma.

The Deterministic Horn

The other horn of the Dilemma Defense is the deterministic horn. How can FSCs not beg the question against the incompatibilist if they assume determinism? First of all, like the indeterministic horn, Fischer argues that "mere flickers of freedom" are the only alternative possibilities left on the deterministic horn. So, it cannot be argued that these flickers ground moral

---

44. Pereboom, *Free Will*, 23.
45. Pereboom, *Free Will*, 24.

responsibility. But the heart of the deterministic horn is the question-begging challenge.[46] Fischer responds,

46. For background on this strategy, note that Fischer first pursued this type of answer to the deterministic horn in Fischer, "Recent Work on Moral Responsibility." Michael McKenna and Ishtiyaque Haji further developed this in Haji and McKenna, "Dialectical Delicacies." In this essay, Haji and McKenna distinguish two interpretations and two dialectical contexts of the deterministic horn. The "broad interpretation" is in the dialectical context of trying to convince someone that is already committed to incompatibilism. On this horn to beg the question means to assume determinism in and of itself. This begs the question because the incompatibilist is already committed to the thesis that determinism is incompatible with the freedom necessary for moral responsibility. On this interpretation, they agree that assuming determinism is question-begging. However, they do not think this interpretation is relevant for the debate.

The "narrow interpretation" is in the dialectical context of trying to convince someone that is NOT committed to compatibilism or incompatibilism. They argue that in this context the assumption of determinism is not illicit. However, they raise a potential issue that could beg the question in this context. It is that determinism already eliminates alternatives. Thus, there is no work for the counterfactual intervener to do. The question-begging might occur in that alternatives get ruled out for reasons other than those introduced by Frankfurt's counterfactual machinery. This is basically the objection that David Palmer raises in Palmer, "New Distinctions, Same Troubles."

Haji and McKenna reply to Palmer's objection in Haji and McKenna, "Defending Frankfurt's Argument." They identify Palmer's objection as follows: "What Palmer's objection requires, really, is the stronger contention that it is not possible for there to be a case in which the counterfactual intervener eliminates alternatives without the assumption of determinism" (Haji and McKenna, "Defending Frankfurt's Argument," 369). The idea is that the intervener alone cannot eliminate alternatives. The Frankfurt defender must provide an example where they show that the intervener alone does this without determinism. Haji and McKenna respond to this challenge in two ways. First, by pointing out that Frankfurt examples have been used to persuade traditional compatibilists (these are compatibilists that affirm PAP), that "compatibilist alternatives" are eliminated. This has been done in Haji, *Deontic Morality and Control*, 68; McKenna, "Does Strong Compatibilism Survive?," 259–64.

Second, by modifying Derk Pereboom's Tax Evasion 2 Frankfurt example. This is an example in which indeterminism is assumed, not determinism and the intervener eliminate all robust alternatives. This shows that the intervener can eliminate alternatives alone, without the help of determinism. Haji and McKenna then wed this to a deterministic context and meet Palmer's objection. They conclude: "Palmer has failed to discredit our view that, in relevant dialectical contexts, prior-sign Frankfurt cases that assume determinism do not beg the question against the Dilemma Defender. . . . Notice that once the dialectical context is specified as the narrow one, and once it is thereby acknowledged that the dispute is to be settled by convincing the fair and theoretically uncommitted voter, it is irrelevant whether the example that is meant to turn the trick is deterministic or indeterminsitic. It is only in what we have identified as the broad dialectical context that the issue of determinism matters. And as we observed in our previous paper, in that case, the background assumption is that the Frankfurt Defender should engage the incompatibilist by beginning the debate on the incompatibilist's turf, granting her, so to speak, the assumption of incompatibilism. But for those who think that the relevance of alternative possibilities should be settled either prior to or independently of the truth of incompatibilism, it is unclear why the Frankfurt Defender

APPENDIX: CRITICISMS OF FISCHER AND RAVIZZA 243

> I do not ask the reader precipitously and straightaway to judge that the relevant agent (say Jones) is morally responsible for the behavior in question.[47]

In other words, it would be blatantly begging the question to move from the deterministic FSC to the conclusion that Jones is morally responsible. Fischer continues,

> Rather, at this stage I simply invite the reader to come to a preliminary conditional conclusion: *if* the agent (say Jones) is not morally responsible for his actual behavior, then it is not in virtue of his lacking freedom to do otherwise. That is, on this more patient and judicious approach, we first get to a preliminary conclusion that does *not* beg the question against the incompatibilist about causal determinism and moral responsibility: that it is not the *mere fact* of lack of alternative possibilities that rules out the agent's moral responsibility, if it is indeed ruled out. Then I would proceed to a second step in which I would seek to argue that causal determination in the actual sequence does not *in itself and apart from ruling out alternative possibilities* threaten moral responsibility.[48]

The first step is to get the person to reach a preliminary conclusion. That conclusion is that the mere lack of alternative possibilities does not rule out moral responsibility. Then Fischer would proceed to argue that actual sequence causal determinism does not alone rule out moral responsibility. He does this by providing another FSC where causal determinism is explicitly assumed and we make no assumptions about causal determinism ruling out alternative possibilities:

> Black checks and sees the "prior sign" at T1 that is associated with a subsequent vote for the Democrat—say, the [raised] *left* brow. Given that Black knows that causal determinism obtains, he can relax, as it were; under these circumstances, Black knows that Jones in fact will subsequently choose to vote for Obama and carry out that choice. It is *also* true, given Black's device and dispositions, that if Jones were to show the sign at T1 associated with voting for a Republican at T2 (appropriately enough, a raised *right* brow), Black's device would swing into action and stimulate Jones's brain so as to ensure that he chooses at T2 to

---

should begin the debate on foreign soil. Why not instead settle the matter on neutral terrain?" (Haji and McKenna, "Defending Frankfurt's Argument," 371–72).

47. Fischer, "Recent Work on Moral Responsibility," 47.
48. Fischer, "Recent Work on Moral Responsibility," 47–48.

vote for Obama and does so vote at T3. I claim that this additional fact, when added to the assumption of causal determinism and the fact that Black can thus be sure that Jones's showing the prior sign at T1 will in fact be followed by his choosing accordingly at T2, renders it true that Jones cannot at T2 choose to vote for [Romney] (or subsequently vote for Romney). These two facts *together* make it the case that Jones cannot at T2 choose to vote for [Romney] or carry out such a choice.[49]

In a recent article, David Widerker and Stewart Goetz challenge Fischer's argument against the deterministic horn of the Dilemma Defense.[50] They do not think that Fischer has provided a deterministic scenario in which all robust alternatives are eliminated. They argue that Fischer's treatment of the deterministic horn leaves the robust alternative possibility of "beginning to choose to vote for McCain." Here is how they state the argument:

> Has Fischer succeeded in disarming the Dilemma Defense, in particular its deterministic horn? We do not think so. Suppose that Jones furrows his left eyebrow at t1. Now consider
>
> (3) The possible act of Jones's beginning (at t1 . . .) to choose to vote for McCain.
>
> Which Fischer regards as a robust alternative possibility. . . . Note that in Fischer's example, Black and his device (and his dispositions) do not rule out this possibility. As mentioned earlier, this alternative is supposed to be ruled out by the fact described in (2), without invoking the assumption that determinism eliminates alternative possibilities. More specifically, it is supposed to be ruled out in that way by the facts:
>
> (2a) There obtains a causally deterministic link between Jones's furrowing his left eyebrow at t1 and Jones's choice at t2 to vote for Obama,
>
> (2b) Jones has furrowed his left eyebrow at t1,
>
> Together with the fact of
>
> (2c) Black's being sure that Jones will choose at t2 to vote for Obama based on his knowledge of (2a) and (2b)

---

49. Fischer, "Recent Work on Moral Responsibility," 48.
50. Widerker and Goetz, "Fischer Against the Dilemma Defense."

APPENDIX: CRITICISMS OF FISCHER AND RAVIZZA 245

We shall now argue that (2a)-(2c) do not satisfy this requirement.[51]

What Widerker and Goetz are arguing is that the robust alternative possibility of "beginning to choose to vote for McCain" is supposed to be ruled out by (2a)-(2c). However, this (2a)-(2c) do not rule out the robust alternative of "beginning to choose to vote for McCain." Therefore, Fischer's argument against the deterministic horn of the Dilemma Defense does not work. He has failed to provide a deterministic FSC where all robust alternative possibilities are ruled out.

The details of their argument showing that (2a)-(2c) do not rule out this robust alternative need not occupy us here. The reason for this is because Fischer agrees with them that (2a)-(2c) do not rule out "beginning to choose to vote for McCain." The problem is not their argument that (2a)-(2c) fail to rule out "beginning to choose to vote for McCain." The problem is that this is not the argument that Fischer gave against the deterministic horn. Fischer writes,

> I have no doubt that (2a)-(2c) do not satisfy the requirement; that is, I agree that (2a)-(2c) do not rule out (3). But I am puzzled as to how Widerker and Goetz could have interpreted me as supposing that (2a)-(2c) rule out (3).... How then could Widerker and Goetz possibly have concluded that I did not contend that Black's device and dispositions are part of the explanation of the fact that (3) is ruled out?... Given this, it should be obvious that the argumentation offered by Widerker and Goetz to show that (2a)-(2c) do not rule out (3) is quite beside the point; it doesn't touch *my* argument ... since my argument explicitly employs the *conjunction* of the presence of Black's device and dispositions and causal determinism.[52]

Widerker and Goetz thus misrepresent Fischer's argument and this leaves Fischer's argument unscathed.

Fischer provides a two-step argument against the deterministic horn. The first step is to ask us not to assume that moral responsibility presupposes freedom to do otherwise. The second step argues that actual sequence causal determinism does not alone rule out moral responsibility. From this we can conclude that a reasonable case can be made that the deterministic horn fails. We can conclude this for three reasons. First, Fischer's two-step argument is reasonable. Second, Widerker and Goetz's response to it is

---

51. Widerker and Goetz, "Fischer Against the Dilemma Defense," 289–90.
52. Fischer "Deterministic Horn," 492.

unsuccessful. Third, there are other approaches to the deterministic horn that support the inadequacy of the deterministic horn.

The Dilemma Defense is one of the most prominent attempted rebuttals to FSCs. Fischer and Ravizza provide a reasonable defense of FSCs. So, we are on reasonable grounds is saying that the Dilemma Defense does not defeat them. Of course, not everyone will agree, but there is nothing on which everyone agrees. Fischer's defense provides the compatibilist with a reasonable response to the Dilemma Defense.

The W-Defense

Another criticism of FSCs is called the W-defense. David Widerker developed this criticism.[53] In order to understand the W-defense, it would be helpful to better understand FSCs. Justin Capes breaks FSCs down into two main components. He writes,

> FR: There may be circumstances that make it impossible for a person to avoid performing a certain action but that in no way bring it about that the person performs that action.
>
> M: A person who performs a morally wrong action in a FR-situation is morally blameworthy for what she has done.[54]

The idea behind the W-defense is to question the truth of M. The claim is made that it is false that the agent in FR-situations is morally blameworthy. If true, this would undermine FSCs because they require that the agent in them be morally blameworthy for what they did. If he or she is not, then we cannot say that moral responsibility does not require alternative possibilities.

In order to see this more clearly, Capes helpfully outlines the structure of the W-defense. He writes,

1. To hold S blameworthy for A-ing essentially involves an expectation that S not have A-ed

2. But to expect that S not have A-ed would be unreasonable if S could not have done otherwise than A

---

53. Widerker, "Blameworthiness and Frankfurt's Argument," 53–73; "Blameworthiness, Non-Robust Alternatives," 292–306. For responses to the W-Defense, see Stump, "Moral Responsibility without Alternative Possibilities" 139–58; Frankfurt, "Some Thoughts Concerning PAP" 339–46; Fischer, *My Way*, 209–10; McKenna, "Where Strawson and Frankfurt Meet," 163–80; "Frankfurt's Argument," 770–93.

54. Capes, "W-Defense," 62.

3. Hence, holding S blameworthy for A-ing when S could not have done otherwise than A would involve an unreasonable expectation on the part of those holding S blameworthy.[55]

The W-defense rhetorically gets at this argument by asking the following question of the Frankfurt defender, "What, in your opinion, should he have done instead?" It seems unreasonable to ask someone to do otherwise, if they did not have the ability to do otherwise. If this is true, then M is false.

Capes's reply to this is very good. First, he helpfully points out two different senses of the word "expectation." The first sense of "expectation" is as "anticipation." He writes, "To expect the storm to pass is to anticipate or predict the storm to pass."[56] This is not the sense of expectation in premise (1) of the W-defense. Instead, it adopts the sense of expectation as demand. He writes, "To expect that a person do something in the sense at issue in the W-defense, however, is to demand or insist that the person do that thing."[57]

Second, Capes questions the truth of (1). Why should we think that holding someone blameworthy essentially requires an "expectation that S not have A-ed?" What reason is there for thinking this?

Third, he helpfully points out that there is a legitimate sense in which we hold people blameworthy, not because we expect or demand that they do otherwise, but because we desire that they do otherwise. He writes,

> To see this, imagine that the devil is evaluating Jones's behavior. The devil might agree with Frankfurt at the cognitive level that Jones is blame-worthy—i.e., that he meets the relevant control and epistemic conditions for moral responsibility—but such a cognitive judgment on the part of the devil does not mean that the devil actually *holds* Jones blameworthy. After all, the devil is no doubt gleeful that Jones has done the morally wrong thing. ... There needs to be a conative element present as well. In order to actually blame Jones, the devil must also desire that Jones not have shot Smith.[58]

Fourth, if you add the intuitive force of the Frankfurt examples themselves in the actual sequence, it adds to the credibility that the agent in FSCs is morally blameworthy. In direct answer to Widerker's question, it is helpful to quote Capes,

---

55. Capes, "W-Defense," 73.
56. Capes, "W-Defense," 66.
57. Capes, "W-Defense," 66.
58. Capes, "W-Defense," 74–75.

So what should Jones have done instead of shooting Smith? Well, if we mean "what *ought* he to have done instead?" then it is open to the Frankfurt-defender to deny that "ought" implies "can" and to insist that Jones should have refrained from shooting Smith. If, on the other hand, we mean "what would it be reasonable to expect (or demand) Jones to have done instead?" then the correct answer, I think, is "there is nothing we could have reasonably expected him to do instead." Since Jones could not have done otherwise than shoot Smith, it would be quite unreasonable to expect him not to shoot Smith. I have argued that this is problematic for the Frankfurt-defender only if by holding Jones blameworthy the Frankfurt-defender is thereby committed to expecting that Jones not have done what he did. But there is no reason to suppose that an expectation that a person not have acted a certain way is essential to our moral disapproval of that person's behavior or to our holding that person blameworthy for what she has done.[59]

The Non-Standard Response

The final category of criticisms to FSCs Fischer calls the non-standard response. He writes,

> The "non-standard" response to the examples claims that even in Frankfurt-type cases the agent has available a robust alternative possibility of precisely the sort normally associated with moral responsibility.[60]

Again, Fischer writes,

> The basic claim of the non-standard response is that insofar as Black's device does not play any actual role in Jones's deliberations or actions, it should be "subtracted" when one is considering whether Jones has a genuine ability to choose and do otherwise.... So if a given agent does X rather than Y in the actual world, but it is intuitively true that the agent could have done Y instead, one looks for a possible world that can differ in certain ways from the actual world prior to the time in question in which the agent does indeed do Y.[61]

---

59. Capes, "W-Defense," 75.
60. McKenna, "Contemporary Compatibilism," 261.
61. McKenna, "Contemporary Compatibilism," 262.

Fischer responds to this in two ways. First, it seems to have implausible results. He writes,

> It would seem to imply that the man who is, unbeknownst to him, locked in the room in Locke's example can leave the room. Or, likewise, if one has secretly been chained to one's desk (perhaps while asleep), it follows that one can leave one's office, despite the chains, as long as one is unaware of the chains.... These results just seem very implausible.[62]

Second, he thinks they are confusing two different senses of the word "ability." He writes,

> I would offer the following diagnosis of the confusion of the nonstandard response. I believe that the nonstandard theorist is conflating general abilities with the sort of ability that corresponds to J. L. Austin's "all-in sense of 'can'" or "can in the particular circumstances." One may have a general ability without having the latter sort of ability, insofar as one does not have the opportunity to exercise the general ability. Although I would concede that the agent in a Frankfurt-type case has the relevant general ability, I would deny that he can under the particular circumstances choose to do otherwise.... It is the particularized notion of ability, and not the general one, that is typically associated with moral responsibility.[63]

This does not exhaust all of the possible objections or actual objections to FSCs. However, it does show that FSCs can be reasonably defended against the main criticisms of them.

Guidance Control

As we have seen, guidance control consists of two parts: (1) moderate reasons responsiveness and (2) mechanism ownership. Fischer and Ravizza's theory of guidance control has not been without criticism.[64] Michael McKenna has a helpful piece where he gives the most recent summary of criticisms against Fischer and Ravizza.[65] In this essay, McKenna identifies six problems for

---

62. McKenna, "Contemporary Compatibilism," 262.
63. McKenna, "Contemporary Compatibilism," 262.
64. Davenport, "Review of *Responsibility and Control*," 384–95; Mele, "Reactive Attitudes," 447–52; Russell, "Critical Notice," 587–606; McKenna, "Assessing Reasons-Responsive Compatibilism," 89–114.
65. See McKenna, "Contemporary Compatibilism."

Fischer and Ravizza. In two of these problems Fischer concedes, but the concession does not destroy the essence of the theory. These are problems with reactivity and the problem of ownership and subjectivity. Regarding the problem with reactivity McKenna writes,

> The upshot appears to be that what Fischer and Ravizza need... is not regular receptivity and weak reactivity, but regular receptivity and weaker reactivity.... In response, Fischer... concedes the point and accepts the proposed emendation.[66]

Regarding the problem with ownership and subjectivity, Fischer does not think that this touches the subjectivity condition required for ownership. So, even if he conceded, his view would basically be intact.

Another problem that McKenna points out also does not destroy Fischer and Ravizza's theory. It is the problem with receptivity. In this problem, all Fischer and Ravizza need to do is add an amendment. McKenna writes,

> Receptivity should include not just an appropriately sane pattern of reasons-recognition, but also receptivity to the actual moral reasons bearing on her context of action.[67]

Thus, far the problems that McKenna has identified do not damage Fischer and Ravizza's theory. This places the theory in a very strong position. However, there are three criticisms that McKenna identifies that could spell trouble with their theory. The first one is problems with counterfactuals and their relevance to guidance control. This issue revolves around the use of Fischer and Ravizza's counterexamples. They are supposed to establish that the agent does not have regulative control, i.e., access to alternative possibilities. The criticism is that this may not be the case. This is the debate within compatibilism between source compatibilists like Fischer and Ravizza and leeway compatibilists, particularly the New Dispositionalists. Fischer's response to the New Dispositionalists was dealt with in the previous section entitled "Non-standard response."[68]

The second problem that could be troublesome for Fischer and Ravizza is problems with mechanisms. This is a problem that Fischer and Ravizza readily acknowledge. The problem is that Fischer and Ravizza have no principled way to establish mechanism individuation. Instead, they rely on intuitive notions of "sameness." McKenna identifies this as a serious problem.

---

66. McKenna, "Contemporary Compatibilism," 192.
67. McKenna, "Contemporary Compatibilism," 192.
68. For further criticism, see Whittle, "Dispositional Abilities" 1–23. For a defense of New Dispositionalism, see Vihvelin, *Causes, Laws, and Free Will*.

Fischer and Ravizza think that it needs work but it is not devastating to their theory. Third is the problem of ownership and manipulation.

Given this brief survey of the potential problems with Fischer and Ravizza's theory, I want to focus on responding to the last three problems. The three problems are (1) mechanism individuation, (2) the subjectivist view of mechanism ownership, and (3) manipulation cases.

Mechanism Individuation

As we have previously seen, Fischer and Ravizza adopt a mechanism as opposed to an agent approach to reasons-responsiveness. One of the reasons they prefer this approach is that it fits well with FSCs. In one such FSC, a person such as Jones is unable to react to a reason to do other than kill Smith. The reason he is unable to react otherwise is the presence of Black. Black is a counterfactual intervener that renders it certain that Jones will kill Smith. Fischer and Ravizza adopt an approach to moral responsibility that says that for someone to be morally responsible, their mechanism must be moderately reasons-responsive (MRR) to reasons to do otherwise. We have already seen the details of this theory. But an apparent problem arises for them. How can a person in a FSC be moderately reasons-responsive to a reason to do other than kill Smith, when Black ensures that this person will kill Smith?

Fischer and Ravizza answer this question in two parts. First, they isolate the mechanism of action from the person who acts. So, it is not the case that the person or agent must be MRR to do otherwise, but the mechanism must be. Second, in order to test to see if the mechanism is MRR, they appeal to possible worlds. They take the mechanism, place it in other possible worlds, and see if it is MRR to do other than kill Smith. In this way, it does not matter that Black is present in the FSC. What matters is that the mechanism is MRR in another possible world. If this is so, then the person is morally responsible.

The benefit of this approach is that it does not have to rely on agents, but mechanisms. In a FSC, the agent is not MRR because of the presence of Black. But if we can isolate the mechanism and test it in other possible worlds, we can have a reasons-responsive theory that fits FSCs. However, as we have previously seen, there is a potential problem. How do we individuate mechanisms? Fischer and Ravizza have already admitted that they have no principled way to do this. They must rely on intuitions in a particular case. Fischer writes,

> I fully admit that I do not have a reductive account of mechanism-individuation, and that, lacking such an account, the theory of guidance control is, at best, incomplete. But an incomplete theory is not thereby an inadequate or fundamentally misguided theory. And my approach to guidance control and moral responsibility is not different from most promising philosophical theories in being incomplete.[69]

This lack of a reductive account has troubled other philosophers.[70] Fischer replies to this worry as follows,

> Further, some important philosophical theories are incomplete in similar respects; theories such as reliabilism in epistemology and generalization in ethics . . . rely implicitly on views about the individuation of the relevant kinds of belief-producing mechanisms or actions without developing explicit, reductive accounts of the sort of individuation at issue.[71]

This is a fair point. Why should we demand so much of Fischer and Ravizza's theory when a good theory can be incomplete? In addition, why demand more of Fischer and Ravizza's theory than that of other theories? After all, Fischer and Ravizza can individuate mechanisms intuitively and on a case-by-case basis. There is just no principled way to do this in advance of a particular instance. Fischer writes again,

> I have suggested a "holistic" methodology whereby one relies on certain "clear" intuitions about mechanism-individuation in provisionally applying the account of guidance control, and then see where it leads. As the theory gets applied to various cases, one will see how mechanisms must be individuated. . . . I do not think this is in itself disturbing or problematic. What *would*

---

69. Fischer, *Deep Control*, 200.

70. Long, "Moderate Reasons-Responsiveness," 151–72; Ginet, "Working with Fischer and Ravizza," 229–53. In this article, Ginet suggests that Fischer and Ravizza move to an agent-based approach. He writes, "Putting it this way suggests an obvious solution, namely, instead of talking about a *mechanism's* being reasons-responsive, to talk about the *agent's* being reasons-responsive at the time of the action. . . . Fischer and Ravizza want the action to issue from a mechanism that is such as to give the agent a certain complex disposition. Why not cut out that middle term and just require that the agent have that disposition? It is not clear that the middle term, the mechanism, is really doing any useful work" (Ginet, "Working with Fischer and Ravizza," 235–36). See McKenna, "Reasons-Responsiveness," 151–83.

71. Fischer, *Deep Control*, 200.

APPENDIX: CRITICISMS OF FISCHER AND RAVIZZA   253

indisputably be problematic is if one individuated mechanisms in inconsistent ways.[72]

Michael McKenna is not satisfied with a mechanistic approach. He draws upon a criticism of Carl Ginet to pose what he calls "A Deep Problem for Any Mechanism-Based Approach."[73] In order to see this problem, McKenna sets it up with a variant of an example that Fischer and Ravizza's theory easily handles. In this variant, the mechanism is unreflective habit. A person is driving and would ordinarily and unreflectively take a certain exit. However, this time the exit is blocked and she is uncertain what other exit she ought to take. The most natural thing would be for her to deliberate. But McKenna says that:

> Fischer and Ravizza hold fixed the mechanism of *unreflective habit*. Hence, they cannot permit that the mechanism of unreflective habit from which this agent acts is plastic enough to allow reflection when conditions call for aborting reliance on habit alone.... The general problem, as I see it, is that any complex system will have "subsystems" that are designed to function precisely by shutting down or by permitting other systems to override in some contexts but not others. Assuming that a person functioning as a practical agent can be understood as a complex system, or at least as relevantly analogous to one, any attempt to whittle down which agential elements are the ones implicated in "the" mechanism of her action is bound to restrict the agent's flexibility as regards reasons-responsiveness.[74]

In the example of the woman driving, there was a shift from unreflective habit to deliberation. The problem as McKenna sees it is that the mechanism consisted of unreflective habit which then gave way to deliberation. Holding fixed the mechanism of unreflective habit would not enable us to account for what happened. We need to be able to identify the mechanism as being "fatter" than simple unreflective habit. But once we do this, we encounter the following problem,

> But once we seek to put more meat on a restriction of a pertinent mechanism of action, we will face problems like the one Ginet has identified. If we back off and allow for the description of the mechanism to be "fatter" so as to allow for shifts between processes like unreflective habit and then reflective habit, we

---

72. Fischer, *Deep Control*, 200.
73. McKenna, "Reasons-Responsiveness," 163.
74. McKenna, "Reasons-Responsiveness," 164.

pretty much have what is the functional equivalent of the agent herself as the mechanism, minus various outlier traits like the ability to do calculus.[75]

The point is that the more we include in the mechanism to account for examples like this one, the more the mechanism looks like an agent. This is a problem that McKenna believes will plague any mechanism-based approach.

I do not find this argument convincing. Why would we think that both unreflective habit and reflective habit constitute an agent or the functional equivalent of an agent? An agent is more than these two faculties, especially on the Christian view of man. Agents also include the *sensus divinitatis*, our emotional faculties, etc. Whatever our view of an agent, it is unlikely that we would identify the agent in such meagre terms. I think this argument is unconvincing and so do others.[76]

Fischer and Ravizza's response to the lack of a principled way to individuate mechanisms may not be satisfying to all, but their response is reasonable and McKenna's argument against them is unconvincing. At the very least, we could call this debate a stalemate. However, for my purposes, I will adopt an agent-based view because I think this more naturally fits with the way reformed theologians talk about man. Michael McKenna shows us a way in which this can be done.[77] McKenna draws upon the resources of the new dispositionalists.[78]

The work of these philosophers is important because they contribute something important that McKenna will use to shift from a mechanism to an agent-based theory. He uses their account of dispositions as complex

75. McKenna, "Reasons-Responsiveness," 164.

76. McKenna also notes two philosophers that he corresponded with that expressed skepticism. He writes: "In correspondence, David Shoemaker has thoughtfully expressed some skepticism about this point—that a more inclusive notion of a mechanism of action will be so inclusive that we might as well identify it with the person, or with the functional equivalent of the person. In conversation, Shaun Nichols has as well, citing the work by Fodor on the modularity of the mind. Here, I have no problem leaving it as an open question whether there is some richer notion of mechanism that would do the work that needs to be done for a mechanism-based view like Fischer and Ravizza's. But I strongly suspect that even if such a kind of mechanism were identified, and even if it turned out to be narrower than the full person qua agent, it would be *much* richer in content than anything like something restricted just to what is actually involved in the causal generation of action" (McKenna, "Reasons-Responsiveness," 165–66n19).

77. McKenna, "Reasons-Responsiveness," 151–83.

78. The New Dispositionalists are a group of leeway compatibilists that have drawn on the work of David Lewis and C. B. Martin. They have tried to account for free-will as the ability to do otherwise by appealing to free-will as a dispositional ability to do otherwise. These philosophers include Kadri Vihvelin, Michael Fara, and Michael Smith.

APPENDIX: CRITICISMS OF FISCHER AND RAVIZZA   255

counterfactuals. Dispositions cannot be accounted for by simple counterfactuals because of finks and masks.[79] The details of finks and masks are not important here. What is important is their account of dispositions.

Their account was developed in order to show that an agent does have the ability to do otherwise, even in a deterministic world. They articulate this free-will ability to do otherwise dispositionally. They think that in a deterministic world, an agent possesses the dispositions to act otherwise and that this disposition is all that is needed to say that an agent has the ability to do otherwise, even in a deterministic world. For example, they would state this disposition in a complex counterfactual such as the following RR_1:

> If Jones were to become aware of R_1, and if Jones retained during the relevant duration of time intrinsic agential properties $P_1—P_n$, and if Jones were not interfered with in a way that would impede the causal efficacy of these properties, then Jones would not shoot Smith.[80]

In this case, Jones is an agent, is reasons-responsive, and has the ability to do otherwise than shoot Smith. This ability to do otherwise is articulated as a disposition or dispositions describable in complex counterfactuals. The reason why this is important is because it helps illuminate that an agent can possess certain intrinsic agential properties or dispositions describable via a complex counterfactual and the agent does not lose these properties or dispositions, even in contexts where they cannot be manifested. McKenna is going to take this insight and use it to argue that an agent (as opposed to a mechanism) can be MRR to do otherwise or reactive to do otherwise, even in an FSC where Black is the counterfactual intervener. This would make it possible to have an agent-based reasons-responsive theory that fits with FSCs and avoids the problem of mechanism individuation.

McKenna's Soulution

Fischer and Ravizza were pushed into the direction of a mechanism-based theory because they thought that an agent in a FSC could not be reactive to reasons to do otherwise. Black rendered this impossible. McKenna questions this idea. He writes,

> The single proposition standing in the way of fitting an agent-based reasons-responsive theory to the contours of source

---

79. An example of a fink is "a glass vase being turned to stone just before it hits the ground." An example of a mask is "a piece of salt encased in wax and placed in water."
80. McKenna, "Reasons-Responsiveness," 168.

freedom is that an agent in a Frankfurt example is not reasons-responsive because, being unable to do otherwise, she is thereby unable to react otherwise when given sufficient reason to do so. I think this proposition should be rejected. I now wish to propose a simple solution to this puzzle. An agent who acts freely in a Frankfurt example, I shall argue, is suitably reasons-responsive despite being unable to react otherwise when given sufficient reason to do so.[81]

In order to understand this, it is helpful to draw a distinction between "being reasons-responsive" and "being able to react otherwise." These are not the same thing and McKenna will show us how recognizing this enables us to adopt an agent-based theory.

We have previously seen that being reasons-responsive in Fischer and Ravizza's sense is MRR. This includes being both receptive and reactive to reasons. McKenna is arguing that an agent can be receptive to reasons to do otherwise as well as reactive to reasons to do otherwise, even if the agent cannot do otherwise because of Black's presence. He illustrates this by considering Jones OUTSIDE an FSC and also considering Jones INSIDE an FSC. Let us first consider Jones outside of an FSC.

Jones Outside an FSC

Smith has harmed Jones's family and Jones seeks revenge. Revenge motivates Jones to actually shoot Smith. Black is not in this situation, so Jones has done this on his own. This situation illustrates certain things about Jones's intrinsic agential properties. Jones satisfies the conditions of MRR. McKenna writes,

> Jones is receptive to reasons R_1 through R_z and is reactive to reasons R_1 through R_n. Assume that the latter is a subset of the former in such a way that Jones's degree of reactivity is weaker than his degree of receptivity.[82]

Jones will be receptive to a larger amount of reasons than those to which he is reactive. Jones is receptive and reactive to reason R_1, namely that Smith has his child with him. In other words, Jones would be receptive to not shooting Smith if he saw Smith with his child and Jones would be reactive to not shoot Smith if he saw Smith's child with him. This would be the case for reasons ranging from R_1 through R_n but not the case for reasons

81. McKenna, "Reasons-Responsiveness," 170.
82. McKenna, "Reasons-Responsiveness," 171.

R_{n+1} through R_z. Consider reason R_{n+1} being the reason that shooting Smith would disappoint Jones's mother. For this latter range, Jones would be receptive but not reactive.

This analysis tells us something important about Jones's intrinsic agential properties. It tells us that in another possible world outside a FSC, Jones (the agent) would be responsive and reactive to not shooting Smith if he saw Smith with his child (R_1). It also tells us that in another possible world Jones (the agent) would be receptive to not shooting Smith if it would disappoint his mother (R_{n+1}) but not reactive to not shooting Smith for this reason. In light of these intrinsic agential properties of Jones (the agent), we need to see how he would do INSIDE an FSC.

Jones Inside an FSC

Smith has once again harmed Jones's family and Jones wants revenge. However, Black also has an interest in Smith being shot. Black installs a device in Jones such that Black can be the counterfactual intervener if he senses that Jones will not go through with shooting Smith. Given what we have seen thus far, we know two things about Jones's intrinsic agential properties. First, we know that he will be both receptive and reactive to not shoot Smith if he is presented with reasons R_1 through R_n. Second, we know that he will be receptive, but not reactive, to refrain from shooting Smith if he is presented with reasons R_{n+1} through R_z. This means that Black does not need to intervene if Jones has reasons R_{n+1} through R_z since Jones will follow through with shooting Smith for these reasons. Black would intervene if Jones were presented with reasons R_1 through R_n since Jones would not follow through with shooting Smith.

From this we see that Black makes it impossible for Jones to react otherwise, yet Jones is reactive to reasons R_1 through R_n. This is very important for McKenna. Jones IS reactive to do otherwise, but unable to do otherwise due to Black's presence. This is Jones as an agent and not Jones's mechanism. McKenna writes,

> But it is nevertheless true that Jones is *reactive* to this spectrum of reasons R_1 through R_n in just this sense: for each reason, were it to become salient for Jones, it is not the case that, given his own intrinsic agential condition, he would act on his own reasons of revenge for shooting Smith. He is at least reactive to reasons in this manner. In reacting to this spectrum of reasons (in

relevant possible worlds), he, by virtue of his own agency and his own reasons of revenge, is not the cause of shooting Smith.[83]

This means that there is a very definite sense, which satisfies MRR, in which Jones is reactive to reasons to do otherwise, yet at the same time he cannot do otherwise because of Black's presence.

What is important here is the language of "intrinsic agential condition." This means that there are certain dispositions that Jones has that render him (not his mechanism) reactive to reasons to do otherwise, even when he is unable to do otherwise. This intrinsic agential condition or dispositions can be analyzed in terms of the complex counterfactuals that the New Dispositionalists utilize.

These types of complex counterfactuals help clarify the sense in which Jones is reactive to do otherwise. For example, consider RR_1:

> If Jones were to become aware of R_1, and if Jones retained during the relevant duration of time intrinsic agential properties P_1-P_n, and if Jones were not interfered with in a way that would impede the causal efficacy of those properties, then Jones would not shoot Smith.[84]

RR_1 and counterfactuals like it tell us something important about the agent. They tell us about the agent's dispositions or modal properties. McKenna writes,

> Jones really is disposed to respond to a reason such as R_1 in certain ways. Were he left unfettered to act as he wished, in relevant contexts, he would act accordingly.... These counterfactuals aid in demonstrating that when an agent like Jones acts as he does on his own, the act he actually does perform is *itself* a reaction or a response to the actual conditions in which he acts. Furthermore, what these counterfactuals collectively help to underscore is not merely that Jones was indeed the cause of his so acting, but that the *manner* of his causing his act was sufficiently sensitive to reasons. In this way, when an agent in a Frankfurt example acts, she is, so to speak, *being* suitably reactive in acting as she does, and so is *exercising* a kind of source freedom, a kind that can be characterized in terms of responsiveness to reasons.[85]

---

83. McKenna, "Reasons-Responsiveness," 171–72.
84. McKenna, "Reasons-Responsiveness," 174.
85. McKenna, "Reasons-Responsiveness," 174–75.

Where Does This Leave Us?

In response to the problem of mechanism-individuation, we have two options. First, we can stand by Fischer's response and argue that we do not need a principle of mechanism individuation. The theory works fine and maybe one day we can come up with a principle. I think that this is an appropriate response. Second, we could follow McKenna and adopt an agent-based approach. This seems more natural in that we typically talk about agents and not mechanisms. It also avoids the problems of mechanism-based models and it fits with FSCs. I adopt McKenna's approach as a more fruitful avenue.

Mechanism Ownership

The problem of mechanism ownership can be stated briefly. McKenna writes,

> According to Fischer and Ravizza, ownership requires that one adopt certain attitudes towards herself. This exposes them to the possibility that a person might not adopt the relevant attitudes, in particular, that the person might not come to think that she is an appropriate object of others' moral demands and expectations as manifested in the reactive attitudes.[86]

The heart of the problem is how we guarantee that an agent has a view of himself as the proper object of others' moral demands and expectations. Fischer and Ravizza do not seem to have the resources to account for this. However, as I will argue in chapter four, the reformed tradition does. I will argue that the *sensus divinitatis* includes an unshedable belief that we are responsible agents. This belief can be suppressed, but it never can be eliminated because God put it there. This view will enable us to address the problem of mechanism ownership that Fischer and Ravizza face.

Manipulation Cases

Another objection to guidance control are arguments from manipulation. These arguments have been around for a while, but they have recently come into prominence in the literature. Perhaps the two most famous manipulation arguments are Mele's zygote argument[87] and Pereboom's four case

---

86. McKenna, "Contemporary Compatibilism," 194.
87. Mele, *Free Will and Luck*.

manipulation argument.[88] McKenna briefly states the general strategy behind these arguments,

1. If an agent, S, is manipulated in manner X to perform act A, then S does not A freely and is therefore not morally responsible.

2. Concerning free action and moral responsibility, there is no significant difference between S's A-ing as a result of being manipulated into doing so in manner X and any candidate for a free and morally responsible action in a deterministic universe.

3. Therefore, any normally functioning agent determined to do A does not A freely and therefore is not morally responsible.[89]

It is important to see from this argument that there can be many instances of manipulation arguments but they all follow the same strategy.

If we were to apply this strategy to guidance control, it would look as follows:

1. Provide an example of an agent that meets the conditions for guidance control via manipulation.

2. Elicit the intuition that the agent is not morally responsible because of the manipulation.

3. Argue that guidance control is insufficient to account for moral responsibility because there is no relevant difference between the manipulated agent and an agent that meets the conditions for guidance control through causal determinism.

If this were successful, then guidance control would be unsuccessful.

Michael McKenna points out that the compatibilist has basically two options in responding to manipulation arguments. He writes,

> A hard-line reply rejects the first premise of a manipulation argument; a soft-line reply rejects the second. What makes one reply hard and another soft is that in the former case, the compatibilist has to take on a hard task. She must argue against an assertion that seems to have a considerable amount of intuitive support behind it; on its face, an agent massively manipulated into conditions ensuring a particular course of action seems not to act freely. In short, a hard-line reply commits a compatibilist to bullet-biting in a way that a soft-line reply does not.[90]

88. Pereboom, *Living Without Free Will*.
89. McKenna, "Moral Responsibility," 151.
90. McKenna, "Moral Responsibility," 152.

A hard-line reply rejects premise one. In other words, he rejects the idea that a manipulated agent is not free and morally responsible. By contrast, a soft-line reply rejects premise two. In other words, a soft-liner holds that there IS a significant difference between a manipulated agent and a causally determined agent. A soft-line reply is also known as a "historicist" position. Fischer and Ravizza hold to this position.

The historicist position argues that the way in which an agent comes to meet the conditions of guidance control is important. For example, suppose that a team of neuroscientists created Dave. Dave comes into existence fully formed and meeting the conditions of guidance control. However, Dave is programed to murder Sally. This act of murder issues from his own moderately reasons-responsive mechanism. Fischer and Ravizza would say that Dave is not morally responsible for this act because he did not come to meet the conditions of guidance control properly. That is, he did not go through the historical process outlined in chapter 2. Fischer and Ravizza would take a soft-line approach to Dave and argue that there is a significant difference between causal determinism and the manipulation of Dave.

Fischer and Ravizza would generally take the strategy of trying to point out a significant difference between a causally determined agent and a manipulated agent. They would try to do this for every manipulation case that the incompatibilist brings their way. In many, perhaps even most cases, they would be able to succeed. However, there is always the possibility that an incompatibilist could bring a case in which there was no significant difference. It is for this reason that McKenna advocates a hard-line reply and that I think we should too.

This does not mean that the history of how an agent came to meet the conditions of guidance control is unimportant. Fischer and Ravizza's approach here is fine as far as it goes. We should try to point out a significant difference between a manipulated agent and a causally determined agent. We will most likely be able to point out a significant difference. However, we do need to address what would happen if the incompatibilist one day does present a case where there is no significant difference. Should we abandon guidance control? I do not believe that we should. Guidance control is highly successful and the hard-line approach to manipulation cases enables us to hang on to the theory even in the face of a manipulation case where we cannot point out a significant difference between a manipulated agent and a causally determined one. For this reason, we should follow the hard-line approach. In McKenna's words,

> If so, a soft-line reply to a well-crafted version of MA (manipulation argument) can only temporarily forestall the inevitable. Let

the compatibilist adopt the soft-line by resisting case after case, showing how in each it falls short of CAS.[91] The trouble point for the compatibilist inclined to avoid the hard-line reply is that *some* credible manipulation case *could* be fashioned.[92]

In order to see how a hard-line approach works let us consider a highly influential manipulation case given by Derk Pereboom.[93]

Pereboom's Four Case Manipulation Argument

Before stating Pereboom's four case manipulation argument, it would be helpful to give a summary of his basic strategy. The strategy conforms to the basic pattern already outlined by McKenna. McKenna summarizes Pereboom's strategy,

> Pereboom's generalization strategy is meant to work by establishing the desired incompatibilist intuitive reaction to the first case. Then, when introducing the second, one that comes closer to a normally determined agent, Pereboom argues that there just is no relevant difference between them, so that the intuitive reaction to the first should generalize to the second. He then introduces a third case that comes yet closer to the case of a normally determined agent. After making the same generalization point as to the relation between the second and third cases, he then introduces a fourth case, which just is the case

---

91. Compatibilist-Friendly Agential Structure

92. McKenna, "Moral Responsibility," 144.

93. A hard-line approach can similarly be taken to the other influential manipulation argument called the Zygote Argument. Mele writes, "Dianna creates a zygote Z in Mary. She combines Z's atoms as she does because she wants a certain event E to occur thirty years later. From her knowledge of the state of the universe just prior to her creating Z and the laws of nature of her deterministic universe, she deduces that a zygote with precisely Z's constitution located in Mary will develop into an ideally self-controlled agent who, in thirty years, will judge, on the basis of rational deliberation, that it is best to A and will A on the basis of that judgment, thereby bringing about E. if this agent, Ernie, has any unsheddable values at the time, they play no role in motivating his A-ing. Thirty years late, Ernie is a mentally healthy, ideally self-controlled person who regularly exercises his powers of self-control and has no relevant compelled or coercively produced attitudes. Furthermore, his beliefs are conducive to informed deliberation about all matters that concern him, and he is a reliable deliberator" (Mele, "Manipulation, Compatibilism, and Moral Responsibility" 263–86). For compatibilist responses, see Fischer, "Zygote Argument Remixed," 267–72; Kearns, "Aborting the Zygote Argument" 379–89.

of a determined agent. A final application of the generalization strategy yields the desired incompatibilist conclusion.[94]

Pereboom gives four examples that form a spectrum. On the one end, we have an obviously manipulated agent (Case 1). On the other end, we have a causally determined agent (Case 4). In between we have two cases (Cases 3 and 4), which slightly move us from Case 1 to Case 4. They do so without being relevantly different from the case that came before. The intuition that the agent in Case 1 is not morally responsible is supposed to transfer through to Case 4. The conclusion to reach is that the agent in Case 4 (the causally determined agent) is not morally responsible even though the compatibilist conditions on freedom and moral responsibility (including guidance control) have been met. In light of this let us turn to Pereboom's four case manipulation argument.

Pereboom's Argument

Case 1: A team of neuroscientists has the ability to manipulate Plum's neural states at any time by radio-like technology, in this particular case, they do so by pressing a button just before he begins to reason about his situation, which they know will produce in him a neural state that realizes a strongly egoistic reasoning process, which the neuroscientists know will deterministically result in his decision to kill White. Plum would not have killed White had the neuroscientist not intervened, since his reasoning would then not have been sufficiently egoistic to produce this decision. But at the same time, Plum's effective first-order desire to kill White conforms to his second order desires. In addition, his process of deliberation from which the decision results is reasons-responsive, in particular, this process would have resulted in Plum's refraining from deciding to kill White in certain situations in which his reasons were different. His reasoning is consistent with his character because it is frequently egoistic and sometimes strongly so. Still, it is not in general exclusively egoistic, because he sometimes successfully regulates his behavior by moral reasons, especially when the egoist reasons are relatively weak. Plum is also not constrained to act as he does, for he does not act because of an irresistible desire—the neuroscientists do not induce a desire of this sort.[95]

94. McKenna, "Hard-line Reply," 145.
95. Pereboom, *Free Will*, 76–77. Fischer's response to this first case is to point out that it is arguable whether or not Plum is morally responsible in this case. He writes,

There are two things to see in this first case. First, all the compatibilist conditions of moral responsibility are fulfilled. In particular, Fischer and Ravizza's conditions on moral responsibility are supposed to be fulfilled when Pereboom writes that "his process of deliberation from which the decision is made is reasons-responsive."[96] Second, Pereboom identifies one reason why Plum is not responsible as, "it is causally determined by the neuroscientist's intervention, which is beyond his control, together with the fact that he would not have decided to kill White had this intervention not occurred."[97] According to Pereboom, this example satisfies compatibilist conditions on moral responsibility, but these conditions are insufficient to render Plum morally responsible. This is because the neuroscientists causally determined his actions. He will next give a second example that reduces the level of manipulation, but also in which there is no relevant difference.

> **Case 2:** Plum is just like an ordinary human being, except that a team of neuroscientists programmed him at the beginning of his life so that his reasoning is often but not always egoistic (as in Case 1), and at times strongly so, with the intended consequence that in his current circumstances he is causally determined to engage in the egoistic reasons-responsive process of deliberation and to have the set of first and second-order desires that result in his decision to kill White. Plum has the general

---

"First, one might think that it is not obvious that Plum is not morally responsible even in the first case. This is because it is not clear how to evaluate the nature of the neural state that is induced by the team of neuroscientists.... To elaborate, if the neuroscientists induce a strong but not overwhelming or irresistible urge to murder White, then it is obvious to me that Plum is not morally responsible; he may, for all that has been said, be acting freely in this context. And this may be so, even if White could not have avoided his decision and act of killing White. (Here the notion of 'irresistibility' is not simply 'cannot be resisted in the particular circumstances.' More, of course, would need to be said fully more adequately to articulate this 'compatibilist' notion of irresistibility)" (Fischer, "Review of *Free Will*," 204–5). Fischer questions whether or not Plum is morally responsible in this case. This is important because it shows that Pereboom's argument, from the beginning, is questionable. However, for the sake of argument, Fischer allows Pereboom's point: "But I shall proceed by simply stipulating, for the sake of discussion, that Pereboom is correct and that Plum is not morally responsible in case 1" (Fischer, "Review of *Free Will*," 205).

96. Pereboom, *Free Will*, 77. John Martin Fischer objects that Pereboom has not actually captured his and Ravizza's account with reasons-responsiveness alone. Pereboom assumes that he has throughout the argument. Fischer writes, "Note again that Pereboom simply refers to "properly reasons responsive mechanisms." But guidance control requires that the agent have taken responsibility for the relevant kind of mechanism. As I wrote above, it is plausible that Plum's mechanism is *not* his own in case 1, as opposed to the other cases" (Fischer, "Review of *Free Will*," 208).

97. Pereboom, *Free Will*, 77.

ability to regulate his actions by moral reasons, but in his circumstances, due to the strongly egoistic nature of his deliberative reasoning, he is causally determined to make his decision to kill. Yet he does not decide as he does because of an irresistible desire. The neural realization of his reasoning process and of his decision is exactly the same as it is in Case 1 (although their causal histories are different).[98]

In this second example, Professor Plum still satisfies all the conditions for moral responsibility as in Case 1 (keep in mind Fischer's objection that ownership is left out). The causal determinism is different from the first case. In the first case, the neuroscientist pressed a button just before Plum began the reasoning process and caused his actions. In Case 2, the causal determinism occurs by programming at the beginning of his life. As in Case 1, Pereboom attributes the lack of moral responsibility to causal determinism. He writes, "Causal determination by what the neuroscientists do, which is beyond his control, plausibly explains Plum's not being morally responsible in the first case, and it's intuitive that he is not morally responsible in the second case for the same reason."[99] In Case 3, Pereboom eliminates the neuroscientists.

---

98. Pereboom, *Free Will*, 77. Fischer does see a difference between Case 1 and Case 2. He writes, "I am (at least sometimes) inclined to think that there is a crucial difference between Case 1 and Case 2; that is, arguably Plum is not morally responsible in Case 1, but is in Case 2. And my approach to moral responsibility is flexible enough to accommodate and explain this intuition. On my approach (together with Mark Ravizza), guidance control is the freedom-relevant condition for moral responsibility. And, importantly, guidance control has *two* components: reasons-responsiveness of the actual-sequence mechanism, and *ownership* of that mechanism. . . . Pereboom tends to focus solely on the reasons-responsive mechanism component, rather than the ownership component. But they are both indispensable, and the ownership part plays a crucial role in a proper analysis of the manipulation cases. . . . The situation in Case 2 is not relevantly different from the ordinary situation in which we are simply "given" a set of dispositions toward feeling and action; and moral responsibility always then is a matter of how one plays the cards that are dealt one, as it were. I think there is an important difference between a case of direct, hands-on manipulation, such as in Case 1, and a case of initial design, such as Case 2; and I contend that this difference lies in the fact that Plum acts from his own mechanism in Case 2 but not in Case 1. . . . On this sort of approach, Plum would be morally responsible for his decision and action in Case 2, but not in Case 1" (Fischer, "Review of *Free Will*," 205–6).

Fischer's strategy here is to drive a wedge between Case 1 and the rest of the cases. This strategy would undermine Pereboom's argument because it would break the transition from Case 1 to Case 4. However, even if this is successful, Pereboom (or others) could simply reinvent Case 1 to accommodate Fischer's criticisms. If this were done, then perhaps, the four cases would hold together and yield Pereboom's conclusion. This is why McKenna's Hard-Line approach is ultimately superior.

99. Pereboom, *Free Will*, 78.

Case 3: Plum is an ordinary human being, except that the training practices of his community causally determined the nature of his deliberative reasoning processes so that they are frequently but not exclusively rationally egoistic (the resulting nature of his deliberative reasoning processes are exactly as they are in Cases 1 and 2). This training was completed before he developed the ability to prevent or alter these practices. Due to the aspect of his character produced by this training, in his present circumstances he is causally determined to engage in the strongly egoistic reasons-responsive process of deliberation and to have the first and second-order desires that issue in his decision to kill White. While Plum does have the general ability to regulate his behavior by moral reasons, in virtue of this aspect of his character and his circumstances he is causally determined to make his immoral decision, although he does not decide as he does due to an irresistible desire. The neural realization of his deliberative reasoning process and of the decision is just as it is in Cases 1 and 2.[100]

Again, Plum satisfies all the conditions for compatibilist moral responsibility. This time, the neuroscientists are removed and replaced with more social and environmental causes. Pereboom says that Plum is not morally responsible in this case either. He writes, "Causal determination by what the controlling agents do, which is beyond Plum's control, plausibly explains the absence of moral responsibility in Case 2, and it's reasonable to conclude that he is not morally responsible in Case 3 on the same ground."[101] Case 4 is a normal deterministic world.

Case 4: Everything that happens in our universe is causally determined by virtue of its past states together with the laws of nature. Plum is an ordinary human being, raised in normal circumstances, and again his reasoning processes are frequently but not exclusively egoistic, and sometimes strongly so (as in Cases 1–3). His decision to kill White issues from his strongly egoistic but reasons-responsive process of deliberation, and he has the specified first and second-order desires. The neural realization of Plum's reasoning process and decision is exactly as it is in Cases 1–3; he has the general ability to grasp, apply, and regulate his actions by moral reasons, and it is not because of an irresistible desire that he decides to kill.[102]

---

100. Pereboom, *Free Will*, 78.
101. Pereboom, *Free Will*, 78.
102. Pereboom, *Free Will*, 79.

Plum meets all the conditions for compatibilist moral responsibility. Pereboom has replaced community causes with those in a physically-determined world. This is exactly what physical determinists think are the ultimate causes of actions. Yet Pereboom thinks that there are no relevant differences between the causes in Case 3 and Case 4. Pereboom concludes that Plum is not morally responsible. The best explanation for this is that causal determinism rules out moral responsibility. He writes, "The salient factor that can plausibly explain why Plum is not responsible in all of the cases is that in each he is causally determined by factors beyond his control to decide as he does. This is therefore a sufficient, and I think the best, explanation for his non-responsibility in all of the cases."[103]

We can see Pereboom's strategy in these four cases. He is starting with a supposedly obvious manipulation case in which Professor Plum is not morally responsible but meets the conditions of guidance control, as well as other compatibilist philosophers. He then moves from case to case changing the situation slightly but arguing that there is no relevant difference from Case 1 to Case 2, from Case 2 to Case 3, and from Case 3 to Case 4. If we follow him along this path, he ends with a case in which causal determinism obtains and all the conditions for compatibilist moral responsibility are met. Yet we are to follow our intuition from Case 1 through to Case 4 and conclude that Professor Plum is not morally responsible in Case 4.

A soft-line strategy of responding to Pereboom would be to argue that one or more of these examples do not actually meet compatibilist conditions on moral responsibility. McKenna writes,

> Several critics have opted for a soft-line reply to Pereboom.[104] ... A soft-line reply seeks some relevant difference between an agent, such as Plum in Cases 1 or Case 2, manipulated into acting from a certain state, and an agent acting from a deterministic history (like Plum in Cases 4). This allows the compatibilist to grant to Pereboom that, indeed, Plum in Case 1 or 2 is not free and responsible. Instead, the compatibilist can argue, there is some further feature of CAS that is lacking in the case of manipulation that is not lacking with relevant agents acting at a determined world. The trouble with this strategy . . . is that it is dialectically unstable. A compatibilist might very well be able to refute some specific formulation of Pereboom's argument. But then it is open to Pereboom to revise his examples so that the feature

103. Pereboom, *Free Will*, 79.

104. Pereboom cites Demetriou, "Soft-line Solution"; Fischer, "Responsibility and Manipulation"; Haji, *Moral Appraisabilty*; *Incompatibilism's Allure*; Mele, "Critique of Pereboom."

of CAS alleged to be lacking in prior iterations of his argument are now present. This compatibilist short-game, it seems to me, eventually leads to a long-game victory for Pereboom—unless compatibilists can show that there is a principled reason why compatibilist sufficient conditions for freedom cannot be replicated by the design of a powerful being (a prospect I think is hopeless). Hence, I think it is best for compatibilists to grant Pereboom that his cases satisfy what they require for CAS. And if his cases fall shy a bit, rather than call him out on this sort of technicality via a soft-line reply, they should just aid him by amending his case(s) so as to get right all that is required for CAS on their favored view. Having dispatched this preliminary work, they should then opt for a hard-line reply. This, at any rate, is how I have elected to take issue with Pereboom.[105]

McKenna's point is that a soft-line reply can often point out shortcomings in an incompatibilist's example. However, the incompatibilist can always come up with another example or a more charitable reading of the example can be given that meets CAS. This is always in principle possible. Thus, a soft-line approach is always in principle capable of defeat.

For this reason, I believe that Fischer and Ravizza's soft-line approach to manipulation cases will be ultimately inadequate. It could be very helpful in showing that this case or that case do not actually meet CAS, but it leaves open the possibility that one day some case will. So, I think McKenna's hard-line reply is ultimately better. Let me outline his hard-line reply to Pereboom's argument.

Mckenna's Reply

McKenna writes,

> I propose a four-step reply to any instance of MA. *Step one: Reject all non-starters.* Consider the example. See if it is in the running for CAS. If not, the jig is up. Reject premise two and be done. *Step two: Help make the manipulation cases better.* If the example gets past step one, if it comes close enough to getting CAS right but falls shy, amend the example. Help out your "good friend" the incompatibilist so that the example does get CAS right. This calls into relief that manipulation can be "just like" determinism. *Step three: Fix attention on salient agential and moral properties.* Illustrate how the agent manipulated in

---

105. McKenna, "Resisting the Manipulation Argument," 470.

APPENDIX: CRITICISMS OF FISCHER AND RAVIZZA 269

manner X to satisfy CAS lives up to a rich sort of agency and genuinely satisfies certain moral properties (for example, does moral wrong). *Step Four: make clear that "manipulation" is not all that uncommon.* Lessen the intuitive uneasiness of the claim that an agent manipulated in manner X is free and responsible by calling attention to mundane causal factors that have a similar result, but are not thought to be freedom or responsibility undermining.[106]

In light of this, let us apply this to Pereboom's argument.[107]

Step One: Reject all Non-Starters

In this section, McKenna provides a more charitable reading of Case 1 in response to Fischer and Mele's criticisms. He writes,

> So, let us suppose that team Plum does not operate by taking Plum, as Mele puts it, "out of the control loop." Let us instead assume that Team Plum operates by providing a very weird causal prosthetic, a causal foundation for the constitution of *Plum's* control (i.e., a foundation different from the foundation provided by typical neural realizers found in normal agents). Reading Case 1 as run by the sophisticated Team Plum should make clear that it is *not* a non-starter. Minimally, it is *in the running* for satisfying CAS.[108]

Step Two: Help Make Manipulation Cases Better

In this section, McKenna improves Pereboom's cases.

Step Three: Fix Attention on Salient Agential and Moral Properties

In this section, McKenna adds two more cases to Pereboom's four in order to make it clearer. McKenna calls Pereboom's Case 4 "Case 6." He adds Case 5:

> In Case 5, causal determinism is replaced by God, who foreknows each of Plum's acts and his entire life history. God brings about the entire state of the world at every moment. God does

---

106. McKenna, "Hard-line Reply to Pereboom," 144–45.
107. McKenna's response to Pereboom is based on an earlier version of Pereboom's four-case argument found in Pereboom, *Living Without Free Will*, 110–17. The version of the four-case argument that I gave earlier is newer but essentially the same.
108. McKenna, "Hard-line Reply to Pereboom," 150.

this by "setting the entire world in motion" in certain ways. Everything else unfolds instead just as it would in Case 6.[109]

To this he adds his Case 4. He writes,

> In this case, God does not do the work, but a deity, Diana, zeroes in just on the introduction of the zygote that will become Plum. Unlike God, Diana cannot foresee the unfolding of every event in Plum's world as applied to every person, but she has just a glimmer of God's knowledge, enough that she can see just how the introduction of this zygote will yield Plum, who will one day kill Ms. White.[110]

Adding these two cases, McKenna now works backward. He writes,

> My challenge to Pereboom is as follows. Since he cannot begin by presuming that determinism rules out freewill and moral responsibility, he cannot begin by denying that Plum is free and responsible in my Case 6 (his Case 4). Now, applying his generalization strategy, it seems that he cannot claim this about Case 5 either, since it seem arbitrary to make theological determination itself have a relevant difference here. But now, Case 4 is just a localized version of the knowledge possessed by God in Case 5. There is no relevant difference as applied to these two cases. Cases 2 and 3 just involve the same causal processes as Case 4 and 5, but via dumb luck. And Case 1 is just dumb luck played out over time instead of Case 2, all up front at the beginning. I conclude that Pereboom is not entitled to presume that in Case 1 Plum is not free or morally responsible. This is so by the light of his own generalization strategy.[111]

McKenna begins with Case 6 and reasonably claims that it is not evident that Plum is not free and morally responsible. He then generalizes back to Case 1. He concludes,

> In my estimation, the disagreement between Pereboom and me plays out in a dialectical stalemate. The intuitions that he seeks to elicit do not demonstrably trump the ones that I seek to elicit. ... If I am correct, if this disagreement does end in a stalemate, then this amounts to a victory for the compatibilist, since *she*

---

109. McKenna, "Hard-line Reply to Pereboom," 153.
110. McKenna, "Hard-line Reply to Pereboom," 153.
111. McKenna, "Hard-line Reply to Pereboom," 153.

was only out to defeat an argument for incompatibilism, not prove her compatibilist thesis.[112]

Step Four: Make Clear that "Manipulation" is not all that Uncommon

McKenna brings up real life cases where manipulation has occurred, yet our intuitions are that the person acted freely and was morally responsible. One such case is the case of Ann. He writes,

> Consider this sort of case. A young child, let us call her Ann, watches up close the deterioration and death of a parent from a crippling disease, leukemia, medically addressed when treatments like chemotherapy were in their infancy, when they were simply barbaric. Suppose that this child, well before the age of mature reason, and so gripped by such an experience, simply came to see life as limited, precious, but also, chocked with prospects of suffering and tragedy. From this she comes to see her life as one that should not be squandered, that should be lived to the fullest, with no promise of a long future or a lovely afterlife. Whether for good, rational reason or not, suppose those experiences settled for that child what would become her deepest unshedable values about how to live. And suppose that as a mature adult she acts upon them. Does she do so unfreely? Is she not responsible for conduct issuing from those values?
>
> I know of such a person and if you were to ask her how this shaped her, she would regard it as something like a real-life manipulation case. But according to her, she regards this not as an impediment of her freedom and her responsibility or, one might say, her dignity, *but as a condition of it*. Thus was she so made. But as she sees it, it surely does not undermine her free and responsible agency. I would propose that the case of Ann is very much like a manipulation case, except that the manipulation is not by the design of a team of scientists like Team Plum, but by the vagaries of life.[113]

This case is intuitively strong. We do tend to think that this person is free and responsible, even though she did not choose her values. Our values and even our character are often shaped by factors outside of our control. But when we act from these values and characters, we are intuitively free and responsible. So, examples like this question the assumption that Professor Plum is not free and responsible in Cases 1 and 2. This

112. McKenna, "Hard-line Reply to Pereboom," 153–54.
113. McKenna, "Hard-line Reply to Pereboom," 156.

would hurt Pereboom's argument because he needs us to think that Plum is not responsible in Case 1 so that we can transfer this non-responsibility through to Case 4.

Another way to question the responsibility of Plum in Case 1 is by using examples that Nomy Arpaly has stated. McKenna writes,

> Nomy Arpaly has recently made similar observations, pointing out that people often find themselves having undergone radical changes but for reasons that were entirely beyond their control and totally unexpected. Some simply discover that their "party animal" life styles no longer interest them, and they become workaholics. Others have no desire to devote their lives to parenting, and are flooded by love upon first seeing their newborns, and experience totally revising their life plans. Still others undergo inexplicable religious conversions. Here again, in these sorts of cases, cases that we do encounter in ordinary life, we have what looks like more mundane cases of manipulation.[114]

It would be helpful to see in more depth a real-life example that Arpaly gives. She writes,

> Consider the case of Patty Hearst—perhaps as close as reality gets to the story of Dr. Nefarious.[115] Brainwashed by her captors, albeit by considerably more arduous methods than those Dr. Nefarious seems to use, Hearst joined their terrorist organization and was eventually convicted for her crimes despite the fact of her nonrational change in motivations. Note that it matters very little to our judgment if she has indeed been brainwashed deliberately or if she just converted, irrationally, due to the duress she was under (the "Stockholm Syndrome"). In either case, a drastic change in her belief-desire set happened irrationally and rather quickly, and in either case the person who stood before the court seems to have been a wholehearted terrorist who was blameworthy for her actions, not an innocent woman acting under great duress. Stress may cause people to act out of character, but it may also truly *change their characters*, and this is what seems to have happened in the case of Hearst.[116]

---

114. McKenna, "Hard-line Reply to Pereboom," 156.

115. Dr. Nefarious is a fictitious character that Arpaly created to illustrate manipulation. He is able to change people's desires so that the act upon them. The point is that the person manipulated comes to these desires or their current psychology in a strange or irrational manner. The case of Patty Hearst is a real life example of this where a court found her guilty even though she was manipulated.

116. Arpaly, *Meaning, Merit, and Human Bondage*, 114.

Cases like these and others that McKenna and Arpaly give rise to very different intuitions about the moral responsibility of manipulated agents. This helps McKenna's hard-line reply. McKenna concludes,

> As far as I can tell, the case of Ann, and cases like the ones Arpaly calls to our attention, or the well-known cases of moral luck featured by Nagel and Williams (Nagel 1976; Williams 1981), are the closest a compatibilist can come to providing a positive intuitive basis for her thesis regarding the possibility of manipulated agents. In these cases, the compatibilist can assert with some confidence that the factors highlighted in these cases do nothing to suggest that such agents are not free or responsible (so long as the factors do not undermine satisfaction of CAS).[117]

Summing Up

Fischer and Ravizza's soft-line approach is good as far as it goes. It could be helpful to deny premise 2 and try to point out how the manipulation example does not mesh with their compatibilist conditions of moral responsibility. Perhaps we should do this. However, McKenna is right to worry about the eventuality of a case that comes up that does meet the requirements. Should we just give up? Or is there a good reply? McKenna's hard-line reply is good. We should reject premise 1 for good reason. It is simply not clear that agents that are manipulated are always not morally responsible. In fact, the case of Ann as well as cases Arpaly gives seriously question this intuition.

Summary

In this analysis of Fischer and Ravizza's theory of moral responsibility we have seen that it holds up well under criticism, especially when supplemented with McKenna's insights. We see this in three ways. First, Fischer's defense of FSCs show us that they do not eliminate all alternative possibilities. However, this is acceptable because they do eliminate all robust alternative possibilities. Second, the criticisms of Fischer and Ravizza on mechanism individuation are not successful. Fischer and Ravizza are within their rights to hold that a principled method of individuating mechanisms is desired but a lack of it is not fatal to the theory. However, if we supplement their account with McKenna's work on agent reasons-responsiveness, we have a superior view. McKenna's work enables us to side-step the desire for a principled

---

117. McKenna, "Hard-line Reply to Pereboom," 156–57.

method of individuating mechanisms in favor of a more natural approach, namely an agent-based theory. Third, Fischer and Ravizza's theory stands up under the threat of manipulation cases. Their soft-line approach is adequate as far as it goes. However, McKenna's hard-line approach enables us to answer the potential threat of a manipulation case that really does satisfy all of Fischer and Ravizza's conditions for moral responsibility. So, we should use the soft-line approach as often as we can, but we should be ready to shift into a hard-line approach upon a manipulation case that meets all Fischer and Ravizza's conditions, if such a case ever appears.

Bibliography

à Brakel, Wilhelmus. *The Christian's Reasonable Service.* Vol. 1. Edited by Joel Beeke. Translated by Bartel Elshout. Grand Rapids: Reformation Heritage, 1992.
Allen, R. Michael. *Reformed Theology.* New York: T. & T. Clark, 2010.
Arpaly, Nomy. *Meaning, Merit, and Human Bondage: An Essay on Free Will.* Princeton: Princeton University Press, 2006.
Audi, Robert. *The Cambridge Dictionary of Philosophy.* Cambridge: Cambridge University Press, 1996.
Bac, J. Martin. *Perfect Will Theology: Divine Agency in Reformed Scholasticism as against Suarez, Episcopius, Descartes, and Spinoza.* Leiden: Brill, 2010.
Bavink, Herman. *God and Creation.* Vol. 2 of *Reformed Dogmatics.* Edited by John Bolt. Translated by John Vriend. Grand Rapids: Baker Academic, 2006.
———. *Sin and Salvation in Christ.* Vol. 3 of *Reformed Dogmatics.* Edited by John Bolt. Translated by John Vriend. Grand Rapids: Baker Academic, 2006.
Beattie, Francis R. *The Presbyterian Standards: An Exposition of the Westminster Confession and Catechisms.* Greenville: Southern Presbyterian, 1997.
Beck, Andreas J. "Gisbertus Voetius (1589–1676): Basic Features of his Doctrine of God." In *Reformation and Scholasticism: An Ecumenical Enterprise,* edited by Willem J. Van Asselt and Eef Dekker, 205–26. Grand Rapids: Baker Academic, 2001.
Beck, Andreas J., and Vos, A. "Conceptual Patterns Related to Reformed Scholasticism" *Nederlands Theologisch Tijdschrift* 57 (2003) 224–33.
BeeBee, Helen. *Free Will: An Introduction.* New York: Palgrave Macmillan, 2013.
Berkhof, Louis. *The History of Christian Doctrines.* Edinburgh: Banner of Truth Trust, 1991.
Berofsky, Bernard. "Classical Compatibilism: Not Dead Yet." In *Moral Responsibility and Alternative Possibilities: Essays on the Importance of Alternative Possibilities,* edited by David Widerker and Michael McKenna, 107–26. Burlington, VT: Ashgate, 2006.
———. "Ifs, Cans, and Free Will." In *The Oxford Handbook of Free Will,* edited by Robert Kane, 181–201. Oxford: Oxford University Press, 2002.
Bratman, Michael. "Fischer and Ravizza on Moral Responsibility and History" *Philosophical and Phenomenological Research* 61.2 (2000) 453–58.
Calvin, John. *Institutes of the Christian Religion.* Vol. 2. Edited by John T. McNeill. Translated by Ford Lewis Battles. Philadelphia: Westminster, 1960.
Capes, Justin. "The W-Defense." *Philosophical Studies* 150 (2010) 61–67.

BIBLIOGRAPHY

Clark, Scott R. *Recovering the Reformed Confessions: Our Theology, Piety, and Practice.* Phillipsburg: Presbyterian and Reformed, 2008.

Craig, William Lane. *The Only Wise God: The Compatibility of Divine Foreknowledge and Human Freedom.* Eugene, OR: Wipf and Stock, 2000.

Crisp, Oliver. *Deviant Calvinism: Broadening Reformed Theology.* Minneapolis: Fortress, 2014.

———. "John Girardeau: Libertarian Calvinist?" *Journal of Reformed Theology* 8.3 (2014) 284–300.

———. *Jonathan Edwards Among the Theologians.* Grand Rapids: Eerdmans, 2015.

———. *Jonathan Edwards On God and Creation.* Oxford: Oxford University Press, 2012.

Cunningham, William. *The Reformers and the Theology of the Reformation.* Edinburgh: Banner of Truth Trust, 1989.

Davenport, John. "Review of *Responsibility and Control* by Fischer and Ravizza." *Faith and Philosophy* 17 (2000) 384–95.

Demetriou, Kristen. "The Soft-line Solution to Pereboom's Four-Case Manipulation Argument." *Australasian Journal of Philosophy* 88.4 (2010) 595–617.

Dennett, Daniel. *Elbow Room: The Varieties of Free Will Worth Wanting.* Cambridge: MIT Press, 1984.

———. *Freedom Evolves.* New York: Viking Penguin, 2003.

Dennison, James T., Jr., ed. *Reformed Confessions of the Sixteenth and Seventeenth Centuries in English Translation.* Vol. 4. Grand Rapids: Reformation Heritage, 2014.

Donnelley, John Patrick. "Calvinist Thomism." *Viator* 7 (1976) 441–55.

Edwards, Jonathan. *Freedom of the Will.* Vol. 1 of *The Works of Jonathan Edwards.* Edited by Paul Ramsey. New Haven: Yale University Press, 1959.

———. *The "Miscellanies" 501–832.* Vol. 18 of *The Works of Jonathan Edwards.* Edited by Ava Chamberlain. New Haven: Yale University Press, 2000.

———. "The Nature of True Virtue." In *The Ethical Writings*, edited by Paul Ramsey, 537–627. Vol. 8 of *The Works of Jonathan Edwards.* New Haven: Yale University Press, 1989

———. *Religious Affections.* Vol. 2 of *The Works of Jonathan Edwards.* Edited by John E. Smith. New Haven: Yale University Press, 1959.

Ekstrom, Larua Waddell. "Protecting Incompatibilist Freedom." *American Philosophical Quarterly* 35 (1998) 281–91.

Feinberg, John S. *No One Like Him.* Wheaton: Crossway, 2001.

Fesko, J. V. *The Theology of the Westminster Standards.* Wheaton: Crossway, 2014.

Fesko, J. V., and Guy M. Richard. "Natural Theology and the Westminster Confession of Faith." In *The Westminster Confession into the Twenty-First Century*, edited by Ligon Duncan, 223–66. Vol. 3. Rosshire: Christian Focus, 2009.

Fischer, John Martin. "Compatibilism." In *Four Views on Free Will*, by John Martin Fischer, et al., 44–84. Malden, MA: Blackwell, 2007.

———. *Deep Control: Essays on Free Will and Value.* Oxford: Oxford University Press, 2012.

———. "The Deterministic Horn of the Dilemma Defence: A Reply to Widerker and Goetz" *Analysis* 73.3 (2013) 489–96.

———. "The Frankfurt Cases: The Moral of the Stories." In *Deep Control: Essays on Free Will and Value*, edited by John Martin Fischer, 33–52. Oxford: Oxford University Press, 2012.

———. "The Frankfurt-Style Cases: Philosophical Lightning Rods." In *Free Will and Moral Responsibility*, edited by Ishtiyaque Haji and Justin Caouette, 43–57. Newcastle: Cambridge Scholars, 2013.

———. "Frankfurt-Type Examples and Semicompatibilism: New Work." In *The Oxford Handbook of Free Will*, edited by Robert Kane, 243–65. 2nd ed. Oxford: Oxford University Press, 2011.

———. "The Freedom Required for Moral Responsibility." Unpublished Paper obtained directly from the author.

———. "Guidance Control." In *Deep Control: Essays on Free Will and Value*, edited by John Martin Fischer, 186–205. Oxford: Oxford University Press, 2012.

———. *The Metaphysics of Free Will*. Malden, MA: Blackwell, 1994.

———. *My Way: Essays on Moral Responsibility*. Oxford: Oxford University Press, 2006.

———. "Recent Work on Moral Responsibility." *Ethics* 110 (1999) 93–139.

———. "Responsibility and Agent-Causation." In *Moral Responsibility and Alternative Possibilities: Essays in the Importance of Alternative Possibilities*, edited by David Widerker and Michael McKenna, 235–50. Burlington, VT: Ashgate, 2006.

———. "Responsibility and Alternative Possibilities" In *Moral Responsibility and Alternative Possibilities: Essays in the Importance of Alternative Possibilities*, edited by David Widerker and Michael McKenna, 27–52. Burlington, VT: Ashgate, 2006.

———. "Responsibility and Control." *Journal of Philosophy* 79 (1982) 24–40.

———. "Responsibility and Failure." *Proceedings of the Aristotelian Society* 86 (1986) 251–70.

———. "Responsibility and Manipulation." *Journal of Ethics* 8.2 (2004) 145–77.

———. "Responsibility and Self-Expression." *Journal of Ethics* 3.4 (1998) 277–97.

———. "Review of *Free Will, Agency, and Meaning in Life*, by Derk Pereboom." *Science, Religion, and Culture* 1.3 (2014) 202–8.

———. "Sourcehood: Playing the Cards that are Dealt You." In *Deep Control: Essays on Free Will and Value*, edited by John Martin Fischer, 163–85. Oxford: Oxford University Press, 2012.

———. "The Zygote Argument Remixed" *Analysis* 71.2 (2011) 267–72.

Fischer, John Martin, and Mark Ravizza. *Responsibility and Control: A Theory of Moral Responsibility*. Cambridge: Cambridge University Press, 1998.

Fischer, John Martin, and Neal A. Tognazzini. "Blame and Avoidability: A Reply to Otsuka." In *Deep Control: Essays on Free Will and Value*, edited by John Martin Fischer, 76–84. Oxford: Oxford University Press, 2012.

Frame, John. "Determinism, Chance, and Freedom." In *New Dictionary of Christian Apologetics*, edited by W. C. Campbell-Jack and Gavin McGrath, 218–20. Downers Grove, IL: Intervarsity, 2006.

———. *The Doctrine of God*. Phillipsburg: Presbyterian and Reformed, 2002.

Frankfurt, Harry. "Alternative Possibilities and Moral Responsibility." In *Free Will*, edited by Gary Watson, 167–76. 2nd ed. Oxford: Oxford University Press, 2003.

———. "Freedom of the Will and the Concept of a Person." In *Free Will*, edited by Gary Watson, 322–36. 2nd ed. Oxford: Oxford University Press, 2003.

———. "Some Thoughts Concerning PAP." In *Moral Responsibility and Alternative Possibilities: Essays on the Importance of Alternative Possibilities*, edited by David Widerker and Michael McKenna, 339–46. Burlington, VT: Ashgate, 2006.

Franklin, Christopher. "Neo-Frankfurtians and Buffer Cases: The New Challenge to the Principle of Alternative Possibilities." *Philosophical Studies* 152 (2011) 189–207.

Ginet, Carl. "In Defense of the Principle of Alternative Possibilities: Why I Don't Find Frankfurt's Argument Convincing." In *Moral Responsibility and Alternative Possibilities: Essays on the Importance of Alternative Possibilities*, edited by David Widerker and Michael McKenna, 75–90. Burlington, VT: Ashgate, 2006.

———. "Review of *Living without Free Will*." *Journal of Ethics* 6 (2002) 305–9.

———. "Working with Fischer and Ravizza's Account of Moral Responsibility." *Journal of Ethics* 10 (2006) 229–53.

Girardeau, John. *The Will and its Theological Relations*. New York: Baker & Taylor, 1891. http://reformedbooksonline.com/american/southern-presbyterians/girardeau-john/the-will-in-its-theological-relations/1891.

Gobelman, Carl F. "To Be Free, or Not to Be Free? An Analysis of Francis Turretin's Doctrine of Free Will." *Mid-America Journal of Theology* 22 (2011) 129–44.

Goetz, Stewart. "Frankfurt-Style Counterexamples and Begging the Question." *Midwest Studies in Philosophy* 29 (2005) 83–105.

Goudriaan, Aza. *Reformed Orthodoxy and Philosophy, 1625–1750: Gisbertus Voetius, Petrus van Mastricht, and Anthonius Dressen*. Leiden: Brill, 2006.

Griffith, Meghan. *Free Will: The Basics*. New York: Routledge, 2013.

Haji, Ishtiyaque. *Deontic Morality and Control* New York: Cambridge University Press, 2002.

———. *Incompatibilism's Allure*. Peterborough: Broadview, 2009.

———. *Moral Appraisability*. Oxford: Oxford University Press, 1998.

Haji, Ishtiyaque, and McKenna, Michael. "Defending Frankfurt's Argument in Deterministic Contexts: A Reply to Palmer." *Journal of Philosophy* 103.7 (2006) 363–72.

———. "Dialectical Delicacies in the Debate about Freedom and Alternative Possibilities." *Journal of Philosophy* 101.6 (2004) 299–314.

Helm, Paul. *Human Nature from Calvin to Edwards*. Grand Rapids: Reformation Heritage, 2018.

———. *John Calvin's Ideas*. Oxford: Oxford University Press, 2004.

———. "Jonathan Edwards and the Parting of Ways?" *Jonathan Edwards Studies* 4.1 (2014) 42–60.

———. "Necessity, Contingency, and the Freedom of God." *Journal of Reformed Theology* 8 (2014) 243–62.

———. "Reformed Thought on Freedom: Some Further Thoughts." *Journal of Reformed Theology* 4 (2010) 184–206.

———. "'Structural Indifference' and Compatibilism in Reformed Orthodoxy." *Journal of Reformed Theology* 5 (2011) 184–205.

———. "Synchronic Contingency Again." *Nederlands Theologisch Tijdschrift* 57 (2003) 234–38.

———. "Synchronic Contingency in Reformed Scholasticism: A Note of Caution." *Nederlands Theologisch Tijdschrift* 57 (2003) 207–23.

———. "Turretin and Edwards Compatibilism" *Journal of Reformed Theology* 12 (2018) 335–55.

———. "Turretin and Edwards Once More." *Jonathan Edwards Studies* 4.3 (2014) 286–96.
Heppe, Heinrich. *Reformed Dogmatics*. Eugene, OR: Wipf and Stock, 1950.
Hodge, A. A. *The Westminster Confession: A Commentary*. Edinburgh: Banner of Truth Trust, 2002.
Hume, David. *An Enquiry Concerning Human Understanding*. Edited by L. A. Selby-Bigge. Oxford: Oxford University Press, 1955.
Hunt, David P. "Freedom, Foreknowledge, and Frankfurt." In *Moral Responsibility and Alternative Possibilities: Essays on the Importance of Alternative Possibilities*, edited by David Widerker and Michael McKenna, 159–83. Burlington, VT: Ashgate, 2006.
———. "Moral Responsibility and Buffered Alternatives." *Midwest Studies in Philosophy* 29 (2005) 126–45.
———. "Moral Responsibility and Unavoidable Action." *Philosophical Studies* 97.2 (2000) 195–227.
Iredale, Matthew. *The Problem of Free Will: A Contemporary Introduction*. Durham: Acumen, 2012.
Judisch, Neal. "Responsibility, Manipulation, and Ownership: Reflections on the Fischer/Ravizza Program." *Philosophical Explorations* 8.2 (2005) 115–30.
Kane, Robert. *A Contemporary Introduction to Free Will*. Oxford: Oxford University Press, 2005.
———. *Free Will and Values*. New York: Albany State University of New York Press, 1985.
———. "Libertarianism." In *Four Views on Free Will*, by John Martin Fischer, et al., 5–43. Malden, MA: Blackwell, 2007.
———. "Response to Fischer, Pereboom and Vargas." In *Four Views on Free Will*, by John Martin Fischer, et al., 166–83. Malden, MA: Blackwell, 2007.
———. *The Significance of Free Will*. Oxford: Oxford University Press, 1996.
Kearns, Stephen. "Aborting the Zygote Argument." *Philosophical Studies* 160.3 (2012) 379–89.
Konyndyk, Kenneth. *Introduction to Modal Logic*. Notre Dame: University of Notre Dame Press, 1986.
Leith, John H. *Assembly at Westminster: Reformed Theology in the Making*. Eugene, OR: Wipf and Stock, 1973.
Letham, Robert. *The Westminster Assembly: Reading Its Theology in Historical Context*. Phillipsburg: Presbyterian and Reformed, 2009.
Locke, John. *An Essay Concerning Human Understanding*. Abridged and edited by Kenneth Walker. Cambridge: Hackett, 1996.
Long, Todd. "Moderate Reasons-Responsiveness, Moral Responsibility, and Manipulation." In *Freedom and Determinism*, edited by Joe Keim-Campbell, et al., 151–72. Cambridge: MIT, 2004.
Macleod, Donald. "Original Sin in Reformed Theology." In *Adam, The Fall, And Original Sin: Theological, Biblical, and Scientific Perspectives*, 129–46. Grand Rapids: Baker Academic, 2014.
McClymond, Michael J., and Gerald R. McDermott. *The Theology of Jonathan Edwards*. Oxford: Oxford University Press, 2012.
McDermott, Gerald R. *Jonathan Edwards Confronts the Gods*. Oxford: Oxford University Press, 2000.

McGowan, A. T. B. *Adam, Christ, and Covenant: Exploring Headship Theology.* London: Apollos, 2016.

McKenna, Michael. "Alternative Possibilities and the Failure of the Counterexample Strategy." *Journal of Social Philosophy* 28 (1997) 71–85.

———. "Assessing Reasons-Responsive Compatibilism." *International Journal of Philosophical Studies* 8.1 (2000) 89–114.

———. "Contemporary Compatibilism: Mesh Theories and Reasons-Responsive Theories." In *The Oxford Handbook of Free Will*, edited by Robert Kane, 175–98. 2nd ed. Oxford: Oxford University Press, 2011.

———. "Does Strong Compatibilism Survive Frankfurt-Style Counter-Examples?" *Philosophical Studies* 91.3 (1998) 259–64.

———. "Frankfurt's Argument against the Principle of Alternative Possibilities: Looking beyond the Examples." *Nous* 42 (2008) 770–93.

———. "A Hard-line Reply to Pereboom's Four-Case Manipulation Argument." *Philosophy and Phenomenological Research* 77.1 (2008) 142–59.

———. "Moral Responsibility, Manipulation Arguments and History: Assessing the Resilience of Nonhistorical Compatibilism." *Journal of Ethics* 16 (2012) 145–74.

———. "Reasons-Responsiveness, Agents, and Mechanisms." In *Oxford Studies in Agency and Responsibility*, edited by David Shoemaker, 151–83. Vol. 1. Oxford: Oxford University Press, 2013.

———. "Resisting the Manipulation Argument: A Hard-Liner Takes it on the Chin." *Philosophy and Phenomenological Research* 89.2 (2014) 467–84.

———. "Where Strawson and Frankfurt Meet." *Midwest Studies in Philosophy* 29 (2005) 163–80.

McKenna, Michael, and Chad Van Schoelandt. "Crossing Mesh Theory with a Reasons-Responsive Theory: Unholy Spawn of an Impending Apocalypse or Love Child of a New Dawn?" In *Agency, Freedom, and Moral Responsibility*, edited by Andrei Buckareff, et al., 44–64. New York: Palgrave Macmillan, 2015.

McKenna, Michael, and Derk Pereboom. *Free Will: A Contemporary Introduction.* New York: Routledge, 2016.

McKenna, Michael, and D. Justin Coates. "Compatibilism." *Stanford Encyclopedia of Philosophy*, December 21, 2018. Edited by Edward N. Zalta. https://plato.stanford.edu/archives/win2018/entries/compatibilism.

Mele, Alfred. "A Critique of Pereboom's Four-Case Manipulation Argument for Incompatibilism." *Analysis* 65 (2005) 75–80.

———. *Free Will and Luck.* New York: Oxford University Press, 2006.

———. "Manipulation, Compatibilism, and Moral Responsibility." *Journal of Ethics* 12 (2008) 263–86.

———. "Reactive Attitudes, Reactivity, and Omissions." *Philosophy and Phenomenological Research* 61 (2000) 447–52.

Mele, Alfred R., and David Robb. "Bbs, Magnets, and Seesaws: The Metaphysics of Frankfurt Cases." In *Moral Responsibility and Alternative Possibilities: Essays on the Importance of Alternative Possibilities*, edited by David Widerker and Michael McKenna, 127–38. Burlington, VT: Ashgate, 2006.

———. "Rescuing Frankfurt-Style Cases." *Philosophical Review* 107 (1998) 97–112.

Moore, G. E. *Ethics.* New York: Oxford University Press, 1912.

Moreland, J. P., and William Lane Craig. *Philosophical Foundations for a Christian Worldview.* Downers Grove, IL: InterVarsity, 2003.

Moya, Carlos J. "On the Very Idea of A Robust Alternative." *CRITICA, Revista Hispanoamericana de Filosofia* 43.128 (2011) 3–26.
Muller, Richard A. *Divine and Human Choice: Freedom, Contingency, and Necessity in Early Modern Reformed Thought*. Grand Rapids: Baker Academic, 2017.
———. "Jonathan Edwards and the Absence of Free Choice: A Parting of Ways in the Reformed Tradition." *Jonathan Edwards Studies* 4.1 (2011) 42–60.
———. "Jonathan Edwards and Francis Turretin on Necessity, Contingency, and Freedom of Will in Response to Paul Helm." *Jonathan Edwards Studies* 4.1 (2014) 268–85.
———. "Not Scotist: Understanding of Being, Univocity, and Analogy in Early-Modern Reformed Thought." *Reformation and Renaissance Review* 14.2 (2012) 127–50.
———. *Prologomena to Theology*. Vol. 1 of *Post-Reformation Reformed Dogmatics: The Rise and Development of Reformed Orthodoxy, ca. 1520 to ca. 1725*. Grand Rapids: Baker Academic, 2003.
———. "Reformation, Orthodoxy, 'Christian Aristotelianism,' and the Eclecticism of Early Modern Philosophy." *Netherkands Archief voor Kerkgeschiedenis* 81.3 (2001) 306–25.
Murray, John. *Collected Writings of John Murray*. Vol. 2. Edinburgh: Banner of Truth Trust, 2001.
O'Conner, Timothy. "Alternative Possibilities and Responsibility." *Southern Journal of Philosophy* 31 (1993) 345–72.
Palmer, David. "New Distinctions, Same Troubles: A Reply to Haji and McKenna." *Journal of Philosophy* 102.9 (2005) 474–82.
———. "Pereboom on the Frankfurt Cases." *Philosophical Studies* 153 (2011) 261–72.
Pelikan, Jaroslav. *The Riddle of Roman Catholicism*. New York: Abingdon, 1959.
Pereboom, Derk. "Frankfurt Examples, Derivative Responsibility, and the Timing Objection." *Philosophical Issues* 22 (2012) 298–315.
———. *Free Will, Agency, and Meaning in Life*. Oxford: Oxford University Press, 2014.
———. *Living without Free Will*. Cambridge: Cambridge University Press, 2001.
———. "Reasons-Responsiveness, Alternative Possibilities, and Manipulation Arguments Against Compatibilism: Reflections on John Martin Fischer's *My Way*." *Philosophical Books* 47.3 (2006) 198–212.
———. "Source Incompatibilism and Alternative Possibilities." In *Moral Responsibility and Alternative Possibilities: Essays on the Importance of Alternative Possibilities*, edited by David Widerker and Michael McKenna, 185–200. Burlington, VT: Ashgate, 2006.
Plantinga, Alvin. *Warranted Christian Belief*. Oxford: Oxford University Press, 2000.
Polluck, Darren M. "Natural Revelation." In *The Jonathan Edwards Encyclopedia*, edited by Harry S. Stout, 392–94. Grand Rapids: Eerdmans, 2017.
Rehanman, Sebastian. "The Doctrine of God in Reformed Orthodoxy." In *A Companion to Reformed Orthodoxy*, edited by Herman Selderhuis, 353–402. Leiden: Brill, 2013.
Russell, Paul. "Critical Notice of John Martin Fischer and Mark Ravizza's Responsibility and Control: A Theory of Moral Responsibility." *Canadian Journal of Philosophy* 32 (2002) 587–606.
Selderhuis, Herman J. "Introduction." In *A Companion to Reformed Orthodoxy*, edited by Herman J. Selderhuis, 1–7. Leiden: Brill, 2013.

Shabo, Seth. "Fischer and Ravizza on History and Ownership." *Philosophical Explorations* 8.2 (2005) 103–14.

Shedd, William G. T. *Dogmatic Theology*. Edited by Alan Gomes. Phillipsburg: Presbyterian and Reformed, 2003.

Strawson, Peter F. "Freedom and Resentment." *Proceedings of the British Academy* 48 (1962) 1–25.

Studebaker, Steven M. *Jonathan Edwards's Social Augustinian Trinitarianism in Historical and Contemporary Perspectives*. Piscataway, NJ: Gorgias, 2008.

Stump, Elenore. "Moral Responsibility without Alternative Possibilities." In *Moral Responsibility and Alternative Possibilities: Essays on the Importance of Alternative Possibilities*, edited by David Widerker and Michael McKenna, 139–58. Burlington, VT: Ashgate, 2006.

te Velde, Dolf. *The Doctrine of God in Reformed Orthodoxy, Karl Barth, and The Utrecht School*. Leiden: Brill, 2013.

Timpe, Kevin. *Free Will Sourcehood and its Alternatives*. 2nd ed. New York: Bloomsbury Academic, 2013.

———. "Trumping Frankfurt: Why the Kane-Widerker Objection is Irrelevant." *Philosophia Christi* 5.2 (2003) 485–99.

Todd, Patrick, and Neal A. Tognazzini. "A Problem for Guidance Control." *Philosophical Quarterly* 58.233 (2008) 686–87.

Trueman, Carl. *John Owen: Reformed Catholic, Renaissance Man*. Burlington, VT: Ashgate, 2007.

Turretin, Francis. *Institutes of Elenctic Theology*. Vol. 1. Edited by James T. Dennison. Translated by Giger George Musgrave. Phillipsburg: Presbyterian and Reformed, 1992.

Van Asselt, Willem J. *Introduction to Reformed Scholasticism*. Grand Rapids: Reformation Heritage, 2011.

———. "Reformed Orthodoxy: A Short History of Research." In *A Companion to Reformed Orthodoxy*, edited by Herman J. Selderhuis, 11–26. Leiden: Brill, 2013.

Van Asselt, Willem J., and Eef Dekker. *Reformation and Scholasticism: An Ecumenical Enterprise*. Grand Rapids: Baker Academic, 2001.

Van Asselt, Willem J., et al. *Reformed Thought on Freedom: The Concept of Free Choice in Early Modern Reformed Theology*. Grand Rapids: Baker Academic, 2010.

Van Dixhoorn, Chad. *Confessing the Faith: A Readers Guide to the Westminster Confession of Faith*. Edinburgh: Banner of Truth Trust, 2014.

Van Inwagen, Peter. *An Essay on Free Will*. Oxford: Oxford University Press, 2002.

———. "Fischer on Moral Responsibility." *Philosophical Quarterly* 47 (1997) 373–81.

———. "Moral Responsibility, Determinism, and the Ability to do Otherwise." *Journal of Ethics* 3 (1999) 343–51.

Van Til, Cornelius *An Introduction to Systematic Theology*. Edited by William Edgar. 2nd ed. Phillipsburg: Presbyterian and Reformed, 2007.

Vargas, Manuel. *Building Better Beings: A Theory of Moral Responsibility*. Oxford: Oxford University Press, 2013.

Vermigli, Peter Martyr. *Philosophical Works: On the Relation of Philosophy to Theology*. Vol. 4 of *The Peter Martyr Library*. Translated by Joseph C. McLelland. Moscow, ID: Davenant, 2018.

Vihvelin, Kadri. *Causes, Laws, and Free Will: Why Determinism Doesn't Matter*. Oxford: Oxford University Press, 2013.

Vos, Antonie. "Scholasticism and Reformation." In *Reformation and Scholasticism: An Ecumenical Enterprise,* edited by Willem J. Van Asselt and Eef Dekker, 99–120. Grand Rapids: Baker Academic, 2001.

Vos, Antonie. "Paul Helm on Medieval Scholasticism." *Journal of Reformed Theology* 8 (2014) 263–83.

Waddell, James A. "Re-examination of Dr. Girardeau's Views of the Freedom of the Will." *Southern Presbyterian Review* 31.4 (1880) 690–716.

Wallace, R. Jay. *Responsibility and the Moral Sentiments.* Cambridge: Harvard University Press, 1994.

Ward, Rowland S. *The Westminster Confession of Faith: A Study Guide.* Melbourne: New Melbourne, 1996.

Warfield, Benjamin Breckinridge. *Calvin and Augustine.* Edited by Samuel G. Craig. Phillipsburg: Presbyterian and Reformed, 1971.

Widerker, David. "Blameworthiness, and Frankfurt's Argument against the Principle of Alternative Possibilities." In *Moral Responsibility and Alternative Possibilities: Essays on the Importance of Alternative Possibilities,* edited by David Widerker and Michael McKenna, 53–74. Burlington, VT: Ashgate, 2006.

———. "Blameworthiness, Non-robust Alternatives, and the Principle of Alternative Possibilities." *Midwest Studies in Philosophy* 29.1 (2005) 292–306.

———. "Frankfurt-Friendly Libertarianism." In *The Oxford Handbook of Free Will,* edited by Robert Kane, 266–86. 2nd ed. Oxford: Oxford University Press, 2011.

———. "Libertarianism and Frankfurt's Attack on the Principle of Alternative Possibilities." *Philosophical Review* 104 (1995) 247–61.

———. "Libertarianism and the Philosophical Significance of Frankfurt Scenarios." *Journal of Philosophy* 103 (2006) 163–87.

———. "Responsibility and Frankfurt-Type Examples" In *The Oxford Handbook on Free Will,* edited by Robert Kane, 323–34. Oxford: Oxford University Press, 2002.

Widerker, David, and Stewart Goetz. "Fischer Against the Dilemma Defence: The Defence Prevails." *Analysis* 73.2 (2013) 283–95.

Williamson, G. I. *The Westminster Confession of Faith for Study Classes.* Phillipsburg: Presbyterian and Reformed, 2004.

Witsius, Herman. *The Economy of the Covenants between God and Man.* Vol. 1. Phillipsburg: Presbyterian and Reformed, 1990.

Whittle, Anne. "Dispositional Abilities." *Philosophers' Imprint* 10.12 (2010) 1–23.

Wolf, Susan. *Freedom Within Reason.* Oxford: Oxford University Press, 1990.

Wyma, Keith. "Moral Responsibility and Leeway for Action." *American Philosophical Quarterly* 34 (1997) 57–70.

www.ingramcontent.com/pod-product-compliance
Lightning Source LLC
Chambersburg PA
CBHW061432300426
44114CB00014B/1649